JOHN A. WILLS

MARINE REINFORCED PLASTICS CONSTRUCTION

MANUFACTURE & REPAIR

TILLER
PUBLISHING
ST. MICHAELS, MARYLAND

About the Covers

Front cover, from top: 80-foot Airex PVC cored one-off yacht designed by Richard Reineman and built by Knight & Carver; 70-year-old **Branta**, a wood-hulled 10-meter sailing yacht salvaged after sinking from a major explosion and restored by resin saturation and microballoon coating; two-man "lay down" mini-sub built by the author for Aerojet and the U.S. Navy; the steam yacht **Medea**, whose deteriorated steel hull was clad in reinforced plastics and restored to seaworthiness.

Back cover, top: production of reinforced plastics recreational boats, courtesy of Bayliner/US Marine; bottom: section of experimental Navy cargo ship produced using VARTM and pre-preg polyester resin using U.V. core system, courtesy of Sunrez Group.

Graphic design and production by:
Words & Pictures, Inc., 27 South River Road South, Edgewater, Maryland 21037.

Printed in the USA by:
The P.A. Hutchinson Company, 400 Penn Avenue, Mayfield, PA 18433.

Questions regarding the content of this book should be addressed to:

TILLER Publishing   or   John A. Wills
P.O. Box 447   32776 Via Del Venado
St. Michaels, Maryland 21663   Valley Center, California 92082
410-745-3750 • Fax: 410-745-9743   760-742-3918 • Fax: 760-742-3167

FOREWORD

In 1939 I had a summer job with Douglas Aircraft. On my first day I was assigned a project to design a fixture for the plexiglass shop where I got my first whiff of acrylic monomer (which smelled like a good martini). That summer introduced me to plastics and, somehow, it has literally stuck with me ever since.

I have been involved with several phases of the plastics industry. Early on, I ran a wartime company whose products were shaped laminates. In those days, if you produced a product, you were either an injection molder, a compression molder, or a laminator. Today, as a laminator, unless you encase ID cards or Aunt Susie's photograph, you would call yourself a reinforced plastics fabricator. I am a reinforced plastics type.

Boats and related marine products came on in volume right after World War II. In a few years the industry produced craft large enough to preclude weekend trailering. In many parts of the country boats were being left in the water all year, which, we realized, could eventually cause some problems — especially the dreaded "boat pox."

The purpose of this book is to introduce you to marine plastics construction, to offer solutions to problems, to present writings from some others in the field, and to present new materials and applications.

The book is divided into three parts:

SECTION I: MATERIALS OF CONSTRUCTION
                 AND MANUFACTURING METHODS

SECTION II: REPAIR OPTIONS

SECTION III: REFERENCES AND APPENDICES

If your principal interest is in repair, you may wish to begin this book with Section II. Originally, I had intended to write only a condensed form of repair options, but after interviewing a cross section of people involved with boats, it became apparent that there is a gap in understanding the materials and construction methods involved in boat building. In order for most readers to comprehend the various repair techniques proffered, a basic understanding of these materials and processes is required.

SECTION I presents the background of conventional materials and manufacturing methods as well as description of the present state of the art.

SECTION II describes types and causes of problems, how damage is rated, and available repair options. Detailed references are included in Section III.

SECTION III affords me the opportunity to share several recent discoveries and investigations in the use of less conventional materials. Some of this is raw information, but much has been tested and evaluated. Papers and comments referred to in the first two sections are placed in Section III so they may be reviewed at leisure without disrupting the flow in reading the main text. This section is certainly not required reading for the owner of a sick boat, though he may find ways to speed repairs; nor will it inspire an insurance company debating a claim. Those of you who enjoy the thrill of a new discovery (new to you and me, at least) may find Section III inspiration enough to pursue further investigation.

You will notice some repetition of subject matter in Sections I and II. This is intentional because these sections are designed to be read independently.

Since you are reading this, you may wish to know you are one of the first to have this book. It has taken me over five slow years to produce this tome. And it will never be really finished because changes occur so rapidly. You will find some glitches which will eventually be corrected by understanding readers and others. I felt that it is more important to get this book into the field now, rather than to wait for perfection — which will never happen!

John A. Wills

OVERVIEW OF CONTENTS

See each section for detailed table of contents.

Acknowledgements

One of the most humbling aspects of trying to be a technical writer is to see if your work can pass muster before your peers. I asked eighteen individuals of different backgrounds to comment on what I thought was a finished draft of this book. Each spent considerable time and offered many suggestions, which resulted in a major overhaul of the draft. None of these people in any way have sponsored or endorsed this book: they are my critics only.

My thanks to all of you for your input!

Donald Begnaud - Owner
Cayacraft Fiberglass Products
Lafayette, LA

Richard Reineman
Industrial Design
San Diego, CA

Ararn Mekjian - Manager
BP Chemicals, Inc.
Keasby, NJ

Daniel Spuur
Practical Sailor Magazine
Portsmouth, RI

Yves Daspet
Norold Composites, Inc.
Fort Washington, WI

Harve Dailey - Group Leader
High Performance Resins
Indspec Chemical Corp.
Pittsburgh, PA

Bud Lincoln - Engineer
Carlsbad, CA

Paul Anderson - Sr. Chemist
Morton International
Woodstock Research Center
Woodstock, IL

Andrew Mar, PhD.
Ciba-Geigy Corp.
Hawthorne, NY

Doug Dennis - President
Dural Plastics, Inc.
Rialto, CA

Alan Thomas
Advanced Piping Products
Houston, TX

Forrest E. Sloan, PhD.
Supervisor, Spectra Lab.
Allied-Signal, Inc.
Petersburgh, VA

Robert Monroe - General Manager
Gougeon Brothers., Inc.
West System
Bay City, MI

Hugo Carver II - Marine Engineer
Corporate Officer
Knight & Carver
National City, CA

Jeff Bootz - Sales
Nida-Core Corporation
New York, NY

Kern Hendricks - Owner
System Three Resins
Seattle, WA

Mark Livesay - President
Sunrez Corp.
El Cajon, CA

Glen Hoover - Engineer
Escondido, CA

Abbreviations and Glossary

(*MS—*)	Materials and Equipment Supplier - listed by number in Appendix A
Ref.	Reference - See Section III
psi	Pounds per square inch
spec.	Specifications
phr	Parts per hundredweight of resin (to 100 parts of resin, add "X" parts of catalyst or activator)
cps	Centipoise - a viscosity term encompassing distance, weight and time
F	Fahrenheit
C	Centigrade
screed	To level or fair, usually with a flexible blade
fair (fairing)	To make smooth to contour
RIM	Reaction injection molding
RTM	Resin transfer molding
stoichiometric	The exact amount of catalyst or hardener required to effect cure of a resin
syntactic foam	A cellular resin compound formed by adding hollow microballoons to a resin matrix
PVA	Polyvinyl alcohol - a water-soluble resin used as a sprayable mold release

MARINE
REINFORCED
PLASTICS
CONSTRUCTION

SECTION I

MATERIALS OF CONSTRUCTION & MANUFACTURING METHODS

SECTION I

MATERIALS OF CONSTRUCTION & MANUFACTURING METHODS

THE HISTORY AND DEVELOPMENT OF PLASTICS

Some people may think that the world of plastics began with the famous statement to Dustin Hoffman in the old movie, *The Graduate*, when it was said, "Get into plastics, young man. It's the coming thing."

But two thousand years ago, the Egyptians made beads from the casein in camel's milk. Casein is still widely used today for wood glue, and long before 1800 Malaysian natives used gutta percha, a vegetable type of gum elastic, to make utensils and artifacts. In about 1820, refined shellac, a natural resin secreted by an insect and used for hundreds of years as a varnish, was made into a practical molding compound by Critchlow.

We've come a long way, baby, from gutta percha to polycyclohexylenedimethylene terephthalate! Here's a general idea of how the industry has developed:

Gutta Percha - no definitive discovery date but was used by Genghis Khan in the 1500s to make composite bows of pine resin and reeds to conquer much of the world.

Shellac - no definitive discovery date, but has been known for three thousand years, when it was first used as a purple-red dye. The United States shellac industry was founded by Zinssen in 1849.

Natural Rubber - first molded in 1820

Melamine - invented by Lieberg in 1834

Nitro Cellulose - first developed by Pelouze in 1836

Vinyl Chloride - developed by Regnault in 1836

Rubber Vulcanization Process - patented by Goodyear in 1839

Gutta Percha Extrusion Process - designed by Bewley in 1848

Polyester - developed by Berzelelious in 1847

Wood Flour-Filled Shellac Molding Compound - developed by Critchlow in 1850

Nitro Cellulose Plasticized with Camphor (to make it moldable) - invented by Cutting in 1854

Formaldehyde Polymers - developed by Butlerove in 1859

Acetylated Polymer - prepared by Schuzenberger, 1865

Styrene - synthesized by Bertholet, 1865

"Celluloid" Basic - patented by Hyatt, 1870

Phenol and Aldehyde Reaction - observed by Bayer, 1872

Plastics Injection Molding - invented by Hyatt, 1872

Vinyl Chloride - first polymerized by Bauman, 1872

Acrylate Esters - first prepared by Caspery and Tollens, 1873

Multi-Cavity Injection Molding - developed by Hyatt, 1878

Screw Extruder - patented by Cray in 1879

Methacrylate - first polymerized by Kahibaum in 1880

Urea Formaldehyde Condensation Products - developed by Holzer, 1884

Synthetic Silk - developed by Chardonnet in 1884

Cellulose Acetate - first industrial process developed by Cross and Bevin, 1894

Cellulose Nitrate Resin Continuous Film Process - inventor unknown

Casein (Plastic) - invented by Spitteler and Kritche, 1899

Alkyd Resin - first observed by Smith in 1901

Secondary Cellulose Acetate (Resin) - first prepared by Miles, 1905

Phenolic Resin Molding Compounds - patented by Bakeland in 1909

As the industry progressed, other basic resins were developed or improved, such as melamine formaldehyde, acrylic, silicone, diallylphthalate, and others. Milestone developments became fewer and the chemistry of plastics became more complicated, yet new resins such as Nylon (polyamide) polybenzimidazol, polyacrylate and polycarbonate emerged.

Thermosets such as the poly- and vinylesters, epoxies, polyurethanes, polytetrafluoroethylene (Teflon), modern phenolics and others came into use.

In the last few years, a miserable habit of using acronyms to refer to a given plastic has become popular.

As well as I try to keep up, I still have to look up the meaning of "PEEK," "PPS," or whatever. Buzzwords are in vogue and I am still not sure which resins are "engineering" and which are not. It would appear that the more expensive they are, the more they qualify as an engineering plastic. The following partial list along with their "call signs" are examples of engineering thermoplastics:

PEEK - (polyether ether ketone) temperature resistance 480°-660°F

PAI - (polyamid-imide) temperature resistance to 500°F

PBI - (polybenzimidazole) resistant to 1400°F

PET - (polybutylene terephthalate) excellent chemical and heat resistance

PCT - polycyclohexylenedimethylene terephthalate) thermoplastic polyester, heat resistant to 500°F

PEI - (polyether imide) long-term heat resistance and good chemical resistance

PMR - (polymerization monomer reactants)

PMR-M - (polyamide) high temperature and fire resistance

PIT - (polyamide thermoplastic) temperature resistant to 700°F

PPS - (polyphenylene sulfide) temperature resistant to 500°F

PAS - (polyarylsulphone) transparent heat resistance to 500°F, oxidative stable

PS - (polysulphone) heat resistance 375°F, transparent, low flammability and smoke

TMA - (ten minutes ago) some "new" resin or alloy was developed

Now, even as this is written, a group of researchers at the University of Rochester has solved the processing problems of very high heat resistant aromatic polyazomethines by adding gallium or ferric chloride, which is later extracted by water or alcohol. Also, polymers and vitreous glass have been compounded resulting in a composite half the weight of glass yet much stronger. Other researchers have inserted an organic molecule into an inorganic chain, thus creating a stiff material by inserting a carbon atom at the center of the polymer.

Few, if any, of these glamorous performers will appear as structural matrix resins in most marine applications because of processing restrictions. Ship's electronic connectors, exhaust components, and engine parts surely will see these high performance materials, but the staples, the low temperature, low pressure liquid or pre-preg materials, will prevail as long as open molding processes, including vacuum bagging, are continued in use.

AN OVERVIEW OF MODERN YACHT CONSTRUCTION METHODS

by Hugo Carver II

A wide variety of modern yacht construction methods are at the disposal of the architect and builder. Most lend themselves to both professional and skilled amateur building, or a blend of each as in kit boat construction. Common to all construction methods is the need to build properly, and most often this means it takes more man-hours than the amateur might initially estimate when compared to other projects: for instance, building a house. With the "proper instruction" out of the way, let's now explore various methods.

Wooden boat construction has a charm all its own, and can retain that feeling for an amazing length of time. There are new methods of wooden construction that are right up-to-date for strength, stiffness, fatigue resistance, weight control, and ambiance that can't be beaten. Traditional, carvel planked boats are still built, but usually for the pride of executing a work of art. Most commonly today, wood boats are built by "cold molding" using thin veneers glued together with an epoxy, sometimes in combination with carbon fibers.

We find boats ranging from dinghies to competitive racing sailboats, to high speed multi-hulls, to high speed, 100-plus-foot motor yachts successfully constructed in this method. The entire vessel is encapsulated in epoxy resin, eliminating the drawbacks of wood, like moisture saturation and rot. Epoxy saturation can also be used to convert a tired old wooden boat to a youngster again, and still retain the charm of the original.

Steel yacht construction is widely used and has some very attractive features. Steel is an inexpensive material, comes in a pre-made high quality sheet, has lots of engineering data available, and, with today's coatings, rust on a well built steel boat can be a thing of the past. Steel is a very heavy material so is rarely used in small boat construction. In displacement vessels, its use starts at about 35 feet, and in planing vessels at about 60 feet. In any case, a steel vessel will take more power to push than where other materials are used, but steel can also give a confident feel in a storm. The key in steel construction is careful detailing and coating of the material to avoid rust; and of course, good engineering and welding techniques. It is interesting that both the lowest cost and the highest cost yachts are built of steel.

Ferrocement can be successfully used in yacht construction. It is generally thought to save cost, but it can require a large number of man-hours to achieve an acceptable degree of finish. Well built ferrocement craft are cruising worldwide, but a concern is that it is impossible to know the mechanical strength of the metal armature imbedded within the cement.

Aluminum is widely used in yacht construction worldwide, from canoes, to racing sailboats, to high speed motor yachts over 150 feet in length. A lot of engineering information is known about aluminum, and with modern paint systems corrosion can be effectively controlled. A great deal of care must be taken to avoid electrolytic attack. Aluminum is moderate in price, easy to work with, relatively lightweight, and is a nice, clean method of construction. In ADDITION to a good system, attention should be paid to careful welding, avoiding structural flexure, particularly at welds, insulation for sound transmission which will not retain moisture, and keeping other metals from contacting the aluminum to avoid electrolysis. Relatively easy construction, light weight, and good engineering properties make aluminum very popular for modern yacht construction.

Fiberglass yacht construction has revolutionized the industry, though it has not been without its problems. Fortunately, there are practical ways of correcting past and preventing future problems, as you will see in reading *Marine Reinforced Plastics Construction.*

The development of the female molding contact process has dramatically reduced costs of producing repeated shapes. Once the female mold is built it is fast and easy to produce parts that can be assembled to create a finished yacht. Because a great deal of the combining of the materials is done at the building site, good engineering and quality control are very important to insure a long lasting and enduring product. Female molded fiberglass boats range from very small dinghies to 150-foot power craft. The majority of production boats are built this way in all price and quality ranges. The basic glass fabrics, resins, and core materials are available in a wide range of price and quality, from materials used 30 or 40 years ago to state-of-the-art materials introduced last week. Construction terminology has changed from the "chopper gun" days to include "vacuum bagging," "unidirectional fabric," "iso-phthalic resin," "vinylester resin," "Kevlar," "carbon fiber," etc. The combinations of materials seem endless, which makes engineering and quality assurance extremely important.

"Cored construction" is commonly used today, often in combination with other building methods. The basic idea is to have two skins of high strength separated by a low density (weight) core of certain desirable properties. We normally think of an I-beam in metal construction as being similar to a cored structure, with two flanges separated by a light web.

A common cored structure would be a surfboard or sailboard using a lightweight foam covered by a thin, strong fiberglass skin. These structures are very light, yet strong. Common core materials are aluminum honeycomb, Nomex and polyetherimide honeycomb, ductile and rigid polyvinyl chloride (PVC) foam, urethane foam, balsa, and quite a wide range of others. These cores must bond reliably and tenaciously to the skin material. Skin materials in common use are polyester-fiberglass, epoxy-fiberglass, epoxy-carbon fiber, and aluminum sheet. Intelligent use of these skin and core materials are producing yachts in every size from dinghies to 200 footers, in cruising, racing, and high performance power craft. Vessels are built combining these materials in different ways to achieve the desired properties for the service intended. Among the results that can be obtained are extremely light weight, high strength, excellent corrosion resistance, and the ability to create any desired shape. As with conventional fiberglass construction, it is critical to combine these materials with good engineering and quality assurance as the materials are combined at the building site. Amateur construction is used in cored construction, but often the man-hours involved are underestimated, as correctly cored construction can be time consuming.

Achieving the state of the art in cored construction can be very expensive. Skins of carbon fiber are $70.00 per pound (versus steel at 30 cents a pound), but entirely worthwhile in certain applications; for instance, aircraft. In some applications, a cored structure can be very cost effective, so again, the correct combination of materials is essential.

A common denominator in all modern yacht construction, no matter what the basic hull's construction, is the use of cored or lightweight interior construction materials. Today, the boat's interior decorator is told to reduce weight, and in response we find thin, laser cut counter tops glued to space age honeycomb core panels. Rather than solid hardwood paneling, we often find thin wood veneers bonded to cored panels which look exactly like solid wood but weigh a fraction, are strong enough for the service intended, and often more stable. That beautiful teak deck may now be 1/10-inch teak with epoxy-carbon fiber in the seams so it doesn't wear out too fast and is a lot lighter than the old standard 3/4-inch solid teak planking.

Seemingly small things save lots of weight on a yacht. A high pressure hydraulic system can save thousands of pounds; changing from standard 12-volt battery system to 24-volt can save a ton. Using titanium rather than stainless steel can be the difference between winning and losing a race. A gas turbine engine is about one tenth the installed weight of a diesel engine and about the same cost per horsepower.

The trend in modern yachts is to reduce the construction weight and avoid a compounding weight increase. In other words, if the boat is heavy, it may need more power (whether sail or engine). That power increase weighs more and requires more fuel. More fuel weighs more and requires heavier tanks. Normal modern boat construction begins with the "mission profile" being established, and then an investigation of what it takes to achieve the desired end results.

Hugo Carver II is a marine engineer. He is corporate officer of Knight & Carver Yacht Center and Custom Yachts, National City, California.

MOTOR YACHT DESIGN FOR THE NINETIES — AND BEYOND

by Richard Reineman

This section is directed only to the general plan and exterior detail of the ship. We leave the all-important underwater hull design, driving system, etc., to the professional marine architect and builder.

In designing a new yacht the first step is to assemble what Hugo Carver calls a "mission profile" — hard facts about how the ship is to be used — accommodations required, speed, cruising range, sea and climate conditions expected, cost limits, etc.

With the foregoing in mind we lay out the general plan — hopefully with adequate walkways all around the ship so docking, mooring, loading, housekeeping, and small boat handling are manageable. Too many new ships give up these features to get a little more salon space or to try for some futuristic look.

The pilot area has a clear view and whenever possible, the front windows slope forward for better visibility, as well as better overhead instrument location and much better sun protection. About every modern naval and merchant vessel is so designed. This is awkward to pull off on a yacht but the practical advantages are worth the effort.

The paid crew, if any, is small but generously housed with their own facilities.

Wiring, air conditioning, and plumbing are ducted in large accessible raceways, using the new fireproof systems.

In organizing the elevations, try to avoid trifling changes in deck level. They are costly to build, weaken the ship, and result in unclean profile appearance.

Once all the above work is satisfactory we at last can get into style and exterior detail.

In this design area we have had quite good acceptance of two example yachts: one 88-footer which made the "Power and Motor Yacht" list of the 100 best designs in the past five years, and a 94-footer which made *Sea Magazine*'s and also *Yacht Magazine*'s cover stories in 1990.

We call this styling system the Andromeda line. In it all components — bulwarks, struts, roof detail, etc. — are made of flat material that can be easily bent, curved and twisted in single plane. These parts are joined at rather sharp edges to make quite rigid closed forms. This lends a sculptural effect strong enough that additional trim, varnished wood, etc., are really not necessary. The two ships described above have no exterior varnish work at all.

The new rigid and semi-rigid foam cored sandwich structures are ideally suited for these structures. They can be compound-formed enough for moderate shapes such as pilot house roofs as well as the main hull. Of course, laminated veneers, steel, and aluminum work fine, too, but the cored system has a higher strength-to-weight ratio, good weathering and no corrosion problems as in metals, but as you will learn in *Marine Reinforced Plastics Construction*, marine structures are subject to hydrolytic attack (a form of corrosion) which within state-of-the-art manufacturing methods is controllable.

Strict adherence to procedures detailed in this book will result in light, strong and durable ships that, together with the new drive systems, will very much improve performance and fuel economy.

Below is a sketch of a proposed new 112-footer illustrating this system.

Richard Reineman - Industrial Design
3698 Zola Street, San Diego, CA 92106
619-225-0869

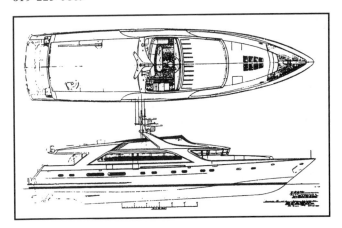

MATERIALS OF CONSTRUCTION

Reinforced plastics products are composites; that is, several items are assembled to make a whole. They are not isotropic (the same all the way through, as is steel). Rather, composites are anisotropic (not the same all the way through, such as wood or reinforced concrete).

Plastics composites must be tested using a different approach, as will be seen later in the text. The following will examine the nature of the ingredients which make up typical marine structures.

REINFORCEMENT FORMS

It is surprising how casually reinforcements are taken for granted. Veil is veil, mat is mat, cloth is cloth, and woven roving is just "heavy" cloth. They are all about the same, so who cares who you buy from? But to the contrary, selection of the proper sequence (schedule) of reinforcement forms, the treatment applied to the fibers which is compatible with the resin chosen and the storage environment used, are vitally important to production of quality laminates.

Surfacing Veils

Veils come in several forms and materials. They are thin, dense webs of non-woven reinforcement not necessarily made of glass. Originally, veils were considered useful primarily for improving the surface of a laminate because they offered some hiding power from the effect of print-through, caused by resin shrinkage around the relatively coarse texture of reinforcement next to the gel coat. This was particularly helpful when using unidirectional or woven roving fabric. Now veils are used for both cosmetic purposes and to absorb or contain up to 90% resin on a volume-thickness basis without the use of a thixotropic agent to provide chemical and water resistance as a result of the resin-rich layer produced. Where the highest glass corrosion resistance is required, corrosion (CR) grades would be selected. Four popular types of surfacing veil are widely available:

1. **C or CR glass.** So-called corrosion-resistant grade. This is available in several thicknesses and, where binder is used, in different binder solubilities. Some suppliers apply coupling agents with or independent of binder. Resin compatibility with binder and coupling agent should always be checked.

2. **A glass.** Usually considered less corrosion resistant and less expensive than the C grade; however, a few products, such as Nicofibers Corporation's *(MS 1)* Surmat 100, offers equivalent corrosion resistance to C glass. Binders are applied which are styrene or non-styrene soluble, and coupling agents are available as well.

3. **E glass.** Used where corrosion resistance is not vital. Manville Corporation's *(MS 2)* 8440 is an example. This particular product is not recommended for polyester resin hand lay-up operations due to intentionally applied low solubility (in styrene) binder. The principal use of this product is for matched-die molding or filament winding where low mat wash is desired.

4. **Polyester.** DuPont's *(MS 3)* Dacron 106 Homopolymer is an example. This type of veil is produced by several manufacturers and is available in two forms: apertured (perforated) and non-apertured. Some suppliers offer heat-bonded binding and stitch binding. Most will supply coupling agents if required.

Structural Reinforcing Mats

Almost all mats used in boat construction are produced from glass fibers similar to veils, but the fibers are larger. Two forms are available: chopped strand and continuous strand.

Chopped strand mat is produced in a felting machine by cutting previously formed roving strands to which an appropriate sizing — usually containing a coupling agent — has been applied. Fibers are randomly cut from 1/2-inch to 2 inches in length and formed into a mat blanket in weights of one half ounce to three ounces per square *foot* by a revolving screen placed over a vacuum chamber. Various widths are available. If the mat thus formed is to be shipped as mat only, then some sort of binder must be applied to facilitate handling by the user. "Powder" binders containing polyester or acrylic resins may be applied dry or wet, then heat fused. Other binders such as starch, polyvinyl acetate, or even bituminous material may be applied, usually in aqueous form. Stitched mat is a knitted mechanical form of binding where no chemical binders as described above are used. The stitching filament may be glass or polyester. This is considered the purest form of mat. The only ingredient other than glass fiber might be a coupling agent which could be combined with a sizing (not binder) previously applied to the roving from which the fibers were chopped.

Continuous strand mats are made by a machine which forms the filaments as a continuous strand into a blanket by a swirling action. These mats are bound in the same way as the chopped form by use of both mechanical and chemical binders.

Mats of both types are often attached to fabrics of many kinds as the mats are formed. A widely used class called stitch mat-woven roving is a combination of mat literally stitched to one or more plies of fabric. This process eliminates the need for a chemical binder, but a coupling agent may be applied to the whole assembly if the fibers had not had coupler previously applied. Mats may be stitched to any fabric, whether it be woven, uni-directional, bidirectional, or tri-axial. The chemical binders in virtually all boat-grade mats are soluble in styrene. This makes them suitable for use with ester resins containing styrene, vinylstyrene, or acrylic as the co-reactant. This also applies to veil mats which may contain a chemical binder.

When it comes to using epoxy or phenolic resin with mats and veils which contain a chemical binder, an uncertain area exists. This has to do with determining resin compatibility. Does this "compatibility" mean that epoxy or phenolic resin will dissolve the binder as does styrene? Or, does it simply mean that the resin is compatible with the coupling agent on the reinforcement but not necessarily soluble in the binder? This should always be checked.

As a general rule, reinforcements containing binder used for ester resins will not be suitable for epoxies or phenolics. Unless the resin will dissolve the binder, the mat will not lay to compound shapes, and the coupling agent which may have been applied with binder will be masked by the insoluble binder. One way to handle this problem is to apply fibers with a chopper gun instead of pre-formed mat. The gun roving should be the type used for filament winding and should contain an appropriate coupler.

Woven Fabric

Glass fibers are made in the same way for yarns as for other glass products. Slender fibers of glass are drawn from molten glass in diameters from 0.05 microns to 25 - 40 microns. As these are formed, the basic glass filaments are gathered into bundles or "strands" of either 102 or 204 filaments each. For woven fabrics where twisted yarn is to be made, various numbers of these strands — also called "ends" — are twisted together to form yarn. *(See the illustrations on page 14.)*

For yarns used in weaving fabrics, a starch-oil textile "size" is applied to protect the fibers during the rather violent looming process. Afterwards, the size must be removed by heat cleaning. At this point the glass is chemically clean but, if used in this condition, will form a poor bond with most resins. Some form of resin-compatible agent (finish) must be applied. This is not a sizing or binder.

There are several styles of weaves available: plain, leno, mock leno, satin, crowfoot, and twill. These are produced in a wide range of combinations of fabric composition with yarns of various twist and ply constructions. These combinations can also involve various filament and yarn weights as well as fabric widths.

The *plain weave* is the simplest form used. As an alternating under- and over-weave, it is usually the least pliable and the most stable for processes requiring easy removal of air during resin impregnation.

In the *leno weave*, yarns are woven into a figure 8 pattern to produce a knotted effect. Because of this, the weave prevents yarn slippage and provides superior stability even though it is a very open weave. It is useful where minimum fiber content is desirable.

The *mock leno weave* resembles the leno in its openness but is not woven the same way. It is used where required strength must be gained through the use of a porous, high-thread-count fabric.

In the *satin weave*, the lengthwise yarns do not interlock with the cross yarns for from four to twelve yarns. The satin weave has a high degree of thread straightness, resulting in a greater laminate strength. It is not as stable as the plain weave but is highly pliable. It is used where maximum drape is required and where high strengths in all directions are needed, along with light weight.

The *crowfoot (uni-directional) weave* is a modification of the satin weave. It is more stable (but less pliable) than the satin weave and is considered difficult to control.

The *twill weave* is a cross between the plain and satin weaves, and the weave pattern gives it a texture of diagonal ridges. This type of fabric is more closely woven than the plain weave.

Some of the satin weaves are standard for high strength aircraft laminating operations. Plain weave fabrics are widely used in tooling and patching applications. Coarse weave fabrics are easier to wet out and thus better for tooling and non-structural applications. *Woven* fabrics of *any* kind should **not** be used for structural applications — more on this later.

Woven roving (not shown) is a plain weave of untwisted rovings and an exception to much of the production process of yarn-formed fabrics. Individual

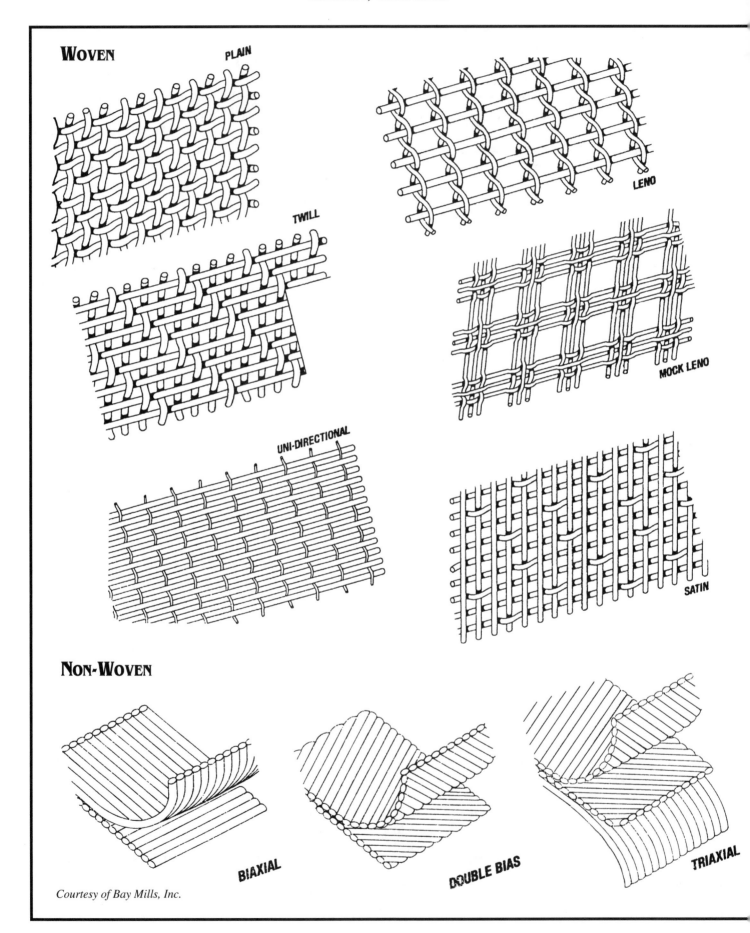

WOVEN

PLAIN

TWILL

LENO

MOCK LENO

UNI-DIRECTIONAL

SATIN

NON-WOVEN

BIAXIAL

DOUBLE BIAS

TRIAXIAL

Courtesy of Bay Mills, Inc.

WOVEN:

Plain:

Warp and filling yarns cross alternately to produce the maximum number of interlacings, the most crimp and the most stable weave. This includes BASKET WEAVE where the yarns run in groups of two or more.

Twill:

Warp and filling yarn interlacings form a distinct diagonal line on the surface giving superior drapeability and high laminate strength.

Uni-Directional:

Offers a concentration of stronger yarns providing maximum strength in one direction.

Leno:

Warp yarns are twisted around one another locking the filling yarns in place. This provides greater dimensional stability of the fabric.

Mock Leno:

Yarns run in groups in both warp and filling, locking each other in place at the interlacings. Mock Leno offers the maximum thickness, good dimensional stability and drapeability.

Satin:

One warp yarn weaves over four or more filling yarns — under one, over four, etc. This process results in a very little crimp and therefore the highest bi-directional strengths for reinforced plastics. Satin is also very drapeable.

NON-WOVEN:

Biaxial:

Yarns in the warp and filling directions are at 90° to each other. This construction maximizes strength in each direction by eliminating yarn crimp.

Uniweft:

Yarns are only in the filling. This allows strength to be concentrated in one direction when required.

Double Bias:

Two sets of yarn are used. One set is oriented +45° from the center line of the fabric and the other set is -45° from the center line.

Triaxial:

Three sets of yarn are used. One set is parallel to the center line and the other two sets are plus and minus 45° from the center line. The strength of the fabric is distributed more uniformly in a laminate.

filaments are first gathered into strands containing either 102 or 204 single fibers. These in turn are gathered into rovings, usually with either 30 or 60 ends (strands), but at this stage are not twisted as in yarns made from roving. A sizing often containing a coupling agent is applied. It is designed for compatibility with the resin to be used and provides sufficient stability to allow construction of a coarse plain basket weave without lubricants. Heat cleaning is not usually performed. Several weights per square yard of woven roving are available.

Non-Woven Fabrics

Modern boat manufacturers and those boat yards performing major structural repairs will (should) tell you there is no place any more for woven fabrics including woven roving except for non-structural and cosmetic applications.

Non-woven fabrics involve directional strands gathered into untwisted flat rovings which are assembled into a fabric form whose rovings are held in position by various means. This fabric, if supplied in a single ply unidirectional form, would require that the roving strands be held in parallel position by some type of mechanical or heat sealing method. Some manufacturers weave a very light filament — usually polyester — across the parallel rovings. Others use a type of glue gun to lay a hot melt thread across the rovings at two- to three-inch intervals. In addition, a non-permanent polyethylene sheet film is under-laid but later discarded to allow the fabric to be rolled. *(See the illustrations on page 14.)*

Bi-axial fabrics are made from two uni-directional plies at 90° to each other.

Tri-axial fabrics are assembled from three uni-directional plies. One ply runs parallel to the centerline. The second is placed at minus 45° and the third at plus 45°.

All of these assemblies are stitched together in some manner, usually with polyester thread. None of these fabric assemblies should be used for marine construction without a mat stitched to the top or bottom of the assembly. Even better, a layer of light chopped or continuous strand mat or veil should be placed between each uni-directional ply. This will assure maximum inter-laminar bond between the rather slick strands of roving. It will be argued that modern "high tech" construction no longer requires this extra step of placing a mat or veil between each layer of uni-directional fabric. However, impact tests show higher results when a non-woven mat type material is used between plies of heavy uni-directional fabric. MIL specifications still read, "mat-roving-roving-mat" where it should read, "mat-roving-mat-roving-mat-roving." Also, the MIL specs should call out uni-directional fabric instead of "roving" which they actually mean to be *woven* roving. (*See Section III, Reference 1.*)

REINFORCEMENT MATERIALS

For certain applications, there is no reason not to use paper, cotton, linen, jute, and other natural fibers impregnated with natural or synthetic resins. Resin impregnated paper honeycomb, cotton or linen fabrics, particle board, and Masonite are some examples.

For so-called fiberglass boat construction, fibers made from E glass predominate. S or S-2 glass, aramid fibers (Kevlar), carbon fiber (graphite), polyethylene and polypropylene fibers, and boron fibers are less frequently used. C and A glass are generally confined to veils.

E, S, S-2, C and A Glass

E glass signifies electrical grade and is made from lime aluminum borosilicate. S or S-2 glass usually means structural grade and is made from finer fibers than used for the E grade. Chemically, these are composed of silicon dioxide, and aluminum and magnesium oxides. C means chemical grade or resistance to strong acids. A glass is also called bottle glass. This is generally lower in mechanical and chemical resistance than the other forms; however, special A glass formulations are available to provide broadband characteristics for radom microwave antennae.

Aramid Fibers

Aramid (Kevlar) is an aromatic polyamide (aramid is the generic name for amide) formed into fibers for construction of rovings and yarns. Products made from aramid are stronger in tension than steel (on a weight basis) and have high energy absorption. DuPont (*MS 3*) makes grades called Type 29 and Type 49. Type 29 is tailored for industrial uses like ballistic fabrics, including bulletproof vests, that are not impregnated with resin. Kevlar is also used to make a high modulus fabric for plastics reinforcements.

Since the aramids have poor compressive strength when used in panel construction, this requires the use of other materials in conjunction, such as S glass or carbon fiber. The aramids are reported to have the highest strength-to-weight ratio of any commonly available fiber. (Makers of polyethylene and polypropylene fibers will dispute this — see "Polyethelene Fibers.") This is not, however, entirely true because its compressive strength is less than 20% of tensile; it has high creep; and it is water-absorbent. Applications of this material should be confined to products where high tensile and impact strength are required.

Aramids are fire-resistant and have good vibration and fatigue resistance. Moisture pick-up can be as high as 7%, but the fibers are not subject to hydrolytic attack.

Aramids are not suitable for use with the polyester resins. Epoxy resin would be the first choice and vinylester resin the second. The cost of aramid fiber is about three times that of E glass.

Carbon Fibers

Carbon (graphite) fibers are formed by first drawing a filament of rayon or polyacrylonitrile stretched, then heated to carbonization (above 1000°F). A coupling agent appropriate to the resin is applied. These fine fibers are assembled into a "tow," which is an assembly of flat rovings which requires 40,000 filaments to form a tape one inch wide by 0.0035 inch thick, or a tape three and one half inches wide which contains 160,000 filaments. Continuous yarns or rovings for fabrics are produced this way. When combined with certain resins — particularly epoxy — laminates of light weight and very high structural strength are manufactured. Virtually any resin may be used with carbon fibers, but careful selection of coupling agents is vital.

Polyethylene Fibers

Extended chain polyethylene (ECPE) fibers represent one of the newer reinforcements introduced to the marine industry. These fibers truly offer the highest *short-term* strength-to-weight ratio of any existing fiber including aramid, carbon, and boron.

The High Performance Products Division of Allied Fibers, Inc. (*MS 6*) produces ECPE in two grades of filament: Spectra 900 and Spectra 1000. Spectra 1000 has a higher tensile modulus than 900 but has a lower strain-to-failure. Allied Fibers produces the raw fibers only. Others process these into rovings for woven roving, cloth, unidirectional fabric, rovings for filament winding, pultrusion, and transfer molding. These outside firms produce yarns and roving for in-house weaving. Some produce a mat.

Polyethylene fibers exhibit their greatest strength in impact and other short-term loading. They have a high creep rate and show poor compressive values. Use of carbon fibers or fiberglass in conjunction with ECPE will produce a composite with lower creep, while retaining good impact strength.

Light weight (specific gravity around 1), virtually zero water absorption, an impact strength more than 20 times that of fiberglass, and excellent abrasion resistance make these fibers candidates for water barrier applications — probably placed just under the gel coat in ECPE mat or fabric form.

A unique method of providing resin coupling to this polyethylene resin is by corona or plasma discharge. This produces an oxide on the fiber surface where chemical coupling agents will not work on polyethylene fibers. I have found the following resins to be compatible with corona or plasma treated SPECTRA fabrics: polyester, vinylester, epoxy, phenolic, phenolic-resorcinol, furfuryl alcohol, polysulfide, and urethane elastomers.

SPECTRA fabric skinned sandwich structures constructed with polypropylene honeycomb offer the highest strength-to-weight ratio possible with any sandwich structure, but beware of creep. One example of this core material is Nida-Core by Nida-Core Corporation *(MS 10)*; other examples of core materials used with SPECTRA fabrics are polyethylene foam by Sealed Air Products Corp. *(MS 11)* and Arco Chemicals Corporation's ARCEL *(MS 12)*, which is a hybrid polyethylene-styrene foam. With SPECTRA fiber placed on the tensile side of these core materials, and S fiberglass or carbon fiber fabric placed on the compression side, most of the creep problems will be solved. Cost of SPECTRA fabric is about the same as Kevlar. *(See Section III, Reference 2.)*

Boron Fibers

Boron fibers are one of the highest strength filaments known. These are made by first drawing a 0.0005-inch diameter tungsten wire, to which boron is vapor deposited, to form a net diameter of 0.004 inch. These fibers may be formed into rovings and yarns also. Because of high cost, both carbon and boron materials would be used only in high-end products such as special marine applications, aircraft, and special performance vehicles.

Quartz Fabrics

Quartz fabrics produced by Hexcel Corp. *(MS 7)* are woven from yarn produced from high purity (99.95% SiO_2) quartz crystals. Quartz makes an outstanding fiber for high temperature use. It is excellent where low dielectric loss properties are required. Quartz fabrics can be used at temperatures much higher than fiberglass — up to 1500°C. Used with phenolic resin, ablative products may be molded.

Ceramic Fibers

Ceramic fibers called Nextel 312 produced by 3M Company *(MS 8)* can withstand long-term use at 2200°F and short term exposure to 2600°F. These fabrics are used in a broad range of applications, from thermal insulation on the space shuttles, to furnace lining, to lightweight fire-walls on the around-the-world *Voyager* and many other experimental aircraft. *(See also MS 18.)*

FIBER REINFORCEMENT COMBINATIONS

Fiberglass-wood, fiberglass-balsa, fiberglass honeycomb (Hexcel), aramid honeycomb (Nomex by DuPont *(MS 3)*, and other impregnated and non-impregnated paper honeycombs are some of the combinations. Others include fibrous skins over structural foams made from styrene *(*Styrofoam by Dow Chemical, *MS 4),* urethane, vinyl, polyethylene and polyester used for making sandwich structures.

Fiber Reinforcement Wood

For many years the value of wood canoes covered with paint or resin-impregnated canvas was well recognized. During World War II many wood structures were fabric-covered and impregnated with some type of lacquer or enamel. Use of high viscosity solvent-based resins such as ethylcellulose over marine grade plywood impregnated into a tough cotton sacking called "osnaberg" provided a high impact-resistant hide for military boats and early pleasure craft. If you're old enough, you'll remember "cracker box" ski boats of the '50s. This method of

18-foot plywood "cracker box" covered with osnaberg cotton cloth and impregnated with ethylcellulose lacquer. Modern wood boats are covered with fiberglass, aramid, carbon, or other combinations.

construction is still in use today, benefited by considerable improvement in materials and technique.

Another form of reinforcement-wood construction is the combination of a fiberglass shell to which end-grain blocks of balsa wood are bonded then covered with an inner shell of fiberglass laminate. Sheets of end-grain balsa wood blocks in any thickness are available. *(See MS 13.)*

Fiber Reinforcement Honeycomb

The earliest honeycomb hulls I am aware of used craft paper honeycomb originally developed for cores in panel doors. This was available only in an un-expanded "log" form, *e.g.,* compressed like an accordion. Sections cut across the log were soaked in water, pulled apart (expanded) and held until dry whereby they would hold their expanded shape. If cuts were made straight across the log, a constant section expanded honeycomb sheet could be produced. If cuts were made diagonally across the log and expanded, a tapered section was produced which aided in fitting to compound shapes such as the turn-of-the-bilge, where the honeycomb core used only on the bottom of a boat could be made to taper to the sides. *(See MS 13.)*

The apparent stiffness of a honeycomb panel is a function of the cube of the thickness. When the span of the sandwich is large, more of the work of bending goes into compressing and extending the faces; while in a short span, the work of bending goes into compressing the core.

Fiberglass Shell-Sheet Foam

This method of sandwich construction is used for construction of Bert Rutan's well known experimental airplanes, the Vari-Eze and the Long-Eze where large blocks of styrene foam are carved to shape then skinned.

Thousands of hulls made by the "one-off" method have been constructed where sheet vinyl foam is used as the core. Vinyl, urethane and, more recently, polyethylene and polypropylene sheet foam account for cores in hulls made in female molds.

Two-skin deck with resin impregnated paper honeycomb. Note taper of expanded honeycomb at edges.

Hatch with paper honeycomb core, fiberglass skins.

Fiberglass Inner and Outer Shells with Injected or Sprayed Foam

Instead of using pre-foamed sheet materials, urethane and polyester foams may be sprayed or injected. The popular Boston Whaler is a prime example of the injection method. The inner and outer pre-fabricated skins are contained in rigid male and female molds and locked together. Then a pre-determined amount of two-part urethane mix is injected. Density is determined partly by the quantity and temperature of the material being injected, which during expansion, develops several tons of internal force until cured.

Single shell parts may be sprayed open with foamable resins whose make-up determines the amount of expansion and thus density. Two-part urethane resins, if to be sprayed in the open, are specified as "2 pound" (per cubic foot), "4 pound," etc. The actual resultant density of open sprayed urethane foam depends upon the accuracy and degree of mixing and the mold and room temperatures at the time of application.

More useful as a sprayed structural foam is a polyester resin which may be applied by a process developed by Venus-Gusmer *(MS 53)*. More details on this process will be discussed later.

Fiberglass Shell-Syntactic Foam

"Syntactic" is a buzzword meaning that each ingredient complements the other. Microballoons such as 3M "glass bubbles" *(MS 8)* mixed with various resins, or microballoons made from synthetic resins such as Union Carbide's *(MS 5)* phenolic resin type may be poured or

injected between structural shells or poured into molds. Cured syntactic foam castings such as sailboat rudders, floats, or underwater craft control fins are examples. These are usually covered with some type of reinforcement, or surface reinforcements may be placed in a female mold next to the mold surfaces followed by pouring or injecting the foam mix. Syntactic foam may also be sprayed or troweled onto a surface where it is allowed to cure. An overlay surface skin may be applied if required.

Syntactic Foam Fairing Compound

This is usually the same foam mix as described above, but it is intended for use as a type of fairing putty and normally contains a thixotrope to prevent sag. One principal use for this material is in surface fairing one-off structures prior to priming and painting.

Another use of syntactic materials is the use of solid granules or beads of numerous materials ranging from mineral sands, metal, glass, scrap metal, granulated wood and nut shell to broken glass and recycled crushed resins. Lead, steel, or glass are readily formed into shot or

Above: Syntactic foam being poured into a mold.

Left: Cast syntactic foam rudder with fiberglass cloth.

Right: Note cast in structure.

Left and below: Syntactic fairing compound is applied.

Right: Large sanding blocks are used to "fair" cured syntactic compound.

granules and when combined with a resin make a very useful compound for castings such as in-place cast keels, tools, and dies. *(See Section III, Reference 3.)*

A different approach to the use of syntactic foam is seen in West Point Pepperell Corporation's Core Mat *(MS 16)*. Core Mat is made up of a random web of non-woven polyester fibers held together by a styrene soluble binder and then "fluffed up" by adding hollow Saran (polyvinylidene chloride) microballoons. This produces thicknesses up to about 5 millimeters or about the thickness of 1½ ounce chopped strand mat. This then is used with chopped strand mat and fabrics including woven roving.

Still another method of using a syntactic material is to pre-impregnate a fabric with a resin in the "B" stage mixed with any type of hollow spheres. When laminated and cured, this will produce a lightweight composite, usually with a density lower than 1.

RESIN FILLERS

Thickening, Bulking-Extending, and Density Change

Minerals such as calcium carbonate, quartz or glass powders, talc, and titanium dioxide are used for bulking, extending and increasing density. Titanium dioxide is also considered a high quality white pigment.

Glass or ceramic microballoons, organic microspheres, and silica glass microspheres such as Perlite serve as resin extenders, thickeners, and bulking agents, also they contribute to lowering density.

Various nut shell powders, ground cork, solid glass beads, and many types of metal granules, beads, and fibers are considered fillers. Almost all of the materials as discussed above are available with some type of surface treatment (coupling agent). None are considered true thixotropes.

For discussion here, fillers include mineral powders of all classes, including fire retardants and thickening agents but not thixotropes. Pigments are also fillers and thickeners, but their prime purpose is to provide color, including black and white pigments. Some of these materials are available with coupling agents added. Pigment usually represents a small percentage of the total filler. One exception to this is pure white or pure black where the color is both pigment and filler.

One of the greatest contributors to polyester degradation is the use of almost any filler placed in the laminating resin. First, to reduce cost; second, to change some physical characteristic or only to provide some fire retardancy. This does provide bulking and thus cost reduction and fire hazard reduction, but with great penalty. The fire retardant fillers are the additive type, *i.e.*, they are added and mixed with the resin. Some of these are aluminum trihydrate, antimony trioxide, chlorinated or brominated wax, and brominated fillers. The second type of fire retardant is called "reactive." Usually chlorine or bromine is chemically added to the backbone of the resin at the time of manufacture.

THIXOTROPIC AGENTS

A thixotrope causes a liquid to be viscous when at rest, *e.g.*, when it is not being stirred, brushed, pumped, or sprayed. When the liquid is moved in any way, the thixotrope allows lowering of the viscosity. An efficient thixotropic agent will lower the viscosity at high shear to the same point as if no agent had been added.

Thixotropes are added to a gel coat or laminating resin for the express purpose of reducing sag or run-off. They are not considered fillers. When a thixotrope is added to the degree that it becomes a thickener, then it would be considered a filler. The miserable habit of adding Cab-O-Sil or other fumed silica to the extent that it becomes a putty is an example of poor workmanship.

Fumed silica, when added in the range of 1/2 to 4% phr to resins with initial viscosities of 200 to several thousand cps, has been the typical anti-sag agent for many years. Until recently, little attention has been directed toward its effect on inter-laminar bond and its chemical resistance. With respect to inter-laminar bond, some investigators have concluded that the long needle-like filaments of silica suspended in the resin are filterable by veil, chopped, or continuous strand mat. It is claimed that, if a dry mat is pressed onto a wet resin which contains thixotrope, a concentrated layer of the thixotropic agent will be formed under the mat (the area between the gel coat and the first mat ply) due to a filtering or blocking action by the mat layer. Evidence of this is claimed from microscopic examination showing a slick, shiny surface easily de-bonded from the reinforcing ply. These same investigators did not address this situation where the matting had been laid dry and when the resin was "pressed" or impregnated through the reinforcement by roller.

While I do not deny the possibility of a concentration of thixotrope anywhere in a lay-up, I question the ability of even a veil mat to become a filter unless such a veil mat had a binder insoluble in the resin which may allow the fibers to remain mechanically intact, thus forming a tight enough network to effect filtration. I routinely run gel coat which contains a high percentage of thixotrope through a conventional paint filter before spraying and have yet to observe evidence of filtered thixotrope.

It is much more likely that the observed concentration (if actually fumed silica) was caused by resin containing an excess of thixotropic agent. Fumed silica is particularly notorious for settling out of resin to the bottom of its container during storage, especially where resin is supplied from drums or large tanks not equipped with circulation. De-bonding between the "layer" of silica may have occurred because neither the resin nor the silica contained a coupling agent.

It is also possible that the "slick shiny surface" previously referred to was not caused by fumed silica at all. De-bonding may have been caused by the use of resin containing dicyclopentadiene (DCPD), a low-cost substitute for some of the acids used in formulating the resin — especially when manufacturing an ortho resin. Some resin manufacturers claim that DCPD backbone resins offer better hydrolytic resistance for marine use than those made with the higher cost acids. I have not seen proof of this.

The DCPD containing resins are generally low in percent of yield strength. They also produce high cross-linking at the air surface, even producing a shiny gloss. Over-laminate bond is poor if the air side is allowed to cure more than an hour or so after the gel. Otherwise, sanding of the resin surface must be performed.

The combination of a highly cross-linked surface improperly prepared for over-laminating — even with the proper use of fumed silica, let alone an excess — could have been another cause of de-bonding. Even if no thixotrope had been used, de-bonding likely will occur if a shiny, smooth surface was observed because it was overlaid after full surface cure of the substrate, or without other surface preparation.

The chemical and hydrolytic attack resistance of fumed silica is poor. Addition of an appropriate coupling agent to either the silica or matrix resin will increase bonding and improve hydrolytic resistance, but will not improve chemical resistance to acids. In construction of corrosion resistant laminates, the use of fumed silica is not recommended.

For any corrosive environment, so-called chemical thickeners as anti-sag agents are preferred over fumed silica. Millithix 925 *(MS 17)* is one of these. *(See also Section III, Reference 4.)* This material is a polyol acetal or substituted sorbitol and does not resemble fumed silica. This is one of the preferred thixotropes for corrosion resistant vinyl esters. Unlike fumed silica, Millithix 925 does not affect corrosion resistance. According to Dr. Russell Harlen of Milliken Chemicals, Millithix 925 is not recommended for use with epoxy resins due to the presence of free hydroxyl sites in its chemical make-up. Its use in liquid phenolics has not been investigated.

Another material useful as a powerful thixotropic agent is Kevlar aramid pulp *(MS 3 and Reference 5)*. This material has the added benefits of providing reinforcement and abrasion resistance. It can be used in high concentrations as a reinforced putty. When used as a thixotrope in gel coat, a slight surface texture may appear. At least for those areas below the boot top, this texture would be tolerable in view of the high abrasion and chemical resistance offered by aramid pulp.

Another material is Pulpas TA 12 by DuPont *(MS 3)*. It is a polyethylene fiber pulp that's very useful as a thixotrope. *(See Section III, Reference 6.)*

The Carborundum Company *(MS 18)* produces a ceramic thixotrope called Fiberfrax for use principally in high temperature and chemical resistant conditions. *(See Section III, Reference 7.)*

REINFORCEMENT ADDITIVES

There is so much confusion and misuse of terms when referring to all the good and bad things which are added to reinforcements that a clear sequential understanding of these terms is called for.

Sizing

"Sizing" is an all-inclusive term representing a "chemical soup" which may include some or all of the following materials to be described. The basic function of a sizing by itself is to hold something together long enough to further process a product. It can be and often is a carrier for other ingredients. For example, when strands are to be held together, particularly if they are not twisted, some sort of "glue" must be applied. Starch as a sizing is widely used for this purpose with most types of filaments including cotton, silk, and flax as well as glass fiber. Starch is not ordinarily used with carbon or boron fibers.

If the next step after forming the fibers is to produce a non-twisted roving which is intended to be used for producing woven or forming non-woven fabrics, then in addition to a sizing a coupling agent would be included in the liquid sizing and applied to the fibers as they are formed at the bushing (the point where molten glass is drawn through a small orifice). The sizing and coupler must be compatible; *i.e.*, the sizing must be capable of being dissolved by the intended resin, and the coupler must be appropriate for the resin specified. Sizing intended for marine use would not contain starch. Whether rovings produced with a starch or other type of sizing are made into woven or uni-directional fabrics or simply used as a roving, they all are made in much the same manner. The important difference is in the type of basic sizing and the type of any coupling agent used. Thus, rovings for high-production chopper guns to make plumbing fixtures will differ from rovings used for weaving. A lubricant, sometimes a vegetable oil, is applied to sized rovings which are to be woven. When weaving woven roving or forming uni-directional fabrics, no lubricant is used.

Schematic 1:
Chopped Glass Strand
Mat Making Machine
Aaron G. Smith, Engineer

MAT MACHINE
For Explanation, the Chopped Fiber Glass Strand Mat Machine
Is Illustrated In General Sections

05-21-1990
Aaron G. Smith

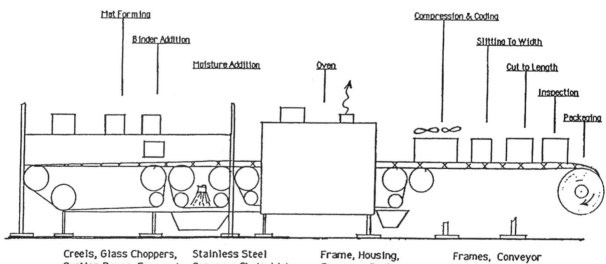

In the weaving of glass cloth (not woven roving), the fibers as formed into roving are sized only — usually with inexpensive starch — as they are twisted into yarns. No coupler would be applied. After drying, a lubricant is applied. Next, these yarns are woven into cloth, wound onto rolls, then "heat cleaned" by high temperature baking, which vaporizes all additives. After cooling, the yarns in the cloth are considered chemically clean but are not useful with most conventional marine resins. A coupling agent intended for use with specified resin(s) is usually applied from an aqueous bath. The fabric is carefully dried, re-rolled, and then bagged in a moisture-proof container.

When strands formed into rovings are intended for use with chopped-strand structural mat formed by a mat-making machine, the rovings would be sized with a resin-compatible material and usually with a resin-compatible coupling agent.

Then they would be chopped and laid down on the felting machine bed with random length fibers up to two inches long. Nominal thickness — thickness is not usually quoted for mats — is a function of the final weight per square foot, and is quoted in ounces *per square foot*. An additional material, now to be called *binder*, is applied in order to contain the very loose fibers being held in mat form by the vacuum bed of the felting machine. *(See illustrations on pages 22 and 23.)*

This binding may be achieved by mechanical stitching with a thread or filament or it may be sprayed using a liquid containing any one or more of a variety of materials; or the binder may be dusted on as a powder then sintered and pressed or rolled to a specified nominal thickness. All of these materials remain with the product, unlike cloth weaving where they would be removed by heat.

Continuous strand glass structural mat is manufactured by applying multiple single strands to form a mat. Sizing and coupler, if specified, are applied in the same manner as chopped strand mat.

Fiberglass veils are usually made from continuous strand, and binder is applied in the same manner as structural mats.

Continuous strand polyester veils are usually bound by a thermal process, *e.g.*, "heat stitched." Coupling agents may be specified, but often are not necessary.

REVIEW OF REINFORCEMENT ADDITIVE DEFINITIONS

Sizing may be plain starch, a resin solution, or a sintered dry resin powder.

Lubricant is applied to twisted yarns for ease of weaving.

A *coupling agent* is applied to provide adhesion to or by the matrix resin.

Binder is used to hold matted material in a usable form which may be applied by chemical or mechanical means.

Heat is applied to woven cloth to remove all additives by vaporization after which a coupling agent only is applied.

Schematic 2:
Method for Continuous Production of Glass Fiber Strand by Electric Melt
Aaron G. Smith, Engineer
Abstract:
Method and apparatus for forming glass fiber strand directly and continuously from raw batch glass-forming material, which includes means for continuously electrically melting raw batch, glass-forming materials, forehearth and fiber forming means for continuously receiving said melted glass, means for continuously attenuating said glass from said fiber forming means in the form of a multiplicity of fiberglass filaments, and means for converging and winding said filaments in the form of a fiberglass strand.

COUPLING AGENTS

These materials — not to be confused with binders or sizings, though often combined with the latter — are substances by themselves. They sometimes are referred to as "treatments."

In general, a coupling agent may be thought of as a molecule with a hook on one end and a loop on the other — material which forms a molecular bridge by covalent bonding. Inorganic fibers such as glass or carbon are polar materials. Resins generally used in marine construction are non-polar, so in a way, they hate polar substances. Therefore, a coupler or "third mutually-compatible ingredient" must be added. Otherwise, wet-strength values may be reduced by as much as 60% due to hydrolytic attack on the raw glass.

Coupling agents are applied to cloth after heat cleaning. Woven roving will have had its coupler added to the roving before weaving. Uni-directional fabrics are formed from previously treated (coupled) rovings.

Coupling agents are definitely not all the same. Each is specifically formulated for a particular type or group of resins. This means some are multi-functional; *e.g.*, one might be suitable for poly or vinylester but not for epoxy. A very few can be specified for phenolic, furfuryl, resorcinol-formaldehyde, or furane resins. Purchasing specifications often neglect or omit specific requirements that pre-treated reinforcements be compatible with the matrix resin to be used.

There are many situations, as will be discussed later, where coupling agents are added to the resin directly in lieu of, or in conjunction with, couplers already applied to the reinforcement or filler, and where a primer type coupler may be formulated to be applied to various substrates. There are dozens of coupling agents manufactured by several firms.

A partial list follows:

For Poly- or Vinylesters

Finish 114	methacrylate type
Volan A	methacrylate type
Dow Corning 6030 *(MS 4)*	methacrylate type
Union Carbide A-174 *(MS 5)*	vinyl type
Union Carbide A-172	vinyl type

For Epoxy Resins

Dow Corning Z-6040	organo silane
Dow Corning Z-6032	organo silane
Union Carbide AM-187	epoxy silane
Union Carbide A-1100	amino silane
Finish 114	
Volan A	
Garan	vinyl silane

For Phenolic Resins

Union Carbide A-1100	
Union Carbide A-1160	ureido
Union Carbide A-1106	amino silane

There are numerous proprietary couplers. Anyone responsible for purchasing pre-treated reinforcements should be careful to discuss with the supplier the compatibility of the coupler with the resin to be used. Many suppliers will not tell you, or their distributors simply do not know, which specific coupler is used, hiding behind the word "proprietary," an all-inclusive term. The manufacturer and/or supplier must at least guarantee compatibility. If you're buying non-treated reinforcements, such as some non-treated veils, microballoons, fillers, and thixos, you should consider adding an appropriate coupling agent directly to the resin, particularly when such reinforcements are subject to hydrolytic attack. When applying reinforced laminates to substrates such as steel or aluminum, a primer-coupler such as Morton International TPR 415 *(MS 15)* should be applied directly to the metal. This material may be thought of more as a primer than coupler since it contains chlorinated rubber as well as an organo-silane coupler. (*See also Section III, Reference 8.*)

CONSTRUCTION RESINS
Solvent Carried

Coatings to impregnate some type of reinforcement applied to a marine structure have been used for hundreds of years. Birch bark, combed palm fronds, grasses, hemp, flax, or cotton fabrics have historically been impregnated with natural gum rosins while melted or thinned in some type of solvent such as turpentine. Parts of the world where only bituminous materials, shellacs, or natural lignins are available serve as sources of "laminating" materials still today.

My first experience with a slightly more modern approach to this was in 1939 with a trade-name material called Chemold, which was an ethylcellulose resin dissolved in lacquer thinner. The solution was adjusted to a viscosity of about that of marine varnish. This concoction was first used as an impregnant for carded palm fibers laid over a crude male mold to produce a small rowboat. One layer at a time was patted on. The solvent was allowed to flash off, then more layers were applied. It was crude, but the product was tough. With enough wood framing, the material could be held together to form a boat shape!

I made some improvements to the process by revising the solution formulation — still using ethylcellulose resin.

The reinforcement was changed to the long staple cotton basket weave cloth called osnaberg, which was originally produced to make coffee bean sacks. Ten to twelve layers of this cloth and resin would produce about a 1/4-inch thick shell. I called this product Lamitex, and by 1943 we (Wills & Roberts Plastics Mfg. Corp.) had produced many droppable boats for the Navy and some droppable airborne containers for the Air Force. Fortunately, we were able to replace this process with fiberglass and polyester resin — then called "plastic resin glue."

Paints of all kinds containing natural rosins or synthetic resins have long been used for canvas-covered small wood boats such as canoes and decks of larger craft. This is still an acceptable practice today.

All oil-based enamels start out as clear "varnish" — a term used by paint chemists to refer to any un-pigmented clear rosin-solvent solution. By adding pigment, varnish becomes "enamel." A classic varnish contains an oxygen hardenable oil. This oil usually contains a catalyst ("drier") and a gum rosin which, in the clear form, is used as such as a clear varnish; but if pigmented, it provides opacity or hiding power. This is called "paint."

Lacquers are natural rosins or synthetic resins dissolved in a volatile solvent. The Chinese have used lacquers for hundreds of years to coat or impregnate many materials for structural as well as decorative or protective coatings. Lacquers are air-dried to form a film and do not depend upon driers and oxygen to cure a film.

12-foot Navy wherry made from Lamitex. These were modified for use as droppable rescue boats during early World War II.

Hot Melt Resins

Reinforced laminates can be constructed by applying uni-directional S glass rovings to polyethylene or polypropylene heavy film or light sheet by heat embedment in a flat or roll press. These sheets are cross-plied in several layers, then hot pressed to form a solid sheet to specified thickness. These laminates are used for some applications where very short-term high impact (ballistic) specifications are required. These composites often replace the glamorous Kevlar for impact resistant applications.

On a less impressive side, hot melt resins ranging from glue-gun types to large scale doctor-knife-applied melted resins are coated on fabrics or papers of many types including fiberglass, and to veneers of wood. Masonite, particle board, wood chip and other similar reinforcements are hot-melt molded using natural lignin rosins and others in sheet forming equipment such as rolls and platen presses.

Thermoformed Sheet

Small craft ranging from paddle boats to rowboats and sailboats are available from thermoformed sheet stock made from a variety of resins and their alloys. When manufactured from properly specified materials, some very useful, long-lasting products are made. Canopies, windshields and cowl vents are typical examples. Aristech Chemical Corporation *(MS 19)* has developed a thermoformable reinforced acrylic sheet suitable for fabricating many marine products, including small boat hulls to 20 feet. (*See Section III, Reference 9.*)

Thermoset Sheet Compounds

Thermoset sheet molding compounds (SMC) are produced by formulating a catalyst-activated, dough-like compound which is extruded cold — but not cured — into conveniently sized sheets. These sheets are then placed into heated-matched dies and press-molded into flat sheets or shapes. The end material is a highly mineral-filled, somewhat heavy product, usually polyester resin-based.

Bulk molding compounds (BMC) are mixed and activated in the same way as SMC and are handled as a dough. The dough is transferred to a hot press as a lump, or forced into closed dies by injection or transfer; occasionally, extrusion of shapes is performed. The physical characteristics of BMC are similar if not identical to SMC.

RIM Foams and Some Structural Foams

Reaction-injection molding (RIM) resins are compounded and activated to provide an in-mold foamable material to be injected into closed, heated dies. A novel feature is that as the material in the mold foams, a structural skin is formed at the mold interfaces, thus producing a flat or compound sandwich capable of producing variable thickness parts. As of this writing, RIM is mostly used to produce automotive panels, but many marine subcomponents will be produced as well.

However, objects like the Boston Whaler boat, which is a two-skin, injected urethane foam product, may eventually be produced by reaction injection molding.

Foamed vinyl resin sheet stock is manufactured in two distinct ways, either aerated or cross-linked. Airex *(MS 20)* and Core-Cel *(MS 54 and Section III, Reference 32)* are air-blown cellular foams made from vinyl plastisol, but it is not chemically cross-linked. Klege-Cell *(MS 21)* is an example of cross-linked vinyl foam which is chemically described as a polyvinyl aromatic polyamid.

Vinyl foams are resistant to water, especially when formed into sandwich structures. They are the basis for the one-off molding process to be discussed later.

Cross-linked vinyl foam tends to be stiffer and somewhat more brittle than air-blown foam. As such, it works well for producing relatively flat structures such as cabinetry and decks.

Non cross-linked foams have high yield high impact and slightly flexible characteristics, which in thick sections are best suited to boat's hulls or other areas subject to high impact.

Polyurethane rigid foams in densities ranging from 2 to 30 pounds per cubic foot are available in sheet form or may be foamed in place by pouring, casting or spraying. This material, unless totally encased (Boston Whaler) is not suitable for marine use, especially when using thin composite shells. All urethane foams absorb water. Rigid foams are friable and easily damaged by impact. They are not advised for flotation devices unless totally encased with heavy skins.

In my view, there is no place for urethane foam in any marine use. I wish this material had never been developed for *ANY* use whatsoever. Flexible upholstery, and rigid roof and wall insulation using urethane foam are absolute potential killers when burned. Both rigid and flexible types soak up moisture like a sponge. In fact, many household sponges are made of urethane. With many, more suitable, materials available, there is no place for urethane foams aboard an aircraft, automobile, boat, or dwelling of any size.

Polyester rigid foams are made from somewhat special ester resins. When combined with a foaming agent and *chemical* activators this material becomes a useful, closed-cell structural foam produced with good impact strength and water resistance. This foam is usually applied by two-component spray equipment but may be poured or cast as well. An example of a chemically activated polyester foam is Luperfoam 329 by ELF Autochem *(MS 22)* (formerly Penwalt Corp.). Luperfoam 329 is chemically described as a blend of t-butylhydrazinium chloride and ferric chloride.

Unlike rigid urethane foam, polyester resin foams may be considered a semi-critical structural material when used with a single shell laminate or as a core material because of its low water pick-up. It is effective for sprayed-on heat and sound insulation because a tight skin is formed on the air side of the cured material. Densities, which range from 10 to 15 pounds per cubic foot, tend to be difficult to control precisely. Very little field experience is available in the use of polyester foams as structural components. So far, the highest usage has been for spray application on the exteriors of thin shelled polyester-fiberglass plumbing fixtures such as shower stalls, where sound deadening and stiffening are required.

As previously mentioned, another approach to sprayed polyester resin foam has been introduced by Venus-Gusmer *(MS 53)* with their MBF-01 gun. *(See Appendix B.)* No chemically active foaming agent is required. Instead, a non-reactive stabilizer is premixed to the main resin supply at about 1½ phr. At the gun, in a chamber with a high speed impeller, carbon dioxide or nitrogen gas is injected. This blends the resin containing the bubble stabilizer with the gas. Separately downstream, MEKP catalyst is injected (still internally) just before the spray nozzle. The encapsulated gas bubbles provide the foam's cells. Thicker sections may be sprayed prior to cure because only conventional catalyst is used, which produces less exothermic reaction than when a chemical foaming catalyst is used.

Foam-to-substrate bond is superior to bonded preformed foam sheet by vacuum bag to a pre-molded shell. It is about equal to a laid-down laminate. "Club sandwich" construction is made possible by using multiple foam-skin layers.

This is a new process introduced in late 1993 by Venus-Gusmer. It is a good candidate for replacement of the vacuum bag method of bonding on foam sheet stock. I am sure that more extensive field tests will vindicate its use as a structural foam core. (*See Section III, Reference 29.*)

Polystyrene foams are manufactured in two ways: by expansion of styrene bead and by continuous extrusion. Styrene beads containing an expansion material must be molded in dies with heat and confining pressure. Shapes may be any form as well as planks. Sheet stock is band sawed or hot-wire cut from large billets. Cut sheet or moldings are found in anti-shock packaging and are characterized by a coarse-grained appearance.

DOW Chemical Co. makes an extruded polystyrene called Styrofoam (*MS 23*). Produced in a continuous process, Styrofoam is a high quality, closely controlled density product. The extrusion process provides a smooth surface skin with no evidence of grain. Thin sheets may be thermoformed into such products as food containers and thin protective packaging sheets. Larger sheets are used for insulation. Extra thick sheets (sometimes called "buns") may be sawed or wire-cut to produce cores for many types of sandwich construction. Burt Rutan's Vari-Eze and Long-Eze aircraft are examples.

Both methods of manufacture provide closed-cell water resistant products useful for flotation and light weight products including sandwich structures. Densities for both types of foam vary from one pound to many pounds per cubic foot.

Styrene foams are highly flammable even when combined with fire repressant. When styrene foams are used as cores for structural composites, it is necessary to carefully avoid contact with styrenic resins, acetone, lacquer thinners and most paints. Epoxy or phenolic resins can be placed directly on styrene foams.

Polyethylene foamed stock is available in board form only in densities of less than 2 pounds to 10 pounds per cubic foot. It can be used in composite construction to a limited extent. Sealed Air Products company (*MS 24*) makes several densities of polyethylene foam plank stock.

Unlike polystyrene foams, polyethylene foams are not affected by water or other solvents, including all resins. Polyethylene materials are not thought of as easily adhesively bonded by or to other resins. Plasma, corona, or other surface treatment or the use of special adhesives is required. Certainly, common resins will not effectively bond. However, I have made an extensive investigation of the bondability of Sealed Air Product's foam and find that little or no adhesive bond is possible, but excellent *mechanical* bond may be achieved if the surface skin of the plank is first removed. This opens highly interlocked openings and spaces between the closed cells which will allow a low viscosity resin (less than 1000 cps) to penetrate. Upon cure of the bonding resin, a phenomenal mechanical bond is developed which exceeds, by far, most adhesive bonds possible on polyethylene. Foam-to-foam bonds which will exceed the strength of the foam itself may be made this way to join sheets in any direction. One word of **CAUTION:** polyethylene foam has a high degree of creep when under load, particularly in thin sections. Make tests for long-term loading.

Polystyrene-polyethylene foam is a hybrid available indirectly from Arco Chemical (*MS 25*) called Arcel. This material is available in densities from about 2 to 8 pounds per cubic foot. Advantages: Arcel is only affected temporarily by common solvents including gasoline and will allow the use of ester resins providing they are cured on the foam surface in a relatively short time. Creep resistance of Arcel is improved over straight polyethylene foam. Bondability is about the same as polyethylene providing the surface skin has been removed. Principal present uses are for high-end packaging where unusually high impact resistance is required. Arcel has about ten times the shock resistance of comparable density polystyrene foam. There is one shortfall. As manufactured by Arco, Arcel must be supplied to fabricators in bead form under refrigeration because of the type of blowing agent used. This runs up the cost. Check with Arco for location of their processors who supply planks.

The Ester Resins
Polyester

Polyester resins are polymers made into chains called "ester linkages." An ester is the result of the formation of an organic acid and an alcohol. Normally, there are two separate acid groups used to make polyesters, and each one will react to an alcohol group. These two acid groups are called "di-functional."

Typical acids are: orthophthalic (phthalic anhydride), fumaric, isophthalic, maleic and adipic. Two of several glycols (alcohols) used are propylene and neopentyl.

Orthophthalic polyester resins were the first to be used in the industry. They are still widely applied where low cost is foremost for such uses as body fillers, "cultured marble," and back-up resin for iso- or vinylester laminates. They are often used alone where hydrolysis would not be a problem.

Orthophthalics are made in what is called a "one stage" process, which provides the lowest manufacturing cost. Lower cost sometimes attracts careless producers as well. If the manufacturing process is not performed precisely, such problems as sublimation of phthalic anhydride occur during the procedure. This produces low molecular weight phthalic esters which have high water solubility, act as plasticizers, and reduce hydrolysis resistance.

In my opinion, careless manufacturing of any resin — particularly polyesters used for marine applications — is responsible for as much structural degradation in boat hulls as that usually attributed to poor workmanship. Attention to proper manufacturing methods answers why some older 100% ortho-based polyester hulls and containers (spas, swimming pools, and tanks) have outperformed even some isos. The resins were simply manufactured to good standards; and we assume workmanship was good also.

Isophthalic polyester resins are an improvement over the orthos because they provide greater corrosion resistance, including resistance to hydrolytic attack, a form of corrosion. These are produced by a two-stage process. The higher corrosion resistant types are usually iso-neopentyl compounds.

Because of the benefit of iso resins, it would be futile for a manufacturer of resins to put together higher-cost materials using a more expensive process and then allow sloppy quality control. Because of this, the end user has come to expect and receive the constant performance the iso esters have shown. There are still a few problem producers, so don't let your guard down.

Another type of polyester is derived from bis-phenol A, which is produced by the reaction of phenol (carbolic acid) and acetone. This, combined with propylene oxide or fumaric acid and certain modifications, produces corrosion resistant resin comparable to vinylesters and epoxies. Another type is chlorendic anhydride polyester, which is highly fire resistant, but should be used only where codes or other specification are required. This type is low in hydrolysis resistance. Environments of intense heat will produce toxic fumes.

Another almost forgotten type of polyester is the powdered form. In this condition, almost any reactive monomer and combination may be added to formulate a liquid laminating resin. Actually, when polyester resins were first produced many years ago, it was common to purchase the powder and scrounge for the solvent — usually styrene or methylmethacrylate monomer. About the only producer today of powdered polyester resin is Reichold Chemicals *(MS 26)* with their Atlac 382.

Vinylester

Vinylester resins contain an epoxy backbone, which is the diglycidyl ether of bis-phenol A. This backbone, which contains vinyl groups, is co-reacted with styrene or sometimes vinyltoluene monomer. This provides a low viscosity, and usually a more corrosion-resistant resin than the polyesters. The chemistry is described as a methacrylated bis-phenol A diglycidyl ether. Chemical attack on all ester-containing unsaturated resins, such as vinylesters and polyesters, will naturally occur at the most reactive sites of their chains, which are the ester linkages and unreacted (unsaturated) vinyl groups (carbon-to-carbon double bonds). Ester groups are subject to hydrolysis, whereas unreacted carbon-to-carbon double bonds can be split through reactions including oxidation and halogenation (hooking on of chlorine, bromine, etc.)

In vinylesters, reactive sites are limited to the ends of the molecule chain *(See Section III, Reference 10)*. You will notice the absence of ester linkages in the backbone of the vinylester, where three occur in the polyesters. The absence of ester linkages within the backbone make vinylester resins less susceptible than polyesters to hydrolysis. Vinylesters are usually co-reacted with styrene monomer. Alpha-methylstyrene and, recently, vinyltoluene monomers also are being used because they offer lower volatile organic compound (VOC) emission.

Though vinylesters contain an epoxy backbone, they should not be confused with epoxy resins.

A Note on Resins Containing Dicyclopentadiene Intermediate

Though by itself not a resin, dicyclopentadiene (DCPD) sometimes is used in compounding marine grade polyester resins. This is used primarily to lower cost. Claims are made that it improves hydrolytic resistance and that it cures with a tack-free surface. Resins containing this product usually show low yield and poor impact strength and are brittle. Because resin air-surfaces with this material will cure to nearly 100%, weak interlaminar bond is likely unless aggressive sanding operations are performed. I do not recommend use of DCPD in marine laminating resins.

Dow Chemical Company *(MS 4)* offers an experimental grade of vinylester resin, XU 71973.00, in which vinyltoluene is used as the sole monomer. Volatile emissions are half of those produced by styrene monomer with no loss of physicals. Dow also offers an experimental emission suppressant, XU 7193, which may be used at about 1% with polyester-styrene, vinylester-styrene, and vinylester-vinyltoluene to reduce emissions below the California standard of 60 g/cubic meter.

Hybrid Ester Resins

Ashland Chemical Company's AME 4000 *(MS 27)* and Reichold's Hydrex 33-250-01 *(MS 26)* are specifically formulated resins for marine use. Both are activated with promoters and methylethylketone peroxide. It is publicly stated that AME 4000 is a modified epoxy resin. Hydrex 33-250—01 is privately described as a modified epoxy also. Both firms use the protection of the word "proprietary" when asked about the true make-up of their product when, in fact, neither is an epoxy resin in the sense they would have you believe. Both are blends of polyester and vinylester resins. The fact that vinylester resin is present allows them to use the term "epoxy" because vinylester resins do contain epoxide background groups. This is a marketing tool which is intended to give you the impression that these hybrids are some type of epoxy resin as you know it, which they are not. You might wish to try blending polyester and vinylester resins for performance and cost comparison.

Both of these resins are pre-promoted and pre-thixed. As discussed in detail earlier, because of the presence (usually) of a thixotrope, which is very likely not chemically coupled, some reservation should be given to using these or any other resins containing untreated fumed silica or equivalent.

Pre-Catalyzed Ester Resins

Pre-catalyzed ester resins are considered hybrids also. Under license from BASF Corporation *(MS 28)*, Sunrez Corporation *(MS 29)* supplies prepackaged ester resins containing a photoinitiator reactive to ultraviolet (UV) or electron beam (EB) sources. Sunrez is a compounder and compounder-contractor who will supply the resin type of their customer's choice, ready to use as a one-component material. With few exceptions, neither Sunrez nor their distributors stock any specific resin. The way this works is that the end user specifies to Sunrez which resin he will use. Then Sunrez contracts with whomever makes the basic resin to make additions which may include certain thixotropes as well as initiator.

Photoinitiators

Unlike conventional initiators, photo-reactive initiators require no peroxide, promoter, or accelerator. The resin is first formulated neat by the basic manufacturer. Then Sunrez adds their ingredients. Thus the resin is completely ready for the end user with the "catalyst" already added. The BASF activator used by Sunrez is an alpha cleavage free radical photoinitiator with the trade name of Lucrin TPO. Chemically, it is called 2,4,6-trimethyl-benzoyldiphenyl phosphene oxide (TPO). This is a true catalyst, as it activates the resin but subsequently

Figure 1 – Manufacturing Process for Bis A-Based Epoxy Resins

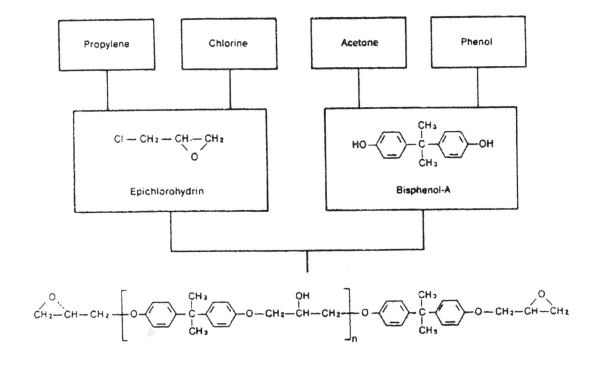

self-destructs, leaving no residue or reaction product in the cured resin. *(See Section III, Reference 12.)* As stated before, be sure none of these resins contain dicyclopentadiene (DCPD).

Epoxy (Epoxide) Resins

The term "epoxy" comes from "ep," the Greek term for over or between, and "oxy" meaning containing oxygen; thus, ep-oxy. Schematically this is:

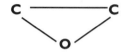

With carbon, this gives the symbol for a reactive site or oxirane group. The epoxy resins discussed here are usually the bis-phenol type. A schematic of the manufacturing process of epoxy resin by Dow Chemical Company is shown in Figure 1 on the previous page.

Compared to the relatively few resins (*e.g.*, the base resin before addition of the hardener or catalyst) there are dozens, if not hundreds, of activators. While basic resins may be diluted with various substances — some co-reactive, some non-reactive or just solvents — they are still only variations or "compounds" of the original basic monomer.

In the United States there are few manufacturers who are truly basic; *i.e.*, who manufacture their own ingredients. All others are considered compounders or repackagers, many of whom disguise their products with trade names or labels. Dow Chemical, USA *(MS 23)*, Shell Chemical Company *(MS 30)*, and Ciba-Geigy *(MS 31)* are the principal basic manufacturers. Except for a few high-performance products, it is not likely that many marine structures — at least large boat hulls — will be manufactured with 100% epoxy resin. Rather, its use will be limited to repairs and application of barrier coats.

Typical ambient temperature hardeners for epoxies will be aliphatic polyamines and polyamides. Use of these and others will be discussed in "Manufacturing Methods" following. *(See also Section III, Reference 12.)*

Modified epoxy resins by Morton International *(MS 32)* are epoxy terminated polysulfides for use as containment (barrier) coatings. Three similar types — FEC 2232, FEC 2233 and FEC 2234 — provide rigid, flexible and elastomeric resins respectively. Suggested film build is 0.030 inch, consisting of two applied passes of 0.015-inch each. All three FEC coatings are filled with titanium dioxide and quartz powder. The color is light gray. I have made long-term osmotic tests with all three of these products showing excellent results.

These modified epoxies could be used as finish barrier coats for boat bottoms over sound, sanded gel coat as well as for a barrier coat over repairs. They are probably best suited for use as top coats over lower viscosity resins used for deep penetration. Use of TPR 415 primer is recommended.

Phenolic Resins

When most writers, including myself, come to the subject of phenolic resins they recite the usual dialog about their use in some glues, automobile distributor caps, brake linings, grinding wheels, light switches, and pipe stems. Read about phenolics in the 1992, 1993, or later issues of *Modern Plastics Catalog* and you will find a description of the chemistry and physical data. It will tell you that the phenolics come in resole or novolac form and that high temperature and pressure are required for cure. You may also be informed that phenolics have joined the ranks of so-called engineering resins. Few if any words are included about liquid phenolics, which can be processed like hand-laid polyesters and epoxies.

Phenolic wet lay-up resins are available for marine construction, but as of 1996 they were being used very little in the United States. I urge you to read my discussion in Section III, References 13 and 30.

Furfuryl Alcohol Resins

Furfural (not misspelled) resins, particularly furfuryl alcohol, is another group of materials overlooked by many in the reinforced plastics industry and, in particular, the marine industry. It is enough that *Modern Plastics* magazine barely mentions liquid phenolics, and then only as a casting resin. For them not to even mention the furfurals as construction resins is a disservice to the plastics industry.

Many who at least know of its existence consider furfuryl alcohol resin to be useful only for its outstanding chemical resistance and for use in making sand cores in the foundry industry. Some will also recognize its fire resistance, which is comparable to the phenolics. Few realize the value of furfuryl alcohol as a marine construction resin.

Although fabrication techniques are similar to polyester, epoxy and phenolic resins, the marine industry so far has made little use of furfural resins for the same reasons that phenolics are not yet accepted. The reasons include unfamiliarity and a concern that new or modified techniques may be required. Again, necessity may change this attitude when regulatory agencies begin to impose emission, smoke, toxicity, and fire propagation standards. I suggest you read more about furfuryl alcohol resins in Section III, Reference 14.

Polysulfide Resins

An interesting barrier coating, RLP 2078 by Morton International *(MS 32)* is a 100% polysulfide elastomeric coating used with a catalyst. RLP is designed to be used with their primer-coupler TPR 415, which is a chlorinated rubber-organosilane. This primer will increase bond to any suitable substrate by several orders of magnitude. I have made several tests lasting more than two years and have found excellent adhesion of RLP 2078 when this primer is used. TPR primer has about the same viscosity as water and should be sprayed in a very light coat, then dried thoroughly. RLP may be sprayed, brushed, or rolled without the use of solvent, but for easier spraying, some methylethylketone (MEK) or xylol may be required. I especially recommend RLP 2078 for bilge coating, and manufacturers should take note because the ideal application time for bilge coating is when the hull is still at the factory.

RLP can be reinforced. Try brush or roller coating to about 0.015 over a sanded polyester gel coat which has been primed with TPR 415. Allow to cure overnight. Next, tailor on dry, a ply of 7- to 10-ounce open weave glass cloth onto the cured film; then coat the fabric with RLP using a serrated roller to smooth. After cure, a third coat may be applied to improve appearance. Allow this to cure for a few days. Then try to peel off the coating with vise grips!

Urethane Resins

Futura Coatings, Inc. *(MS 67 and Section III, Reference 35)* makes a high modulus urethane-polyester hybrid structural laminating resin compatible with all gel coats. Urethane foams are used with other resins as cores for sandwich structures. They may be used as co-polymers with ester and epoxy resins. Gel coated and un-gel coated polyester, vinylester and epoxy-based hulls are often coated with two-part urethane resins as a barrier and/or appearance finish. Almost all one-off hulls are coated with a urethane paint over the entire hull. *(See Section III, Reference 15 and MS 31.)*

Marine Paints

Of course, conventional marine paints are not used as structural materials, except possibly when used with canvas to cover a canoe, but are confined to use as barrier and appearance coatings. Marine air-dried paints are not conventionally used on fiberglass products for moisture barriers. Paints are, nevertheless, resins in solution. They are not considered usable as a laminating resin at present standards, but may be considered as barrier coatings. If you want to believe the second University of Rhode Island report *(Section III, Reference 24)*, you may.

GENERAL CURING SYSTEMS FOR THE RESINS DISCUSSED

Any thermoset resin will require some form of initiation to accomplish cure. Cross-linking occurs through condensation (phenolics) or polymerization (esters). Heat alone is the primary initiator. True catalysts will cause a reaction but will not usually become part of the reaction product. An initiator is just that; it is not considered a catalyst in the strict sense. An initiator may be a chemical, another resin, whole sunlight, or a specific wavelength of radiation such as ultraviolet light used for photoinitiating. *(See Section III, Reference 12.)*

Some curing systems, depending upon the type of resin being used, provide only a "kick in the apogee," *i.e.*, they initiate the first part of the reaction, which then causes the resin to auto-cure, usually with the production of heat, which provides completion of the reaction.

Catalysts for the Esters

For all practical purposes, the catalyst, more properly called initiator, will be methylethylketone peroxide (MEK or MEKP) carried in a semi-reactive solvent-plasticizer such as dimethylphthalate or equivalent. A promoter, usually cobalt napthenate, which is a paint drier, is almost always added to the resin by the manufacturer. An accelerator such as dimethylaniline (DMA), diethylaniline (DEA) or dimethylacetoacetamide (DMMA) can be added to the resin before catalysis to speed gel time. Almost all vinylesters and their hybrids *require* one of the anilines with cobalt napthenate in order to cure. The anilines react with MEKP only in the presence of a metal salt such as cobalt napthenate (CN). The addition of DMA, DEA, or DMMA to a resin not containing CN will have little effect on gel time when using MEKP alone.

Benzoyl peroxide (BZP) is another widely used catalyst. It is usually mixed into the resin as a 50/50 paste made by grinding BZP granules in a plasticizer. ***WARNING:* Do not attempt this grinding operation as it is extremely dangerous!** This paste is the so-called hardener you get in a tube with a can of Bondo™ or its equivalent. "Liquid" forms of BZP are now available, especially for catalyst injection equipment.

Exactly opposite MEKP, benzoyl peroxide does not react with the cobalt napthenate in the resin — only with the aniline. When you open a new undisturbed can of Bondo™ or other polyester "body putty," you will notice the purplish color of cobalt napthenate floating on the surface. While BZP is used as the activator, the purpose of the CN is to act only as an inhibitor to premature curing of the polyester resin. It happens that almost all Bondo™ type putties will also self-cure with MEKP as the activator. In my opinion, this offers much better control of gel time than when BZP is used. When BZP is selected, there are liquid forms available for polyester and vinylester resin curing.

Because gel time is not easily controlled when using BZP-aniline as the curing means, this method is not widely accepted in manufacturing hand lay-up of structural parts. I feel more effort should be placed on practical ways of using BZP as a hand lay-up activator if for no other reason than there is no retained water in its formulation. I know of no published information where BZP-aniline used as the activator was, by itself, determined to contribute to hydrolysis of the resin.

It was not until the blister problem appeared in spas that we began to look for the sources of either water contained in the gel coat before spraying or water that somehow got onto the mold. Air lines were carefully purged and compressed air refrigerated to remove moisture. Molds were kept dry and sometimes heated for this purpose. But the blisters — especially short term — still persisted. Eventually we turned to the MEKP catalyst and found it as a source of water. The use of MEKP will continue to be the principal activator used in hand lay-up operations for some time. MEKP containing the lowest percentage of water must be used.

As has been stated before, one of the most common problems is caused by misuse of the initiator and/or by molding under high humidity conditions. Unless initiator is added in stoichiometric amount, there will always be reduced chemical resistance, low heat resistance, and high warpage tendency. However, if the basic process of producing the resin in the first place is not carefully controlled, no amount of initiator — stoichiometrically correct or not — will correct an improperly formulated resin.

MANUFACTURING METHODS

WOOD CONSTRUCTION

Hollow out a log. Don't knock it — it's still being done. Even the natives benefit today from a good epoxy glue! We are still using logs for boats. The only difference is that we cut the log up first then put it back together to form a shell. Many a strip-planked hull has been covered with impregnated canvas. Plywood panels and "cold molded" veneers are routinely overlaid with a reinforcing surface. Of course, my old 40-ton trawler planked with 3-inch mahogany has only paint for its surfaces.

Marine plywood is shaped over some type of forming structure, which may be constructed as a permanent fixture or used one time only. The hull design generally provides for forming the hull from developable flat sheets with some goring allowed. A reinforcing skin is usually applied.

Before World War II ended, some of us used thickened lacquers of ethylcellulose and cotton fabric as the reinforcing and exterior surface. When the first polyesters and glass fabrics became available, we had no so-called room temperature curing catalysts except for a miserable ultraviolet-reactable benzoin compound generally known as sunlight catalyst. As long as true sun or UV bulbs could "see" the resin, it might cure. Let it hide in the shade or under something and be left without a source of UV even for a short time, then you have a sticky mess on your hands. For the first two or three years after World War II, many a wood hull and deck were covered using polyester resin and this catalyst.

I had the good fortune to perfect the use of cobalt napthenate as a promoter for methylethylketone peroxide (MEKP) in about 1947.[1] This resulted in a true low-temperature curing system for polyesters, and it is used without a source of ultraviolet light or other external energy. Because this curing system was obviously so easy to use and the word spread rapidly, some poor workmanship resulted mostly because it was thought that the "magic" of fiberglass could make up for poor construction. Well, if you slapped enough on? Many did.

Blisters and delaminations were common in those early days. Wood boats, regardless of size, were usually covered with only one ply of 10-ounce woven glass cloth on the outside of the hull only. Rarely was the bare wood primed with resin before application of the fabric. Practically unknown was the necessity of using a mat of some form under the cloth to assure adhesion. Consider a casually constructed 40-foot hull relying on its one-ply woven skin to hold it together — you are visualizing a disaster.

Today, good manufacturing practice for wood panel construction will require pre-laminating inside surfaces of the panels before assembly to the form. Often, standard-length panels are scarfed joined end-to-end in long lengths before being laminated with reinforcement. Before applying any reinforcement, however, the panel must be thoroughly primed with resin. Resin must be applied until there are no dull spots. Then the first ply of reinforcement is applied as soon as possible after the last prime coat. The construction is a light weight, non-bound, non-sized but coupled underlay veil, light chopped strand mat, or a light application of chopped roving from a gun over which at least one ply of uni-directional fabric is placed.

Applying reinforcement to the inside of panels for hull and deck before assembly provides many obvious advantages. It's also an excellent opportunity to use a phenolic or furfuryl resin for both fireproofing and structural improvement. This applies to both sides of cabin structures as well. For the bilge, after the panels have been installed, you should also consider a type of containment barrier coat such as polysulfide, which has excellent moisture permeation resistance.

The outside covering laminates, depending upon design requirements and location on the hull, will be scheduled by the designer. For a typical well-built 30-foot fiberglass reinforced plywood hull, one ply of tri-axial fabric would be applied. This fabric assembly weighs about 40 ounces per square yard and consists of one ply of uni-directional fabric at 0°, one ply at minus 45°, one ply at plus 45°, and one (bottom) ply of 1-ounce chopped strand mat. The whole assembly comes stitched together. This construction would probably suffice for hull sides and both surfaces of deck panels. Additional layers of tri-axial fabric may be applied to the bottom. In place of or in addition to some of the outside reinforcement, you might consider using two or more plies of ECPE polyethylene fabric for the outside at the bottom to provide outstanding impact and abrasion resistance. (*See Section III, Reference 2.*)

All the usual resins may be applied with these fabrics. A good high grade, medium elongation iso-polyester is a good economical choice, particularly if fiberglass is the only reinforcing material. If areas of high strength are required where aramid or carbon filaments would be indicated, then a medium elongation vinylester may be chosen. An epoxy modified to produce medium elongation could also be used. Polyesters should not be used with aramid fibers since they do not bond well, and though possible, they should not be used with carbon fibers. If epoxy or vinylesters are used above the waterline, a UV protective coating must be applied as the top coat.

Planked construction including glued-up veneers does not lend itself to pre-application of reinforcement to the inside surface of the planks or veneers prior to attachment.

If new construction is monocoque (*i.e.*, no ribs or bulkheads yet installed), a laminate could be applied to the inside prior to installation of other structure — this is exactly the procedure when finishing the inside of a one-off foam cored hull.

The laminating schedule for the outside of planked hulls would be similar to plywood construction discussed previously. If no reinforcement is to be applied to the inside of the hull and decks, then an impregnant should be applied liberally to reduce water absorption. If the boat is either new or older and dry, a low viscosity epoxy or one diluted with furfuryl or benzyl alcohol will provide deep penetration for the first saturation coats. Follow these with undiluted epoxy resin. If a hull has a high percentage of absorbed water and epoxy saturation is desired, use a hardener which tolerates moisture.

Laminating schedules for the outside of new or older dry planked hulls must include a more elastomeric (higher elongation) resin than for panel or solid strip veneer ("cold molding") construction. While woven fabrics may be used for cosmetic reasons such as cabinetry or joinery — or where used for abrasion and impact surfaces such as polyethylene cloth — woven materials have no place in structural reinforced plastics.

---

1. Before 1947, Dr. Muscat of Muscat Resins Co. found that cobalt napthenate — a well known paint drier — would produce a gel in ester resins when used with MEKP. For reasons never explained to me, he insisted on adding the CN in small amounts to the resin only after the MEKP had been added. Very long gel time was encountered and, often, complete cure did not occur. Also, I suspect that the quality of his MEKP may not have been high.

An acquaintance, Dexter Benner, had tried Muscat's process and had given up in frustration. However, he offered to give me his stock of cobalt napthenate. Being a bit of a paint chemist myself, I knew that, like building a good martini, you've got to age the mix to achieve perfection. As it proved out, by adding at least ½% of 6% strength cobalt

napthenate (this worked out to be about 1 quart of CN per 500-pound drum of resin) drier to the **uncatalized** *resin with thorough mixing, the CN dispersed (aged) in the resin. We also discovered that the additional CN increased the shelf life of the resin many months. The resin companies already used a small amount for this purpose.*

At room temperature then, by adding 1 to 1½% MEKP (at the time we used "Uniperox." then a product of Union Oil Company, which had a high oxygen content), we produced gel and full cure within about an hour.

I believe perfecting this process alone may have been the launching pad for much of the polyester wet lay-up industry as we know it today.

CORED CONSTRUCTION

If strip-planked, carvel-planked, or plywood hulls are covered with reinforcement on both sides, this would technically be cored construction. In this discussion, the definition of "core" also includes structural foams, honeycombs, end-grained wood (balsa), and syntactic materials (microballoon-resin mixes).

STRUCTURAL SHEET FOAM CONSTRUCTION

The term "one-off" means just that. When it is contemplated that a design will be produced one time only, then only one part will be pulled off the form, mold or jig. More specifically, the term "one-off" is used when referring to structural sheet foam

85-foot Airex vinyl foam core one-off by Knight & Carver, designed by Richard Reineman.

The black hull is an 85-foot one-off Airex PVC foamed core construction. Knight & Carver decided to make a female permanent mold from this hull. Photos show the female mold being removed from the one-off, which acted as a temporary plug. This is an unusual two-for-one gain.

construction. Rigid vinyl resin sheet foam is the most widely used today. Planking procedures for foam sheet stock follow the same path as planking with plywood panels.

Cross-gored foam panels are applied to suitable forms to allow compound shapes to be made. The most reliable system of applying reinforcement is by the lay-down method. Here, the hull is to be planked in the inverted position. The core sheets are placed, gaps and seams are filled with syntactic putty, and the entire outside surface of the hull is primed with resin. Then the appropriate laminations of reinforcements are applied. No vacuum bagging or other assist is required. The same

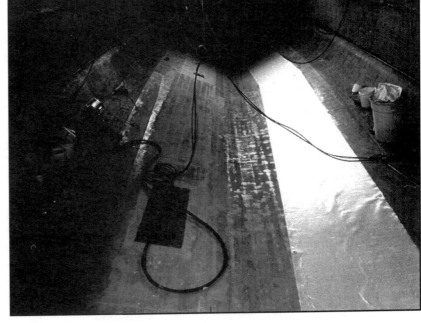

In one-off construction, the hull is placed upright after installation of the outer skin. Then, the inside of the hull is laminated with reinforcement by hand lay-up.

procedure is followed after the hull is placed upright. Gaps and seams are again filled, the entire surface primed with resin, then reinforcement is applied — again, by lay-down. A fireproof resin (phenolic or furfuryl) should be considered as the main interior structural resin or, at least, used as a cladding. All these procedures apply to any core material.

END-GRAINED BALSA BLOCKS

This type of core is discussed in the sheet foam category because of its similarity to foam. Balsa blocks may be laid over solid forms or molds, then seams and gaps properly filled and sealed, laminations applied, the hull rolled over and completed as in foam construction — all by the lay-down method, of course.

STYRENE FOAM

Styrene foam is not often used for marine structures — particularly hulls — because of its solubility in ester resins and many common solvents including gasoline. But styrene foam may be used, for example, as core material in surfboard blanks, aircraft parts, building panels etc., where non-styrenic resins or other bonding materials are used.

POLYETHYLENE, POLYPROPYLENE, AND POLYETHYLENE-POLYSTYRENE HYBRID FOAMS

Polyethylene, polypropylene, and polyethylene-polystyrene hybrid foams are new candidates for marine structures which will accommodate any resin; however, these are not yet widely used.

URETHANE FOAM

Urethane foam — whether flexible as used in upholstery, rigid sheet stock, or poured in place — has no business aboard any boat large enough to have enclosed cabins. First, it produces toxic fumes when burned. Second, it has high water absorption, regardless of density or rigidity.

STRUCTURAL SHEET FOAM CONSTRUCTION USING ONE-OFF METHOD WITH A FEMALE MOLD

When sheet foam stock is used in conjunction with a female mold, the one-off method of molding does not usually apply. The use of a female mold implies that a number of duplicate parts would be molded. If the structure is to be a cored sandwich, the core must be bonded to an outer skin followed by an inner skin. This operation might not be repeated for some reason so could be considered a one-off. An example of this might be that a manufacturer who usually makes single shell structures could offer a "custom" cored sandwich part. The method of using a female mold for sandwich construction applies to other types of cores, as well. All cores, regardless of type, are usually bonded to the outer skin using vacuum assist when this process is used.

STRUCTURAL SYNTACTIC CONSTRUCTION

Syntactic foam is usually just a mix of microspheres and a resin. In this form it provides a "pourable" core stock in just about any viscosity required. In a stiff thixotropic form it is used as a screeding putty for filling and fairing. It may also be used in a limited way as a structural core material. It can be sprayed to give almost any thickness. Syntactics become structural cores when poured into a mold, cured, and covered with a reinforcement. Rudders, keels, and flotation devices are examples. Other syntactic combinations may use solid beads, pellets, granules, or scrap made from almost any material, along with a suitable matrix resin. An example would be a keel poured in place in the hull of a sailboat. The mix may be steel or lead shot encased in a resin or discarded nuts and bolts — even gravel, wheel weights, or anything small and heavy. So-called polymer concrete — marble chips, sand, or ground metal scrap imbedded in a resin — all of these will work.

STRUCTURAL SHEET HONEYCOMB CONSTRUCTION

Expanded honeycomb cores are available in many materials. Most metals, impregnated paper, fiberglass, polyethylene and polypropylene are examples. Most of these are supplied without solid scrim faces, so some technique must be provided to prevent cells from filling with resin. Attachment of honeycomb sheet must almost always be applied with vacuum blanket assist. Honeycomb should not be used for hulls, particularly below the waterline, because of water permeation into the open cells. Decks and cabin structures are their place.

Nida-Core Corporation's Nida-Core (*MS 10*) is the source for lightweight polypropylene honeycomb. Offered in 3/8-inch (8mm) cell size only, it is extruded into 4x4x18-inch logs. These are stacked and welded ultrasonically into a billet which is then hot-wire cut into sheets of various thicknesses. A non-woven polyester scrim with a polyethylene barrier film is thermofused to the surface of the core sheets, thus locking the ends of the cells to the scrim fibers. The barrier film is available in either non-permeable form for resin transfer products, or semi-permeable for bedding a vacuum bagged compound curved sheet. The semi-permeable film normally will not pass thixotropic or filled resin into the cells; yet it will prevent bubbles from being trapped under the core.

Virtually any width or height may be assembled into sheet form. Thickness is determined by cutting crosswise (perpendicular to the axis of the cells). Sheets of basic core are 4x7 feet long and thicknesses are available from 3/8-inch to 18 inches. Sheets up to 1 inch thick may be ordered with 2-inch scoring to allow forming to compound shapes.

Polypropylene is flammable, but a brominate may be added to the polypropylene base resin before extrusion to provide some fire retardancy. The core weight is approximately 4.8 pounds per cubic foot. As of 1994, cost including scrim faces for 1-inch stock is around $2.00 per square foot.

Just about any laminating resin may be used for wet lay-up work. Nida-Core makes flat panels with skins of various materials including aluminum, Formica (phenolic), wood, steel, and various RP skins. Cells may be ordered filled with phenolic or urethane foam for insulation and sound deadening, but water absorption into these filler foams should be checked even for marine joinery.

The core and faces of Nida-Core are transparent to ultraviolet light, so they are suitable for use with resins using photoinitiators. This core is relatively inert to chemical attack. Also, it will not rot. Cell stock is available with hot-wire scoring to provide inter-cell connection. This opens the opportunity to use the cells for storage of liquids such as water, fuel, and other chemicals. Burt Rutan's around the world *Voyager* airplane used DuPont's Nomex *(MS 3)* scored aramid honeycomb for fuel tanks as well as for structure.

SINGLE SKIN (SOLID) CONSTRUCTION

Before the industry had developed a practical female molding process, almost all open fiberglass work was performed on male molds. They were often made of plaster of Paris. You might think this process is *passé* but don't forget, just about every female mold is made over a male form (mold). If the part to be made requires a finish surface only on the inside, then the mold is male. This becomes logical whether the part is to be used as a mold or is a production part. If a part or duplicate mold requires a finish surface on the outside then the mold is female. Whether the part is male or female, an opportunity to use a fireproof barrier presents itself. Except to repeat that no woven fabrics should be used in molding structural parts, no further description of this well-known process is required.

FAIRING AND FINISHING OF APPEARANCE SURFACES

Except for repair, there is little need for most major finishing operations with parts made with an on-mold gel coat surface. When the appearance surface is not created by the mold, hand finishing is required. Any one-off molding, particularly a boat hull which is formed over a male mold or form, will require surface finishing by hand.

Reasonable attention to butt and lap joints at the time of lay-up of fabric blankets will determine the amount of preliminary rough grinding prior to application of fairing materials. Judicious use of "peel ply" and careful roll-out will reduce grinding requirements. In any event, overall fairness must be achieved during power sanding operations. Only minor high spots are to be removed and these should be very local. If large continuous areas require removal, then considerable structural material will be lost. This would indicate the existence of a flaw in original lofting or form construction; or that more material may have been applied in some areas than necessary.

Once the part has been "trued" and all flaws are low spots, initial fairing with a microballoon-resin screeding material will be performed. The amount of surface that can be reasonably expected to be covered by the initial fairing pass is first sealed with the same resin as used in the fairing material. This is applied and brought to the gel. Fairing material is applied as soon as possible.

No attempt is made to create a final faired finish surface on the first pass — only filling of low spots, and this will never be complete the first time. As soon as the fairing compound has gelled, additional material may be added to obvious low, local areas. When the material has cured to sandability, fairing is begun using a long sanding block. The surface again is re-sealed with resin and additional compound is applied until the surface is deemed fair enough to finish with surfacing sanding primers. Final sealing with resin should be done prior to applying sanding primers.

FAIRING COMPOUNDS

For initial heavy fairing, glass microballoons such as 3M Company's Glass Bubbles *(MS 33)* are the preferred micros (avoid substitutes), and the preferred matrix resin, vinylester or epoxy. Sealing resin should be the same as the microballoon matrix resin.

Depending upon the quality of the surface after clear resin sealing, a number of options are open for semi-finishing with primer-surfacer. Commercial high-build, sanding-grade paint-type primer surfacers are available. Resinous types which are based on epoxy or vinylester are top-coated with urethane or conventional marine paint. It is my opinion that reverse polyester gel coating (discussed later) provides one of the most reliable semi- and final-finish methods providing, of course, that the hull and all fairing materials use the same class of resin. Whatever the semi-finished base, it may be followed by any conventional top coat and/or barrier coating. These fairing and finishing operations apply to all major repairs as well as new construction.

Durall Corporation's "Duratec Vinylester Surfacing Primer" *(MS 34),* unlike commercial repair options described later, uses vinylester as the base resin rather than epoxy, as do most commercial repair procedures. Durall does not offer or claim this product as the sole material for the repair of blister damage. They also do not wish to imply that it should be used in place of those coatings that are commercially advertised as moisture barrier coatings.

The principal use of Duratec vinylester is for high build and fairing, much like reverse gel coating. It may be used in place of gel coat over newly repaired laminate; or when resurfacing sound laminate where the gel coat has been removed. Above the waterline, some type of top coat must be added because vinylesters, even if pigmented, have poor resistance to sunlight. (*See Section III, Reference 16.*)

There is apprehension among many regarding the hand labor to screed and finish fair, one-off products as just described. If sufficient production of one design justifies the cost of a female mold, and the product requires only a single shell, and even if the product is very large, then this may be the best choice. If a cored product is specified using a female mold, the extra cost and possible reduction in quality of core attachment to the outer shell must be considered.

If hand finishing the appearance surface of a product appears worrisome, it is likely that the planner has not done his homework. Hand fairing certainly is an art, but it is widely used today and it would be wise of a manufacturer or boat repair facility to master this art.

Any manufacturing process that produces a hull having a polyester gel-coated final surface is a candidate for additional barrier coat before it is ever launched. This applies to replacement gel coating on older hulls as well. I recommend it for added protection.

RESIN TRANSFER MOLDING

"Resin transfer" is a general term used to describe the movement of a liquid or liquefiable resin from a fixed volume chamber to some type of cavity which will be a closed die of some type. The means of transfer of the resin will determine the actual molding method. Here is a little history:

Upon the invention of phenolic molding compounds in 1909, the first molds were constructed as male and female compression dies, which provided high molding pressure by the telescoping action of closely fitted heated metal molds. The mating of the telescoping parts was critical yet, of necessity, was required to produce some flash since the cavities had to be slightly over-filled to ensure complete filling of the cavity and removal of voids.

Depending upon the formulation of the molding compound, often the two halves of the die had to be "bumped" early in the cure cycle. Phenolics are condensation curing resins which produce water-of-reaction in the form of steam and gas, which must be vented by slightly opening the two halves of the dies momentarily to allow the vapor-gas to escape, then the molds are quickly closed while the resin is still soft. Pressure is again applied until cure is completed.

Because flash can be a nuisance, and certain shapes are costly to make with telescoping molds, necessity required a better molding method. Thus, resin transfer molding (RTM) was developed.

RTM offers the advantage of not requiring telescoping molds. A closed, flat surface at the parting line and sufficient mechanical force (usually in tons) to tightly close the two halves are all that is required. Unlike compression molding, no flash is produced. A port(s) is provided to allow injection of molten resin by means of a short tube (gate) connected to a transfer chamber which, in turn, is fitted with a close-fitting piston. All components are usually incorporated within the die block so that an even temperature on all parts of the mold may be maintained.

The press is usually vertical simply because presses in general, by convention and necessity, were vertical. The injection (transfer) piston is usually operated mechanically by a compound motion on the closing of the press platens. The stroke of the injection piston and its cylinder provide the exact volume of resin to fill the mold cavity. Because very high hydraulic action can be held on the resin within the cavity until cure, no bumping or breathing of the die is necessary and, of course, no flash is produced.

Resin transfer molding was early adapted to thermoplastic resins by making some relatively simple modifications. Mold design remained nearly identical to thermoset resin molds, *e.g.,* two halves are clamped shut mechanically. An injection port is provided externally. Instead of having an injection cylinder and piston as in integral part of the die set to provide an exact volume for the "shot" as required with thermoset resins, a separate large heated cylinder or "barrel" driven by a hydraulic cylinder or screw is provided. This is constructed to allow placement of resin granules within the cylinder, which then become liquefied. The delivery end of the barrel is fitted with a nipple and is aligned with the injection port on the die through which melted resin is shot into the cold die and held under pressure until the resin has cooled to solidification. Eventually, because presses no longer had to be two stories high and also for convenience, presses were constructed in the horizontal position. Today, presses processing either thermoset or thermoplastic resins can be made to operate in any position.

At the advent of zero-pressure, room- (or slightly elevated) temperature, thermoset resins suitable for open lay-up molding, it became quickly obvious that the principal of injecting low viscosity resin into very lightweight, inexpensive closed molds containing some form of reinforcement (not necessarily fibrous) preplaced within the mold cavity was entirely practical.

By 1948, having developed a practical room temperature cured polyester resin, developed a pigmented gel coating system, and perfected hand lay-up open molding to a routine, some of us saw the need to provide two finished surfaces to some parts and to eliminate hand operations. The chopper gun had yet to be developed. At the time we were not much concerned with volatile emissions (VOCs). There was no EPA!

I was an early developer of gel coated fiberglass plumbing fixtures such as shower stall bases, lavatories and bathtubs. As a result, I became the author of the first United States Bureau of Standards voluntary standard for gel coated plumbing fixtures.

At one of the various meetings in Washington, DC, I met the owner of a firm who had just received a patent to produce bathtubs by infusion of polyester resin into a chopped fiberglass preform contained by two shells to form a male and female mold. The service side — the male mold — contained a gel coat. Both molds were inverted. A continuous trough was provided around the perimeter of the male mold which became the resin supply source. The outer mold shell was placed over the male mold into which was placed a chopped strand preform. The outer shell was positioned so its edge extended into the resin trough. One or more ports were provided at the top of the assembly to provide vacuum access. Thus, an early buzzword evolved — infusion molding. I learned later that this gentleman and his patented process were abandoned because of financial problems and the requirement for rapid design changes. Also, plumbing fixtures required only one finished surface.

The perfection of the chopper spray-up gun and the serrated roller at about this time allowed unskilled workers to "roll out" small parts over single male molds without the need of preforms, a far more productive system. In the plumbing fixture industry, this is still true today, 50 years later. As we also recognize today, there is an

Marbleized gel coat on thin single skin mat and cloth shell. Each complete lavatory required 7 minutes to hand lay-up, including gel coating.

optimum size, or breaking point, where one process will prevail over another.

Going back to the late '40s and early '50s, simple vacuum bag processes were being used. They never really could compete with hand lay-up. Many start-up firms learned the hard way by refusing to learn the hand lay-up art. They tried to complete using simple wet vacuum bag processes where hand lay-up methods could win hands down. Military specifications rarely allowed crude hand laid parts because they rarely understood the process. MIL specs often required the use of pre-pregged materials which required the use of vacuum bags, so vacuum bagging techniques were relatively fine-tuned.

Now enter on the stage run-of-the-mill open molded parts so large that they were becoming labor intensive, inefficient to produce, and often unreliable in quality. I am talking about large parts such as boat hulls in the 50- to 100-foot range. Ordinary bag molding over a large wet or dry pre-preg represents obvious problems. Infusion molding over pre-placed dry reinforcements under a cover sheet (bag) has recently appeared attractive. Up to a short time ago, many technical problems with this process remained to be solved and open lay-up still prevailed.

Today, aside from the hope of achieving better quality control by infusion molding, the pressure by the EPA and the various air quality agencies to lower airborne volatiles becomes one of the driving forces to make infusion molding workable on very large parts.

This, of course, requires some form of closed mold system. Inner and outer rigid molds would obviously be totally impractical. So, the problem reduces to the use of one rigid mold and one mating flexible mold. This boils down to some form of vacuum assisted bag molding.

To infuse even low viscosity resin into massive volumes of dry reinforcement using conventional flexible bags often requires more time than even an extended gel time catalyzed resin may allow. Even though this problem has recently been reduced by development of novel flexible bags, with one exception, one serious problem remains. To provide extended gel time, much modification in resin formulation and catalyst adjustment is required. Exceptionally long gel time can drastically reduce structural strength even if post-cure heating is performed. The popularity of vinylester resin further compounds the structural problem in that this resin prefers to be gelled and

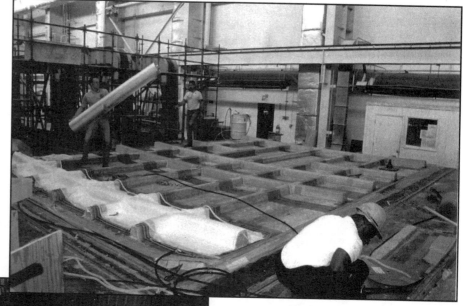

Deck structure being progressively molded by infusion. Note reinforcement in place. The bag has not yet been installed.
Courtesy of Sunrez Corp.

The bag is first loosely placed over the dry, previously placed reinforcement. Then resin is pulled in by vacuum assist. Curing is by ultraviolet light.
Courtesy of Sunrez Corp.

cured as rapidly as possible, so infusion time must be reduced to a very few hours at most, or a practical method of partial molding must be developed. Mold temperature must remain constant and post-cure heat should be applied as soon after gellation as possible at a temperature high enough and long enough well above any end use environment the product may experience, no matter how far in the future.

In general, present technology has not solved these problems to my satisfaction. I mentioned above an exception. The use of certain catalysts which may be activated by ultraviolet light does solve the problem of

Deck plate base made using infusion molding by VARTM (vacuum assisted resin transfer molding). An ultraviolet light sensitive catalyst is used which provides unlimited time for infusion. Courtesy of Sunrez Corp.

Resin progressively saturating reinforcement under patented Quick-Draw transparent film. Courtesy of Sunrez Corp.

infusion time for three basic reasons. First, they provide unlimited gel time — weeks, if necessary. Second, UV catalyzed resin is insensitive to moderate heat or cold, thus viscosity may be adjusted by increase or reduction of heat. Third, full structural value is achieved almost instantly upon exposure to a UV source. Post curing is not usually required. There are drawbacks, but these are solvable. Because the structural value of this type of resin curing is not affected by gel time, it is my opinion that this system is the most advanced so far.

Now we get into the acronym business again. Today, the overriding acronym is "VARTM" (vacuum assisted resin transfer molding). Three contenders of record appear to be out to capture the VARTM market (and each other's neck, in court) by waving the almighty patent. I smile at the dozens in the past who have created the "prior art" that some of these tend to ignore. To keep the attorneys employed, eventually, some of these souls will surface.

Then we will see what hits the fan! I also chuckle about those individuals who will quietly make the present art obsolete in short order.

Three visible contenders are:

SCRIMP. Seeman Composite Resin Infusion Molding Process is part of a joint venture firm called Scrimp Systems, L.L.C., of Cazenovia, NY (*MS 64*). This consortium licenses several patents, principally Patent # 5,439,635 dated August 8, 1995. Inventor, William Seeman. I suggest you obtain a copy for study.

Ultraviolet VARTM. Sunrez Corp. (*MS 29*) of El Cajon, CA, uses UV activated catalysts along with their patented Quick Draw vacuum bag. The molding process is straightforward. Contact Sunrez for details.

LPRM. LeConte USA (*MS 63*) calls its system Low Pressure Infusion Molding. Again, this firm relies on their patented bag material for their system and licensing.

The resin injection tube has almost filled the area in the foreground. Tubes to the right and left will be connected to the resin supply.

The first section of deck base is completely saturated with resin and the areas to the left and right will be injected.

One variation is the use of a slight positive pressure on the resin supply and the use of foam cores to assist in resin distribution. This infusion process requires a very long time.

OITW Process. "Others In The Woodpile." Watch for them!

(Please see Section III, Reference 33.)

NOTE TO MANUFACTURERS & RE-HULLERS

At the time of manufacturing a new hull or major re-hulling, a removable test panel should be molded from the same materials as used in the hull and inserted at an area in the bottom at a flat section. If a female mold will be used, it is best to mold a gel-coated panel in the mold at the insertion area approximately 1/2x16x18 inches. After removal from the mold, this panel is cut in two lengthwise. One half is cut into structural test specimens for dry structural tests then data recorded in the ship's log as "reference dry control." The second half of the panel is beveled and the cut edges applied with gel coat or epoxy. Appropriate mold release is applied to all surfaces; then using one or two blobs of modeling clay, the panel is temporarily attached to the mold. The hull is then molded as usual over the test panel. Upon removal of the hull from the mold, the test panel is removed, the cavity cleaned and the panel drilled with oversize holes to provide for attachment with stainless steel sheet metal screws. Holes and

countersinking are coated with sealing resin or gel coat. Then the panel is installed in the cavity in the hull. This will provide a flush panel which may be removed at appropriate times for structural wet tests. The space previously occupied by the one or two strips cut for tests may be filled in with syntactic putty.

In one-off construction, or if creating a cavity in the hull is a concern, the test panel may be attached to the stern or other appropriate location below the waterline.

MOLDS AND TOOLING

Before leaving the subject of manufacturing methods, some discussion regarding mold and tool construction is appropriate.

For duplicate product construction, some type of permanent mold must be produced. Except for jigs and fixtures, the one-off process does not utilize permanent molds. For repeat production, either a male or female tool is made.

For repeat hull production a female mold is used, while a male mold (often the original "plug") is used to produce one or more production female molds.

It is not my purpose here to detail methods of mold construction except to say that in general, materials and construction methods are similar to those used in the product. I wish to point out that one of the most challenging problems — particularly with very large molds — is the requirement for even temperature control during molding operations and the requirement for elevation of mold temperature for post-curing.

I am a great believer in post-curing any so-called room temperature cured product. To remove a "green" part from a mold when it has never seen an in-mold shop floor temperature higher than ambient and rarely over 90°F, then send it to the dealer's parking lot to post-cure on one side only in the sun, under load three-point on a trailer or chocks, is not my idea of proper post-curing!

It is vital to have the capability of mold heating for obvious reasons, whether by sunlight, infrared lamps, heated circulating air, convection oven, heated autoclave, or imbedded or jacketed heating elements. Very large molds are impractical to heat in an autoclave or a convection oven. Sunlight heat is intermittent and it is unreliable. Infrared lamps are unwieldy and, other than for pre-heating a mold, they are impractical during lay-up operations. To perform molding operations with personnel in a heated autoclave or convection oven is unlikely.

Embedded heating elements have been used with limited success. Examples include liquid or steam tubes, jacketing, solid metal resistance wires or mesh, conductive carbon fibers, or powder. In most instances, uneven heating is the result, and heating rate is slow.

Composite Materials, L.L.C. (*MS 50*), and their distributor, Technical Fiber Products Ltd. (*MS 51*), supply metal coated carbon fibers which may be fabricated into roving, tow and yarns, woven fabrics, mat, and chopped roving. Plain weave cloth made from nickel coated yarns formed from carbon roving is available for use as both a heating element and an integral reinforcement. When used as a single ply placed anywhere in the lay-up and connected to a low voltage source, it will provide a variable temperature, evenly heated mold. It allows ideal through-cure because the part is cured from the mold side out rather than by a heat source directed at the air side of the part contained by a cold mold. (*See Section III, Reference 17.*)

Buying Used or New Boats

While I have offered you an overview of the materials that may be used in constructing marine products, it would seem reasonable that I stick my neck out by providing suggestions to those of you contemplating the purchase of a new or used boat. This discussion will include any boat where structural reinforcements and resins are used including composites. Let's start with used boats.

You probably will consider using a marine surveyor. We will assume that the boat has been hauled. If you have read the first two sections of this book, I would like to think that you could very well be your own surveyor — at least you will know what to look for. It might not be a bad idea to ask your surveyor if he has read this book also!

The surveyor should report only what he sees. Besides the usual list of equipment, he should report any corrections required and any observable damage resulting from physical or chemical action. He should not offer correction procedures other than suggest options if he knows them. You should always realize that his findings will be based on just a few hours' work.

Used Boats

1. Before hiring a surveyor, ask the owner or owner's agent to let you read the boat's log. Rarely will the log be of much help in determining what repairs have been made; but if you do find any useful information, feed it to your surveyor. If you know who built the boat, you might find out how it was made.

2. Certain makes of boats have consistently had more blister problems than others. Ask around, and you

might find out which ones they are, either avoid these or buy cheap enough that even re-hulling would pay off.

3. If you find evidence of blister repair, the owner is required to divulge this. He is not obliged to tell you who made repairs or how they were made, but he may. Check this out yourself.

4. If you find a boat you like but that it has a present or past history of hydrolytic damage, then follow the guidelines offered in Section II and stay on top of the repair process as much as possible.

5. You may find an all-wood boat that you like. Determine if it has been resin-saturated and how the resin was applied. Has a barrier coat also been applied? If reinforcements were used, determine what they are and how applied and what resins were used.

6. You may also find a previously owned steel or aluminum hulled boat that you like. Chris Craft's "Roamer" is a good example.

It would be unusual to find any metal boat, new or used, which may have been "fiberglassed." It would be rare to find one to which a resin-composite had been applied properly, but there are some. The steam yacht **Medea** was saved from salvage by having its bottom laminated with a PVC foam and vinylester resin skin. This marvelous old lady is part of the San Diego Maritime Museum and is berthed in top operating condition at the Museum Pier for public viewing. *(See Section III, Reference 34.)*

If you find a metal boat which has been repaired only with a resin-reinforcement patch, be wary. Consider it a candidate for restoration only. *(See Section II, Boat Restoration.)* If the hull has been laminated with resin and

reinforcement as a complete skin at least over the bottom and above the boot top, then ask how the metal surface was prepared prior to laminating. Was it sandblasted to bare (gray) metal? How, and with what, was it primed? What laminating resin and what reinforcements were used, and how many plies? Was the reinforcement mat only, mat and fabric, fabric woven or uni-directional? Above all, what was the laminating schedule and what net thickness was produced?

There are only about three ways to prepare a metal hull for laminating: sandblasting (including grinding), metal etch with priming, and priming only. The best preparation — especially for a new hull — is to sandblast, then apply metal passification and primer. An older hull, for many reasons, may not have been sandblasted or etched but still may have been suitable for fiberglass laminating if it had been cleaned sufficiently and a corrosion resistant coating applied to protect the surface of the metal under the laminate. Many a badly corroded aluminum boat or canoe has been covered with 1/16-inch to 1/8-inch skin with little more preparation than scuff sanding the metal surface, but the entire hull must be covered.

If the purpose of resin reinforcement was to protect or smooth the contours of a metal craft without adding strength, then a high degree of bond is necessary and a thin lamination would suffice. If the purpose is to provide a heavy-duty working skin that is expected to correct structural deficiencies, then a laminating schedule would read like a composite hull made from a mold or form and then "slipped" over the metal hull with a net fit.

On metal boats large enough to require leaving them in the water, it is recommended that a thin lamination not be applied above the boot top because expansion and contraction of the metal above the waterline may de-bond a thin laminate. If thick laminate had been used (thicker than 3/16 inch), good bond is not required.

It may seem unusual for you to find a composite clad metal hull. It is unusual, but consider the thousands of leaky containers for fuel, plating, acid, etc., which have been skinned. Why not metal boats?

The steam yacht **Medea.**

New Boats

If you're considering buying a new boat, you most likely will not use a marine surveyor. Get your dealer or factory representative to answer the following:

1. What type of resin was used? There may be at least four: vinylester, iso-ester, ortho-ester, and blends of the latter two with dicyclopentadiene (DCPD). What is the laminating schedule? Is woven roving the principal reinforcement, or has uni-directional fabric been used partially or exclusively? What coupling agents are on the reinforcements?

2. If the hull was made in a female mold, what gel coat was used and who was the manufacturer? What reinforcing or anti-print-through fabric was used next to the gel coat? Was the resin for at least the first few plies vinylester? Who was the manufacturer? What is the core resin? Who made it? Is it ortho resin? Are any of the resins based on dicyclopentadiene? What resin and reinforcement was used for the inside plies of the hull? Was any fire resistant resin such as a phenolic used with the inside plies as an overlay?

3. Was a laminate made to the exact schedule of the hull, one half of which provided dry reference test data recorded in the boat's log? Was the other half attached to the bottom or stern below the waterline for future structural tests?

4. What additional barrier coat was applied to the hull on the bottom below the boot top? Was a bilge barrier coat applied? Who made these materials?

If you are considering a cored boat, in addition to the above, ask:

1. What construction process was used? Was a female mold used or was it one-off laminated lay-down? If a female mold was used, was the core attached to the outer shell using vacuum assist?

2. What type of core? Plank, plywood, foam, balsa, honeycomb (a no-no for hulls), or other? If planked, how was the wood hull prepared? What sealing resin was used prior to laminating? If the inside was not laminated with resin and reinforcement (such as some types of plywood construction), was it sealed? What with? If balsa core (female mold technique), how thick? How was it attached?

3. If cored with honeycomb (hopefully only decks and cabin structures), what materials were used? How thick? How was the honeycomb attached to the skins?

4. What fabrics were used in general and where were they placed? Was any woven material used? Where?

The Ideal Boat for All Construction Methods

With the exception of a planked wood boat which will not be laminated, the construction resin should be at least be 100% high grade iso-ester. Ideally, the outer plies will be vinylester resin, no orthophthalic resin will be used anywhere and no resins should contain DCPD. The reinforcing fabrics should all be uni-directional. Mat used anywhere should contain no binder. All reinforcements, including mats, must contain coupling agents appropriate to the resin being used.

In the female molding method where a gel coat is used, a high grade isophthalic is required and 0.020-inch to 0.030-inch should be applied. A 0.020-inch to 0.030-inch veil mat or light chopped filament winding grade roving with appropriate coupling agent would be applied to the gel coat within two hours of the time of application of the gel coat. This would be carefully rolled out (saturated) followed within two hours by a layer of tri-axial uni-directional fabric and vinylester resin. Resin will be Dow Chemical Company's 411-415 vinylester *(MS 23)* or equivalent. Inner laminate resin, if not vinylester, will be a high grade isophthalic such as Reichold's 6631T *(MS 26)* or equivalent. The final 1/8-inch on the inside will have a fire retardant added to the resin. But because fire retardants can be a source of hydrolysis, it would be better to use 1/8 inch or more of tri-axial fabric impregnated with phenolic resin to serve as fire retardant and structure.

A test panel will be made, one half of which will be attached to the hull.

A vinylester barrier coat consisting of Durall's vinylester primer surfacer (*MS 34*) or equivalent is applied to the sanded gel coat on the bottom below the boot top. An epoxy barrier coat may be applied over this if desired.

For cored construction, my choice would be the one-off method using the lay-down system with Airex (*MS 20*) or Core-Cel (*MS 24*) vinyl foam for the core other than where wood (plank or plywood) is used as the core. Balsa core is obsolete for most boats which will remain in the water months or years at a time. Exceptions might be high performance craft where they are usually hauled after use. As stated before, honeycomb should not be used below the water line, if at all on the hull.

Laminating resin would be an isophthalic or medium-yield vinylester such as Dow's 411-415 (*MS 4*) or equivalent. This same resin would be used for the inner laminates. A phenolic fire resistant cladding should be applied. Finally, a bilge coating such as polysulfide or epoxy should be applied.

If the core is plywood, the outside of the hull would be laminated with at least one ply of 42-ounc-per-square-yard triaxial glass fabric and impregnated with Dow resin 411-415 vinylester, Reichold's 6631-T (*MS 26*) iso-polyester, or equivalent. Fairing would be performed using 3M's glass bubbles (*MS 8*) with Dow's 411-415 vinylester. The final outside barrier coat would be Durall's Vinylester Primer Surfacer (*MS 34*) or Gougeon Brothers, Inc.'s West System epoxy (*MS 35*) or equivalent. The inside of the hull would be laminated with the same skin as the outside, or preferably laminated with the same fabric but with a phenolic resin for fire protection. The final application on the inside would be a spray or brush coat of Morton International's RLP polysulfide (*MS 32*).

In a loose way, a new or thoroughly dry older planked boat, before any coating is applied, and after thorough sanding or blasting, may be considered a core. A penetrating epoxy may be applied in several coats both inside and out. When a definite film has been built up on both sides of the hull, and after thorough cure, the outside surfaces are scuff-sanded with 80 grit paper and then faired with an epoxy-microballoon compound. Final sealing would be with an epoxy paint type primer followed by a tight urethane paint top coat. This process can produce a product which will look like it had been made in a female mold. A good example of this may be seen at the San Diego Yacht club in California, where the 70-year-old 10-meter **Branta** owned by the Reineman family is slipped. Work was performed by Knight & Carver of National City, CA.

62-foot yacht **Branta**. *In 1987,* **Branta** *suffered a violent hull explosion which blew a five-foot diameter hole below her waterline, sinking her at the dock in less than 10 seconds. Two years later, she emerged as a 72-year-old "youngster" after being restored using Gougeon Brothers' West System epoxy saturation technique.*

MARINE
REINFORCED
PLASTICS
CONSTRUCTION

Section II

Repair Options

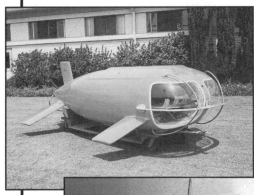

SECTION II:
REPAIR OPTIONS

BACKGROUND

Boats did not inspire the first general awareness of problems caused by the degradation of polyester resin-fiberglass containers. Tanks of all sorts containing or immersed long term in various liquids, including water, showed problems considered peculiar to individual circumstances. Strong chemicals could rightly have been blamed, but severe problems surfaced even with water. Fiberglass boats, although water containers, were not yet built large enough to require being left in the water because of size, so were not considered long-term storage containers and, therefore, did not appear to have a degradation problem at that time.

The first large-scale appearance of visible problems came with the fiberglass spa which had nothing to do with size — it was simply a long-term hot water container. Problems of all sorts had been experienced earlier with fiberglass swimming pool shells, but most of these problems were focused on degradation of the outside (soil side) due to chemical reaction with the soil. Deterioration here was so rapid that any problem with the interior or working side, usually gel coated, went unnoticed or, if observed, was not considered a problem. Also swimming pools usually contained cold or tepid water. The problem with chemical reaction with the soil has since been resolved by use of epoxy resins throughout the structure or at least on the soil side. Underground tanks including septic, water, and fuel presented the same problems unless epoxy resins were used.

THE SPA STORY

The spa craze began in the mid 1960s. At the same time, the marine industry was just starting the serious production of all-fiberglass non-trailerable boats over 25 feet — those hulls large enough to require being left in the water for extended periods.

Both industries were plagued with what were thought to be gel coat problems. Blisters, bubbles and gel coat separation were common and inevitable. The repair business was excellent. Demon gel coat (resin) was universally considered the problem. After a few years of this with no solution in sight, many spa manufacturers either stopped producing polyester fiberglass shells or simply went out of business.

Blind alleys of investigation led to few answers. The "turtle box" test was popular (*see Figure 1*). Hundreds of samples of every conceivable kind were run, but no test was better than the giant turtle box itself: the spa.

Experiments with a limited production of spas having thick vacuum formed liners such as acrylic, ABS, and others reinforced on the back with chopped fiberglass laminate produced some sales and did reduce the problems of using polyester resin gel coat, but other problems occurred which made this approach unacceptable. The use of these liners produced another effect also. Since the gel coat was considered the culprit in at least the blister problem, and the use of liners in spas seemed to eliminate the blisters, it reinforced the general contention that *all* problems with gel coated products containing water, including some plumbing fixtures and boat hulls, were caused by the gel coat.

By the time the gel coated or lined spa was phased out to ceramic or porcelain enameled cast iron, boat owners were beginning to see what somebody dubbed "boat pox" in areas below the waterline. For several years the boatyard painters simply sanded off the pox and maybe plastered on some Bondo™. On the next haul-out, many more blisters usually were found.

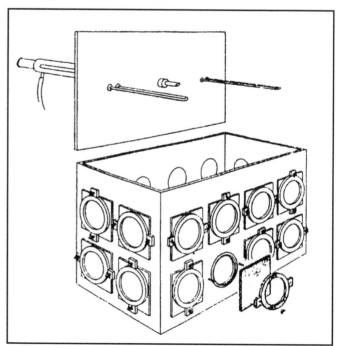

Figure 1: Apparatus for Testing Boiling Water Resistance of Gel Coat Laminates
1/4-inch aluminum sheet; overall dimensions 14x14x24 inches. Drawing does not show stirrer, or heaters and condensers on cover.

I have made hundreds of turtle box tests, but for several years, I do not recall testing any samples of non-gel coated panels for blisters. What good would this do? After all, we all knew the problem was in the gel coat. Too bad. I ignored my previous training and experience in evaluating any panel by not performing "wet strength" and "dry strength" structural tests (more on this later). In the dying days of gel coated spas, we did come up with some interesting observations of other test results. Unfortunately, test procedures were nowhere near standardized. Partly by accident and plan I did standardize all my turtle box tests using distilled water at 150°F. It happens that this temperature is now accepted as standard. Remember, we were looking for observable blisters and our eyes were focused on coatings only.

I remember testing some fiberglass panels of iso and ortho resin gel coated panels molded on glass plates. This was in a boat factory, so to duplicate the typical gel coating practice used on the factory production line, all panels were made by the gel coat operator. Window glass and polished metal plates (flat molds) were waxed and buffed. Approximately 0.020 inch of gel coat was sprayed on and allowed to cure for four hours at 65°-75°F. Another set of window glass plates were chemically cleaned on one side, and an equal number of glass plates, which were dry sandblasted on one side, were prepared. A coating of clear, carefully catalyzed laminating resin was applied by draw plate to the prepared side of these glass plates, then immediately placed on the previously gel coated plates (molds). Light pressure was applied to squeeze out air until the resin had gelled. Final cure was overnight or 12 hours at about 70°F.

The mold plates were removed and any wax remaining on the test panels was intentionally left on. All panels were tested in a turtle box using distilled water at 150°F. Testing was continued until all panels failed (within two weeks, as I recall). These tests were run using iso and ortho laminating resin respectively. All gel coats were made from isophthalic resin. Remember, we tested a layer of gel coat and a layer of resin bonded to the glass plates. No reinforcement was used.

We were surprised that the high quality gel coat blistered very soon — the side which had been next to the waxed mold plates. So we duplicated all of above except to substitute a gel coat made with ortho resin. We found that the ortho gel coat did not blister as rapidly but appeared to lose bond eventually.

The test results of the surfaces of the test panels next to the sandblasted or chemically cleaned plates were the same. These produced a few small blisters and very little delamination was observed. Flat blisters (delamination) usually occurred between the gel coat and the laminating resin.

The time was in the late 1960s, early 1970s. Fiberglass boat blistering was considered a cosmetic problem then. In hindsight, it is unfortunate that the boat industry did not take some lessons from the spa industry while they were still making gel coated fiberglass pieces, each one of which was its own turtle box.

FORTUNATELY, THERE IS NO FIBERGLASS HULL THAT CANNOT BE REPAIRED!

Only by systematic examination and evaluation can a true condition of a fiberglass product be determined. The purpose of Section II is to assist in attaining that goal. The degree of apparent damage can be determined in a relatively short time by informed persons. The following looks at those who make these observations and those who are affected by them.

MARINE SURVEYOR

The marine surveyor must report his findings without prejudice. He lists all items he sees. He reports defects as well as positive conditions. He may list items which, in his opinion, are in need of repair. He does not (should not) specify *how* a repair should be made. He may offer a list of repair options without prejudice. He should leave the choice of repair procedure to the other parties involved.

REPAIR FOREMAN

It is the repair foreman — whether he represents a boatyard, a tank manufacturer, or a spa and plumbing fixture factory — who is responsible for the administration of the chosen repair procedure.

OWNER

The owner of an affected product, unless an insurance company intervenes, makes the final decision on the repair method. If he can learn to ask the right questions and know what to observe, he will be well ahead.

BUYER AND SELLER

When a used product is being sold, the biggest game of deceit in town begins. This is especially true with boats! The owner, and particularly the broker, hope the surveyor doesn't report all the problems the seller, and usually the broker, know are there. Only the best informed buyer can deal with this. Avoid any surveyor who refuses to allow a prospective buyer to accompany him on his inspection. If you must put up with a broker, use him to negotiate repairs.

INSURER AND LENDER

If the insurer and/or lender must depend upon a surveyor to decide whether or not to lend and insure, then you are at the mercy of someone who can only report what he sees in one or two hours of poking and prodding.

NEW BOAT MANUFACTURER

It might not be a bad idea for you, the manufacturer, to be as well versed in repairing your product as you are in making it in the first place. Your expertise in the first instance will determine the amount of your efforts which will be required in the second instance!

TYPES & CAUSES OF PROBLEMS

BLISTERS

There are really only two distinct types of blister problems, observable blisters and those which are non-visible but can result in structural damage.

Observable Blisters

By themselves, gel coat blisters are harmless. If the substrate is impervious, inert or unaffected, such as in the window glass test plates previously described, then a blister is only a nuisance which does not improve the appearance of the structure.

A fiberglass hull made in a female mold is molded absolutely backwards. The very first thing in the production process is to paint a hull which does not yet exist. This, of course, is the sprayed gel coat in the mold. This paint job lies in the mold under various kinds of process and quality control, and is subject to wide atmospheric conditions. Even in the best of situations, the subsequent reinforcing layer applied to the gel coat does not form a very good bond.

The term "gel coat" is one of the most inaccurate descriptions of first coat or mold coat ever invented. So be it. The term represents the first construction step for most hulls made in a female mold. A "good" gel coat is supposed to produce a long lasting beautiful "customer" (outside) surface, be impervious to chemical attack, prevent water penetration, and bond 100% to whatever is slapped on it. Of course, it is none of these things. The more carefully a gel coat is formulated and the more carefully it is applied and the tighter the film it forms, the more likely it will produce blisters! The poorest quality gel coat properly applied is least likely to produce blisters! And no gel coat at all will produce no external blisters.

There are no polyester gel coats, iso or ortho, which can form a non-penetrable coating. There may be no visible pin holes. Any hole the size of the point of a pin would not cause a blister: osmotic action cannot occur at a pin hole. Smaller micro-defects or imperfections in the gel coat can cause convective flow or capillary action. This action can cause blisters to form in a high quality, properly applied gel coat, sometimes within months.

Another longer-term problem in the surface coating is caused by solubility. In a water environment, this is called "hydrolysis," which is the result of diffusion of water through the gel coat, resulting in plasticization and corrosion of the resin. Stated another way, hydrolysis is the chemical addition (reaction) of water to a substance. Hydrolysis of a polyester resin results in partially reproducing the starting materials from which it was made, an alcohol and an organic acid.

The amount and/or degree of diffusion is determined by the molecular free volume (space between molecules) of the film. In other words, in order for a blister to form there has to be a channel. Generally, if the film is tight, this channel will be a molecular one. A gel coat should be regarded as a semi-permeable membrane and through it — by diffusion and/or osmosis — the water on the outside of the hull will pass. This water is pure after passing through the membrane regardless of source. But it immediately becomes combined with whatever is reactive inside, thus becoming more dense than the liquid on the outside of the membrane. This reaction on the inside need not be a chemical one; it may only physically combine with water soluble impurities in the substrate. The "pure" water coming through the membrane tries to dilute the material inside.

A given *volume* of fresh water will pass through an osmotic membrane faster than contaminated (salt) water. The higher the concentration of salt water on the outside and the colder, the slower will be the osmotic effect. Once inside, if there is no reaction with any impurity in the substrate, then this osmotic liquid will be virtually pure water regardless of its source on the outside. Pure or fresh water

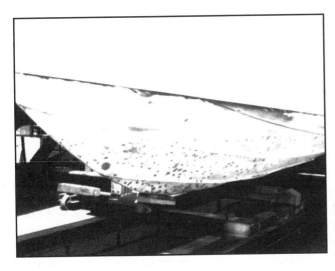

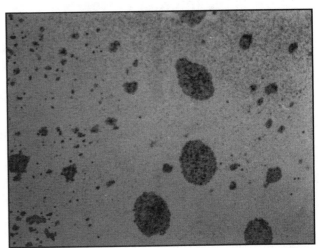
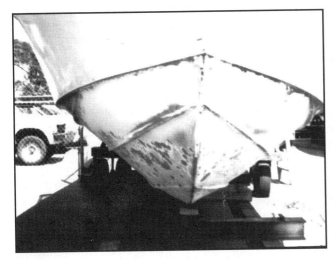
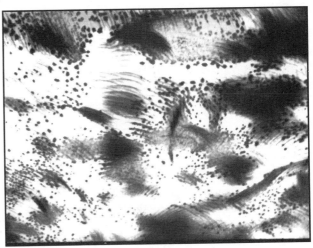

Each pair of photographs above shows a different type of blistering on a boat hull on the left and a close-up of the blistering on the right.

will react with polyester resin; the degree depends upon the quality and type of resin. This may not cause a surface blister. Also any liquid trapped under the gel coat regardless of source — whether it be pure water or contaminated — will permeate through fissures in the laminate. More on this later.

The osmotic pressure created in a blister between the gel coat and substrate or within the substrate can be impressive — in pounds per square inch. By whatever cause a blister is formed, the pressure of the liquid within the blister causes the gel coat to shear from the substrate, and until broken, the pressure can force the liquid into the voids or channels within the laminate. Now, capillary action begins. Mere removal followed by filling and patching of what may appear to be only surface blisters rarely stops hydrolysis started in the laminate due to the presence of surface blisters.

Non-Visible Internal Blisters

Non-visible internal blisters (delaminations) cause structural strength reduction. In the process of designing a good structural laminate of resin-glass, calculations for working wet-strength retention should always be made prior to manufacture. It should be realized that any boat constantly immersed in water will have a gradual (hopefully) loss of structural strength over a period of time, say 20 years, so extra material might be required at the time of manufacture to compensate for this inevitable strength loss. Many years ago the practice by some was to guess what was adequate, then double it! This is one of several reasons why some of the older hulls are still structurally sound though they may suffer some other ills. Many of the Taiwanese hulls manufactured in the 1980s were "engineered" with very heavy laminates and extra thick gel coats.

Test Coupons and Testing for Potential Problems

Test coupons should be made with the same materials, preferably cut from the product at the same time it is being produced. All test results should become part of the hull records. Wet-strength tests are standard procedure and should not be accelerated; *e.g.*, at temperatures above 150°F or above the heat distortion temperature of the laminate — whichever is lower. If in doubt, run at 125°F. The use of boiling water will accelerate tests, but this does not represent conditions encountered with a boat hull. I don't know anyone who boils boats to test them. Generally, what happens in a short-term (100 hours or less) boiling water test, if the laminate appears to stay intact, is that water will enter the laminate by capillary action and diffusion causing some structural strength loss, especially in wet-strength tests. This same laminate, subsequently dried, often will regain most of its original dry strength. Very little hydrolytic action will have occurred, only a temporary physical one.

The only reliable way to know the real present structural strength is to perform destructive mechanical tests on sections taken from the area of the boat's bottom most likely to be affected. If original structural tests are available (which usually they are not), these can be used to compare the wet samples taken from hull. If original test data are not available, then take a sample from a non-immersed area above the waterline as the dry sample reference. Because the samples must be kept small, the ASTM Short Beam test method is generally used. If you wish to determine what type of resin was used, *e.g.*, ortho or iso, have your test lab run Fourier transformer infrared spectrometry on the sample. (*See Section III, Reference 18.*)

Water Absorption

A typical 40-foot fiberglass hull with five years in the water will absorb hundreds of pounds in weight of absorbed water, blisters or not. Depending upon the type and quality of the materials used in constructing the entire hull, along with acceptable structural strength loss, *hydrolysis* can be a real killer. As stated before, hydrolytic action causes the original chemical reaction from which the resin was produced to reverse. Hydrolytic action varies dramatically with the type of resin used, the care with which it was made, and the water temperature of the hull's environment. In the final states of decomposition, the resin in the laminate granulates, resembling fine sand. The glass fibers become limp and broken. This is a terminal condition (*see photos on page 53*).

It would be easy to say that all hulls constructed with orthophthalic-based resin will deteriorate within X years. Still today, some manufacturers use the cheaper orthos as their main laminating resin. Of course, up to the time of the availability of isophthalic-based resin, all fiberglass boats were made with ortho resin. Why then the confounding fact that many, many old as well as reasonably new craft made with ortho resins do not show any problems and pass cut sample structural tests? The principal answer to this lies in how well the resin was manufactured, be it ortho or iso. Equally important is how carefully was the hull constructed? What quality control was used in determining the type of binders and coupling agents applied to the reinforcements and especially catalyst control?

Misuse of Catalyst — Water In

Catalyst misuse and molding during high humidity conditions causes problems. The polyesters appear to be forgiving in the amount and type of catalyst used — a little for slow, a whole lot for fast. Of either of these extremes, less is better if thorough mixing is performed. Within limits, an under-catalyzed polyester will cure. It's pretty hard to un-cure an over-catalyzed resin.

Some water is present in all methylethylketone peroxide from water-of-reaction when the catalyst was compounded. Carelessly handled catalyst will absorb water from highly humidified air. This entrained water can cause blistering and other problems. Only those catalysts with lowest water content should be used. (A test for excessive water in MEKP is to combine equal volumes of catalyst and styrene. If water is present, the solution will turn milky.)

Misuse of Chopper Spray Guns

The misuse of spray guns used to apply gel coat or resin spray guns used with chopper equipment is a widespread problem when producing any fiberglass product. Early internal or external catalyst mixing guns were crude and temperamental. Most chopper guns depended upon the roll-out or squeegee operation to provide mixing if the catalyst got to the laminate at all. It's rather hard to depend upon this type of "mixing" when applying gel coat! Addition of a dye to the catalyst from a chopper gun at least provided evidence that the catalyst got there, but how much was a good question. Of course, dyes cannot be used in gel coat application. Many of these guns still in use today have a considerable lag between the time the gun trigger is first pulled and the time the catalyst gets into the resin stream.

Generally with the older equipment, when a gel coat or chopper gun operator first starts to spray with an external mix gun, he will squirt catalyst first, then turn on the resin. I have seen many an operator perform this "test" while pointing the gun at the mold! Spattering catalyst either under or on top of a gel coat will absolutely guarantee blistering. This procedure applies to external mix guns only. There is no sure test to determine if catalyst is being injected in an internal mix gun except by the use of a dye or observing some type of flow meter. Watching a flow meter while you are spraying is a neat trick! Modern spray equipment will be discussed later.

Batch mixing, whether for gel coat or laminating resin, is still the most accurate method of adding catalyst. Volume ratios are simple. Good mechanical mixing is possible and vital. Because batch cure rate is dependent on temperature, some pot temperature control may be required.

Dependence on Gel Coat as the Moisture Barrier

A gel coat cannot be depended upon to serve as a moisture barrier to a boat hull. Structural problems with the laminate, including blisters, are often blamed on the gel coat. From the standpoint of preventing water absorption by the hull, the quality of the gel coat takes last place. The only contribution a gel coat makes (along with any sealant applied over it such as an epoxy) is to slow down the *rate* of water absorption by the hull laminate. This is not to say that these materials should not be used — especially sealer on new boats — but they should not be considered a protection against structural damage which may have already occurred on a hull in service or will occur on a new boat.

It must be realized that a hull with a serious blister problem most likely suffers from a loss of structural strength in the laminate. Drying the hull and applying a sealant simply will not restore structural strength. If by some method of repair such as epoxy sealing or re-gel coating, the hull is kept drier than before, further structural damage may only be slowed.

FAULTY LAMINATE SCHEDULING BY THE DESIGNER

The boat designer or his engineer should take into account a worst case basis over at least a ten-year period where continuously wetted surfaces of a hull might lose over 50% of original dry strength. Having this in mind, he could have specified adding more material at the right places to extend the useful life of the craft. Unfortunately, not all of this foresight in boat design is evident even today. It is interesting to note that the largest percentage drop in strength of the wetted portion of the hull occurs in the first year regardless of the quality of the laminate. Some laminates will not even go a year before serious problems, usually hidden, may occur.

Resin Choice

King resin has generally been the whipping boy for all fiberglass ailments, particularly boats. This includes resin for gel coat. It is time to recognize that the catalyst and reinforcement manufacturers should take some of the flak.

It is generally agreed that the *quality* of a resin is as important as its chemical make-up. This is why a top grade of orthophthalic may outperform an inferior iso. From a practical standpoint, assume that most available resins are made to high standards. Then, considering the resin alone, the useful life of the manufactured product will increase starting with ortho, iso, vinylester and modified epoxy hybrids.

Incorrect Specifications for Binder, Sizing, Coupling Agent, and Lubricant

Binders on chopped strand mat should not be water soluble because these are the source of most osmotic blisters. Acrylates or powdered polyester resins must be used. Stitching is the best binder.

Sizing is used in the fabric weaving process to stabilize twisted yarns for the loom.

Lubricants are applied to sized yarns to aid weaving. Both sizing and lubricant must be removed by heat cleaning after completion of weaving. This must be followed by application of an appropriate coupling agent.

Incorrect Use of Filler, Pigment, Fire Retardant, or Thixotrope

Fillers should not be used with hand lay-up resins. While use of these may reduce costs, the quality of a hand-laid part is reduced because of inability of the molder to see entrained air which produces voids. Also, many fillers chemically react with the acid formed from osmotic action. Pigment, especially titanium dioxide or carbon black, is necessary for gel coat resin but has no place in laminating resin. Fumed silica thixotrope is widely used but may cause delamination and other problems if it does not have a coupling agent applied. So-called chemical thixotropes should be considered.

Fire retardants are fillers and can cause the same problems as fillers. Also, toxic gas, produced when a fire is hot enough to activate the retardant, is often more hazardous than the fire itself. Some fire retardants contribute to early hydrolytic action. (*See Section III, Reference 20.*)

Warpage Due to Incomplete Cure

Post-heat cure is vital to all resins. To reduce warpage and to increase chemical resistance, any resin system must be fully cured. Some resins will complete curing with time, but warpage can be expected during the interim. A post-curing temperature should be selected which is higher than any service temperature the product is likely to encounter but should be kept below the heat distortion temperature of the resin.

DAMAGE ASSESSMENT

The following rating system is my attempt to standardize the *degree* of damage as determined by a marine surveyor or his equivalent.

The rating scale is 0 for no damage (new) to 10 for near total loss. (*See Condition Ratings below.*)

A competent surveyor should **not** recommend a repair procedure during the rating process. He should refer his client to the available repair options only.

This scale is intended to rate degree of damage including impact and abrasion. Blisters, including cracks or crazes, weeping fluids, soft or dead spots, and flaking gel coat are other examples.

A rating of 0 would be expected on a new boat. I don't mean a reading of 0 on a moisture meter! This would be expected to apply to a new boat at the factory, or one which had not yet been launched. A surveyor may rate a hull at 1 or 2 initially after launching. At some time later, particularly during repairs, he may be asked to partially re-survey and re-rate.

In addition to the usual tools of the inspector's trade, a syringe for collecting blister fluid and containers for collecting gel coat flakes should be included. The inspector should have the equipment and be knowledgeable in the procedure for taking cores for short beam structural tests,

Moisture Meters

A moisture meter can be a useful tool if used properly. It is almost always a part of a surveyor's kit. (*See Section III, Reference 21.*)

CONDITION RATINGS (SCALE: 0 TO 10)

Rating 0 to 1

(a) Relative moisture readings approximately equal.

(b) No visible blisters.

(c) No soft or "dead" spots — usually checked with surveyor's hammer.

(d) No visible cracking, crazing, or pin holes.

(e) No evidence of abrasion from impact.

Structural strength data to be recorded on report if available. All relative moisture readings recorded.

NOTE: A rating of 0 to 2 might be found in a hull manufactured after 1988 or later state-of-the-art and having been continuously in the water for one year or less. This would be an example of a well constructed boat.

Rating 1 to 2

(a) Increase of relative moisture content in various areas of the hull, not necessarily just the bottom. Without actual testing of plugs taken from the indicated "wettest" area, no accurate determination of actual moisture content can be made. If there are any moisture readings higher than the dry control, there is water absorption. This should be expected of any hull having been in the water one month or more, or even in dry dock during or after a condition of high humidity. Record the readings and locations. These readings are not percentage of moisture content.

(b) No apparent blisters. Other cosmetic defects may be noted.

(c) No soft spots or delaminations using hammer test.

(d) If structural strength retention tests are to be run, and original factory test data are available, results should show approximately 75% retention of original structural values on a hull built to minimum standards. If a hull appears to have been built with a high reserve strength (usually meaning extra thick), a 50% strength retention would be acceptable.

NOTE: In no way are these ratings related to age. The highest drop in structural strength will occur during the first year of immersion. A rating of 5 could be assigned to a boat six months old. Except for moisture absorption with subsequent loss of structural strength, a rating of 1 or 2 could be expected of many craft 20 to 30 years old. If factory structural data are not available, a structural dry reference should be established by taking a test plug above the waterline. This requires taking this plug one time only for present and all future test comparisons. Obviously, to determine structural strength retention at any given time, a sample from the hull, or a specially installed test panel below the waterline, must be taken. If it is cut from the hull, use an area indicated from a moisture meter to be the wettest known area.

Rating 2 to 3

(a) Definite variation of relative moisture readings (indicating some moisture absorption). If available, compare moisture meter readings (with the same type of meter) from a previous haul-out. A modest increase would be expected.

(b) Occasional blisters less than 3/8 inch in diameter. On a 30-foot sailboat, for example, no more than 20 blisters total.

(c) No soft spots or apparent delaminations. No visible mechanical damage.

(d) Retained structural strength approximately 65% (*see note above*).

(e) If possible, collect fluid from blisters for analysis. Remove a few blister skins and probe for laminate deterioration. If deterioration appears evident, advance the rating to 3 or 4 and advise repair options.

Rating 3 to 4

(a) Numerous blisters (20 to 60 on a 30-foot boat). Sizes varying from pinhead to 1 inch in diameter. Check also for blistering above the waterline especially on the deck and exterior cabin walls where fiberglass-covered wood is used. To retain this rating, no soft spots anywhere on the hull, deck or cabin should be found. When wood has been covered with fiberglass improperly, bubbles may form between the wood and fiberglass skin. These would not be considered osmotic blisters but bubbles caused by gassing. Small bubbles of this type usually are only a cosmetic problem; however, wet rot may be found underneath the blister. Have the boat repairman remove one or two bubble skins to investigate. Advise repair options, if necessary.

(b) Cracking and crazing in any area of the hull. Cracks are usually caused by stress or a one-time impact. Impact stress cracks will often radiate from the center of the impact. Stress cracks due to poor construction or overload such as a flexing bottom will usually be long and parallel. Crazing looks like the pattern on a dry lake and is caused by long-term exposure to sunlight. This type of damage is caused by ultraviolet radiation and should not be confused with cracking which is caused by mechanical action. Blistering will not occur in areas of cracking or crazing, but water (or anything else) will enter these defects readily.

(c) Hulls determined to be in this rating should be suspect of laminate deterioration as well as serious gel coat delamination due to osmotic blistering. Moisture *content* (not "measured" with a moisture meter) and structural retention tests should be run.

(d) Use the same procedure as in Rating 2 and perform the following important procedure:

Have the boat repairman select two or three large blisters. Take blister fluid samples if possible, then remove the blister skins. Probe extensively with an ice pick. If no softness or granulation is observed, then light feather sanding with a disc will be sufficient to open up the damaged area for observation. If any softness is noticed, grind out the area with a square ended rotary burr to the boundary of the surface blister. The depth of the cavity should be to solid material. Don't pull any punches on this operation; go as deep as degraded material is indicated. The purpose of using a square-ended rotary burr is to produce a shoulder around the perimeter of the blistered area much the same way a dental cavity is prepared.

Immediately after the cavity has been dug out, wipe away any noticeable liquid. With a wood tool such as the end of a hammer handle, and with as much pressure as possible, press up and down all around the cavity perimeter to see if liquid can be pumped out. Try light hammering around the edge for the same effect. If any liquid is produced, delamination is likely.

With a flat screwdriver on small cavities or a putty knife on larger ones, pry the laminate at the square shoulder all around to see if any lamination separates easily. Do not be aggressive with this operation; use hand pressure only. Even the best of sound laminates bone dry will delaminate with surprisingly little force.

(e) If no moisture can be pumped into the cavity and the depth of the cavity is less than 10% of the hull thickness, then the edges may be feather sanded for repairs. Repair options should be offered.

Rating 4 to 5

(a) Countless blisters of all sizes, suspected soft or dead spots found with a survey hammer, cracking and crazing are evident. *(See photos on page 53.)*

At this point great consternation and trauma set in. Owners call lawyers, manufacturers deny liability, boat yard operators wish everybody would go away and everybody blames everybody. Frankly, I blame the owner(s) for allowing the hull damage to progress this far. The owner has probably delayed hauling the hull for observation, has not listened to his diver if he had one at all, ignored his boatyard's advice or accepted poor advice without checking options. Usually at this point there is a great rush to blast off the gel coat, get on with the drying process, patch the holes, slap on some sealant, "paint it blue and call it new," then get rid of the dog. There should not be a rush to remove the gel coat at this point. All operations should first be performed as in rating 3. If it is determined that the rating should be increased to 4 or 5, you will know that the hull moisture is high due to long-term absorption and possible delamination, and that extensive further examination will be necessary.

When a blistered area is probed (explored), it will not be unusual that an area indicated by a 1-inch surface blister turns out to signal an area of damage several times the size of the blister in some form of degradation. This interior damage will not appear in blister shape. Usually it will appear as delamination sometimes filled with a liquid to form a flat "blister." Often these delaminations are many plies deep. Ruling out mechanical damage due to impact or other causes, hydrolytic action has set in. If one area on the hull is determined to be internally delaminated, it is very likely there will be many others. Use the surveyor's hammer over 100% of the bottom or other suspected areas to look for dead spots. Unfortunately this is not a conclusive method, but certainly any dead spots should be investigated.

If delamination has been detected, all material around and down to unaffected laminate must be removed. Except for the local areas being examined, do not yet remove the entire gel coat. If several affected areas are found in the 2- to 4-inch diameter range, none of which requires removal of more that 10% of the local thickness of the original laminate, the rating should be placed at about 5.

Once the decision has been made to remove the gel coat (and probably some of the laminate as well), it will be almost impossible to see where the original blistering had been. If abrasive blasting is used to remove the gel coat, it is likely that OSHA will require wet blasting. And even if dry blasted, the hull will be washed, wetted by rain or otherwise, thus hindering further observation of blister location and internal liquid exudation. Surface abrasion such as sanding, blasting or use of a "gel coat peeler" will not always reveal sub-laminate delamination.

Before general gel coat removal, it is vital that structural strength loss tests be made. This will require removal of a test plug from an area of the hull which appears to be most affected, yet the plug must be taken from what *appears* to be sound material. Strength retention as low as 50% would not necessarily indicate a serious problem providing a lot of "iffy" things can be satisfied. These will include the hope that the designer provided for at least 50% of eventual loss of structural strength; that the manufacturer followed the directions of the designer; and above all, that this 50% figure is consistent throughout the hull.

It is recommended that so far as is practical, the surveyor have the repairman remove all blister skins, probe for deterioration, remove all necessary material, and complete operations through feather sanding (when performed) — all of this prior to removal of the entire gel coat. ***THE GEL COAT IS THE ROAD MAP TO WHERE THE PROBLEMS BEGAN.***

Offer repair options if requested.

Rating 5 to 6

At this point it is presumed that all operations in 3 and 4 have been performed and that the gel coat will be removed. After removal of the gel coat is the time when extensive poking and probing is required. Too often at this point, only the gel coat is removed with few if any repairs. Then after a little atmospheric drying, something is slapped on as a "sealer"; depressions are filled with whatever-you've-got; some paint and anti-foulant are thrown on; and then back she goes in the water.

When all material removal operations are completed, a drying period is necessary. Other than early one-time thorough wash-down with water, no sealer, putty or other material should be applied during the drying period. Unless many weeks of dry storage can be justified, some form of vented shrouding should be recommended to accelerate reduction of moisture from the laminate.

Rating 6 to 7

If, besides gel coat removal, considerable structural material has been removed, the surveyor should recommend that structural strength *retention* (or loss) tests be made. These should be performed at the beginning toward what is considered to be the end of the drying period.

If the hull appears to be repairable by extensive patching and re-sealing, repair options should be offered. If soft spots remain and/or oil-canning is evident, the hull should be rated at 7 or higher.

RATING 7 NOTE: A rating of 7 or higher is a matter of degree of damage. In no case should a hull at this rating be recommended to be simply patched then returned to the water. In no event should air intentionally heated over 100°F be applied to hulls in the 7 to 10 category. The saturated, soggy hull is barely able to hold its own shape by surface tension of the moisture within the glass fibers. As the hull dries, the tendency will be for it to collapse on the ground supports, so hang it by its ears! More and more support will be required as the hull dries. Use poles, slings, diapers or timbers wherever possible; especially use supports under the gunwales to the ground.

A rating of 7 would be assigned if, no matter what its appearance, the hull has retained its shape after extensive drying. This is a fair indication that considerable structural value remains and that less than extraordinary repair is possible.

I suggest that the surveyor should recommend, the owner and the insurance company should insist, and the boatyard should CYA that structural strength tests be run by a certified laboratory at least after all repairs have been made. The boat should be re-rated on this scale of 1 through 10.

Rating 8 to 10

A rating of 8 would be assigned to a hull with extensive soft spots which, before drying at least, appears to be able to retain its shape. Very careful shoring must be provided during further operations.

A rating of 9 would be assigned to a hull which collapses in the process of drying. The hull may be salvageable. *(See Major Repairs, this section.)*

A rating of 10 would usually mean loss of the hull by shipwreck or simply tied to the dock due to extensive deterioration but recovered for evaluation. Under some circumstances, the hull may be repaired.

THE DAMAGE ASSESSMENT OF DOUBLE-SKIN (CORED) HULLS

Damage assessment of each shell would be made in the same manner as if each were single thickness hulls. Beyond the usual determination of blisters, soft spots, cracks, and crazes would be a careful examination for separation of either shell from the core material. If the outer shell appears relatively sound, it may be difficult to determine delamination by hammer tapping alone.

Obviously, a dead sound, a soft spot, or oil-canning would indicate immediate problems. If a *delamination* due to severe stress does actually exist but has yet not been found by hammer tapping from the outside because the outer shell is usually thicker than the inner one, then it might be found by tapping the inside shell.

Any suspect area should be drilled from the outside with an 1/8- to 3/16-inch drill to see if any liquid is exuded. If no liquid is observed, after making several survey holes, then a low exotherm resin can be injected in the survey holes (this applies to solid cores, not honeycomb). Use an epoxy resin if the type of core material is unknown. If one or more of the holes accepts more than 1/4 of an ounce, then delamination or lack of bond exists.

If no history of severe impact or stress has been reported, yet lack of bonding has been determined and both shells appear to be sound, then the diagnosis may be *de-bonding* or *no bonding* in the first place. If test holes have not produced any moisture, then injection of bonding resin could be performed. This remedy cannot assure that the same problem will not recur if the de-bonding was originally caused by stress due to structural deficiency. If there had been no bonding in some areas when the hull was manufactured, and the survey holes showed the core to be dry, then injection of bonding resin may solve the problem.

If definite soft spots are found, survey holes will almost always produce moisture. This often will indicate a condition of hydrolysis which will require major repair, possibly involving both shells in the area affected. One rare but possible fix is to use an injectable hydrophilic "water loving" resin. (*See Commercial Barrier Coat Options, following.*)

WHY DRY THE BOAT?

The standard answers to this question are:

1. To stop all those chemical reactions that had been going on in the presence of water. It is not possible to remove all of the water; therefore, chemical reaction will continue but at a slower rate. This will be true even after extensive sealing.

2. No resin-fiberglass repairs can be made in the presence of moisture because the resin will not cure. Not true! Proper selection of repair or sealing resins *will* allow repairs in the presence of moisture. Some resins require moisture to cure and some may even be applied underwater.

3. Get rid of all those foul smelling, purplish blister liquids. True, but those which remain will simply be dried temporarily.

4. Resin-starved (leached) areas show up better when dry. True.

5. The structure may become stronger (stiffer), impact strength will be regained and the hull will become lighter. This would be true of a hull where it was determined that it had absorbed water only and no apparent hydrolytic damage was evident. It would be a rare instance that no hydrolytic action had occurred in a wet hull.

There are many other possible reasons for drying a hull. Certainly the hull should be washed (leached) and dried to as low a moisture content as is practical. There is no way that entrained moisture can be removed completely.

A book published by A is A Publishing Company (no misprint) entitled *A Manual for the Repair of Fiberglass Boats Suffering from Osmotic Blisters* describes in extraordinary detail their methods for drying boats prior to application of a barrier coating. The authors are the two brothers McLean, who have collected numerous citations, and together with their field experience in yacht maintenance, have produced a manual useful for boatyard drying. (*See MS 52.*)

The use of vacuum bag methods for drying is covered in an article by Gougeon Brothers, Inc. (*See Section III, Reference 22.*)

This 10-meter carvel-planked wood hull was air dried for one year, then saturated with epoxy resin. Water absorption was reduced by more than 1 ton.

COMMERCIAL BARRIER COAT OPTIONS

It is appalling how inadequate most of the product application instructions are among the trade name products offered as barrier coatings.

The rat maze which a prospective user must go through to make reasonable decisions on preparation procedures, the sequence and type of materials, how long he should wait for this and what to do after that, is frustrating to say the least.

In the following pages is a sampling of what sellers of kits of materials and profferers of procedures offer. I have critiqued each as fairly as possible. Some instructions are so poorly presented and have such gross omissions, possibly intentionally, that I cannot suggest using them. I wish that choosing the right materials and process were as simple as deciding which new automobile to buy. All the automobiles are guaranteed to get you there. You will not find one established supplier of a barrier coat who will guarantee much more than the fact that something was put in his container.

Read what these samples of a few suppliers tell you and consider my comments. Beware of any supplier who purports to guarantee his material with a carload of hedges. You will rarely find one who will guarantee that you or your applicator will put the stuff on correctly. You will more likely find a yard and/or applicator who will come closer to offering a limited warranty. I would rather spend my time and money looking for owners of boats who have had problems similar to mine, find out which "system" seemed to work, whether he or a yard or contract applicator did the job, and most important, what is the track record of such a yard or applicator making good the repair of his defects.

To be expected, producers of barrier materials all claim their product is better than the other guy's. Many say to use solvent, or that theirs already contains solvent. Others say solvent is not "100% solids." Another puts shingles in his product. One puts tar (coal tar) in his product. Still others put in some pigment or aluminum. Which one is best? Again, "ask the man who owns one."

The average non-chemist attempting to research the virtues of mostly epoxy-type barrier resins for "boat pox" will very quickly become swamped with chemical jargon. Even if he understood the meaning of stoichiometric quantities, EEWs, AHEW, HDT, glass transition temperature etc., etc., he will likely become turned off. This is exactly what all suppliers of kits or re-packagers want you to do. To a considerable extent, the few suppliers of basic materials will not want to deal with you, the layman. Fortunately, there are a few exceptions, so for those of you who may want to go it alone, or at least ask the right questions, see *Other Barrier Coat Options* near the end of this section.

With the exception of the University of Rhode Island reports, the following is a description of some of the repair methods offered commercially; *e.g.*, in package form. I will comment on each of these. The order in which they appear is random.

THE UNIVERSITY OF RHODE ISLAND REPORTS

The University of Rhode Island reports, though not considered commercial options, are recommended reading at this point. These are reproduced in their entirety in *Section III, References 23 and 24*. See also *Reference 25* and *Reference 26*.

Why WEST SYSTEM Brand Epoxy?

Technology and Products You Can Rely On

For two decades, Gougeon Brothers, Inc., has been devoted to providing low-cost building alternatives, safer chemical compounds and a versatile epoxy system for a variety of situations. WEST SYSTEM Brand products are an easily used chemistry set that gives the professional and amateur the ability to tailor the epoxy mixture to meet the project's specific needs.

Most fiberglass boats are built with low-cost polyester resin in matrix with fiberglass cloth. It's a system which works well when all of the resin is allowed to cure together. We call this primary bonding. Problems can occur, however, when you try to bond polyester resin to a laminate that is already cured (secondary or post-bonding).

WEST SYSTEM Brand epoxy, on the other hand, forms a superior chemical and mechanical bond with the cured polyester base when used in secondary bonding situations. Since the epoxy is more durable than the polyester, the epoxy repair may actually be stronger than the original structure. WEST SYSTEM Brand epoxy also has a much higher resistance to moisture than polyester: an important characteristic in reducing moisture permeability through the resin matrix, which could result in gelcoat blistering and/or interlaminate failure. (See chart at right.)

WEST SYSTEM Brand epoxy may be more expensive than polyester resin, but the cost of the epoxy is usually only a small fraction of the overall cost of most repair jobs. The peace of mind that comes from knowing your repair is much less likely to fail at an inopportune time and result in inconvenience and additional costly repair, is well worth your investment in WEST SYSTEM epoxy.

WEST SYSTEM Brand products include a complete line of epoxy materials and supplies developed to meet a wide range of building and maintenance needs for fiberglass, wood, steel and aluminum structures. Anywhere an extremely strong, water-resistant bond or coating is needed—WEST SYSTEM Brand products provide an affordable, efficient and high-quality solution.

Protect Your Investment

A boat represents a substantial investment; when left unchecked, many of the maintenance problems unique to the fiberglass structure can threaten your investment. Although many of these problems can be intimidating, with the correct techniques and materials, they are not difficult to solve and are within the capabilities of the average boater. WEST SYSTEM Brand epoxy can save the boat owner expensive labor repair costs while getting professional results.

The problems and solutions outlined here give you a step-by-step procedure for using these versatile products to solve each of the seven common problems associated with fiberglass boats.

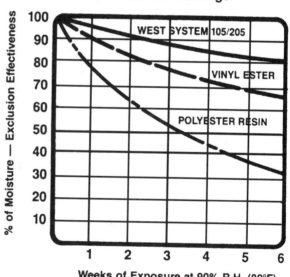

Moisture Protection Capability of Various Marine Coatings

% of Moisture — Exclusion Effectiveness vs. Weeks of Exposure at 90% R.H. (80°F)

WEST SYSTEM 105/205 — VINYL ESTER — POLYESTER RESIN

```
GOUGEON BROTHERS, INC.
P.O. BOX   X908
BAY CITY, MI 48707
    (517) 684-6881
```

Author's Comment on West System

Gougeon Brothers, Inc. promoted the West System - Wood Epoxy Saturation Technique in the 60s. For reasons of their own, they would rather not have you consider their resins today as only a saturation material.

Meade Gougeon wrote a book in 1979 entitled *Wood and West System Material*. This very detailed volume is recommended especially for wood boat builders or just those working with wood.

It is generally known that any coating resin may be made to penetrate a semi-porous material such as wood, Cellotex, concrete, glass fibers, particle board, dry rot — you name it. If you want varnish to penetrate, add turpentine. If you want tar to soak into concrete, add kerosene. If you want epoxy resin to soak into something, add a material to lower viscosity. In this connection, I quote from a statement by the Gougeon people: "in our MEE test matrix we used epoxy resin systems that contained non-

Solution 5a
Prevention and Repair of Gelcoat Blistering

1 Prepare the hull for drying by opening all blisters and abrading the bottom with 50-grit sandpaper. For extensive blistering, grinding or sandblasting the gelcoat surface down to the fiberglass laminate may be necessary. The entire surface below the waterline should be sanded to a dull finish, with all bottom paint removed.

2 After the blisters have been opened and the hull sanded, allow the hull's moisture content to stabilize. Two weeks at 50% or less relative humidity is ideal. If more humid conditions prevail, a hot air gun or heat lamps may speed the job. A heavy plastic skirt hung around the boat will keep rain from the work area should conditions deteriorate. A dehumidifier or fan placed under the skirt may speed drying.

3 Salt deposits or other contaminants may have been left on the surface as the moisture evaporated from the laminate. Wash the surface with fresh water and immediately dry with clean paper towels. When dry, sand the surface once again to provide a clean bonding surface.

4 Apply a single coat of WEST SYSTEM epoxy to the surface with a foam roller. Be sure the inner surfaces of blisters and pits are well coated.

5 Within 6 to 8 hours of applying the first coat, trowel a non-sagging fairing mixture of epoxy and 407 Low-Density filler into the blister cavities.

6 After 24 hours, sand the entire surface to a dull, smooth finish with 80-grit sandpaper. Repeat steps 5 & 6 as necessary.

7 Follow instructions 3 and 4, under **"Solution 5b Barrier Coating— New or Repaired Hulls."**

Solution 5b
Barrier Coating — New or Repaired Hulls

1 If the bottom has not yet been painted, wipe the entire surface with a cloth dampened with a wax and silicone remover or solvent to remove remaining mold release agents or waxes.

If the bottom has been painted, the paint must be completely removed with chemical strippers and/or sanding prior to coating.

2 Abrade the gelcoat surface below the waterline with 80-grit sandpaper. When completed, there should be no glossy areas. Mask freeboard at the waterline with electrician's tape.

3 Apply a minimum of three coats of WEST SYSTEM epoxy to the surface with a foam roller. For optimum moisture exclusion, we recommend a total of 20-mils of epoxy, which is usually five or six coats. Note: For best results, apply at 60-70°F; (15-21°C) 40-60% relative humidity.

The first coat should be applied with no additives. Each successive coat should include 10% 420 filler (an aluminum-based barrier coat additive which increases the epoxy's resistance to moisture permeability) blended with the resin/hardener.

All coats may be applied in one day. Apply the next coat as soon as the first will support its weight. If epoxy is allowed to cure overnight, wash with water and a 3M Scotch Brite® pad; then sand before re-coating. **Do not thin WEST SYSTEM epoxy; doing so will seriously diminish the epoxy's moisture barrier effectiveness.**

4 Thoroughly sand with 220-grit sandpaper before application of the antifouling paint. Follow the paint manufacturer's instructions for final surface preparation and application.

reactive dilutents, mono and di-functional glycidyl ether dilutents, and bis A and bis F epoxy blends. We found that there were noise-level variations in the performance when considering most of the resin formulation and that non-reactive dilutents performed equal to or better than the 100% solids (undiluted) resins." From this statement it may be reasonably concluded that the West product contains non-reactive dilutent.

For those of you who are willing to accept, or prefer, a pre-packaged product without exact knowledge of its ingredients — which will be the case with many other packaged products — you will find the West System comparable to others. The West System is not less labor intensive than many other methods. However, it is widely used and they have an excellent customer service department.

Gougeon Brothers, Inc. produce excellent brochures and documents relating their products to hull repairs. Especially informative is their booklet "Gel Coat Blisters Diagnosis, Repair and Prevention." Thanks to the Gougeon people, parts of this document are reproduced or referred to in other parts of the book you are now reading. For the complete text of their blister book and their other documents, I suggest you write or call them directly.

PRO-LINE PAINT CO.

MARINE, MILITARY & INDUSTRIAL

PAINT MANUFACTURERS

2646 MAIN ST. • SAN DIEGO, CA 92113-3967 • TEL: 619-231-2313
1168 HARBOR AVE. • LONG BEACH, CA 90813 • TEL: 213-432-7961
TELEX NO. 695085 PRO LINE SDG

PRODUCT SPECIFICATIONS

Pro-Line 5070 Series

Resin Blister Blocker

Series

Description:
Pro-Line 5071/5079 Series is a multicoat system for fiberglass surfaces. When used as directed it will help to minimize gel coat blistering.

Gel coat blistering can be avoided if sufficient mil thickness is applied to protect the surface from coming in contact with water. Remember the more coats you apply the better the chance of avoiding blistering.

Advantages:
  * User Friendly, Easy to apply
  * 1:1 mixing ratio
  * May be applied at up to 20 wet mils
  * Maximum overcoat time is 6 plus months over a clean substrate

Surface Preparation:
1. If the mold release compound was water based or you are not sure, first wash the surface with a solution of T.S.P. and fresh water and rinse thoroughly, then proceed as follows.
2. Wipe the complete surface with Pro-Line #25 Fiberglass Prep, changing rags frequently (this is very important).
3. Sand the surface with #60 or #80 sandpaper to remove all of the gel coat sheen.
4. Remove all sanding residue with compressed air or clean rags.
5. Again wipe the complete surface with Pro-Line #25 Fiberglass Prep, changing to clean rags frequently.

Mixing:
Mix equal parts of component "A" with Component "B", if possible use a Jiffy-type mixer to insure proper blending. May also be mixed by stirring.

Application:
May be applied by brush, roller or spray; spray application gives the best results. When applying with roller use a short nap roller sleeve. When rolling, a smoother finish may be obtained by following with a brush.

(Rev. 2-12-90 AFB)

Colors: 5071, Tan
5079, Gray

Finish: Low sheen

Service: Interior and exterior

Component Ratio: 1 to 1 by volume

Pot Life: 4 hours minimum @ 70F.

Solvent: Pro-Line Y18, thin as required

Solids By Volume: Approximately 60%

Recommended Wet Film Thickness: 8 mils minimum

Recommended Minimum Number Of Coats: Four

Recommended Total Dry Film Thickness: 20 mils

Flash Point: 100F., C.C. method

Overcoat Time @ 70F.:
Epoxy 5070 series: 2 hours minimum - 6 months maximum.

Antifouling: Must be applied before the epoxy is hard (as soon as you can touch the epoxy firmly without having it stick to your finger) within 2 to 8 hours.

These products meet A.P.C.D. & E.P.A. requirements.

PRO-LINE PAINT CO.

MARINE, MILITARY & INDUSTRIAL

PAINT MANUFACTURERS

2646 MAIN ST. • SAN DIEGO, CA 92113-3967 • TEL: 619-231-2313
1168 HARBOR AVE. • LONG BEACH, CA 90813 • TEL: 213-432-7961
TELEX NO. 695085 PRO LINE SDG

PRODUCT SPECIFICATIONS

Pro-Line 5070 Series

Resin Blister Blocker

Series

HOW TO REPAIR GELCOAT BLISTERS

Over the last few years gelcoat blistering has become a major concern to boat owners of fiberglass hulls. This problem appears on most makes and has been especially prevalent in hulls constructed with fire retardant resins.

Although the actual cause of blistering is still being debated, it is generally recognized that it can be stopped or at least greatly reduced with the proper coating system. The best method to stop gelcoat blistering is to stop it before it becomes a problem. This can be done when the vessel is new and will require the least amount of work and expense.

NOTE: Although we will be discussing the exterior of the hull, it is recommended that as much of the interior of bilges be coated with the same system.

SURFACE PREPARATION

1. Remove all old paint by sandblasting or with a power grinder; be sure to break all blisters. On hulls that have not started to blister see "How To Prevent Gelcoat Blistering."

2. After sanding, sandblasting or grinding, wash the complete hull with high pressure fresh water. This process will help insure that all dust and free styrene is removed.

3. Allow the surface to dry. (This should be checked with a moisture meter and the moisture content should be 14% or lower.) The lower the moisture content the better the results you will achieve. Depending on the hull and climatic conditions, this can take from 4 to 30+ days. For fast and controlled results, dehumidification equipment can be used to insure a fast low moisture content. This can reduce the time to 1 to 3 days.

Author's Comment on Pro-Line Barrier Materials

As you can see, Pro-Line's instructions for preparation and use of their barrier materials is not exactly overdone!

Again, if you have concern about materials which contain solvents and/or pigments, and if you are convinced that solvents cannot be used successfully, then avoid Pro-Line's two systems. It is my view that it is more important to determine if the effectiveness of the cured barrier coat — even if applied with solvent — has been proved in the field. The only way to do this is to track down owners who have used the system, not just the boatyard foreman.

Pro-Line 5070 series has been used for several years, especially in new boat construction. Their newer 3060 series is designed for low temperature application use; it can be applied in fewer coats and has the same over-coat time as the 5070 material, which is claimed to be up to six months without preparation.

Be careful you are not misled into applying a second coat using either of these systems if the cured coat has produced a hard surface and/or glaze. This will be evident after only a few hours and will remain so thereafter. In spite of what they don't tell you, *dry* sand with 60 -100 grit discs or paper only. Do not wipe with any solvent or wash with water. Blow off dust with oil- and water-free air.

If you have scheduled application of anti-fouling paint, note that Pro-Line requires for both systems that the anti-foulant be applied before the last epoxy barrier coat has cured.

TECHNICAL BULLETIN #900A

InterProtect™

THE INTERPROTECT SYSTEM
PROTECTS FIBERGLASS HULLS FROM WATER ABSORPTION.

X. Interlux®

Issued 4/88

THE INTERPROTECT™ SYSTEM TO REDUCE WATER ABSORPTION BY A FIBERGLASS HULL

I. CAUSES AND PREVENTION OF BLISTERING

The use of fiberglass laminate and resin as construction materials for boats has created one of the most dramatic changes in the industry since man first hollowed a log. Fiberglass boats are efficient to manufacture in large numbers, are light in weight, allow flexibility in design and have a long and relatively maintenance-free life. Simply described, most fiberglass hulls are made in molds of the desired hull shape from the outside in. This means the surface of the mold is coated with gelcoat (pigmented resin), then layers of resin saturated fiberglass (laminate) are laid against the gelcoat and allowed to harden. When hard, the gelcoat, resin and fiberglass laminate bind together and conform to the desired shape of the hull. The resulting combination of materials provides a very durable and strong structure.

However, throughout the history of fiberglass boat construction, it has been discovered that these marvelous materials have limitations just as any other material. The bright, shiny topside gelcoat surfaces of fiberglass boats will fade, crack, become porous and oxidize with age. In short, the surface loses its "new" brilliance. Fortunately, when this occurs, topside gelcoat regains brilliance by the application of two-part polyurethanes such as INTERTHANE PLUS® It has been discovered that underwater gelcoat and fiberglass laminates **can absorb water** which can cause changes in the physical makeup of the hull. These changes can affect hull performance, physical appearances and sometimes result in blistering of the underwater surfaces of the hull. It is the purpose of this Technical Bulletin to address the subject of water absorption by a fiberglass hull, the problems created and the preventative and repair measures necessary to reduce these problems.

HULL BLISTERING

Gelcoat was, at one time, thought to be an almost indestructible surface and impervious to water. Field experience and extensive testing have proven that, like many other "waterproof" materials at some point in the life of a hull, water will pass through the gelcoat and reach the laminate layer.

Once this water permeates the gelcoat, and if conditions are right in the laminate, hull blistering can occur. Specifically, there must be a residue of material in voids along the gelcoat/laminate boundary which will form a solution dissimilar to the existing water on the outer skin of the gelcoat. It is this difference which causes a pressure. The liquid solution behind the gelcoat wants to reach equilibrium with the water on the outer skin of the gelcoat. During the attemped equilibrium process, pressure increases and is responsible for distension of the gelcoat in the form of blisters. Without going into great detail, this is how gelcoat blistering occurs. The whys are more complicated and are of little importance from a pragmatic point of view and beyond the scope of this Technical Bulletin.

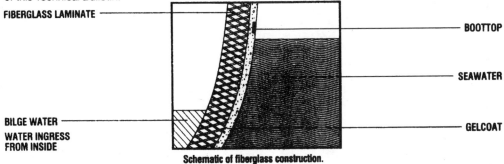

FIBERGLASS LAMINATE —   — BOOTTOP

    — SEAWATER

BILGE WATER —   — GELCOAT
WATER INGRESS FROM INSIDE

Schematic of fiberglass construction.

EFFECTS OF WATER ABSORPTION

It is difficult to determine how much water a fiberglass hull laminate must absorb to cause gelcoat blistering. Documentation has shown the gelcoat and laminates absorb water. (Not only does the gelcoat allow exterior water to pass, but exposed interior laminate can absorb bilge water, too.) Therefore, it is reasonable to assume that keeping water from the gelcoat and laminate is an effective method of preventing water weight gain by the hull, reduce the potential of gelcoat blistering and other forms of laminate degradation from taking place. This penetration or absorption process can take days, months or years. Regardless, the hull steadily gains weight, loses efficiency through the water, suffers increased fuel consumption and can result in hull blisters.

MINIMIZING WATER ABSORPTION

There are several methods of reducing water from saturating the hull. Proper thickness of gelcoat will provide a degree of prevention but increasing gelcoat thickness is not an answer. Gelcoat tends to be brittle and crack. Thick gelcoat cracks easier, providing a direct water path to the laminate. Other techniques include "drysailing" (storing the boat on land and launching for each outing), spot repairing during seasonal (winter) hauling, or sealing the hull with two-part epoxy coatings. The latter approach is gaining support from many authorities within the marine industry. It is accepted that water absorption decreases by increasing the barrier (gelcoat and epoxy) between the laminate and the water.

There is a popular misconception that epoxy coatings and resins are "waterproof". This is not true. Better stated, epoxy coatings survive well underwater and well formulated epoxy coatings have better water resistance than the average gelcoat. Simply, to delay water absorption, a hull requires an additional epoxy water barrier which effectively increases the thickness of the gelcoat and retards water migration to the laminate.

TRADITIONAL EPOXY TECHNOLOGY

Applying an epoxy coating which is specifically formulated to delay water absorption gives the boat owner the best option to seal the gelcoat and hull. In the past, epoxy coatings were adopted from other uses. Technological limitations of the formulations made the application process an extremely difficult and time-consuming task, reserved for the most competent and skilled professional. Many epoxy products required four to five coats, applied at 24-hour intervals to achieve 10 mils (.010 inch) of dry film. Only after as much as a week of application could antifouling paint be applied. These coatings required experienced and controlled applications to avoid runs and sags, which require many hours of tedious sanding to remove. To say the least, not a job for the do-it-yourselfer.

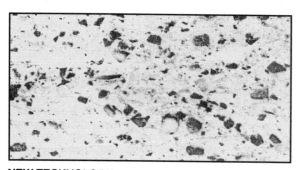

Traditional two-part epoxy coatings were adaptations of products designed for other applications which were not specifically developed to resist water permeation. This electron microscope photograph of a conventional epoxy coating enlarged 900 times shows the pigment randomly dispersed, creating no uniform barrier to water permeation. Water can find almost a direct path through and around these randomly dispersed particles.

Photo #1

NEW TECHNOLOGY

When International Paint set out to specifically design an epoxy coating to reduce water absorption, the following characteristics were required:
☐ Fast drying characteristics to enable the applicator to achieve 10 mils of protective epoxy coating over the gelcoat *in one day*.
☐ A coating easily applied by a do-it-yourselfer, as well as the highly skilled applicators.
☐ Improved sag resistance allowing film build without runs or sags.
☐ A natural structure within the epoxy coating to create a barrier against water permeation.

With the above in mind, International Paint chemists have developed a unique two-part epoxy coating, INTERPROTECT 2000,™ specifically to reduce the potential of water absorption by the hull. INTERPROTECT 2000™ allows the do-it-yourselfer to apply 10 mils of epoxy in one working day, rather than one week. In addition, INTERPROTECT 2000™ has a unique protective barrier within its film to retard water permeation. Technically, the INTERPROTECT 2000™ MICRO-PLATE™ formula provides millions of overlapping microscopic plates. When bound in the epoxy coating, they create an overlapping barrier similar to shingles on a roof. Enlarged 900 times in this electron microscope photo, the overlapping MICRO-PLATES clearly eliminate any direct path for water migration, Photo #2.

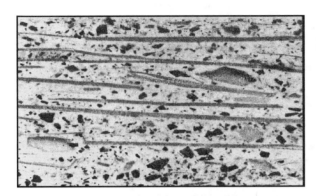

Magnified 900 times, the Micro-plate™ effect of Interprotect™ is demonstrated in this electron microscope photo. The overlapping micro-plates create a material barrier against water migration yet provide a smooth, hard epoxy finish.

<u>Photo #2</u>

INTERPROTECT 2000™ provides exceptional advantages over older epoxy technologies. In addition to the technical advantages, application of INTERPROTECT 2000™ is beyond compare. This product is applied by brush or roller without tendencies to sag or run. Not only can the entire system (10 mils) be applied in one day, but the antifouling paint can be applied without additional surface preparation. (Be sure to follow label directions.)

INTERPROTECT 2000™ is a preventative maintenance system. Just as undercoating one's new car will delay the onset of rust and decay, proper application of INTERPROTECT 2000™ will substantially delay water penetration and its effects. It must be pointed out, **the key to protection against water absorption is the early application of INTERPROTECT 2000™.** The proper application of INTERPROTECT 2000™ enhances fiberglass hull's long term performance, integrity and resale value.

To complete the INTERPROTECT™ System, International Paint has formulated a complementary product to seal bare laminate and badly blistered gelcoat prior to the application of INTERPROTECT 2000™. This sealer coat is called INTERPROTECT 1000™ and is described in detail in Section VI of this Technical Bulletin.

II. CHOOSING THE RIGHT INTERPROTECT SYSTEM

1. INTERPROTECT™ AS A PROTECTIVE SYSTEM
   INTERPROTECT 2000™ should be used as a preventative measure to protect new or used boats from water permeation. If the gelcoat is generally intact or has minor blistering, INTERPROTECT 2000™ can be applied without INTERPROTECT 1000/1001. Refer to Section V for detailed application instructions.
2. INTERPROTECT™ AS A REPAIR SYSTEM
   If the hull has experienced serious gelcoat blistering, surface weeping or gelcoat detachment, it is recommended that the laminate and gelcoat be sealed with INTERPROTECT 1000™. Boats with severely damaged gelcoat should be inspected by a competent Marine Surveyor to determine if the gelcoat can be sanded or must be removed. Refer to Section VI for detailed application instructions on the INTERPROTECT 1000™ and Section V on INTERPROTECT 2000™ systems.

III. THE IMPORTANCE OF PROPER HULL DRYING

The importance of having a moisture-free hull laminate cannot be overemphasized. The drier the laminate, the lighter the hull, better the performance, the more efficient-fuel use and longer gelcoat life. If INTERPROTECT™ is applied to a wet hull, it could trap moisture in the laminate and the gelcoat blistering may continue. When convinced of dryness, proceed to Section IV. For used boats without any visible signs of water absorption, remove all antifouling paint with Interlux 299 Fiberglass Antifouling Paint Remover and then sand with 80 grit production paper. Allow the hull to completely "dry", two weeks to two months, badly blistered hulls will take longer to dry. Atmospheric conditions and boat age will affect drying time. Older boats in cold, damp conditions will dry slower than newer boats in hot, dry conditions.

A technique to help determine the hull dryness is to tape a clear plastic sheet, one foot square, over the cleaned surface. All edges of the square must be sealed with tape to the hull. If after 24 hours the inside of the plastic is free of condensation, the hull is ready for INTERPROTECT™. If condensation is present, repeat until plastic remains dry. If there is any doubt that the hull laminate is not dry, allow more time.

For boats with visible signs of water absorption (blisters, weeping, etc.) remove antifouling paint with Interlux 299 Fiberglass Antifouling Paint Remover and then sand with 80 grit production paper or professional sandblasting. Open all blisters by grinding to solid laminate. Scrub and rinse these areas with fresh water. Water may penetrate the laminate from the inside (bilge). Be sure bilges are dry. Allow hull to dry as long as possible. (A saturated hull may require a minimum two-three months or longer to dry.)

Typical Dehumidifying Tent
Note: Be sure plastic is laid under boat to reduce moisture being drawn from the ground.

Photo #3

In areas where boats are stored out of water during the off season, complete the surface preparation when the boat is hauled. Apply INTERPROTECT™ system prior to seasonal launch. In this way, the hull will have a long drying cycle. The recurrence of gelcoat blistering cannot be completely assured, although longer drying times decrease the possibility of future blistering.

Complete removal of gelcoat should be undertaken only under the advice and recommendation of a competent Yacht Surveyor. Gelcoat removal is only necessary to eliminate a questionable gelcoat surface and does not reduce drying time.

Some owners or yards will provide a dehumidified environment for the hull within a shed, or they will build a plastic tent around the underwater portion of the hull. Check for dryness with clear plastic patch as previously outlined.

IV. CALCULATING WETTED SURFACE AREA

Applying the proper film thickness of INTERPROTECT™ is critical in keeping hull laminate dry. The following is designed to help estimate the amount of material required for a specific hull. **Proper film thickness will improve the performance of the INTERPROTECT™ system.**

It is best to actually measure the wetted surface area of the hull. If this is difficult to do, a close approximation can be made by multiplying the length overall, times the beam, times 85%. (L.O.A. x Beam x .85 = wetted surface area.) The following chart is offered as an approximation.

POWERBOATS

Boat Size	Estimated Surface Area	INTERPROTECT 2000™ 4-5 Coats Total	INTERPROTECT 1000™ If Required
18' Runabout	120 sq. ft.	8 qts. (2 gal.)	3 qts.
21' Runabout	150 sq. ft.	10 qts. (2½ gal.)	4 qts.
28' Cruiser	240 sq. ft.	16 qts. (4 gal.)	5 qts.
32' Sportfisherman	300 sq. ft.	20 qts. (5 gal.)	7 qts.
36' Cruiser	350 sq. ft.	23 qts. (5¾ gal.)	8 qts.
42' Cruiser	500 sq. ft.	34 qts. (8½ gal.)	11 qts.
53' Cruiser	650 sq. ft.	43 qts. (10¾ gal.)	15 qts.

SAILBOATS

Boat Size	Estimated Surface Area	INTERPROTECT 2000™ 4-5 Coats Total	INTERPROTECT 1000™ If Required
18' Day Sailer	120 sq. ft.	8 qts. (2 gal.)	3 qts.
24' Trailerable	160 sq. ft.	10 qts. (2½ gal.)	4 qts.
28' Racer/Cruiser	250 sq. ft.	16 qts. (4 gal.)	5 qts.
31' Racer/Cruiser	270 sq. ft.	18 qts. (4½ gal.)	6 qts.
36' Cruiser	330 sq. ft.	22 qts. (5½ gal.)	8 qts.
41' Cruiser	435 sq. ft.	29 qts. (7¼ gal.)	10 qts.
53' Cruiser	590 sq. ft.	40 qts. (10 gal.)	13 qts.

Wetted surface areas and product volume requirements for boats listed above are approximate and are supplied as reference only.

Because a thick coating provides greater protection against water penetration, all quantities should be rounded up.

☐ Average expected coverage of INTERPROTECT 2000/2001™ is 60 sq. ft. per gallon kit to achieve 10 mils of dry finished coating.

☐ Average expected coverage of INTERPROTECT 1000/1001™ is approximately 175 sq. ft. per gallon kit to achieve 8 mils of dry finished coating. Surface condition may greatly affect the coverage.

V. APPLYING INTERPROTECT 2000™

Proper hull preparation prior to the application of INTERPROTECT 2000™ is essential. The procedures outlined in Section III on hull drying should be followed carefully to obtain best results. It is also important to carefully calculate the amount of material needed for the hull. Refer to Section IV for details.

PRODUCT DESCRIPTION: INTERPROTECT 2000/2001™ is a unique two-part epoxy coating developed to protect new and used fiberglass hulls from water absorption which can lead to poor hull performance and possible hull blistering. It can also be used to repair gelcoat blistered hulls. This product makes it possible to apply a complete underwater barrier and antifouling system within two (2) days. On boats where the gelcoat has been removed and bare laminate is exposed, use INTERPROTECT 1000™ as a sealer coat prior to the application of INTERPROTECT 2000™.

FILM THICKNESS: Recommended dry film thickness is 10 mils (.010 inch). To determine how many gallons of INTERPROTECT 2000/2001™ are required to obtain this thickness, divide the wetted surface area of the boat by 60 square feet per gallon kit. This will result in the total number of gallons required for the entire system. Normally, 4-5 coats will be required. See Section IV.

MIXING AND THINNING: Thoroughly mix 3 parts of INTERPROTECT 2000™ to 1 part INTERPROTECT 2001™ by volume, allow to set for 20 minutes (induction time) before use. INTERPROTECT 2000/2001™ can be brushed or rolled. *DO NOT SPRAY.* Normally, thinning is not required. However, if necessary, product can be thinned up to 10% by using #2316 REDUCING SOLVENT.

Due to the fast evaporation rate of the solvent in INTERPROTECT,™ pour small amounts into the painting tray. The remainder of the mixed paint should remain in the closed can to prevent evaporation and maximize pot life. **The INTERPROTECT 2000™ should not be left overnight if reacted. Mix only enough product which can be used in 4 hours.**

ESTIMATED DRY TIMES: INTERPROTECT 2000/2001 should only be used at temperatures of 50°F and above. Additional coats of INTERPROTECT 2000/2001 may be applied a minimum of 2 hours and a maximum of 18 hours without additional surface preparation (if beyond 18 hours sand last coat with 80 grit paper). By applying every 2-4 hours a complete protective coating system can be applied in one day. The first coat of INTERLUX antifouling paint may be applied after the last coat of INTERPROTECT 2000/2001 as detailed below.

Temperature	Hours Between Last Coat of INTERPROTECT 2000 and Antifouling Paint
50° - 60°	6 - 8 Hours
60° - 80°	4 - 6 Hours
80° - 90°	2 - 4 Hours

Beyond these times, sand with 80 grit paper or apply another coat of INTERPROTECT 2000 before application of the antifouling.

SURFACE PREPARATION FOR NEW BOATS
When used as a preventative measure against water absorption or gelcoat blistering.

1. Thoroughly clean hull with 202 INTERLUX FIBERGLASS SOLVENT WASH, as per label directions.
2. Lighty sand with 80 grit paper.
3. Apply one coat of INTERPROTECT 2000 every 2-18 hours.
4. Apply antifouling paint as per dry times above.

SURFACE PREPARATION FOR USED BOATS WITH MINOR BLISTERING
1. Remove all antifouling from the gelcoat with Interlux 299 Fiberglass Antifouling Paint Remover and then sand with 80 grit production paper. If small amounts of blisters exist, open and expose all cavities.
2. Flush thoroughly with fresh water to remove all residue in the cavities.
3. Allow to dry as long as possible (2 weeks–2 months). If drying period is less than two weeks, moisture may be trapped in hull. Moisture trapped in hull may cause continued blistering.
4. Apply 417A/418B EPOXY FAIRING AND SURFACING COMPOUND to cavities. Allow to cure overnight. Sand smooth with 80 grit paper.
5. Apply INTERPROTECT 2000, as described above.
6. Apply antifouling paint as per above.

VI. APPLYING INTERPROTECT 1000™ and INTERPROTECT 2000™ AS A REPAIR SYSTEM

Proper hull preparation prior to the application of INTERPROTECT™ is essential. The procedures outlined in Section III on hull drying should be followed carefully to obtain best results. It is also important to carefully calculate the amount of material needed for the hull. Refer to Section IV for details.

PRODUCT DESCRIPTION: INTERPROTECT 1000/1001™ is a primer coating for use when gelcoat is removed and fiberglass laminate requires sealing. It is a two-part, high build, clear epoxy coating which enables the applicator to see that all dry fibers are saturated and sealed. This product should be used in conjunction with INTERPROTECT 2000/2001™.

FILM THICKNESS: Due to the varying conditions of the laminate layer, it is impossible to predetermine the exact amounts of materials to be used for saturation. Average expected coverage is 175 square feet per gallon kit.

MIXING AND THINNING: INTERPROTECT 1000/1001™ should not be thinned. Mix thoroughly Base 1000 with reactor 1001 (5:2 ratio). **Mix only what can be used in twenty (20) minutes.** *Pour mixed material into a wide, flat tray to prevent premature curing.* Mix only *small* amounts until application technique is determined. Do not spray. For clean up use #2316 REDUCING SOLVENT.

ESTIMATED DRY TIMES: If overcoating with 1000/1001, minimum overcoating time is 4 hours. Maximum is 24 hours, without sanding. If maximum time is exceeded, scrub and flush with fresh water, then sand with 80 grit paper.

SURFACE PREPARATION: (1). Remove all antifouling paint from the bottom of the boat with Interlux 299 Fiberglass Antifouling Paint Remover and then sand with 80 grit production paper and open all blistered areas either by physical grinding or by professionally sandblasting. Complete removal of gelcoat is not necessary, provided the remaining gelcoat is solidly attached to the underlying laminate. Complete removal of gelcoat should be done *only* after the advice of a competent Marine Surveyor. (2). Wash frequently the entire underwater surface with fresh water and rinse clean. (3). Grind out any blistered areas which are not solid laminate. (4). Allow hull to dry as long as possible (2 months - 3 months) to insure all water has left the hull. Moisture in hull may cause additional blistering.

GENERAL APPLICATION: INTERPROTECT 1000/1001™ must be applied above 50°F. Coat the exposed laminate with one coat of INTERPROTECT 1000/1001.™ It is suggested to apply first coat by brush (subsequent coats by roller or brush) to be sure INTERPROTECT 1000™ is well saturated into exposed fibers and bare laminate. After INTERPROTECT 1000/1001™ has cured 4-24 hours, scrub with fresh water to remove any chemical blush or sweat. Allow the surface to dry thoroughly. If any bare laminate fibers extend up through the first coat of INTERPROTECT 1000/1001,™ it is necessary to sand these fibers flat with 80 grit paper. Apply a second coat to completely seal the bare laminate and gelcoat. When dry, and before overcoating with INTERPROTECT 2000/2001,™ flush with water and <u>sand entire surface.</u> Fill voids with 417A/418B EPOXY SURFACING AND FAIRING COMPOUND. <u>When dry, sand fairing compound with 80 grit production paper.</u> Apply first coat of INTERPROTECT 2000/2001™ following directions (see Section V). If antifouling paint is applied directly to INTERPROTECT 1000,™ wash with fresh water, dry and use AL200 NO SAND PRIMER as a tie coat.

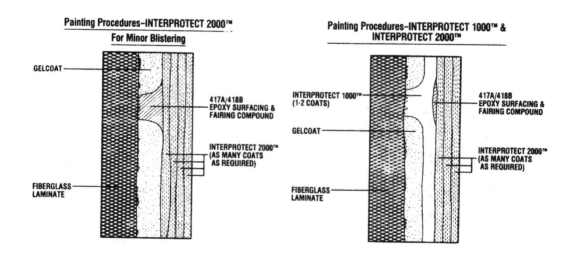

Painting Procedures–INTERPROTECT 2000™
For Minor Blistering

GELCOAT

417A/418B EPOXY SURFACING & FAIRING COMPOUND

INTERPROTECT 2000™ (AS MANY COATS AS REQUIRED)

FIBERGLASS LAMINATE

Painting Procedures–INTERPROTECT 1000™ & INTERPROTECT 2000™

INTERPROTECT 1000™ (1-2 COATS)

GELCOAT

417A/418B EPOXY SURFACING & FAIRING COMPOUND

INTERPROTECT 2000™ (AS MANY COATS AS REQUIRED)

FIBERGLASS LAMINATE

VII. INTERPROTECT AS A UNIVERSAL PRIMER – SPECIAL SYSTEMS

The excellent results obtained from INTERPROTECT has expanded the areas and applications for which this product is useful. INTERPROTECT has been used as an epoxy primer for every part of a boat with outstanding results. Listed below are specific systems for steel keels, lead keels and aluminum.

STEEL KEELS: 1. Blast surface to bright metal or sand steel keel thoroughly using 36 grit wheel. Be certain all old antifouling paint has been removed. 2. Apply one coat of INTERPROTECT 2000 within one hour after sanding or sandblasting directly to bare steel. 3. Allow at least 4 hour dry under normal weather conditions. Fair with 417A/418B or 4496/4497 depending on condition of keel. 4. Sand fairing compound until smooth and blended with surrounding area. 5. Apply at least 4 coats of INTERPROTECT 2000. 6. Refer to page 5 for approximate dry times between the last coat of INTERPROTECT 2000 and the first coat of antifouling paint.

LEAD KEELS: 1. Blast surface to bright metal or sand lead thoroughly using 36 grit wheel. Be certain all old antifouling paint has been removed. 2. Apply one coat of INTERPROTECT 2000 directly to freshly sanded lead. 3. Allow at least 4 hour dry under normal weather conditions. 4. Fair with 417A/418B or 4496/4497 depending on condition of surface. 5. Sand fairing compound until smooth. 6. Apply at least 4 coats of INTER-PROTECT 2000. 7. Refer to page 5 for exact dry times between the last coat of INTERPROTECT 2000 and the first coat of antifouling paint.

ALUMINUM: 1. Sand blast to bright metal or sand aluminum with 60-80 grit emery paper. (Aluminum should be solvent wiped to remove grease and/or dirt, prior to this step.) Be certain all old paint has been removed. 2. Apply one coat of INTERPROTECT 2000 within 1 hour after sanding or sandblasting directly to bare aluminum. 3. Allow at least 4 hour dry under normal weather conditions. Fair with 417A/418B or 4496/4497 depending on condition of surface. 4. Sand fairing compound until smooth and blended with surrounding areas. 5. Apply at least 4 coats of INTERPROTECT 2000. 6. Refer to page 5 for exact dry times between the last coat of INTERPROTECT 2000 and the first coat of antifouling paint.

ABOVE WATERLINE: INTERPROTECT 2000 can be used as a priming system for the two-part INTERTHANE PLUS polyurethane.

VIII. EXPECTATIONS OF SUCCESS

All yachts which are well built with high-quality materials and good workmanship are likely to perform in a completely satisfactory manner for many years. However, there are many reasons why water absorption can occur. The causes and contributory factors have been analyzed and not completely understood. What seems to be clear is that nearly all blistering problems arise from the presence of water in the laminate. INTERPROTECT 2000/2001 will reduce water absorption. Its success is directly related to your following of the application guidelines.

The performance of any marine paint or coating depends on many factors outside the control of International Paint, including surface preparation, proper applicaiton, and environmental conditions. Therefore, International Paint (USA), Inc. cannot guarantee this product's suitability for your particular purpose or application. IMPLIED WARRANTIES OF FITNESS FOR A PARTICULAR PURPOSE AND OF MERCHANTABILITY ARE EXCLUDED. INTERNATIONAL PAINT SHALL NOT, UNDER ANY CIRCUMSTANCES, BE LIABLE FOR INCIDENTAL OR CONSEQUENTIAL DAMAGES. By purchase or use of this product, buyer agrees that the sole and exclusive remedy, if any, is limited to the refund of the purchase price or replacement of the product at International Paint's option.

HEALTH AND SAFETY RECOMMENDATIONS
1. Be sure to follow all instructions properly.
2. Wear protective clothing, eye protection and appropriate mask when working with any paint or gelcoat.
3. Apply INTERPROTECT™ in well-ventilated areas.
4. If rash or skin irritation occurs with the use of INTERPROTECT,™ discontinue use and thoroughly wash with soap and water. SEE APPROPRIATE LABEL FOR FURTHER DETAILS ON THE SPECIFIC FORMULA.
5. Do not spray INTERPROTECT.™ If not handled correctly, INTERPROTECT may cause injury if sprayed through improper equipment. Please consult Interlux Representative.

✕Interlux®
YACHT FINISHES
International Paint (USA), Inc.

2270 Morris Avenue
P.O. Box 386, Union, New Jersey 07083
(201) 686-1300

19500 Transcanada Highway
Baie D'Urfe, (Quebec) H9X 3S8

✕ COURTAULDS COATINGS

INTERPROTECT™
3000/3001

PRODUCT DESCRIPTION: INTERPROTECT 3000/3001 is a unique two part epoxy coating designed to offer many of the properties of INTERPROTECT 2000/2001 and **meets** the most restrictive V.O.C. regulations in the country. INTERPROTECT 3000/3001 is a high solids (80%) epoxy coating developed to protect old and new fiberglass hulls from water absorption, which can potentially lead to hull blistering. Due to the high solids content of the product it is possible to apply a complete barrier system and antifouling paint within a 2-3 day period. On boats where gelcoat has been removed or large areas of fiberglass laminate are exposed, use INTERPROTECT 1000/1001 as a sealer coat prior to application of INTERPROTECT 3000/3001. INTERPROTECT 3000/3001 contains the same unique Micro-Plates™ Technology as INTERPROTECT 2000/2001 which substantially reduces water migration through gelcoat.

V.O.C COMPLIANCE: The V.O.C of INTERPROTECT 3000/3001 is 166 grams/liter (1.4 lbs./gal.) as supplied. With a 10% volume reduction with either INTERLUX 2316N or INTERLUX 2333N, the V.O.C. is increased to 233 grams/liter (1.94 lbs./gal.).

FILM THICKNESS: The recommended dry film thickness is 10 mils (.010 inch). To determine how many gallons of INTERPROTECT 3000/3001 that is required to achieve this thickness, divide the wetted surface area of the boat, by 110 sq. ft. per gallon when brushing and rolling or by 90 sq. ft. per gallon when spraying. This will result in the total number of gallons required to properly complete a 10 mil dry brush and rolled 3 to 4 coat system or a spray applied 2 to 3 coat system.

MIXING AND THINNING: Thoroughly mix 4 parts INTERPROTECT 3000 base with 1 part INTERPROTECT 3001 reactor by volume. After mixing and before application allow a 30 minute induction time. When brush or roller application is desired the best results have been by using the roll and tip method. If a thinner is required, use 5 to 10% **maximum** of INTERLUX 2333N brushing solvent. For larger surfaces spray application is recommended to provide a more desirable finish. Airless spray is the preferred method, using no solvent. If conventional spray is necessary (pressure pot only) use 5 to 10% **maximum** of INTERLUX 2316N spray solvent.

ESTIMATED DRY TIMES: Interprotect 3000/3001 may be applied at temperatures ranging from 40°F to 95°F. Low temperatures below 65°F will result in longer cure and overcoating times.

Beyond these times, sand with 80 grit paper before applying another coat of INTERPROTECT 3000/3001 or before application of the antifouling.

NOTE: INTERLUX AL200 PRIMER can also be used as a tie coat between the antifouling and the INTERPROTECT 3000/3001.

SURFACE PREPARATION FOR NEW BOATS: When used as a preventative measure against water absorption or gelcoat blistering.
1. Thoroughly clean hull with 202 INTERLUX FIBERGLASS SOLVENT WASH, as per label directions.
2. Lightly sand with 80 grit paper.
3. Apply one coat of INTERPROTECT 3000/3001 every 3 to 16 hours. (See chart above) A total of 3 to 4 coats are necessary.
4. Apply antifouling paint as per dry times above.

SURFACE PREPARATION FOR USED BOATS WITH MINOR BLISTERING
1. Remove all antifouling from the gelcoat with INTERLUX 299 FIBERGLASS ANTIFOULING PAINT REMOVER and then sand with 80 grit production paper. If small amounts of blisters exist, open and expose all cavities.
2. Flush thoroughly with fresh water.
3. Allow to dry as long as possible (a minimum of 2 months). If drying period is less than two months, moisture may be trapped in hull. Moisture trapped in hull may cause continued blistering.
4. Apply 417A/418B EPOXY FAIRING AND SURFACING COMPOUND to cavities. Allow to cure overnight. Sand smooth with 80 grit paper.
5. Apply INTERPROTECT 3000/3001, as described above. A total of 3 to 4 coats are necessary.
6. Apply antifouling paint as per above.

If large amounts of gelcoat have been removed and bare laminate is exposed, use INTERPROTECT 1000/1001 as a sealer coat prior to the application of INTERPROTECT 3000/3001. Refer to INTERPROTECT 1000/1001 label for details. Additional information is available on the above systems in INTERLUX Technical Bulletin No. 900.

Dry Time:				Overcoating Interval for Interprotect 3000/3001			
Substrate Temperature	Pot Life	Touch Dry	Hard Dry	3000/3001 Over Self		Interlux Antifouling	
				Min	Max	Min	Max
41° F (5° C)	6 hrs	10 hrs	24 hrs	16 hrs	3 mths	16 hrs	20 hrs
73° F (23° C)	4 hrs	4 hrs	8 hrs	6 hrs	2 mths	6 hrs	10 hrs
95° F (35° C)	2 hrs	2 hrs	4 hrs	3 hrs	1 mth	3 hrs	6 hrs

INTERPROTECT 3000/3001 AS A UNIVERSAL PRIMER - SPECIAL SYSTEMS

INTERPROTECT 3000/3001 can be used as an epoxy primer for every part of a boat with outstanding results. Listed below are specific systems for steel keels, lead keels and aluminum.

STEEL KEELS: 1. Blast surface to bright metal or sand steel keel thoroughly using 36 grit wheel. Be certain all old antifouling paint has been removed. 2. Apply one coat of INTERPROTECT 3000/3001 within one hour after sanding or sandblasting directly to bare steel. 3. Allow at least 6 hours dry under normal weather conditions. Sand with 80 grit paper then fair with 417A/418B or YAA840/YAA841 depending on condition of keel. 4. Sand fairing compound until smooth and blended with surrounding area. 5. Apply at least 3 coats of INTERPROTECT 3000/3001. 6. Refer to chart above for exact dry times between the last coat of INTERPROTECT 3000/3001 and the first coat of antifouling paint.*

LEAD KEELS: 1. Blast surface to bright metal or sand lead thoroughly using 36 grit wheel. Be certain all old antifouling paint has been removed. 2. Apply one coat of INTERPROTECT 3000/3001 directly to freshly sanded lead. 3. Allow at least 6 hour dry under normal weather conditions. 4. Sand with 80 grit paper then fair with 417A/418B or YAA840/YAA841 depending on condition of surface. 5. Sand fairing compound until smooth. 6. Apply at least 3 coats of INTERPROTECT 3000/3001. 7. Refer to chart above for exact dry times between the last coat of INTERPROTECT 3000/3001 and the first coat of antifouling paint.*

ALUMINUM: 1. Sand blast to bright metal or sand aluminum with 60-80 grit emery paper. (Aluminum should be solvent wiped to remove grease and/or dirt, prior to this step). Be certain all old paint has been removed. 2. Apply one coat of INTERPROTECT 3000/3001 within 1 hour after sanding or sandblasting directly to bare aluminum. 3. Allow at least 6 hour dry under normal weather conditions. Sand with 80 grit paper then fair with 417A/418B or YAA840/YAA841 depending on condition of surface. 4. Sand fairing compound until smooth and blended with surrounding areas. 5. Apply at least 3 coats of INTERPROTECT 3000/3001. 6. Refer to chart above for exact dry times between the last coat of INTERPROTECT 3000/3001 and the first coat of antifouling paint.*

***NOTE:** INTERLUX AL200 Primer can also be used as a tie coat between the antifouling bottom paint and the last coat of INTERPROTECT 3000/3001.

Author's Comment on Interlux InterProtect Products

Interlux Bulletin 900-A published in 1988 is a well-written document outlining the hull degradation process along with good field instructions for using their products. This bulletin describes the use of their hand (non-spray) applied 1000 and 2000 series resin. Product 2000 contains a solvent.

Product Code 3000/3001 is a 1990 development of a sprayable, VOC compliance coating containing approximately 20% solvent. This product allows the use of airless as well as conventional spray equipment and has an increased self-overcoat time of up to several weeks.

Product 1000

For hulls other than new but with undamaged surfaces, the 1000 clear "sealer" will likely be required. This is an un-pigmented, low viscosity epoxy cured with what appears to be an amine hardener, since it is stated that all "blush or sweat must be washed off with water and sanded if over-coat time exceeds four hours" (at a presumed temperature of 72°F). Amine hardeners characteristically produce a carbonate blush when cured in open air. It is not clearly stated whether or not Product 1000 contains any solvent as supplied. Bulletin 900-A says only that it should not be thinned.

Product 2000

This is a "pigmented" product in the sense that by the addition of micronized plates of mica, a shingled effect is produced, thus reducing water permeation in the same manner that shingles prevent penetration of water on a roof. (This simile appears to me to be rather farfetched.) Product 2000 contains a solvent as supplied and can be further thinned if required. Probably because of the type of hardener and solvents, it should not be sprayed, apparently not even with airless equipment. It is not clear whether Product 2000 produces an amine blush but it should be presumed that it does and that washing and sanding operations should be performed if cured beyond recommended schedules.

Product 3000

Product 3000 contains the same pigmentation as Product 2000 but is designed for more convenient and rapid build-up by spray application. Depending upon the degree of damage being corrected, this method offers a final finishing step by spray and allows re-coating time to be greatly extended. It can be used over Products 1000 and 2000.

PRODUCT INFORMATION

PETTIT PAINT COMPANY
16 PINE STREET, ROCKAWAY, NJ 07866 • 201-625-3100

Tech Sheets: P420/Rev. 12/89 • P410/Rev. 9/89 • P430/Rev. 9/89 • Tech Bulletin 580

P240 - BLISTERED FIBERGLASS TWO-PART EPOXY REPAIR SYSTEM

Research on the problem of gel coat blistering indicates that the cause of blistering can be traced to the manufacturing processes and materials used in the original construction of the boat. Therefore, post-production barrier coatings may slow the blistering process; they will not prevent it. Similarly, coatings used in the repair of blistered gelcoat cannot be guaranteed to prevent a recurrence of blisters.

Pettit's materials and application techniques will aid in protection against, and repair of, gelcoat blisters but are not insurance, nor ever were, against future blistering problems.

Two-part epoxy materials are the most moisture-resistant, and Pettit makes two specifically for gelcoat blister prevention and repair:

7020/7025 Epoxy Fairing Compound is designed specifically for filling and resurfacing blister-infected areas. Its tough adhesion and water resistance provide exceptional durability. The fast drying characteristics enable quick recoatability for leveling deeply pitted surfaces. And it sands to a powder easily for a super smooth, flush finish.

4171/2084 All-Temp Epoxy Undercoater forms a protective barrier against moisture penetration of the gelcoat. It has, in comparison to standard epoxy coatings, a higher solids content by volume for greater film density and superior moisture resistance. And All-Temp's fast drying times permit rapid, multiple applications to quickly achieve the recommended film thickness.

Application Instructions

1. Puncture all blisters; permit them to drain, then rinse with fresh water to remove contaminating residue.

2. Remove all old antifouling paint by sanding, sandblasting or using Pettit 9030 Fiberglass Paint & Varnish Remover. Grind out all blisters, then sand the entire bare surface well with 80 or 100 grit sandpaper until a dull, clean surface is obtained. Wash the surface thoroughly with Pettit 15095 Fiberglass Dewaxer.

Allow the bare hull to stand in a protected area for as long as possible to dry out. We strongly recommend the use of a moisture meter to accurately measure the moisture content of the hull material. Do not proceed until the moisture level is below 10%.

In extreme cases of gelcoat blistering, it may be necessary to completely remove all the gelcoat. In this case, and especially if there is evidence of fiberglass cloth or mat that was not properly saturated with resin during the boat's construction, apply at least two coats of Pettit 7035/7040 Polypoxy Epoxy Glue to the entire surface where the gelcoat was removed. If the surface is uneven, smooth with 7020/7025 Epoxy Fairing Compound, followed by 4171/2084 All-Temp Epoxy Undercoater.

3. Mix 7020/7025 Epoxy Fairing Compound components together, in a 1:1 ratio. Apply with a putty knife or squeegee to all blister-infected areas. After the first application has cured 1-2 hours, reapply the compound to deeply pitted areas. After final curing (4 hours), sand flush with 80 grit sandpaper.

4. Mix 4171/2084 All-Temp Epoxy Undercoater components together, in a 3:1 ratio (three parts 4171 Base to one part 2084 Hardener). Apply undercoater, at 4 mils wet, with a short nap roller over the entire bottom surface. Allow to dry 2-8 hours* (depending upon temperature), then apply the next coat. Four to five full coats are recommended for best results.

It is advisable to tint each alternate coat of undercoater with Pettit Resin Colorant (for a white-blue-white color sequence, for example). You need add only that amount of colorant which enables you to distinguish the fresh coat of paint from the previously applied one. This will visibly aid in avoiding "holidays," or missed areas, and insure that a complete overall film thickness has, in fact, been achieved.

5. After the final coat of undercoater has dried only until tacky, apply the first finish coat of antifouling paint.* Apply the second finish coat after an overnight dry.

* All-Temp Epoxy Undercoater need not be sanded between coats if it is recoated within 2-8 hours of the previous coat. However, the final coat of All-Temp should dry only until tacky (1 hour or less, depending on temperature) before the application of antifouling paint. If All-Temp is allowed to dry hard, it must be thoroughly sanded with 80 grit paper before the application of antifouling paint or a coat of Pettit 6004 Skipsand Fiberglass Primer, or 6999 Sandless Primer can be applied to eliminate the need to sand.

P410 - BOTTOM PREP 4171/2084 "ALL-TEMP" EPOXY UNDERCOATER

4171/2084 All-Temp Epoxy Undercoater represents a significant development two-part epoxy technology, as demonstrated by both the application convenience and physical attributes of its composition. The special blend of epoxy and urethane resins cures at any temperature above freezing, unlike standard epoxy coatings. This unique ability affords a much more flexible painting schedule; work can now be performed in the colder months of the year, giving an all-season versatility to a previously temperature-restrictive type coating.

Once applied, All-Temp's drying times are considerably faster than those of its standard epoxy counterparts, thereby permitting rapid, multiple applications in a short period of time. And, when prescribed recoat times are met, All-Temp eliminates the need for sanding or tie-coat primers before overcoating.

All-Temp Epoxy Undercoater has a higher solids content by volume for greater film density. This tight, "high-build" chemical structure has very low water permeability — with superior resistance to moisture and osmotic pressure. It is, therefore, highly recommended as an underwater barrier coat for sealing gelcoat against blistering and as a part of the repair system for blistered gelcoat, as described above.

NOTE: Although our systems are highly effective in preventing gelcoat blistering, it must be kept in mind that no coating is completely impervious to moisture penetration. In addition, manufacturing processes by the boat builder have been shown to be a major factor in a boat's susceptibility to blistering, which no post-production coating will prevent.

Above the waterline, 4171/2084 is ideal for resurfacing cracked, crazed or porous gelcoat and for smoothing rough metal surfaces. It sands easily to provide a uniform, durable base upon which Pettit Dura Thane or Easypoxy topside enamels can be applied.

Mixing Ratio: 4171/2084 All-Temp Epoxy Undercoater is formulated as a 3:1 mix. 3 volumes of Part A (4171 Base) must be thoroughly blended with 1 volume of Part B (2084 Hardener) prior to application.

Finish Color: Flat White

Coverage: 400 square feet per gallon by brush or roller; 250 square feet per gallon by spray gun.

Film Thickness: 4 mils wet; 2 mils dry, per coat

Dry Times: Set to touch 1 hour. Dry to recoat (without sanding) 2-8 hours, depending on temperature. ***IMPORTANT NOTE:*** This dry-to-recoat time is for successive coats of All-Temp only. The final coat of All-Temp should be allowed to dry only until the surface becomes tacky before the application of antifouling paint. If All-Temp is allowed to dry hard, it must be sanded with 80 grit paper before the application of antifouling paint or a coat of Pettit 6004 Skipsand Fiberglass Primer or 6999 Sandless Prep Coat can be applied to eliminate the need to sand.

Pot Life: 8 hours

Temperature Cure Range: 32 degrees F to 85 degrees F.

Thinner/Cleanup: 12097 Polypoxy Thinner, Toluol or Xylol.

Product Stability: Keep A and B cans tightly sealed to keep out moisture.

Systems

Bare Fiberglass: Wash the fiberglass with Pettit 15095 Fiberglass Dewaxer; sand with 80 grit sandpaper to a dull finish and rewash. If the boat is new and has not yet been placed in the water, or if the gelcoat is in good, unblistered condition and dry (we recommend the use of a moisture meter to check for proper dryness — less than 10% moisture), apply at least two coats of undercoater as a barrier against moisture penetration and possible blistering.

Blistered Gelcoat: Puncture blisters and rinse with fresh water. Remove all antifouling paint by sandblasting or using 9030 Fiberglass Paint and Varnish Remover; sand the entire bare surface with 80 grit sandpaper and solvent wash with 15095 Fiberglass Dewaxer. Allow the hull to dry thoroughly; we recommend the use of a moisture meter to check for proper dryness — less than 10% moisture. Patch all infected areas with Pettit 7020/7025 Epoxy Fairing Compound. Sand the compound smooth with 80 grit paper, then apply 4 to 5 coats of Undercoater.

Aluminum Hulls & Lead Keels: Abrade to bright metal; solvent wash with 12097 Polypoxy Thinner to remove contamination. Apply one thin, complete coat of 6455/044 Metal Primer. Then, if surface defects exist, apply 7020/7025 Epoxy Fairing Compound as required; sand final application smooth with 80 grit paper. Follow with two coats of Undercoater.

Cast Iron or Steel Keels: Abrade to bright metal; solvent wash with 12097 Polypoxy Thinner to remove contamination. Immediately apply two coats of 6980 Rustlok Primer, allowing only 1-2 hours drying time before overcoating. Then, if surface defects exist, apply 7020/7025 Epoxy Fairing Compound as required; sand final application smooth with 80 grit paper. Follow with two coats of Undercoater.

580 - 7035 POLYPOXY GLUE PART A
7040 POLYPOXY GLUE PART B

Polypoxy Glue is a highly durable, clear epoxy adhesive which can be used to bond wood-to-wood, wood-to-metal, metal-to-metal, metal-to-plastic, plastic-to-plastic, and plastic-to-wood. The bond tensile strength is over 4,000 PSI. The glue has a pot life of about one hour and sets in four hours. After overnight curing, the bond achieves full strength. The Part A is a pale blue color, and the Part B is a pale yellow color. When blended properly, a pale green color results. The Polypoxy Glue can be used as a fiberglass resin or as a surface resin on a rough gelcoat where a new surface has to be built up.

Working Temperature: 60 degrees F minimum

Working Time: One hour maximum

Set Time: Four hours

Cure Time: Overnight

Clean-Up: Use denatured alcohol, Xylol, or 12097 Polypoxy Thinner.

Systems

Blend the Polypoxy Glue Part A and Part B on a one-to-one volume basis. Mix thoroughly to a pale green color. Add the Part A to the Part B for easier mixing. Make sure the surfaces to be bonded are thoroughly clean and have no loose material on them. Apply a thin coat of the glue to the surface and join together. Remove any excess from the joined edge. Pressure should be kept on the bond for at least four hours under good curing conditions. Curing can be speeded up by heating the glue or the glue joint.

On surfaces where Polypoxy Glue is used as a coating, such as fiberglassing the boat hull or bottom, the glue can be thinned about 5% with denatured alcohol or Pettit 12097 Polypoxy Thinner for easier brushing.

On plastic or metal a light sanding of the surface will improve the adhesion of the glue.

Any Polypoxy Glue joint or surface coating can be sanded lightly and painted after curing overnight. Use any Pettit undercoater or finish enamel.

430 - BOTTOM PREP
7020/7025 EPOXY FAIRING COMPOUND

Designed for filling and smoothing surface imperfections above and below the waterline, 7020/7025 Epoxy Fairing Compound is a pure, two-part epoxy putty. The overall physical attributes which make this compound superior to other types are its tough durability, excellent solvent and water resistance, and its rapid curing time for quick overcoatability and sanding.

In particular, 7020/7025 is the only compound suitable for below-waterline application and is recommended for properly repairing blistered gelcoat and for fairing metal keels. Above the waterline, 7020/7025 is excellent for leveling uneven metal surfaces and filling gouges, scratches, or other indentations on fiberglass.

7020/7025 Epoxy Fairing Compound's non-sagging, non-shrinking properties sand to a "powder" easily for a super-smooth finish. Its fast drying characteristic allows multiple applications for patching deeply pitted areas in a short period of time. 7020/7025 can then be overcoated with any type of undercoater, including strong, solvent-based products.

Mixing Ratio: 7020/7025 is formulated to be mixed in equal parts. Therefore, 1 volume of Part A (7020 Base) and 1 volume of Part B (7025 Hardener) must be thoroughly blended together prior to application. Do not use extra Part B to speed cure. A soft compound will result.

Mixed Color: Gray

Application: Apply the mixed compound with a putty knife or squeegee. Spread out to an even, uniform layer and let dry. Reapply, if necessary, until the area is flush with the surface. Sand the final application smooth with 80 grit sandpaper prior to painting.

Dry Times: 7020/7025 will be tack free in 2 hours and ready for reapplication in 1 to 2 hours. Prior to sanding and painting, allow 4 hours to cure.

Application Temperature: Do not use below 55 degrees F.

Author's Comment on Pettit Two-Part Epoxy-Fiberglass Repair Systems

Pettit offers four bulletins which I will critique separately.

P420 / Rev. 12/89 - Blistered Fiberglass Two-Part Epoxy Repair System

Application Instructions, Item 2:

After grinding and sanding damaged areas, the thing you should not do is recontaminate the surface with a dewaxer.

The use of a moisture meter will not provide a percentage of moisture. This can be accomplished only by removing test plugs from the hull. If you are restricted from using 4171/2084 All Temp Epoxy Undercoater until the true moisture content of the hull (presumably only the wetted portion) is below 10%, then you are in for drilling a lot of test plugs and have a lot of time to wait! Better stated would be: Barrier coating operations should be delayed until the moisture meter readings have stabilized; *i.e.*, no longer rise or fall appreciably as compared to a dry standard moisture reading above the water line.

Application Instructions, Item 3:

If there is "evidence of fiberglass cloth or mat that was not properly saturated with resin during the boat's construction, apply at least two coats of Pettit 7035/7040 Polypoxy Epoxy Glue. . . ." In my more than 50 years of shop experience with boat hull lay-up, I find it very, very rare to discover an unimpregnated portion of a laminate. A molder would have to really work at it, even if intentionally, to under-saturate — to over-saturate? Yes.

If there is evidence of what appears to be under-saturation, then the red flag should go up. It is far more likely that what appears to be under-impregnation is actually evidence of hydrolytic degradation which application of some "magic glue" will not correct. Serious structural repairs may be required.

P410 / Rev. 9/89 - Bottom Prep 4171/2084 'All Temp' Epoxy Undercoater

"Bare Fiberglass" I assume is intended to mean an uncoated, bare *gel coated* fiberglass surface.

Again appears the mis-stated use of a moisture meter.

"Blistered gel coat" — after sanding, why recontaminate with a dewaxer?

580 - Standard Two-Part Epoxy Glue 7035/7040

This epoxy "glue" is principally designed for adhesive bonding. It is also recommended by Pettit for use as an initial or primer coating where heavy grinding operations have been performed. Pettit states: "On surfaces where Polypoxy Glue is used as a coating such as fiberglassing the boat hull or bottom, the glue can be thinned about 5% with denatured alcohol . . . ." You may be able to get away with using denatured alcohol as a thinner for this resin when applied as a coating, but to use any solvent — especially denatured alcohol — in any resin for laminating is asking for much trouble caused by solvent entrapment.

430 - Bottom Prep 7020/7025 Epoxy Fairing Compound

After sealing sanded or ground areas, this method of filling voids is suitable. In no circumstances should this be substituted for filling voids where structural laminate should be replaced.

These repair procedures as written by Pettit appear to have been composed by someone who has never set foot in a fiberglass boat repair yard. The materials offered may be as good as any, but you are advised to research better repair instructions.

MARINE PAINTS & FINISHES

Product: **POXITAR® TAR EPOXY**

DESCRIPTION: A two-component, high solids, high build Coal Tar Epoxy.

USE: FOR MARINE/INDUSTRIAL/PROFESSIONAL USE. NOT FOR USE IN THE HOME.

Z-Spar Poxitar is designed for the protection of fiberglass boat bottoms prior to the application of copper or tin based bottom paints and for repair of fiberglass bottoms damaged by "Boat Pox."

"Boat Pox" is blistering of gel coat finishes caused by permeation of water through the gel coat and into the underlying resin/glass laminate. While the theories and causes of blistering are still being researched, Z-Spar Poxitar, when applied according to instructions, has demonstrated a remarkable ability to alleviate and retard the occurrence of blistering and to restore and repair badly blistered fiber glass surfaces. Poxitar forms a thick dense film of very low permeability in a minimum number of coats (normally 2) which substantially reduce the water permeability of the gelcoat finish. When used with appropriate preparation techniques, Poxitar will restore and renew blister-damaged gel coats below the waterline for years of additional service.

Poxitar can be used in a "wet-on-wet" system with copper and tin based bottom paints to form an extremely durable long-term base for protection against fouling. Poxitar will discolor non-copper bottom paints and all common types of marine finishes; Poxitar should be used in conjunction with darker color copper-containing antifoulant coatings for non-discoloration. Use with tin based bottom paint will cause some initial discoloration, but subsequent coats will have minimal if any discoloration.

Among some suspected causes of "Boat Pox" are the presence of bubbles or voids in the gel coat or resin/glass laminate. Using Poxitar on gel coat surfaces which have not been visibly damaged by blistering does not insure blistering will never occur. The potential cause of blistering will not be eliminated. Blistering will however be significantly retarded by substantially increasing the water resistance of the gel coat. When blistered surfaces are properly repaired and coated with Poxitar, the potential for reoccurrence of blistering can be minimized. Elimination of blistering depends on thorough examination and preparation of the surface to insure all existing blisters are opened and patched.

See Surface Preparation Section for additional information.

TECHNICAL DATA:

Number of Coats: Two

Application Rate: 90 to 115 sq. ft./gal. per coat (includes a 20% loss factor). Expected film thickness at this application rate is 8 to 10 dry mils per coat (11 to 14 wet mils per coat).

Drying time at 70°F and 50% Relative Humidity:

To touch: 3 to 4 hours

Before applying Second Coat of Poxitar: Overnight to 24 hours maximum.

To topcoat "wet-on-wet" with bottom paint: 2 to 6 hours, while Poxitar film is still uncured and slightly soft.

Before Submersion: 3 to 5 days minimum.

Koppers Company, Inc., Pittsburgh, Pennsylvania 15219

IMPORTANT NOTES:

1. For boats just hauled let the hull dry no *less* than 10 days, preferably 2 weeks, during which the preparation for application of the Poxitar system can be done. Opening the blisters, if any, and abrading or removing the gelcoat if necessary will speed the drying.

2. Application in direct sunlight will cause very rapid cure of the film. The recommended dry times are adequate for temperatures up to 90°F only. At higher temperatures and in direct sunlight, faster recoat times are required to avoid delamination between coats.

3. Do not delay application of the second coat of Poxitar beyond 24 hours because inter-coat adhesion may be severely reduced. If the second coat of Poxitar can't be applied within the recommended time limit, the existing coat of Poxitar must be coarsely and thoroughly abraded before application of the second coat.

4. Some bottom paints dry quickly enough that the boat can be launched as soon as 6 hours after the last application of bottom paint. Poxitar however must have at least 3 to 5 days curing time at 70°F., longer if cooler, before submerging. Therefore, apply the first of two coats of bottom paint to Poxitar within 2 to 6 hours using the "wet-on-wet" technique. Delay the application of the second coat of bottom paint until the Poxitar coating has received recommended curing time.

Color: Black.

Topcoats: Z-Spar Bottom Paints that can be used with Poxitar are: The Protector, Supertox, Vinyl-Cop, Multitox, and Colortox*.

Thinner: Z-Spar Thinner T-892.

Cleaner: Z-Spar Thinner T-892. Thoroughly clean equipment immediately after use or if to remain unused longer than 30 minutes at 70°F (10 minutes at 90°F or higher).

Surface preparation: There are three systems in which Poxitar may be used:

1. To coat gel coat surfaces below waterline which are not blistered.

2. To coat gel coat on blistered fiber glass bottoms after all blisters are cut out and patched.

3. To replace all gel coat on fiber glass bottoms in cases of severe blistering.

NOTE: Severe blistering is defined as when blistering is dense over all surfaces below waterline, includes numerous large blisters, or when blistering has occurred on a new hull within three years. Blistering can be prevented from recurring only when all active and potential blister sites are treated.

Preparation to coat existing blister-free gel coat:

1. On new gel coat surfaces, use Z-Spar T-1132 Fiberglass Prep Solution to remove wax and similar contaminants.

2. Scrub and wash surfaces to remove dirt and fouling. Let dry thoroughly.

3. If coated with a bottom paint, remove all bottom paint.

4. Thoroughly sand gel coat surface with 80 to 150 grit sand paper.

5. Remove dust by vacuuming, dry wiping, or "tac rag." DO NOT wet surface with any solvent or water after sanding.

Preparation and patching blistered gel coat:

1. Scrub and wash surfaces to remove dirt and fouling. Let dry thoroughly.

2. Remove all existing bottom paint.

3. Remove all visible blisters by power disk sanding or grinding. Cut under blisters and remove all uncoated glass fiber. If blisters contain liquid, be sure liquid is drained and removed from blisters.

4. Scrub blister sites with 5% ammonia in water. (Do not use commercial or household cleaners that in part "contain ammonia"). Rinse thoroughly and let dry thoroughly, at least overnight.

5. Thoroughly sand remaining gel coat with 80 to 150 grit paper.

6. Remove all dust by vacuuming, dry wiping, or "tac rag." DO NOT wet surfaces again with solvent or water after sanding.

Colortox is a TBTF based bottom paint and may discolor over Poxitar. (The Poxitar may "bleed" through the Colortox.) Blister reduction and anti-fouling protection are not affected.

TECHNICAL DATA
  (Continued):

7. Patch and fill blisters with Z-Spar No. 5 Polyester Putty. Use also to "fair" surfaces.

8. Sand cured putty for uniform surface. Remove dust as before.

Preparation when removing gel coat:

1. Scrub and wash surfaces to remove dirt and fouling. Let dry thoroughly.

2. Remove gel coat with heavy duty rotary or belt sanders. Use extreme care to avoid contaminating work site with and inhaling of dust from bottom paint. Cut out all visible blisters with power disk sander or grinder. A 40 to 60 grit sand paper is appropriate. Cut under all blister sites, also under voids revealed when gel coat is removed. Cut away all exposed dry, uncoated glass fiber. If blisters contain liquid, be sure liquid is drained and removed. Avoid unnecessary scoring and gouging of resin surface. Abrasive blasting to remove gelcoat is acceptable; care must be taken to avoid excessive damage to the softer underlying resin/glass laminate.

3. Wash and scrub entire surface with 5% ammonia in water. (DO NOT use commercial or household cleaners that in part "contain ammonia").

4. Rinse thoroughly and let dry thoroughly, at least overnight.

5. Patch all blisters, voids, gouges, with Z-Spar No. 5 Polyester Putty. Do all expected filling and fairing at this time; reputty where necessary until all surfaces are satisfactorily faired.

6. Sand cured putty with 80 to 150 grit sandpaper. Remove dust by vacuuming, dry wiping, or "tac rag." DO NOT wet surfaces again with solvents or water.

Mixing Ratio by volume: 4 parts Component A (Black) to 1 part Component B (Transparent).

Mixing instructions:

1. Mechanically mix Component A until uniform.

2. Continue mixing while adding Component B; mix thoroughly at least two minutes.

3. Pour some of mixture into Component B can, mix to incorporate remainder of Component B, and return to bulk of product with mixing.

4. Let mixture stand 10 to 15 minutes before use.

5. Add thinner only with mechanical mixing to insure proper incorporation.

Pot life after mixing: At 50°F-10 hrs.; at 60°F-6 hrs.; at 80°F-2 hrs.; at 100°F-1 hr. Do not mix more Poxitar than can be used within pot life time limits. Discard all unused material, in accordance with applicable local regulations, after pot life limit is exceeded. Do not add thinner to restore original viscosity after pot life limits are exceeded.

Methods of application: Brush, roller, or air atomized spray. Use only natural bristle brushes and phenolic cored rollers with maximum 3/8" to 1/2" nap. Thinning for brush or roller application should not be required. To spray use:

Air-Atomized Spray	Airless Spray
Material Pump: 8:1 ratio (or use pressure pot)	Pump: 30:1 Ratio
Material Hose: 3/8" to 1/2" i.d.	Line Pressure: 50 to 90 psi
Pressures:	Tip: 0.021" to 0.031", use reversible tips
Material: 30 to 55 psi	Tip Filter: None
Atomization: 40 to 80 psi	Manifold Filter: 30 Mesh
Fluid Tip: up to 1/8" to 1/4"	Hose: 3/8" to 1/2" i.d. high pressure; 50' maximum recommended length; 3/8" H.P. whip end with swivel.
Atomization	
Cap: up to 3/16" External mix.	

Thin as necessary to obtain proper atomization when spraying. Maximum recommended amount of thinner is 10 to 12% by volume (one pint per gallon). If thinner is added, do not try to get extra coverage from Poxitar. Material must be applied at recommended mil thickness per coat.

DO NOT mix or apply Z-Spar Poxitar at temperatures below 50°F or if rain is expected before the coating is dry.

81

TECHNICAL DATA
(Continued):

Application instructions:

1. By Brush: lay on in full wet strokes.
   Do not overbrush. Brushmarks are unavoidable; do not overthin the product in attempting to eliminate brushmarks.

2. By Roller: lay on with fully wet roller. Do not roll excessively. Slight dimpling (orange peel) is characteristic and will be hidden by bottom paint application. Do not overthin to reduce orange peel.

3. By Spray: apply in multiple thin passes with 1/3 to 1/2 overlap. Slight orange peel is characteristic. Thin only enough for adequate atomization and application. Do not overthin in an attempt to reduce orange peel.

Packaging: One gallon units, 1.25 gallons net yield, packaged as 1 gallon Component A Black plus 1 quart Component B Clear. 5 gallon pails yielding 5 gallons net.

Shelf Life: One year minimum. Viscosity of Component A will increase during storage, but product will return to original viscosity with mechanical mixing.

PRECAUTIONS: Take these precautions during application and before the coating dries: See Material Safety Data Sheet for this product.

(APPLIES TO THE MIXTURE OF COMPONENTS A AND B).

DANGER!

Flammable. Harmful or Fatal is Swallowed. Vapor Harmful. Skin and Eye Irritant. May Sensitize Skin to Sunlight. Contains xylene and tri(dimethylaminomethyl) phenol. Keep away from heat, sparks and flame. Avoid breathing of vapor or spray mist. Avoid contact with eyes and skin. Use an ultraviolet barrier cream on exposed skin.

Wash thoroughly after handling. Keep closures tight and upright to prevent leakage. Keep container closed when not in use. In case of spillage, absorb and dispose of in accordance with local applicable regulations. Do not take internally.

KEEP OUT OF REACH OF CHILDREN.

Use with adequate ventilation during application and drying. In tanks and other confined areas, use only with adequate forced air ventilation to prevent dangerous concentrations of vapors which could cause death from explosion or from breathing. Use fresh air masks, clean protective clothing and explosion-proof equipment. Prevent flames, sparks, welding and smoking. Follow OSHA regulations regarding ventilation and respiratory equipment.

FIRST AID: In case of skin contact, wash thoroughly with soap and water; for eyes, flush immediately with plenty of water for 15 minutes and call a physician. If sunburn occurs, treat symptomatically. If affected by breathing of vapor, move to fresh air. If swallowed, CALL A PHYSICIAN IMMEDIATELY. DO NOT induce vomiting.

IN CASE OF FIRE: Use dry chemical, foam, water fog or CO_2. Cool closed containers with water.

IMPORTANT! Any mixture of Components A and B will have hazards of BOTH components. OBSERVE ALL APPLICABLE PRECAUTIONS.
Photochemically Reactive.
Volatile Organic Compounds content (VOC) of the mixture of Components A and B as supplied, no thinner added, is under 2.2 lb./gal. (265 grams/liter).

MARINE PAINTS & FINISHES

Product: P-646 EPOXY PRIMER

DESCRIPTION: A two-component, polyamide cured, corrosion inhibiting primer and electrolysis barrier for steel hulls. Also for use on fiberglass for prevention and repair of osmotic blisters.

USE: FOR MARINE USE ONLY. NOT INTENDED FOR USE IN THE HOME.

P-646 Epoxy Primer is suitable for priming steel above or below the waterline. It is high-building and has excellent adhesion. It is compatible with a variety of undercoats, enamels, and antifouling bottom paints. Can also be used as a barrier coat in three-3 mil applications for prevention of "Boat Pox" for a smooth, racing finish on fiberglass.

TECHNICAL DATA:

Number of coats: 2 or more depending on service.

Coverage per coat: 250 sq. ft. per gallon (allows for an approximate loss of 20%).

Drying time at 70°F. and 50% relative humidity:

To touch: 2 hours

Between coats: As soon as the solvent is released or the coating hardens.

Color: Brown

Thinners: None necessary if high build is desired. T-1187 Thinner may be used if needed to reduce viscosity.

Cleaners: T-1187

Surface Preparation:

Steel: Remove all dirt, grease, form oil. Other interference materials must be completely removed from steel by sandblasting to a Near White Blast. To maximize adhesion, a 1 to 2 mil blast profile should be obtained.

Fiberglass: 1. Prevention of Boat Pox on new fiberglass.

Remove all traces of wax with T-1132 Fiberglass Prep Solution. Sand entire bottom with 120-150 grit paper.

Koppers Company, Inc., Pittsburgh, Pennsylvania 15219

TECHNICAL DATA (Continued):

2. Repair of fiberglass bottoms with blisters.

Remove all existing paint, primers, and fillers with coarse disc grinder. All blisters must be ground out and emptied. Wipe blisters with T-1187 Thinner or acetone and let dry. Fill all blisters with #5 Polyester Putty and sand with 120-150 grit paper.

Coating system:

Steel Bottoms: After sandblasting, apply three coats of P-646 Epoxy Primer to a minimum 9 dry mils film thickness. While the last coat of P-646 is still tacky (usually within 2-6 hours), apply a first coat of antifouling bottom paint. This is the "wet-on-wet" technique that provides the most durable system. If the P-646 Primer dries overnight or longer, apply another coat of P-646 Primer and use the "wet-on-wet" technique, or apply one coat of P-619 Non-Sanding Fiberglass Primer before applying finish coat. For topside surfaces, see specific instructions for topcoats being used.

Fiberglass: Apply a minimum of 3 coats — 3 mils each P-646 Primer, waiting 6-12 hours between coats. Topcoat with any Z-Spar bottom paint using the "wet-on-wet" technique.

Mixing instructions:

Stir components A and B separately, then mix two components together in equal volume. Mix thoroughly and allow the mixture to stand 30-60 minutes before using. Do not mix more material than can be used in an eight hour period. All extra admixed material must be discarded after that period.

Methods of application:

Brush may be used, however, conventional or airless spray is recommended. Do not apply when temperatures are expected to drop below 50°F. or if rain threatens before the coating is dry.

Packaging:

One-gallon units with 2 gallon net yield. One quart unit with 2 quart net yield.

PRECAUTIONS:

Follow precautions as listed on label for P-646 EPOXY PRIMER.

Protective Coatings Technical Data Sheet

BARRIER PROTECTION ON NEW BOATS:

1. Dewax with Woolsey's 624 Dewaxer. Apply liberally, using a constant motion. Select an area that can be completed in five minutes or less. Do not leave the dewaxer on the surface for longer than five minutes. After applying the dewaxer, wash off with plain water to remove all traces of dewaxer, wax and other contaminants. Wipe all water with clean rags. Let dry. Note: If you wish to be doubly certain that all foreign matter has been removed from the surface, wash the surface once again with Woolsey's 625 Heavy Duty Fiberglass Wash.

2. Sand entire bottom with 80 grit sandpaper or use Woolsey's Sandnomore Fiberglass Primer (W749). Be certain that the bottom is completely free of contaminants before applying Sandnomore Primer. Shake can of Sandnomore before using. Apply one thin coat by brush or roller. Important: Sandnomore Fiberglass Primer must be overcoated within one-half hour. Do not apply to an area larger than you are able to overcoat in one-half hour.

3. Apply two to three coats of Woolsey's SUPER HI-BUILD EPOXY PRIMER W 340 . Super Hi-Build will give you seven (7) mils dry thickness with each coat. Your first coat will be dust free in 25 to 30 minutes. Apply subsequent coats in 4 to 16 hours. Use wet-on-wet system to apply more than one coat. Test surface with your hand. If paint does not come off, and you can still indent it with your fingernail, it is ready for your next coat. If perchance the epoxy should cure completely, then it will be necessary to sand lightly before applying your next coat.

4. Apply the Woolsey Antifouling paint of your choice, following label instructions.

REPAIRING GEL COAT BLISTERING:

1. Open all blisters and allow them to drain. Where extensive blistering exists, it may be necessary to sandblast or sand those areas.

2. Then wash entire hull with fresh water to remove all salt deposits.

3. Allow the hull to dry. The boat should be in a dry place or at least protected from the rain. The longer the drying period—the better. Two weeks minimum—no maximum.

4. Gouge, grind or carve out any soft laminate. Be careful not to damage good laminate.

5. Sand the entire bottom to remove all of the bottom paint to prepare the hull for the epoxy barrier coat.

6. Use Woolsey's Epoxy Putty (W660/661) to fill all holes. When putty is dry, sand to obtain a smooth finish.

7. Apply two to three coats of Woolsey's Super Hi-Build Epoxy Primer (340 Gold)

8. When surface has cured according to label instructions, apply a Woolsey Antifouling paint of your choice.

THE ROYAL TREATMENT

Woolsey Marine, Unit of KOP-COAT, INC., Newark, N.J. 07114 1-800-221-4466

Author's Comment on Z-Spar Poxitar & P-646 Epoxy Primer

NOTE: This product is now being produced by Woolsey Z-Spar, unit of Kop Coat, 36 Pine St., Rockaway, NJ 07866 Ph: 1-800-221-4466

The Koppers brochure, OM 642 October 1985, tells you how a fiberglass boat is made (in 1985), how to maintain it, about the beginning signs of gel coat osmosis blistering ("boat pox"), and how these blisters are formed. If you have not read anything else about osmosis and hydrolysis damage, this is good basic information and there are some excellent photos and drawings. Thirteen general causes of blistering are listed. Write to Woolsey for a copy.

The repair information is very sketchy and you are told: "Poxitar is a time-tested protective coating that can be used to prevent blisters and repair blister-repaired damaged hulls by waterproofing. Z-Spar Poxitar, when applied according to instructions, has demonstrated a remarkable ability to alleviate and retard the occurrence of blistering and to restore and repair badly blistered surfaces subject to water immersions."

Z-Spar's September 1986 brochure which is reproduced here (see note above) states: "Poxitar is easy to apply, just two coats at 10 mils. each, give maximum protection forming a thick waterproof barrier." For instructions, they ask you to see your marine dealer or yard. They do go so far as to say "to cure boats that already

have the pox, all blisters should be removed and cleaned [I assume they mean the cavities left by the blisters!], filled with #5 polyester putty and coated with Poxitar prior to applying standard, anti-fouling paint."

If you ask further, you may be offered the yard applicator's February 1987 technical data sheet instructions for Poxitar epoxy application and his May 1986 technical data sheet for P-646 Epoxy Primer. Both data sheets are included here (see note above).

You will discover that Koppers (Woolsey) is touting two separate barrier coating systems, neither of which refers to the other. With either system, the instructions offer inadequate advice mostly by omission. For example, in the Poxitar data sheet, "surface preparation," items 4 and 5 are destructively misleading. It takes a lot more preparation of a blistered area requiring removal of reinforcing fiber than simply washing with ammonia, then applying Poxitar. The fiberglass repair instructions for product P-646 Epoxy Primer are even more nebulous than for Poxitar.

In all, I regard the instructions for both systems as poorly done. The materials offered are good, rather standard available items not unique to Koppers, but be cautious in accepting all the claims made for the product.

If you are willing to look for much more detailed and accurate information found elsewhere or in other sections of this book, then the two products offered by Koppers may be used as barrier coats after proper preparation of the product being repaired.

GELCOAT BLISTER REPAIR
A MANUAL FOR THE APPLICATION OF MARINE EPOXY RESIN FOR THE REPAIR AND PREVENTION OF GELCOAT BLISTERS ON FIBERGLASS BOATS

PUBLISHED BY:
SYSTEM THREE RESINS
P.O. BOX 70436 • SEATTLE, WASHINGTON 98107
206-782-7976

REPAIRING GELCOAT BLISTERS

I. INTRODUCTION

The cause of gelcoat blistering is beyond the scope of this book. For those interested in the causes of this problem we suggest that they obtain a copy of the McLean booklet referred to in Step 3 and consult the bibliography. System Three Resins does not pretend to be an expert in this field. We have written

this booklet because many people and boatyards use our product in the repair of gelcoat blisters. This booklet describes the method of repair. We do not claim that this is either the only method or the best method available. Our only claim is that the method described herein is being used and the track record has been generally good. There have, however, been a few failures using our products just as there have been using others' products and methods. This booklet has not been written as an inducement to sell our product for this purpose. Blister repair, being an inexact science, is one where you "pays your money and takes your chances." Please read the warranty on the inside front cover of this booklet before deciding to use our products.

This is not a "stand alone" booklet. It is designed to be used in conjunction with *The Epoxy Book* published by System Three Resins. Be sure to read it and this booklet before beginning.

We caution that gelcoat blister repair is a dirty, labor intensive job. This is why the price the yard quoted may seem so high. Compared to the labor cost the materials are cheap. Unless you have more time on your hands than money in your pocket, you might want to accept the yard's offer and have them do it. Or, you might have the yard do the gelcoat removal and you do the rest with some occasional hired help. If you do plan to do the job yourself, make sure your haulout yard knows what you plan to do and allows it.

II. UNDERSTANDING EPOXY RESINS

The most important product for a successful repair job is the epoxy resin and hardener system you use. You should know a little about epoxy resins before you get started. *The Epoxy Book*, published by System Three Resins, will provide detailed background on epoxy resins and their use in the unit operations involved with blister repair. You should read the entire booklet with the exception of Sections VI B, VI D, and VIII before starting a blister repair job.

System Three epoxy is an unfilled 100 percent solids marine grade epoxy resin with a very low water extractables content. This is the only type of epoxy resin that should be used.

Always mix System Three resin and hardener at the correct ratio of two parts of resin to one part of hardener by volume. Never vary this ratio under any conditions for any reason. You can not "speed things up" by using more hardener. Nor, can you "slow things down" by using less hardener. Remember: Always use the right ratio — Two parts of resin to one part of hardener by VOLUME.

The only factor that will change the cure rate is temperature. Warmer means faster, cooler means slower. If you're working in cool weather, you'll need more time until you can go on to the next step in the repair process. Short of somehow heating the hull there is nothing much you can do except wait. You should not use the epoxy resin unless the hull temperature is above 40°F.

If the resin is curing too fast because it is a very warm day, you can do several things to slow it down. First, make sure the containers of resin and hardener are as cool as possible. Avoid storing them in a hot car or leaving them in the sunlight to warm up. Wait until evening or for a cooler day to do the work.

As epoxy resins cure they give off heat. In thin sections, or films, this heat is given off to the environment almost immediately and the resin cures at ambient temperatures. In thicker

sections some of the heat produced is retained, heating the resin which causes it to cure faster, thus giving off even more heat, raising the temperature, etc.

You can avoid this rapid curing by working in smaller batches and by increasing the surface area for a given volume. For example, if the putty you'll be working with in Step 4 is curing in the cup before you get it into the blister, then spread it out on a piece of cardboard or plywood and use it there like an artist uses a painting palette.

Epoxy resins are combustible but not highly flammable. The solvents you may be using are extremely flammable. For safety's sake do not use any of these products around an open flame.

Epoxy resins have caused skin irritation problems in certain susceptible people. This is almost always the result of repeated skin contact with uncured epoxy resin and/or hardeners. Always wear disposable gloves when handling either of these materials. If you get either resin or hardener on your skin, clean it off immediately with good waterless handsoap. Do not attempt to remove it with solvents. This will only drive the uncured resin and hardener into your skin. If the epoxy is too far cured to be soluble in the waterless handcleaner, then let it cure and peel it off the next day. Cured epoxy resins are not known to cause problems. Work cleanly and you won't have problems.

Avoid breathing sanding dust. Bottom paint sanding dust is potentially lethal because of the toxins it contains. If you don't own one, buy a good dust mask. Be sure to wear it whenever you're creating sanding dust.

III. INSTRUCTIONS

Step 1: Clean Hull — Remove Bottom Paint

Remove all marine growth, scum, barnacles, etc. Your yard may do this upon haulout by hydroblasting or steam cleaning. It may be necessary to use a scraper to get the barnacles off.

If your boat lacks a boottop strip you'll want to develop a technique for marking the top of the bottom paint line. Running masking tape above the line on the topsides is a good method. It will become frayed when sanding and you'll want to replace it for Step 7. Making small grease pencil marks right above the tape on the topsides every foot or so will serve as a guide for the new tape. These are easily removed with soap and water or paint thinner when the project is finished.

When the hull is dry you've got to make a decision whether you are going to remove the gelcoat or merely abrade it by sanding and opening the blisters as discussed below. The decision will largely hinge on the extent of the blistering. Removal offers the greatest chance of a complete cure but it also requires great labor to bring the hull back to its original fair condition. Merely sanding but not removing gelcoat eliminates a lot of the fairing problems but may miss some of the small blisters. They may show up on next haulout and you'll have to patch them then.

Sandblasting is the easiest way to remove the gelcoat. It is worth paying a professional to do it. Your yard may know of someone who does this. Be sure to check with your yard to see if they even allow sandblasting. Some do and some don't. If sandblasting, be careful to remove only the gelcoat and any damaged mat. Digging into the hull with the sandblaster will weaken it as it removes structural fabric.

A 1500 to 2500 rpm sander polisher with an eighth-inch foam backed pad is the best way to sand gelcoat. Be advised that this is dirty, strenuous and tedious work. You will get very tired and may spend as much money in time and materials as you'd have paid to have someone come in and sandblast it.

Hulls with gelcoat removed seem to dry faster than those with the gelcoat intact.

CAUTION: Bottom paints contain toxic materials. Avoid breathing dust or getting dust in cuts or open sores. Always wear suitable dust masks. Wash contaminated clothing separately from other clothing.

Step 2: Open Blisters — Remove Damaged Fiberglass

If you have elected to go the sandblasting route, you have already completed this task. Skip on to Step 3. If you have only sanded the gelcoat and do not plan to remove it, read on.

Now is the time to open the blisters and clean them out. Use the point of a utility knife to puncture each blister. Insert the knife and with a twisting action, cut out the damaged gelcoat and fiberglass. Remove all the "rotten" material. Keep cutting until you get it all out. Don't worry about cutting good fiberglass. It is highly resistant to cutting. Use the knife to get rid of all undercuts as they will make filling more difficult.

Other tools may be used also. Small rotary files attached to electric drills have been successfully used. The idea, whatever you use, is to open up the blisters and remove damaged gelcoat and fiberglass.

CAUTION: Blisters generally contain acidic water under pressure. The water may contain dissolved material which could cause eye irritation. Wear safety goggles and stand back out of the line of fire.

Step 3: Wash and Dry Boat and Blisters

Wash the boat thoroughly from the boottop stripe down with fresh water to remove all traces of salt, blister fluid, sanding dust and other dissolved material. Rinse the hull well. Be sure to squirt the water into the exposed blisters to remove any contaminants in the blister. Let the boat drain and air dry for several hours. Look and see if any purple-brown colored vinegar smelling liquid is oozing out of the opened blisters. This is blister fluid. If it is, then dig out those blisters even more and rewash. Repeat this step as necessary.

The next step, drying the hull, is the single most critical operation to affect a cure that lasts. It is of paramount importance that the hull be as dry as possible. Start by emptying the bilge of standing water. In 80°F weather at 40 percent relative humidity, the average blistered hull will take three weeks to dry to a steady low level. You may not be able to achieve these

conditions without "skirting" the boat and using heat and a dehumidifier. If you plan to do it this way, we recommend "A Manual for the Repair of Fiberglass Boats Suffering from Osmotic Blistering" by Richard and Roger McLean. It is available from Systems Three Resins or by writing to A is A Publishing Company, P.O. Box 11500, Piedmont, CA 94611. The booklet costs $15.00.

Some people have suggested that the hull drying process can be accomplished by vacuum bagging. We have studied the results of this process and talked with those who have done it. While there is some initial drop in hull moisture content, this method will not properly dry a hull even at safe elevated temperatures. We can not recommend this method of drying a hull.

Step 4: Fill the Blisters

When the hull and blister cavities have completely dried, you should roll on a sealer coat of mixed System Three epoxy resin/hardener. Work the mixed resin into each cavity to wet out the damaged fiberglass. Allow it to soak in for an hour or two. Then mix up some more epoxy and make a filling putty by the addition of microballoons and silica thickener. The details appear on Section VI E and Appendix E of The Epoxy Book. This material makes a non-sagging putty which will replace the material you removed in Step 2. Try to perform this step on the shady side of the hull if possible as you will have longer working time.

Initially, mix small batches until you get the hang of working with an epoxy-microballoon mixture. You can always mix more but once mixed, you've got to use it within a short period of time or it will go off in the pot. Fill each blister from the bottom (otherwise you will trap air) using a putty knife or similar tool. Fill flush with the gelcoat surface with a slight overfill which will be sanded down later. Finally, use the edge of the putty knife to scrape off any excess around the perimeter of the hole. Get it now before it cures or you will have to sand it off later.

Fill all the blisters and allow to cure at least overnight if the temperature is above 60°F or for two nights if the temperature is below 60°F before proceeding to Step 5.

If you have had the hull sandblasted, you may not have blister pockets to fill. Your job is to begin fairing. Section VI E and Appendix E of The Epoxy Book will guide you. Before beginning, roll on a coat of mixed resin to seal the exposed fiberglass surface. Allow several hours to cure before fairing. The idea in fairing is to restore the surface to the gelcoat level prior to removal. You will do this with the same microballoon mixture but use a broad knife or similar tool to apply it. In effect you will be plastering the hull with the epoxy microballoon mixture and sanding it to get it fair. A careful job applying the "mud" will save hours of sanding later.

CAUTION: Always protect your skin with disposable gloves when working with epoxy resins and hardeners. If you get the resin on your skin, use a good waterless handcleaner to remove it. Do not use solvents to remove resins from you or your tools. Wipe your tools off with a paper towel when through using and sand any remaining cured epoxy off the next day. Roller covers, brushes and cups are to be discarded and not cleaned.

Step 5: Sand the Filled Cavities

Use 60 grit aluminum oxide paper and sand the filled cavities fair with the surrounding hull. Blocks or sanding pads help avoid sanding the cured putty below the surrounding hull surface. The putty will sand faster than the fiberglass. Refill any concave holes or exposed air bubbles with the putty blend. Allow to cure and resand.

If you have removed the gelcoat and puttied the entire hull bottom, you will now sand fair. This is best done by two people using a longboard. This is just a long sanding block with paper glued to it. The flat part of a straight 2x4 about 3 feet long works well. You may find that the sanding will reveal low spots that require additional microballoon mix. Fill them, resand and continue in this fashion until the entire hull is without ridges, bumps or hollows.

CAUTION: While the sanding dust from Step 5 is not toxic, you should wear a dust mask to avoid breathing this or any other sanding dust.

Step 6: Prepare Hull for Epoxy Coating

After the cavities have all been filled and the hull is fair, it is necessary to prepare the hull for epoxy coating. It is this coating that will help prevent the hull from blistering in the future as the epoxy coating is much more resistant to water penetration than the polyester resins used to build your hull.

Begin by sanding the entire hull to be epoxy coated with 60 grit paper if you have not sanded it in the filling/fairing process. You may hand sand it or use a vibrating sander. Rotary high speed sanders should only be used if you are confident about your ability to use them. They are heavy and cut fast and you may end up gouging the hull. Sand the hull until there is no gloss left; sand right up to the old bottom paint line. Avoid breathing the dust.

After the hull has been thoroughly sanded, wash it with water to remove the sanding dust. Really get in there and scrub it with a clean brush to remove all traces of sanding dust. Rinse and allow it to dry well, at least overnight.

Step 7: Coating the Hull with Epoxy

You will need resin and hardener, disposable gloves, graduated cups, stirsticks, roller covers, roller frame, disposable brushes and a 9" roller paint tray for this step. Use only the roller covers supplied by us. They are designed for our product. Reread Section VI A of The Epoxy Book before continuing.

The idea here is to get on a minimum of four coats of epoxy without the runs and sags that will require a lot of sanding later. It is this coating that provides the barrier that helps prevent the future intrusion of water into the hull.

First, run the masking tape around the boat so that the bottom edge of the tape is right at the top of the old bottom paint line.

This will help prevent rolling epoxy on the topsides or the boottop stripe.

Put on the gloves and mix up about six ounces of resin/hardener. Pour the thoroughly mixed material into the roller pan and "paint" the hull using the yellow foam roller covers. Put on as thick a coating as possible but not so much that it will run and sag. Experience will teach you how much you can get away with. Better to spend the time putting on an extra coat if the previous coats have been a little thin, rather than sanding out runs later. If you see a run developing, go back and roll it out. The resin/hardener mix contains no solvent so you won't leave marks if you do this. Brush out any air bubbles with a foam brush using light strokes. Just use enough pressure to break the bubbles and not disturb the uncured epoxy.

Remove the masking tape right after you finish the first coat. Do it before it cures or else it will be difficult to remove later. Wear gloves since the masking tape will be wet with epoxy.

Apply the next coat as soon as the previous coat is set enough so the combination of the two coats will not run and sag. This is about 2 to 3 hours with fast hardener on a 60°F day; less on a warmer day, longer with slower hardener. You may wait up to 72 hours between coats without sanding as long as the hull does not become contaminated in the meantime.

Put the succeeding coats on the hull right up to the top of the first coat. By catching the light right you'll be able to see where the first coat ended and the new coat starts.

If you wait longer than 72 hours between coats, you'll have to give the epoxy a light sanding to give the new coat some "tooth" to tie into the previous coat. Prior to this time the coats will bond chemically to each other.

Allow the last coat to cure overnight before proceeding to the next step; even longer if the temperature is below 60°F during the cure cycle.

Step 8: Sanding for Bottom Paint

Hose and sponge the hull with water to remove any oily surface film on the cured epoxy. This is a water soluble film and will be thicker if you applied the coating in humid weather. It is a byproduct of the epoxy curing reaction. Solvents do not remove this film.

Sand the cured epoxy with 80 grit paper to smooth any runs and kill the gloss. A sanding block helps to prevent over sanding when removing cured runs. Be careful not to sand through the epoxy coating and re-expose the gelcoat, thus losing the epoxy protection. If you desire an even smoother bottom, you may want to use finer grades of wet and dry paper. If the sand paper clogs excessively, then the epoxy coating has not sufficiently cured. Wait another day. Wet sanding helps prevent paper clogging and keeps the dust down. Use wet or dry paper and dip in into a bucket of water occasionally.

After sanding, wash the dust off with a sponge and water. Allow the hull to dry. Wipe with acetone, MEK or the solvent recommended by the bottom paint maker for preparation to applying this paint.

Step 9: Applying the Bottom Paint

Follow the manufacturer's recommendations when applying bottom paint to the epoxy coated hull. Most bottom paints will adhere well to the sanded epoxy coated hull with no primer. Keep in mind, however, that bottom paints are formulated for polyester gelcoat hulls and some may not work well on epoxy coatings. You should do a small test patch on your hull to make sure that the bottom paint dries properly and adheres well to the epoxy coating. Never apply bottom paint to uncured epoxy resin.

Author's Comment on System Three Resins' Gel Coat Blister Repairs

You will immediately learn that you will be advised to get the *McLean Book* ($15.00) and *The Epoxy Book* ($5.00) — both available from System Three Resins.

The Epoxy Book is an excellent treatise for the layman and is well worth the price; however, much of it is devoted to wood construction. A mention is made of "Phase Two" literature which is recommended reading but has little to do with blister repairs. You will find this is a resin system used in building composite structures which involves elevated temperature curing. *If you have read Section I, you know that I really concur in this*.

The only reference to repairs in *The Epoxy Book* is the very last paragraph, where in essence, it refers you to the *System Three Gel Coat Blister Repair Book*. This gives you instructions about as good as you will get with a commercial blister repair package. Of course the *McLean Book* is recommended by System Three for drying procedures.

Author's Comment on Travaco Laboratories, Inc., GLUVIT

This is an outstanding example of an absolutely atrocious repair procedure and misuse of epoxy resin. Read Travaco's "instructions" which are reproduced here. If you are willing to settle for this so-called repair system, you do not need this book!

COMMENT ON COMMERCIAL BLISTER REPAIR SUPPLIERS

My experience with most marine stores who stock the several brands of "barrier" materials is that they do not maintain or offer the manufacturer's full literature — no matter how meager — for each product. You cannot repair a boat properly by only reading the instructions on the can label!

All of the barrier coat suppliers discussed so far, and most others not reviewed, fall dangerously close by omission in giving the impression that the repair or refurbishing which has physical evidence of osmotic blistering simply needs some digging and some putty with a coating over it to correct the problem.

Few of the firms I have investigated address the absolute necessity of determining structural strength retention before repair procedure is specified. Even in the mildest cases of blistering, cracking, or crazing, structural tests should be performed. Like skin cancer in animals, any visible form of surface damage on marine structures signals some degree of damage below the surface. Specimens properly removed from the structure should be analyzed by a competent laboratory, the results of which will determine the repair procedure.

It is my opinion that all suppliers of barrier coatings would be better off to simply state: "*Our materials are*

SIMPLIFIED INSTRUCTIONS:

Open the Blisters.....Sand exposed area.....Clean with Toluol or "GLUVIT THINNER".
Over shallow sections, apply 1 or 2 coats GLUVIT.
In deep sections, either fill with "Marine-Tex" or a scrap piece of fiberglass in conjunction with "GLUVIT".
Lightly sand cured area and Paint with Epoxy or Urethane coating.

Travaco LABORATORIES, INC.
345 EASTERN AVENUE
CHELSEA, MASSACHUSETTS 02150

designed to be applied as a sealant and/or barrier coat for fiberglass marine structures immersed in or containing an aqueous medium. For specific preventative maintenance or repairs, seek professional advice." Let the professional advisor stick his neck out when it comes down to specifics. No entity can generalize repair procedure, especially materials suppliers.

All of the above products discussed here and many others not mentioned produce similar results if properly applied. This is not to say that all barrier coat systems offered are all the same. When the term "resin" is used (almost always it is an epoxy), it is assumed to be a resin-hardener combination. It is the hardener which most affects the physical end result. There are literally hundreds of epoxy hardeners, but there is only a handful of basic epoxy resins.

There are really only four major suppliers of "epoxy" resins in the United States and only two of these, Shell and Dow, are truly basic, *i.e.*, manufacture their own raw materials. You might be interested to know that none of the majors get into such mundane things as offering materials kits or field advice on marine fiberglass repairs. Since they don't, but very well could and do if approached properly, they supply their formulator and re-packager customers and let them take the heat from the field. Later, I will present some guidelines for you to become your own formulator.

Practical Sailor Magazine, June 15, 1991, has an article by Dan Spurr which created quite a stir. He describes a commission given to Rick Strand of Comtex Development (no longer in existence). Strand performed two types of tests on several commercial barrier coats including one vinylester, one iso-ester, one ortho-ester, and several epoxies.

The first test was called "Water Vapor Transmission — Moisture Gained." The test involved applying a film onto a glass plate to the thickness prescribed by the supplier. After curing per specifications, the rim of a Petri dish which contained a mixture of dry salts was bonded to the test film using an epoxy resin. All test specimens were accurately weighed and then placed in a water bath at 80°F and weighed again at intervals.

The second test, "Overcoat Exposure Series," required that gel coat-laminated panels be prepared by coating an 0.018-inch-thick gel coat onto a glass plate. The gel coat was allowed to cure to a tack-free condition, thus ostensibly creating a weak interface with subsequently applied

laminate. Each lay-up was allowed to cure at room temperature, then removed from the plate. Next, the gel coat surfaces were sanded with 100 grit paper. Each panel was coated with one of various commercial barrier coat products at thicknesses specified by the supplier and allowed to cure at room temperature for two weeks. Then, all were post-cured for three hours at 150°F and then exposed to water at the same temperature. Though the article did not specify, it is presumed that only the test coating side was exposed to the water (*e.g.*, "turtle box" tank).

According to Strand's tests, a vinylester was the leader in the water vapor transmission trials; and the West System was the leader in the overcoat exposure series. Vinylester was reported to be below most of the epoxy barrier coats in this test.

While these tests are informative, they can be misleading. I feel it is necessary to take some issue with the test procedure. In the water vapor transmission trials, I feel that the Petri dishes should have been completely encapsulated with the same coating being tested and to the same thickness as the test film rather than depending on a possibly foreign epoxy as the method of sealing. The very arbitrary use of an epoxy as the seal only presumes that it will at least be equal in resistance to water permeation as the test film. Also, the chamber containing the salts should be vented to the atmosphere.

In the overcoat exposure tests, oven post-curing of test panels at any temperature above ambient and the use of water at 150°F skewers test results. There is no question that post-curing any resin-hardener system will produce results different from those where the product has seen ambient temperature only. Most epoxy-hardener systems are improved by post-curing. Even when heated dry above its heat distortion temperature (HDT) and then cooled, an epoxy's physicals are usually improved, but heating by hot water above its HDT usually will be degrading. For the sake of accelerating test time results only, the use of temperatures above the maximum environmental temperature that the product is likely to encounter does not produce realistic test results. I therefore put more credence in the water vapor transmission tests than I do the overcoat series described; in fact, I feel that Strand's second test should not be regarded as valid.

I suggest you write to *Practical Sailor* magazine for the complete text of this article. Write to: *Practical Sailor* Magazine, P.O. Box 619, Newport, RI 02840.

OTHER BARRIER COAT OPTIONS

POLYESTER RESIN

Polyester resin is not usually specified as a final barrier coat, but under some conditions it is used for major repairs and re-hulling. Of course, when polyester resin is used as a gel coat and no other protection is added, then a polyester gel coat would be considered a barrier coat.

Before application of any coating intended principally as a barrier material, repairs must be made first if they are required. There is much argument about the use of polyester resin *vs.* epoxy for repair and re-hulling. Peddlers of epoxy repair kits will argue, "Why repair with a material that failed in the first place?" My answer to this is why not make repairs with the same type of resin which was used in the original manufacture but with improvements, especially a full re-hull? This can and should include a reverse gel coat. If the epoxy boys claim they can protect a new or undamaged gel coat then why won't their stuff work over new polyester resin repair, especially with a new gel coat? Also consider that any repairs above the waterline will not usually have a barrier coat applied. If repairs have been reverse gel coated, no further coating is necessary. If repairs have been made with epoxy (or vinylester), marine paint or two-part urethane will be required above the waterline because these resins must be protected from ultraviolet light.

If repairs are required only to the extent that minor reinforcements are needed in the ground-out areas, and an epoxy barrier coat will be used, then I have no quarrel with using an epoxy all the way providing a coupler such as Union Carbide's A-1100 *(MS 5)* has been added to the resin. Any fairing compound used on top of the epoxy repairs should have an inert filler added such as glass microballoons or quartz powder also containing A-1100 or equivalent. In no case should a polyester gel coat be applied over an epoxy substrate. Use Ultrachrome Gelcoat *(MS 67)* as a tie-coat, then apply polyester gel coat; or use Ultrachrome or two-part urethane paint only as the finish.

If repairs are major and deep requiring several plies of reinforcement — yet complete re-hulling is not required — then use a high grade iso-polyester and add to the resin 1/2 to 1% coupling agent such as Union Carbide's A-174. Reinforcements will have had their coupling agents applied.

All grinding and feather sanding operations should be followed by a re-coat of polyester resin (always with coupler). Apply as little fairing compound as possible, and then only with glass microballoons and a little thixotropic

agent if necessary. It is far better to take the extra time to fill deep low spots with resin and reinforcement than to use an excess of fairing compound. Do not use veil or chopped strand mat for fairing; instead, use an open weave 7- to 10-ounce glass cloth which has a compatible coupler applied. Feather sand and add more resin and cloth if necessary. If the area to be re-coated is resin which has been cured for several hours beyond the gel, then sand with 80 grit paper before adding more resin and reinforcement. Use this process to bring the area reasonably fair, ending with a final coat of clear resin. Under no circumstances use wax or so-called "surfacing" resin for this coat. If you feel the need to apply a microballoon fairing compound at this point, use a wet mix and use as little as possible.

After complete 80-grit sanding, start the reverse gel coat process. Apply 0.030 inch in one continuous pass if possible. As soon as this coat becomes tacky (5 to 10 minutes, maximum) spray on a water soluble mold release in about three passes. Use a light mist spray all around on the first pass; then follow on the second pass with a slightly heavier application, on the third and final pass sufficient mold release should be applied to detect the color of the mold release. Allow the gel coat to come to a hard gel or longer; then wash off with water. You are now ready for block sanding. Repeat the above process until you are satisfied with the results. The last applications of gel coat may be any color. White is best for block sanding operations and it allows viewing the guide color in the mold release as it is being applied. If no other materials such as a barrier coat and/or bottom paint are to be applied above the waterline, then a surfacing wax additive may be added only to the absolute final application of gel coat. The water soluble mold release method is the safest.

VINYLESTER RESIN AND HYBRIDS

These resins may be used as barrier coats and repairs in the same way as are polyesters using the same technique and the same coupling agents, and may be used under isophthalic gel coats. A vinylester gel coat could be used if available, but only below the waterline. Vinylesters are not UV resistant, even when pigmented.

WARNING: Always use SCBA (Self Contained Breathing Apparatus) when spraying any resin.

A presentation by Paul B. Burrel, David. J. Herzog, and R. Terrance McCabe presents an excellent case for vinylester resins including use as barrier coats. *(See Section III, Reference 27.)*

Durall Corporation's Duratec Vinylester Primer is a primer-surfacer which also may be used as a barrier coat over gel coated or non-gel coated ortho or iso-polyester substrates. One-thousand-hour exposure tests in boiling water on panels of orthophthalic resin-mat substrate show no blistering of the Duratec coating. *(See MS 34 and Section III, Reference 16.)*

EPOXY RESIN AS A BARRIER COAT

Almost all epoxy-hardener combinations are standardized by being compared to a resin base that is produced by only a few manufacturers. Two in particular are most often referenced; Shell Chemical Company's Epon 828 *(MS 30)* and Dow Chemical Company's D.E.R. 331 *(MS 23)*. Both have an epoxy equivalent weight (EEW) of about 200.

The type and amount of hardener, and in some cases catalyst, will determine the initial application viscosity at any given temperature. For example, Pacific Anchor Chemical Corporation's Ancamine 1784 *(MS 61)*, a modified aliphatic amine hardener, mixed with either 828 or 331 in a ratio of 40 phr will produce a viscosity at 75°F which is ideal for high-build films. No solvent or dilutents are required. This produces a very light colored, clear film and cures free of blush even in high humidity. Pot life is two hours and thin film set time is 12 hours.

For a faster gel and thin film set time you can use Ancamine 1769 at 25 phr. This also provides a greatly reduced level of skin irritation and is the basis for many packaged so-called safety epoxy resins.

Either of these resin-hardener systems may be used with inert filler such as aluminum powder or micronized mica to increase build and possibly reduce water permeation.

Ancamine 1922 at 25 phr will produce a very tough, impact resistant, low viscosity coating with outstanding bonding quality.

I suggest adding 1/2 of 1% of an epoxy-compatible coupling agent such as A-1100 to all of these compounds.

If you are interested in compounding coal-tar extended coatings, look into Ancamine 1978, Ancamine 2031, and Ancamine 2071 hardeners. If you would like to compound an injection type resin for re-bonding cores or for injection of voids where there are damp conditions, check out Ancamine 1942. Where a known damp or water saturation condition exists, look at Pacific Anchor's SUR-WET R hardener where water actually accelerates the cure. This is also a good candidate for an injection resin. Doesn't the possibility of using some of these hydrophilic hardeners, which depend upon water for cure, lessen some of your concern about retained moisture when making repairs or applying coatings to the hull?

Be sure to ask Pacific Anchor Chemical Company for their product guide. You will have a field day! I also suggest you ask Henkel Corporation *(MS 36)*, Ciba-Geigy Corp. *(MS 31)* and Tremont Chemicals, Inc. *(MS 13)* for their data sheets. There are many other suppliers of excellent hardeners for molding and coating too numerous to list. *(See Appendix B.)*

MODIFIED EPOXY RESINS

Morton International Corporation *(MS 32)* produces a line of epoxy-terminated polysulfide resins for use as barrier coatings. Three similar types — FEC 2232, FEC 2233, and FEC 2234 — provide rigid, flexible and elastomeric types respectively. Suggested film build is 0.030 inch consisting of two passes of 0.015 inch each. All three FEC coatings are filled with titanium dioxide and quartz powder. The color is light gray. I have made long-term osmotic tests with all three and have achieved excellent results.

These modified epoxies could be used as finish barrier coats for boat bottoms over sanded, sound gel coat as well as for a barrier coat over repairs. They are probably best suited for use as top coats over lower viscosity resins made for deep penetration.

POLYSULFIDE

Another interesting containment (barrier) coating by Morton International is their RLP 2078 100% polysulfide elastomeric coating when used with their chlorinated rubber-organosilane ester primer TPR 415. This primer is, of course, a coupling agent which increases bond to any substrate by several orders of magnitude. I definitely recommend this to be used with RLP 2078, especially on metal. I have made several semi-long-term tests with these materials and have found excellent adhesion to sanded gel coat.

TPR 415 primer is water-thin. It should be sprayed in a very light coat and then dried thoroughly. RLP 2078 may be sprayed, brushed or rolled on without the need for solvent, but it may require some xylol or methylethylketone solvent for better handling when spraying. I especially recommend this for bilge coating, and manufacturers should take note because the ideal application time for bilge coating is when the hull is still at the factory!

RLF 2078 can be reinforced. Try brush or roller coating this material over a sanded, TPR 415 primed gel coat to about 0.010 inch thick. Allow this to cure overnight. Next, tailor on dry, a ply of 7- to 10-ounce open weave glass cloth onto the cured film; then coat the fabric with

RLP using a serrated roller to smooth and remove air. After this has cured, a third coat may be applied to improve appearance. Allow this to cure a few days. Then try to peel off the film with vise grips!

URETHANE (TWO-PART) AND MARINE PAINT COATINGS

Gel coated and un-gel coated polyester and vinylester hulls are often coated with two-part urethane coatings as a barrier and as an appearance finish. Almost all hand finished exterior surfaces of one-off hulls are coated with a urethane paint over the entire hull to serve both as a barrier coat for the bottom as well as appearance finish for the rest of the hull. Certainly, urethane coatings may be used over any properly prepared surface.

Marine air-dried paints are not conventionally used on fiberglass products for bottom moisture barrier coating, but if you are ready to believe the second University of Rhode Island Report *(Section III, Reference 24)*, then you may want to try using marine enamels for barrier coating. I am not ready to buy the idea yet until I see some more test results.

PHENOLIC & FURFURYL ALCOHOL RESINS AS BARRIER COATS

Insufficient test data and incentive yet exist for most manufacturers to consider the use of these materials as barrier coat resins until the time comes when perhaps an entire hull would be constructed of either of these resins.

There is no question that the phenolics, at least, will be widely used very soon as an overlay structural material on the inside of polyester or epoxy hulls or for decks and wood structures such as cabins. In this sense, the resin itself would be considered as a barrier coating for the surface of the laminate. Although these resins do not have a hydrolytic problem, their laminates do absorb water. So, if for no other reason, they should be given a barrier coat to prevent absorption and thus weight gain. RLP 2078 is ideal for a bilge coating in this case and could be used on the outside bottom as well. Otherwise, an epoxy barrier coat might be used.

In a broad sense, a phenolic or furfuryl laminate used as an overlay may be considered a chemical barrier as well as a barrier to prevent fire from reaching a hull constructed of otherwise fire-prone materials such as wood and all practical structural resins, particularly poly and vinylester and epoxy.

MAJOR REPAIRS

RE-HULLING

I consider a major repair to be one where structural damage has occurred to the extent that replacement and/or additional reinforcement are required, and where all paint, gel coat, and affected material have been removed. This may include complete removal and replacement of a large section, or at least removal and replacement of more than 50% of any single skin thickness. If the damage has been caused solely by physical impact or stress, such damage would likely be local. It is not the purpose of this book to present repair procedures for this type of damage except to say that repair of damage caused by chemical means would be similar.

You should plan to replace as much thickness as was removed. Replacement reinforcements will be considerably stronger on a thickness basis because no woven fabrics would be used for structural repairs.

Re-hulling, generally only the bottom, is probably the most radical of all repairs; yet it offers an opportunity to gain the assurance that the result will be virtually a new boat based on modern materials and methods.

One of the most efficient and time saving procedures is to invert or careen the hull if at all possible. This allows all operations to be performed "lay-down" in the same manner as discussed in one-off molding. Gel coat, ply removal, and sectioning operations are made easier.

The following is offered as a theoretical example of replacing the entire bottom including the boottop by overlay of a 40-foot power boat.

It is assumed that the hull has been careened to 45° so work will be performed on only one side at a time. A gel coat peeler has been used, and either an average of 50% of the original thickness remains as solid material or laminate has been removed to solid material. The inside of the hull is force-vented continuously.

At this point the hull bottom is considered to be little more than a mold or form over which a new bottom will be fitted and bonded to the contour of the old structure.

Vinylester has been selected as the matrix resin, and a 40-ounce triaxial fabric has been specified as the reinforcement throughout. A laminating schedule has been decided.

No chopped strand mat will be used for build-up, and no filling putty, including syntactic putty, will be used until all structural reinforcing materials have been applied.

It has been determined that a five-square-foot section of laminate requires complete replacement because of advanced chemical deterioration. It has been found that this area may be accessible from the inside. The area to be removed is a compound shape. Before complete removal of the section it will be decided whether the panel will be replaced by first cutting out the area or using one of two types of molds to provide the contour for repairs.

1. It has been determined that the outside area can be ground down to 1/8 inch of the inside and can be scarfed to sound material around the edges at about a 30:1 ratio, the remaining laminate, though perhaps soft and having no structural value, may yet be sound enough to allow application of a penetrating resin to stiffen the remaining laminate and thus produce, in a sense, a mold. This method must be used if access to the inside is not possible.

It is important that any type of resin contain an appropriate coupling agent if it is to be used for the above purpose or in any other part of the hull where resin is first applied to the old laminate. This applies to resin used to impregnate the first reinforcing layer over any of the old laminate. Subsequent layers need not have the coupling agent added to the resin if the new reinforcement has been treated with a coupling agent appropriate to the resin specified.

2. If it is determined that the area would not hold its own shape if damaged material were to be removed down to 1/8 inch, then before removal of any material a structural repair laminate must first be applied to the inside. This is either intended as a permanent inner structural laminate or as a mold which would be removed later. If there will be no interference inside, it is recommended that this laminate serving as a mold remain to add further strength to the repair area.

3. If it is decided that the inside repair laminate is to serve as a mold only, then an appropriate mold release is first applied and the area is laminated to the outside of the scarf line — the area of sound material. The resin may be of any quality and the reinforcements may be woven cloth and/or chopped strand mat. When cured, the perimeter of the mold around the scarf is temporarily but firmly attached with sheet metal screws where there is sound hull material. After the mold is cured it is removed, the damaged hull material is cut out to sound material, and the edges are scarfed from the outside. The mold is first coated with mold release and reinstalled over the now open hole.

4. If it is decided that this mold is to become a permanent part of the hull instead of only a mold, then the entire area of repair inside the hull including the scarf line is thoroughly ground before laminating. Again, it is vital to add a coupling agent to the initial laminating resin to insure bond to the hull. Though this add-on is presumed bonded to the inside of the hull, it is suggested that corrosion-resistant sheet metal screws be installed around the scarf line and left in place. The damaged hull material is then completely removed by grinding including the surface of the overlay mold.

Regardless of which method of repair is selected, the repair area will be laminated and contour-ground flush to the average thickness of the remaining hull. The initial application of resin *must* contain a coupling agent. This operation will be first performed on all areas required, if not the entire hull, until all repairs have been brought flush to the base hull thickness; *i.e.*, the minimum overall thickness of the stripped hull before application of the main rehull laminate.

A vinylester such as Dow Chemical's Derakane 411-415 has been selected for the laminating resin. Vinylester resins have excellent "natural" bonding ability to untreated (raw) or depleted previously coupled fibers. Any coupling agents which may have been added to the glass fibers when manufacturing the original hull are presumed to have been leached out at the area of repair. Though vinylester resins have good inherent bonding ability to glass, the addition of a coupler as little as 0.005% 2.4 pentanedione or 0.1% of Union Carbide's A-174 will increase bond and hydrolytic resistance dramatically. Vinylesters are generally superior to polyesters in water resistance.

From this point on the replacement of the hull laminate will follow the one-off process previously discussed.

STRUCTURAL FOAM AS OVERLAY

Vinyl foam may be applied to a repaired, sound single skin hull over which a sandwich would be molded in one-off fashion except in reverse order; *i.e.*, the inner skin pre-exists (the old hull) where in true one-off the inner skin is applied last. This method may be applied to virtually any hull material whether it be fiberglass, wood, steel, or aluminum. A perfectly sound but flabby hull can be made stiffer and at the same time more buoyant. It certainly is worth considering in any re-hull planning.

STRUCTURAL FOAM REPAIRS

The inside and outside of any cored hull structure are subject to the same hydrolytic deterioration as a single shell. There may be some differences in major repairs. As would be expected, the inner skin would likely suffer less hydrolytic attack than the outer one; however, the inner skin is usually thinner. A 60:40 thickness ratio is about optimum. Only if the bilge had been kept dry or if no moisture had passed through defects in the foam core from the outside, would the inner skin show no hydrolytic attack.

I consider the paper by Thomas J. Johannsen of Torin, Inc. *(MS 20)*, presented at the MACM conference in March 1990, to be one of the best discussions on this subject. I certainly could not improve on it except to point out the obvious advantage of male form one-off construction. *(See Section III, Reference 28.)*

It would appear, then, that if repairs to a cored hull are ever required, the damaged area will likely be confined to the outer skin. Also — depending upon the type of core which had been used in manufacture — delamination between the core and outer skin would be expected.

If it is suspected that delamination had occurred between a sound outer skin and possibly the inner skin as well, in an area no more than a few square feet, then injection of a low exotherm resin may suffice. If the area will accept any injected resin at all, a void exists. If proper injection technique shows the void to accept only a few cubic centimeters, then the area may be considered re-bonded. If the area requires a large or endless amount of resin, then one skin or the other in the affected area should be removed in order to make repairs in the manner outlined in Johannsen's paper.

BOAT RESTORATION

Boat restoration is very similar to performing repairs. The big difference is that restoration is based on a lot more love than when you're forced to make repairs. A lot of us are car collectors. We have them for the pride of possession and often, just to save a classic for posterity. It can be the same with boats.

You may already have a candidate for restoration. If not, certainly you can find one on the market. Make your selection as outlined in the *Degree of Damage Assessment* section. Don't be dissuaded from selecting a boat everyone else has given up on. It can be restored. Here are some examples.

WOOD BOAT

You have found a 38-foot fully formed keel wood sailboat. The planking is carvel; *i.e.*, the plank seams are butted and contain no caulking. You want a boat made of wood but you don't want the water-soaked heavy hull so common with wood boats. You have selected a resin saturation process.

You have wet blasted the inside and outside completely. A lot of furniture will have to be removed from the inside first. You find some rot and some planks will have to be replaced. By the time all of this operation has taken place, the wood should be reasonably dry, down to 12 to 15% (true) depending upon atmospheric conditions.

The outside of the hull must be power sanded and the moisture content low enough to produce dry sanding dust. The hull ultimately will have been dried to 12 to 15% before application of any resin.

You have decided to use epoxy resin only for all operations except for a urethane top coat on the outside of the hull. No laminating will be performed. The penetrating resin will be a low viscosity, moisture-tolerant, two-part epoxy which you may select from those previously described — including the commercial ones! Sufficient resin must be applied to both the inside as well as the outside to eventually bring up a slight glaze. Fairing, if required, may be performed with an epoxy microballoon mix. After final fairing, clear resin is applied to bring up a near glossy surface (the barrier coat). Then, finally a high quality two-part urethane top coat is applied. If you prefer to take advantage of the outstanding water permeation resistance of vinylester resin, consider using the previously described Duratec vinylester primer-surfacer directly on top of the epoxy microballoon-faired surface mentioned above. Then apply urethane top coat.

METAL BOAT

You have found a steel Chris Craft "Roamer" and the bottom up to the boottop is in bad shape and the topsides not much better, but it's all there and you can buy it at almost salvage price. On haul-out you determine there might be some metal left after sandblasting so you decide to use vinyl foam and structural fiberglass cladding.

You choose vinylester resin throughout because of its excellent ability to bond to steel — even without primer — and because of its hydrolytic resistance. Dow's 8084 vinylester is a good choice. Foam thickness will be 3/8- to 1/2-inch and must be bedded onto the hull with resin-microballoon mix by vacuum bag. You may want to consider using Morton International's TPR 415 Primer applied just prior to attaching the foam. Check the use of this primer for increased bond over bare metal; if no improvement, then delete. After all foam sheets have been installed, all voids are thoroughly filled with microballoon mix and the foam surface faired in preparation for the fiberglass skin. The latter will be a triaxial unidirectional fabric. Skin fairing will be as in one-off and will utilize vinylester resin in the microballoon fairing material. After fairing by final sanding, Duratec's primer-surfacer could be used or a clear epoxy barrier resin might be applied. Top coat will be two-part urethane.

An aluminum hull is processed in the same manner.

FIBERGLASS BOAT

You have found, say, a 42-foot power cruiser that is perfect inside but terrible on the outside. It's riddled with blisters, delaminations and some soft spots. Let's just say this boat with a hull in sound condition would sell for $200,000, but you can buy it from the insurance company for $25,000. This 42-foot boat is a well-known "B———" or "H———-" or "U———-." It doesn't look great, but it has held its shape. You should not have to spend more than $75,000 for restoration costs to have yourself a new boat in which you will have confidence and which will last a long time.

It is very likely that immediate heavy ply peeling will be required — up to 50% of original thickness. And, in some areas, major structural repairs will be required. Dry the hull within reason. Rough fair it by peeling and lots of grinding, then plan to lay on a solid reinforced vinylester hull to at least the original thickness. Use triaxial uni-directional fabric and a medium elongation resin.

CONCLUSION

If you're still with me at this point I will have rung you through a lot of options. Be careful of the scare tactics practiced by some. Picking at the surface when attempting repairs will often cost more even in the short run than if you jump straight into major repair. Even re-hulling may prove to be the most economical route. Any hull rated at 4 or higher on my scale is an immediate candidate for re-hulling. There is no over-kill in going this way and you will wind up with a boat in which you will have full confidence.

MARINE
REINFORCED
PLASTICS
CONSTRUCTION

SECTION III

REFERENCES & APPENDICES

Section III
References & Appendices

References

Reference 1

The Effective Use of Directional Reinforcements

by
Marvin Luger
Director of Research and Development
Proform, Inc.

Introduction

For many years designers of reinforced plastics products have recognized that their laminates were dissimilar to metals and other crystalline materials in several important ways. One of these differences is that unlike metals, a laminate is "non-isotropic," that is, the strength and stiffness change with the change in direction within a laminate. Although nearly everyone recognizes this fact, the great majority of designs are made using a single set of property values which ignore the fact. An important minority, meanwhile, have developed some very advanced mathematical techniques (e.g., directional finite element computer analysis) to optimize laminate designs permitting sophisticated designers in those industries (e.g., aerospace) to design laminates that become the most efficient product components possible today. Between these two extremes there seems to be a great knowledge gap. This presentation is designed to give those designers who have no experience with directional materials some simple design approaches that will improve their designs while introducing them to directional materials.

In addition to presenting simplified design approaches, I will introduce a number of our Knytex Division reinforcement products. Most of these products are already in use by large firms using computer designs. They have also been in volume use in applications where low cost and high handling volume are pre-requisites. As the original large user of Knytex reinforcements, Proform/Knytex, Inc. large structural product laminating plants have perfected the structural applications and the placement of these materials with impregnators and chop/hoop winders.

Types of Directional Reinforcement

The directional reinforcements of interest in this presentation are variable in two ways: They vary in their fiber arrangement and they vary in the material from which the fibers are made. There are some structural advantages of non-woven fiber reinforcements compared with woven ones. If we assume each fiber is loaded horizontally with a tension force T, the maximum woven fiber force becomes $T/cos.d$ which is greater than T of the straight fiber. The average stress $T/area$ of the straight fiber becomes $T/(cos.d \times area)$ in the woven case which is also greater but in addition to that disadvantage the stress in the woven fiber, unlike that of the straight fiber, is non-uniform; thus the woven fiber stresses reach limiting values at lower values of T. The geometry of the weave also creates shear and bending moment values which are absent in the non-woven construction.

Cross ply material properties exceed the woven properties, and this would be true in both the warp and weft fiber directions. The unidirectional properties are highest, of course, in the fiber direction and that is the property direction desired. Unidirectional materials are the most efficient supplementary stiffening and strengthening reinforcements to use in the frequently occurring case where a laminate is deficient in only one direction. Our objective in this paper is to show several methods to use directional materials as partial or total replacements for standard laminates. It should be noted that other values (e.g., shear, bearing, etc.) are needed in most designs and some of these values differ considerably with directional materials. The methods shown can be extended to cover these considerations.

Design Approach Purposes

In designs of one reinforcement, one merely uses the allowable stresses and modulus values for the substitute material. These will show basis of comparison. Equivalent strengths are then computed by multiplying the cost per cubic inch of each laminate type by the ratio of the strength of the basis material to that of the laminate type being compared. Equivalent costs can be found for any strength of interest.

The logic of this approach is quite simple: if a material is twice as strong, then it takes only half as much of the material to carry the load. The laminate cost of each type is multiplied by the ratio of the basis material stiffness to that of the laminate being computed. Cost comparisons for Kevlar and hybrid materials are not extended for strength and stiffness. Although stronger and stiffer than glass, they are not cost justified on a single property basis. If one is interested in weight saving, impact strength, fatigue resistance, or other of the high performance properties of these materials, then similar performance ratios for each property can be formed and a weighted percentage for each according to its relative importance used to determine the most cost effective laminate overall. It is even possible to consider handling qualities, drapability, and other considerations if it is possible to quantify the relative performance of each laminate.

Among the most promising material alternatives are some of the hybrids which can be mixed within a strand or by alternating strand materials. These materials frequently out perform single material reinforcements and provide considerable design flexibility.

OTHER DESIGN CONSIDERATIONS

It should be noted that this discussion is not a complete coverage of all important design considerations. It is meant to show some simple approaches that will introduce directional materials into a design.

One point of caution in handling shear forces — directional materials tend to resolve shear forces in the fiber direction. As a result, cross ply shear planes should be examined more carefully than shear planes between woven layers.

CONCLUSION

It is our hope that this presentation will convince those who have never considered the use of directional reinforcements that they can obtain many useful benefits and efficiencies by such use. Although truly optimum results require fairly complex mathematical analysis, it is nonetheless possible to make major design improvements on many simple and ordinary products by using the methods outlined. *(See the design sketches below.)*

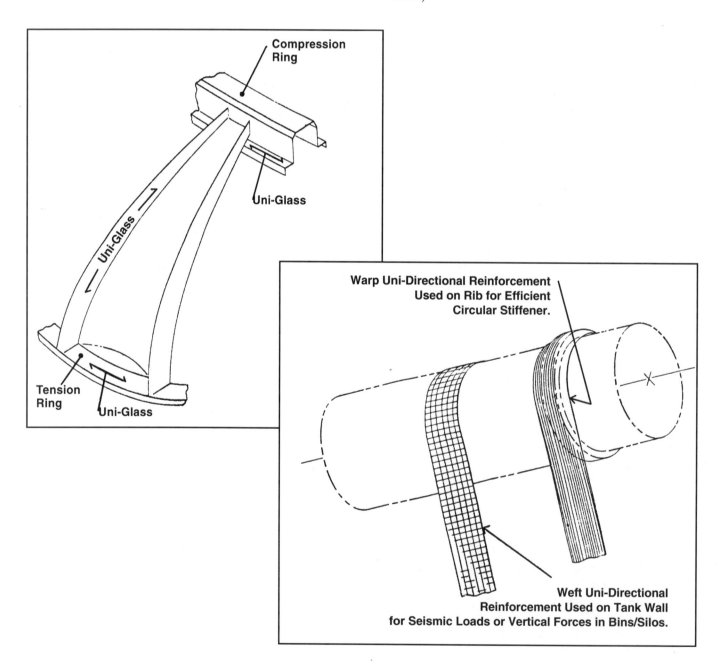

Compression Ring

Uni-Glass

Uni-Glass

Tension Ring

Uni-Glass

Warp Uni-Directional Reinforcement Used on Rib for Efficient Circular Stiffener.

Weft Uni-Directional Reinforcement Used on Tank Wall for Seismic Loads or Vertical Forces in Bins/Silos.

REFERENCE 2

APPLICATION OF SPECTRA™ FIBERS IN THE MARINE/BOATING INDUSTRY

by

Forrest Sloan and Huy Nguyen

Composite laminates reinforced with Spectra extended-chain polyethylene (ECPE) fibers are being used increasingly in the marine composites and boating industries. In addition to having the highest specific strength and stiffness of any man-made material, these fibers have low moisture uptake and outstanding resistance to impact and abrasion. Low dielectric constant and loss tangent (for low losses and less distortion of radar signals) and density close to that of seawater (for low acoustic insertion losses for sonar signals) are also attractive properties in many marine applications. The development of ECPE fibers as well as the properties of unidirectional and fabric composites are reviewed. Several applications of ECPE/polymer composites in the marine/boating industry are discussed.

Allied-Signal, Inc., Spectra Composites Group,
P.O. Box 31, Petersburg, VA 23804 • 804-520-3288

INTRODUCTION

The use of fiber-reinforced composite materials has become synonymous with the boat-building industry, which was once dominated by more traditional materials such as wood and steel. Glass is by far the most common reinforcing fiber, but high-performance fibers such as carbon and aramid are also used. One of the most recent fibers to be introduced is extended-chain polyethylene (ECPE), e.g., Spectra® from Allied-Signal Inc. The purpose of this paper is to compare the properties of Spectra ECPE fibers with other high-performance reinforcing fibers used in boatbuilding, and to examine applications of ECPE in the marine industry.

BACKGROUND

Historically, boats have been built from wood, which was one of the few bulk materials available to man which floated. The advent of high explosives brought about the deployment of heavy steel armor plating on wooden ships, and eventually to the development of the so-called "ironclads" of the American Civil War. Today large warships (with the exception of mine-countermeasures ships) are built almost entirely from high-strength steels.

The first glass fiber-reinforced plastics (GRP) boats were built at the beginning of World War II. Initial problems with fiber/matrix adhesion were overcome in the late 1950s with the advent of silane coupling agents, and mass production of glass fibers is common today. GRP remains the material of choice for boatbuilders because of its low cost and extensive use history. Glass fiber has also been greatly improved since its first inception, and now many high strength grades such as S-2 and R-glass are making inroads into the high-performance fibers market.

The use of more advanced fibers such as carbon and boron began in the early 1960s but was restricted to the aerospace market for cost considerations. The price of carbon fibers has since dropped dramatically as consumption has increased but boron remains a prohibitively expensive aerospace material. In 1972 the first high-performance organic fiber appeared, aramid (aromatic polyamide), but high material cost limited its use.

Although these materials remain much more expensive than standard E-glass fiber, the life cycle costs (which include fuel consumed, power requirements, repair frequency, etc.) often dictate their use in boating applications. For example, in 1980 a boat constructed of aramid fibers rather than glass increased the fuel economy and thus cruising range by more than 50%.[1] Today the use of high-performance fibers is most common in racing boats, which gain the most from light weight and high strength.

PROPERTIES OF POLYETHYLENE FIBER

The latest high-performance fiber to enter the marine market is extended-chain polyethylene (ECPE), which was introduced in 1985 under the trade name Spectra.[2] The mechanical properties of ECPE fibers are compared with other reinforcing fibers in Table 1. ECPE fibers have the highest strength-to-weight of any known fiber, and are extremely resistant to cutting and abrasion. Their outstanding properties are direct attributes of the gel spinning process which was patented in 1983.[3,4] In general, a solution of an ultra high molecular weight polyethylene (UHMWPE) feedstock is used in the spinning process. The spinning and subsequent drawing steps lead to a highly crystalline, extended chain morphology in the fiber.

Polyethylene has the simplest chemical structure of any polymer:

$$\left[-\underset{\underset{H}{|}}{\overset{\overset{H}{|}}{C}} - \underset{\underset{H}{|}}{\overset{\overset{H}{|}}{C}} - \right]_n$$

This simple structure, coupled with the highly crystalline, extended chain morphology, makes Spectra fibers resistant to chemical attack. The lack of hydrogen-bonding sites also prevents significant moisture absorption by the fibers. In contrast, aramid fibers (e.g., poly(paraphenyleneterephthalamide) or Kevlar™) have a relatively complex chemical structure.

$$\left[-\overset{\overset{O}{\|}}{C} -\bigcirc\hspace{-1.5em}\bigcirc - \overset{\overset{O}{\|}}{C} - \underset{\underset{H}{|}}{N} -\bigcirc\hspace{-1.5em}\bigcirc - \underset{\underset{H}{|}}{N} - \right]_n$$

It is the nature of the amide linkage and hydrogen bonding of this structure which make it inherently prone to chemical attack and moisture absorption. Table 2 compares the performance of the fibers against exposure to various solvents. In this set of experiments, neat fibers were submerged in the desired solvent for 6 months and 24 months and then tested in tensile mode for breaking strength. The breaking strengths of the exposed fibers were normalized with those of the original fibers for comparison purpose. Note in particular the susceptibility of aramid fibers to concentrated chlorine, a commonly used anti-mildew and cleaning agent used by most boat owners.

Another attribute of ECPE fiber is its electrical properties, as shown by the data in Table 3. Of the reinforcing fibers frequently used for radome applications, Spectra has the lowest loss tangent and dielectric constant. The very low loss tangent (0.0002) and dielectric constant (2.2) of Spectra allow composite radomes to be made with over 90% signal transmission and minimum signal distortion. It is important to note that plasma treated Spectra products are recommended for applications where good shear and compressive strength are required.[5-7] On the other hand, unmodified fibers are employed in applications where damage tolerance, impact protection or ballistic protection are important.[8-10] Since UHMWPE has a melting point of 150°C, it is also recommended that ECPE fibers be used in applications and fabrication techniques which do not exceed 120°C.

PROPERTIES OF ECPE/EPOXY COMPOSITES

The static properties of a typical unidirectional Spectra/epoxy composite are listed in Table 4 along with the properties of other fiber-reinforced epoxies. Spectra properties are for unidirectional plasma-treated (PT) Spectra 1000 fiber in an Epon 828 epoxy with 8% TETA cured at 105°C. Data for other materials was taken from Fiberite technical bulletins (1990). Table 4 also lists composite properties normalized with respect to laminate density (specific strength and specific modulus).

Spectra composites are characterized by high tensile strength and modulus. The specific tensile properties of Spectra composites compare favorably with composites reinforced with aramid or glass. However, the compressive strength of ECPE fibers, as with other organic fibers, is relatively low. The compressive strength limits flexural properties in ECPE composites, as failure occurs on the compression side of a flexural specimen. Laminates which will see significant compressive or flexural loads can be optimized by hybridizing Spectra with glass or carbon to increase the flexural and compressive properties.[11-12] Hybridization creates a composite which synergistically combines the structural properties of graphite fibers with the abrasion and impact resistance of Spectra fibers.

The tensile strength and modulus of Spectra are even higher at high strain rates, making it an ideal choice in ballistic and impact sensitive applications. Table 5 shows drop weight impact properties of Spectra as compared with other materials. (The specific peak force, specific energy absorbed, and specific total energy were normalized by dividing the peak force and energy values by the areal density.) The high strain-wave velocity of the ECPE fibers also makes Spectra an ideal material for vibration damping.[13] This property has important implications for vibration or noise abatement programs in airborne and undersea applications.

Spectra composites have electronic and acoustic properties which can be very desirable in a variety of applications. The low dielectric properties discussed previously allow composite parts to be tailored, in combination with other materials, for low transmission losses (e.g., in shipboard or airborne radomes) or for low reflectivity.[14] In underwater applications, the low density of Spectra allows the construction of composites with densities close to that of seawater. With the appropriate selection of resin, sonar enclosures made with Spectra exhibit some of the lowest insertion losses (signal loss on transmission through the wall of the enclosure) available for acoustic applications.[15] Other resin matrices could be used with Spectra to provide very high reflection losses, which becomes important in applications where echo reduction is paramount. Figure 1 shows the low insertion loss and high reflection loss in a Spectra/polymer composite tested at normal incidence.[16]

Another important characteristic of polyethylene that sets it apart from other organic reinforcing fibers such as aramid is its low moisture uptake. Spectra composites absorb very little moisture (<1%) even at hydrostatic pressures of up to 140 MPa for 28 days, as shown in Table 6.[17] More importantly, the static mechanical properties are unaffected by the small weight gain. This is in contrast to aramid composites which absorb significantly more moisture (4-5%) and are known to be adversely affected as a result.[18-20]

MARINE APPLICATIONS OF ECPE COMPOSITES

Several characteristics of ECPE (in addition to light weight and high strength) make it an ideal choice for racing boat applications, but the primary advantage is in impact. As discussed above, ECPE fibers have the highest available strain-wave velocity, which means that impact energy is distributed very rapidly. In addition, the very high ultimate strength of the fibers makes hull penetration extremely difficult. Both of these attributes make boats with ECPE-reinforced hulls unlikely to fail catastrophically upon impact. Thunderboats, Inc., has produced several crash resistant safety cells from Spectra, for use in racing boats.[21] Other powerboat racing applications are under consideration. In the world of wind-powered racing boats, a more recent application of Spectra is in several of the 1992 America's Cup class boats, which utilize Spectra composites to provide light-weight impact protection for the graphite reinforcing fibers in the hull.[22] The low moisture absorption of ECPE is an additional benefit. When Spectra fibers are used as an exterior surfacing mat just behind the gel-coat in composite boat hulls, the tendency for osmotic blistering to occur may be reduced.[23]

104

ECPE is also used in small unmanned vehicles which require low mass to reduce power consumption. For example, several airborne remotely piloted vehicles (RPV) utilize Spectra fibers in the wing skins and fuselage.[24] The largest single use of Spectra composites in a marine remotely operated vehicle (ROV) is in the free-flooded fairings of the Naval Ocean Systems Center's new autonomous underwater search system (AUSS) submersible, where it serves as the forward, Doppler, and tail fairings. Spectra has been used in the construction of several research vehicles, including the ALVIN/JASON system where it is used for impact resistance on the primary vehicle as well as in JASON's umbilical cables.

CONCLUSION

Extended-chain polyethylene (ECPE) fibers are the latest in a long line of high-performance reinforcing fibers to be considered for use in marine applications. ECPE fibers offer high strength and stiffness as well as low weight and many other attractive physical properties such as low moisture absorption and high transparency to electromagnetic waves. Small boat and underwater vehicle construction using ECPE-fiber-reinforced composites have been very successful because of the light weight and high impact resistance of the material. More complex marine applications utilizing ECPE/carbon or ECPE/glass hybrid constructions should become more common as the experience base expands and new applications are discovered.

REFERENCES

1. DuPont Magazine, *75* (6) 26 (1981).

2. Tam, T.Y., Boone, M.B., and Weedon, G.C., Polym. Eng. Sci., *28*, 871 (1988).

3. Smith, P., and Lemstra, P.J., U.S. Pat. 4,422,993, Dec. 1983.

4. Kavesh, S., and Prevorsek, D., U.S. Pat. 4,413,110, Nov. 1983.

5. Kaplan, S.L., Rose, P.W., Nguyen, H.X., and Chang, H.W., SAMPE Int. Sym., *35*, 551(1988).

6. Nguyn, H.X., Riahi, G., Wood, G., and Poursartip, A., SAMPE Int. Sym., *33*, 1721 (1988).

7. Nguyen, H.X., Weedon, G.C., and Chang, H.W., SAMPE Int. Sym., *34*, 1603 (1989).

8. Zimmerman, R.S., and Adams, D.F., SAMPE Int. Sym., *32*, 1416 (1987).

9. Chang, H.W., Lin, L.C., and Bhatnagar, A., SAMPE Int. Sym., *31*, 859 (1986).

10. D.C. Prevorsek, G.A. Harpel, Y.D. Kwon, H.L. Li and S.A. Young, SAMPE Int. Sym., *33*, 1685 (1988).

11. Cordova, D.S., and Cordova, C.W., ANTEC '87, 767 (1987).

12. Peijs, A.A.J.M., Catsman, P., Govaert, L.E., and Lemstra, P.J., Composites, *21*, 513 (1990).

13. Mantena, P.R., and Gibson, R.F., SAMPE Tech. Conf., *22*, (1990).

14. Cordova, D.S. and Collier, L.S., SAMPE Int. Sym., *37*, (1992), in press.

15. Huang, H.A., Hahn, H.T., Nguyen, H.X., and Chang, H.W., SAMPE Int. Sym., *36*, 1879 (1991).

16. Broding, M.S., and Miessler, J.D., Syntech Materials, Inc., private comm., July 1991.

17. Nguyen, H.X., SAMPE Int. Sym., *36*, 1836 (1991).

18. Allred, R.E., in *Environmental Effects on Composite Materials*, G.S. Springer, Ed., Technomic, *27* (1984).

19. Wang, J.Z., Dillard, D.A., and Kamke, F.A., J. of Materials Science, *26*, 5113 (1991).

20. Haque, A., Mahmood, S., Walker, L., and Jeelani, S., J. of Reinf. Plast. and Comp., *10*, 132 (1991).

21. La Banco, S., Thunderboats, Inc., private comm., March 1990.

22. Meldner, H., America³ Foundation, private comm., October 1990.

23. Wills, J.A., private comm. October 1992.

24. Allen, E.H., Daedelus Research Inc., private comm., July 1991.

MACM '92 CONFERENCE PROCEEDINGS

TABLE 1. Tensile Properties of Spectra and Other Fibers

Fiber	Density (g/cm³)	Diameter 10⁻⁹ m	Strength GPa	Specific Strength 10³ m	Modulus GPa	Specific Modulus 10⁶ m
E-Glass	2.6	16	3.5	140	72	2.8
S-Glass	2.5	7	4.6	190	90	3.7
Graphite[1]	1.75	7	2.8	160	230	13
Aramid[2]	1.44	12	2.8	200	130	9.2
Spectra[3]	0.97	38	2.1	220	90	9.5
Spectra[4]	0.97	27	2.5	260	130	14

[1]*High Strength, T300*　　[2]*Kevlar 49*　　[3]*SPECTRA 900*　　[4]*SPECTRA 1000*

TABLE 2. Solvent Resistance of Fibers (Percent Retention of Breaking Strength)

Agent	Aramid 6 months	Aramid 24 months	Spectra 900 6 months	Spectra 900 24 months
Seawater	100	98	100	100
Hydraulic Fluid	100	87	100	100
Kerosene	100	97	100	100
Gasoline	93	No Data[1]	100	100
Toluene	72	No Data	100	96
Glacial Acetic Acid	82	No Data	100	100
1M Hydrochloric Acid	40	No Data	100	100
5M Sodium Hydroxide	42	No Data	100	100
29% Ammonium Hydroxide	70	No Data	100	100
Perchloroethylene	75	No Data	100	100
Chlorox	0	0	91	73
10% Detergent Solution	91	No Data	100	100

[1]*Not enough material remained to test.*

SPECTRA
HIGH PERFORMANCE FIBERS

An introduction to SPECTRA® high performance fibers

SPECTRA® 900 and SPECTRA® 1000 are two new, ultra-tough fibers developed by Allied Corporation's polymer research group. Pound for pound, SPECTRA fibers are stronger than steel. Made from polyethylene, SPECTRA high-performance fibers combine a very high degree of molecular orientation with a very low density to provide a unique and extraordinary performance profile. Brief lists of SPECTRA fibers' attributes and potential applications are provided below and more detailed information can be found on the pages that follow.

Product Attributes

- Low specific gravity
- High specific modulus
- High specific strength
- High energy to break
- High abrasion resistance
- Low dielectric constant
- Excellent chemical resistance
- Low moisture absorption
- Excellent damping characteristics

Potential Applications

- Sail cloth
- Marine ropes and cables
- Impact shields
- Medical implants
- Radomes
- Sports equipment
- Pressure vessels
- Boat hulls
- Soft and solid anti-ballistic shields
- Fish netting
- Aerospace composites
- Industrial composites

Allied's Customer Technical Support team stands ready to discuss with you the suitability of SPECTRA 900 and SPECTRA 1000 fibers for your high performance end-use applications. We look forward to hearing from you.

We welcome your inquiries. Please contact:

SPECTRA Customer Technical Support
Allied Fibers Technical Center
P. O. Box 31
Petersburg, Virginia 23803
(804) 520-3321
Telex: 710-9572331
Telefax: (804) 520-3388

ALLIED Fibers

TABLE 3. Electrical Properties at 10 GHz of Various Materials

Material	Dielectric Constant	Loss Tangent (10[4])
E-Glass	6.00	5.2
Quartz	3.78	2.0
Aramid	3.85	10.0
SPECTRA	2.20	2.0

TABLE 4. Static Properties of Unidirectional Fiber Reinforced Composites

Property	SPECTRA[1]	Aramid[2]	S-2 Glass[2]	HS-Carbon[2]
Tensile Strength, MPa	900	880	1200	1400
Specific TS, 10^3 m	88	66	61	93
Tensile Modulus, GPa	50	65	52	140
Specific TM, 10^6 m	4.9	4.9	2.6	9.3
Compressive Strength, MPa	70	210	810	1300
Specific CS, 10^3 m	6.9	16	41	87
Compressive Modulus, GPa	52	41	67	130
Specific CM, 10^6 m	5.1	3.1	3.4	8.7
Flexural Strength, MPa	210[3]	530	1700	1600
Flexural Modulus, GPa	42[3]	56	57	124
Short Beam Shear[4], MPa	21	34	72	48
Density, kg/m³	1040	1350	2020	1530
Fiber Volume %, V_f	0.50	0.60	0.60	0.60

[1]SPECTRA 1000PT in Epon 828 w/8% TETA

[2]Fiberite 948A1 epoxy. Data from Fiberite technical brochure.

[3]ASTM D790, l:d=16:1. Ultimate strength.

[4]Data from Tsai, Composites Design (1991).

TABLE 5. Drop Weight Impact Properties of Composites

Reinforcement	Laminate Density Kg/m³	Laminate Thickness mm	Specific Peak Force N-m²/g	Specific Energy Peak Force J-m²/Kg	Total
SPECTRA 900 (Fabric 902PT)	1050	2.1	2.1	7.4	17.4
SPECTRA 1000 (Fabric 951PT)	1040	0.7	2.7	22.1	29.6
SPECTRA 1000-PT (cross-ply laminate)	1050	1.2	2.6	15.8	19.5
Aramid, K-49 (cross-ply laminate)	1300	2.0	1.5	6.0	9.9
E-Glass (cross-ply laminate)	2000	2.7	1.9	6.3	11.3

TABLE 6. Water Absorption in SPECTRA Fabric Composite[2] and Effect on Mechanical Properties

Sample (Time, Pressure[1])	Weight Gain %	Tensile Strength MPa	Tensile Modulus GPa	Compressive Strength MPa	Compressive Modulus GPa
Dry (control)		440	35	59	11.3
7 days, 69 MPa	0.12	440	36	60	14.3
28 days, 69 MPa	0.20	430	30	55	13.8
7 days, 140 MPa	0.64	460	34	58	12.2
28 days, 140 MPa	0.62	430	32	56	12.8

[1]Hydrostatic pressure, fresh water, room temperature

[2]Style 951PT, Epon 826 resin cured with 8% TETA.

REFERENCE 3

EXCERPT FROM *INDUSTRIAL RESIN PUTTYS*

by John A. Wills

The Library of Congress
United States Copyright Office
Registration Number TXU 166-250

Sailboats often require weighted keels which are usually cast from lead. Special molds — usually concrete whose surface is heavily rubbed with carbon black for a mold release — are made to cast the slug which is then fitted by embedment into the hull shell. Depending upon closeness of fit, one of the mineral filled puttys could be used. For perfect alignment and balance, consider placing or suspending the slug into its cavity but not touching its walls or bottom. Pour in dry steel or lead shot around the perimeter. It will fill every crevice and irregularity. Pour on the top a slow cure batch of resin either from the top by gravity or by injection from the bottom through a port in the hull. Control of the final weight required is accomplished by adding a few more shot encapsulated with resin. This way you can eliminate the lead melting operation or even "pour" the keel weight while the hull is still in the mold or jig. If you have been melting lead, you probably buy scrap wheel weights, battery lead and odds and ends of other shapes.

The very hull to receive the keel weight is the best possible mold. It is the only mold if the hull is a "one-off" or one of a kind. Instead of melting the scrap and pouring it directly into the hull (it's been done, but it's a "no-no"), place the individual pieces with reasonable care into the hull, fitting them as closely as possible. From time to time lead or steel shot is distributed around with vibration, if possible. No more than six inches in height should be placed before encasing with a slow cure polyester poured over the top. Complete saturation is not necessary. This process is repeated until the final ounce is placed. Weigh everything as you go, including the resin, and you will be able to place the design weight within an ounce.

Photo shows simplest possible castings. Cylinder at left is resin with steel beads. Cylinder at right is resin with steel grit. Both were cast in a jelly jar.

You are not restricted to the use of lead scrap. Use whatever is available and in any combination. All materials are encased in resin and should present no corrosion problems.

All of the above will work in molds too. If a slug is to be precast, use a fiberglass mold with proper mold release. If a fiberglass gel-coated shell bolt-on keel is to be made, the casting of metal scrap and resin is performed the same way as if poured in place in the hull.

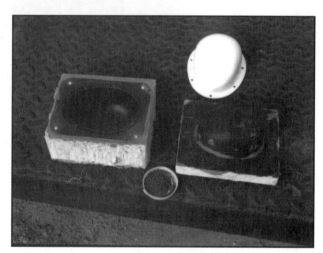

Typical male, female mold and part. Mold is cast from polyester resin and steel beads shown in small cup in foreground

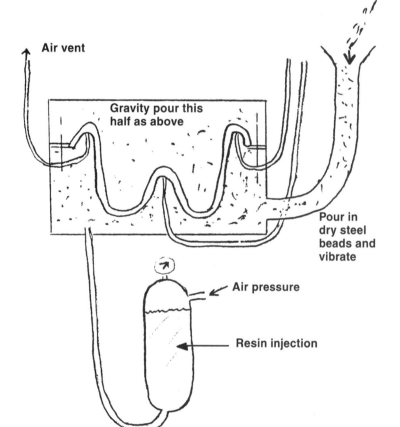

Air vent

Gravity pour this half as above

Pour in dry steel beads and vibrate

Air pressure

Resin injection

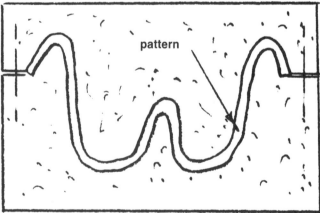

pattern

This is an easy one if the assembly can be turned over. The top half could be cast with resin using steel beads and/or grit, then turned over and the other half cast the same way.

REFERENCE 4

SPECIALTY INTERMEDIATES

MILLITHIX® 925

Millithix 925 is an organic thixotrope for use in unsaturated polyester and vinyl ester resins. It is effective at relatively low levels and has little effect on the cure, appearance or corrosion properties of the resin. Millithix 925 can be used either as a powder or as a solution for easier incorporation. It has been·found very effective as a gelling agent and makes an attractive, clear antiperspirant.

FEATURES

—Effective at low levels

—No cobalt absorption

—Non-hygroscopic

—Does not require polar activator

—Non-settling

—Minimal effects on corrosion properties

—Excellent clarity achievable

—Does not require heat to incorporate

PROPERTIES

Millithix 925 derives its thixotropic properties from the formation of a weak three-dimensional network within the resin. Under low shear conditions this network greatly increases the resistance to flow of the resin trapped within the network. Under high shear this loosely associated network is broken down, allowing the resin to flow much more freely.

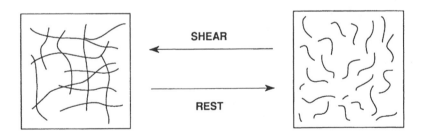

When the shearing forces are removed and the Millithix 925/resin system is allowed to sit undisturbed, the network immediately begins to rebuild and resistance to flow increases. This shear thinning effect is commonly measured by dividing the low shear viscosity by the high shear viscosity; the quotient of which is termed the "Thixotropic Index" of the system.

$$\text{Thixotropic Index} = \frac{\text{Low Shear Viscosity}}{\text{High Shear Viscosity}}$$

The high shear rate is typically 10 times greater than the low shear rate. For example on a Brookfield LVT viscometer, the thixotropic index might be taken as the 6 RPM viscosity divided by the 60 RPM viscosity. The higher this number, the greater the shear thinning properties of the system.

7/88   1/8

INCORPORATION

When incorporating Millithix 925 into a resin, it is necessary that the powder be wetted and swollen by the resin to form agglomerates of primary particles and resin. These agglomerates must then be broken down to the primary rheologically active particles and dispersed uniformly throughout the resin. This is accomplished by the application of high shear mixing over a period of time (Figure 2).

Figure 2

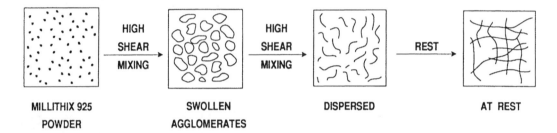

| MILLITHIX 925 POWDER | SWOLLEN AGGLOMERATES | DISPERSED | AT REST |

After the high shear mixing has been discontinued and the system allowed to rest, the three-dimensional network is formed which imparts to the system its thixotropic characteristics.

As with most thixotropes, the viscosity and thixotropic index which one obtains is dependent on a number of factors. These factors include time and intensity of mixing, the composition of the resin system, and the presence of any materials which might act as dispersing agents in general. Increasing the time and intensity of mixing increases the degree of dispersion of the thixotropic additive and therefore lowers the viscosity of the system (see Figure 3). Table 1 shows the effect of increasing concentration and increasing degree of dispersion on the viscosity of a vinyl ester resin containing Millithix 925.

7/88 ® Registered Trademark of Milliken & Company

TABLE 1

Viscosity Versus Concentration And Mixing Time In A Bisphenol A Type Vinyl Ester Resin

Sample	Concentration	Viscosity, CPS LVT #3 @ 6 RPM
A	0.3%	3800
B	0.4%	6900
C	0.4%	4140
D	0.4%	1720

A,B—Cowles Dissolver, 300 RPM, 15 min.
C—Cowles Dissolver, 3000 RPM, 30 min.
D—Cowles Dissolver, 3000 RPM, 60 min.

Figure 3.

WETTING SWELLING — DISPERSION / FLOCCULATION — DISPERSION / FLOCCULATION

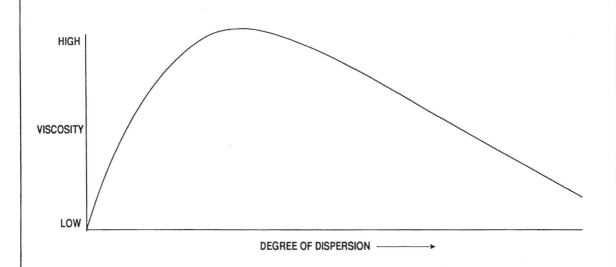

The inclusion of dispersing agents or polar activators such as glycols or glycerin also lower the viscosities obtained with Millithix 925 by increasing the degree of dispersion and interfering with the formation of the three-dimensional network. Their use is not recommended.

Due to its organic nature, Millithix 925 has some limited solubility in resin systems. Its solubility is highly dependent on temperature. Subjecting Millithix 925 to excess temperature during incorporation may result in particle solubilization of the material in the resin. On cooling, this dissolved material comes back out of solution as swollen agglomerates and results in a semi-solid or gel-like resin consistency. This material can be converted back to a smooth, thixotropic liquid by re-dispersion with a high shear mixer (Figure 4).

Figure 4.

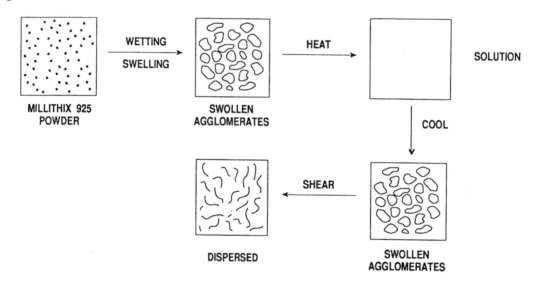

This situation can generally be avoided by keeping the temperature during incorporation below 40°C (104°F).

PERFORMANCE

Figure 5 and Table 2 show the performance of Millithix 925 in a typical Bisphenol A based vinyl ester resin (45% Styrene). The Millithix 925 was incorporated by stirring the powder into the resin and then mixing with a Cowles Dissolver (1.75 inch diameter blade) at 3000 RPM for 30 minutes at 25°C.

Figure 5.

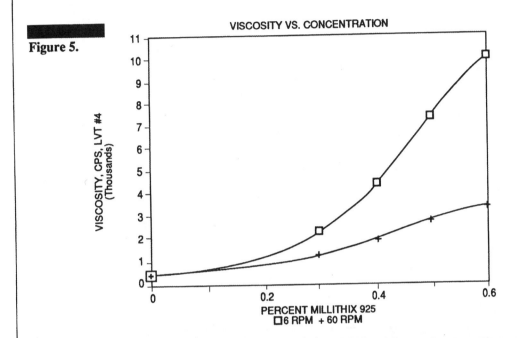

TABLE 2

Viscosity Vs. Concentration In A Bisphenol Based Vinyl Ester Resin

Concentration	Viscosity, 6 RPM	CPS. LVT #4 60 RPM	Thix Index
0	468	500	—
0.3	2400	1310	1.8
0.4	4400	2170	2.0
0.5	7700	2890	2.7
0.6	10500	3500	3.0

It should be noted again that increased mixing intensity and time will result in a lower viscosity and thixotropic index.

7/88   5/8

An alternate method for the incorporation of Millithix 925 involves the use of Millithix 925 as a 25 percent solution in N-Methylpyrrolidone. The advantage of using this solution is that the wetting and swelling step in the incorporation process is for the most part by-passed. After addition, the Millithix 925 is present in the resin in the form of swollen agglomerates which require significantly less energy to properly disperse. Figure 6 and Table 3 show the performance of Millithix 925 in a typical Bisphenol based vinyl ester resin (45% Styrene) when used as a 25 percent solution in N-Methylpyrrolidone. This liquid form makes incorporation easier in situations where high intensity mixing is not available.

Figure 6.

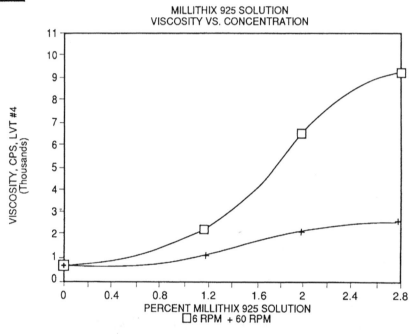

TABLE 3

Viscosity Vs. Concentration Of Millithix 925 In A Typical Vinyl Ester Resin

Viscosity, CPS LVT #4

Concentration of Millithix 925 Solution	6RPM	60RPM	Thix Index
0%	500	500	—
1.2%	2300	1090	2.1
2.0%	6700	2290	2.9
2.8%	9100	2680	3.4

 7/88 ® Registered Trademark of Milliken & Company

The use of Millithix 925 as a powder or as a solution does not significantly effect the cure of vinyl ester resins as demonstrated by the data in Table 4.

TABLE 4

*Gel Times In Vinyl Ester

Additive	Gel Time	Peak Exotherm	Time To Peak Exotherm
NONE	35 Min.	196°F	77 Min.
0.4% M-925	34 Min.	197°F	75 Min.
1.6% M-925/NMP	35 Min.	182°F	83 Min.
0.75% M-925	35 Min.	189°F	73 Min.
3.0% M-925/NMP	36 Min.	178°F	86 Min.
1.0% M-925	36 Min.	195°F	80 Min.
4.0% M-925/NMP	39 Min.	180°F	85 Min.

M-925 = Millithix 925
M-925/NMP = 10:25 PM 925 in N-Methylpyrrolidone
*@ 0.5% Dimethyl Aniline, 0.75% Methyl Ethyl Ketone, 0.2% Cobalt Napthenate.

Certainly the most outstanding property of vinyl ester resins is their ability to withstand an attack by corrosive materials. It is important that any additive used in these resins not diminish this very important property. Due to the organic nature of Millithix 925 and the fact that it can be used in very small amounts, Millithix 925 has no significant effect on the corrosion properties of vinyl ester resins. Table 5 shows a comparison of the weight gain over time between a typical Bisphenol A based vinyl ester resin containing no Millithix 925 and Millithix 925 in a 25% solution with N-Methylpyrrolidone.

TABLE 5

Millithix 925
Corrosion Performance
0.4% in Bisphenol A Type
Vinyl Ester Resin

	% WEIGHT GAIN	REFLUXING WATER	REFLUXING 4% NaOH	REFLUXING 20% HCl	NaOCl @ 150° F
CONTROL	1 Week	1.06	0.76	1.08	0.55
	5 Weeks	1.07	0.80	1.31	0.59
M-925	1 Week	0.93	0.85	1.23	0.54
	5 Weeks	1.00	0.87	1.35	0.60
M-925/NMP	1 Week	0.59	0.67	1.16	0.61
	5 Weeks	0.63	0.68	1.31	0.67

NMP = N-Methylpyrrolidone

Due to the critical importance of the corrosion performance of parts fabricated with vinyl ester resins, it is strongly recommended that formulations containing Millithix 925 or any other additives be tested for their performance in the application for which they are intended. The resin manufacturer's guidelines should be followed and they should be consulted on any questions pertaining to the corrosion performance of these systems.

STORAGE AND HANDLING

When not in use, Millithix 925 should be stored in a closed container in a dry environment away from sources of ignition. When handling, an approved dust mask and eye protection should be worn. As with many other dry powders, a static charge may accumulate during handling. Proper safety precautions should be observed when using around flammable or explosive liquids.

REFERENCE 5

KEVLAR® ARAMID PULP FOR THIXOTROPY AND REINFORCEMENT IN SEALANTS, ADHESIVES AND COATINGS

Arnold Francis - Research Associate
John Dottore - Marketing Representative

E.I. du Pont de Nemours & Company
Textile Fibers Department
Kevlar® Special Products
Sealants and Adhesives Group
Fibers Marketing Center
Wilmington, DE 19898
1-800-441-2637

ABSTRACT

Kevlar® aramid pulp has been shown to be a safe asbestos replacement for thixotropy in sealants, adhesives, and coatings and a more economical alternative to fumed silica. Kevlar® is easily processed and will maintain its thixotropic properties, even under high shear mixing, unlike other thixotropes which break down. Furthermore, its inherent strength and thermal/chemical resistance also impart mechanical reinforcement and wear resistance to various resin systems over a wide range of temperatures and service conditions.

INTRODUCTION

Today's sealants, adhesives, and coatings must perform under a wide range of loads and environmental conditions. In addition, these compounds must be cost effective, safe to handle and process well. A number of materials have been used for thixotropy and reinforcement in resin systems. These include asbestos and fumed silica. With the health hazards associated with asbestos and government action threatening the availability of future supply, many manufacturers are using substitutes to produce asbestos-free products. Fumed silica also has its limitations, which will be discussed.

BACKGROUND

Kevlar® aramid fiber was commercially introduced by Du Pont in 1972 as a continuous filament reinforcement for tires and mechanical rubber goods. With strength six times that of steel on a pound-for-pound basis, and other excellent mechanical properties, Kevlar® was soon being designed for applications in bullet resistant vests, ropes, and advanced composites for the aircraft and aerospace industries.

The structure of Kevlar® is unique in that it is an organic fiber that is crystalline with a high degree of orientation. Kevlar® pulp is produced by fracturing this crystalline structure. Pulp products are very short, highly fibrillated fibers available in wet or dry forms. Figure 1 shows Kevlar® pulp. Figure 2 shows the degree of fibrillation or "hairy" nature of the pulp. It is this combination of high surface area and degree of fibrillation that gives the pulp its unique reinforcing properties. These properties, along with the excellent thermal and chemical resistance of the fiber (Kevlar® does not shrink or melt and has a degradation temperature around 500°C) led to its use as an asbestos replacement in a number of applications. These include: friction products (such as brakes and clutch facings), gaskets and rocket motor insulation. Kevlar® pulp has also been used commercially as a thixotrope and reinforcement in various sealants and adhesives.

With the growing trade interest in Kevlar® pulp for sealants and adhesives, we set out to better understand the merits of Kevlar® pulp for these applications. Our primary focus was to establish its effectiveness as a thixotrope in various resins. In

Figure 1
Kevlar® Aramid Pulp

Figure 2
Kevlar® Aramid Pulp
(magnified)

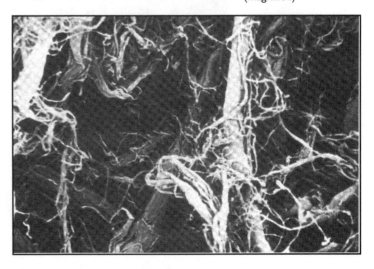

addition, we have begun to investigate whether the addition of Kevlar® will improve bond strength, tear strength and/or wear resistance.

THIXOTROPY

We've found the term thixotropy or thixotrope to mean different things to different people. These interpretations include:

1) a material that only thickens a fluid,

2) more often, the definition of pseuoplasticity — a material that thickens and also shear thins, independent of time, or

3) the true definition of a thixotropic fluid, which is one that shear thins like a pseudoplastic material, but exhibits a time dependency. Upon removal of shear, a thixotropic fluid exhibits a time lag in regaining its viscosity. This phenomenon is described in Figures 3a and 3b. The area between the curves in Figure 3a is a measure of the fluid's thixotropy.

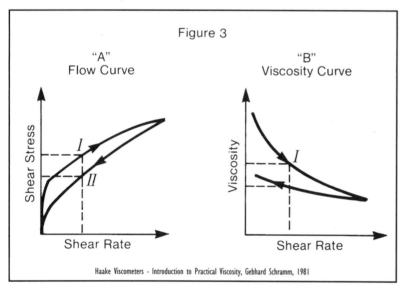

Figure 3

"A" Flow Curve

"B" Viscosity Curve

Haake Viscometers - Introduction to Practical Viscosity, Gebhard Schramm, 1981

In the sealants and adhesive industry, the primary need is for a pseudoplastic material which will be viscous at low shear for "sag" or "slump" resistance and thin under high shear so that it can easily be pumped or even sprayed. To conform to common industry usage, we will refer to this description as thixotropy and any additive which imparts this behavior will be called a thixotrope.

To evaluate Kevlar® pulp as a thixotrope, we blended it into an epoxy and studied its rheology. The pure epoxy resin and the epoxy with fumed silica were tested as controls. Due to the health hazards associated with asbestos, we did not evaluate it as a thixotrope. We tested Kevlar® in a number of sealants and adhesives including: epoxy, neoprene, PVC plastisol, asphalt, polybutadiene, polyurethane, and silicone. Our findings were similar for all the resins tested, but for this report we will concentrate on the epoxy and briefly mention some of the others where appropriate.

Initially, we selected 1.5 wt. % Kevlar® and 4.9 wt. % fumed silica to put both materials on an equal cost basis. Figure 4

shows how much more effective Kevlar® pulp is than fumed silica at building viscosity.

To quantify these differences in viscosity and to determine the extent to which these materials shear thin, we measured the viscosity as a function of shear rate (Figure 5). Since shear rate, in reciprocal seconds, is something not too many people can relate to, we included some processing conditions to help put this in better perspective. Specifically, the very low shear rates are typical for gravitational sag or drip, whereas the highest shear rates are typical of those encountered in a spraying application. As shown in Figure 5, the pure epoxy is Newtonian (no shear dependence) with a viscosity of about 11,000 centipoise (cp). Adding 4.9% fumed silica to the epoxy increased its viscosity at low shear to about 300,000 cp. However, adding only 1.5% Kevlar® pulp, or an amount equal in cost to the 4.9% fumed silica, increased the viscosity at low shear to 4,000,000 cp — over a tenfold increase with about one-third the amount of thixotrope.

In addition to high viscosity at low shear for "sag" or "slump" resistance, these materials are very often metered and even sprayed. Therefore, it is important that the viscosity be low at high shear to permit easy handling and application. Looking again at Figure 5, we see that the viscosity of the epoxy with fumed silica thins to about 25,000 cp at a shear rate of 10^3 sec[1]. Although the epoxy with Kevlar® has a viscosity at low shear that is more than 10 times greater than the epoxy with fumed silica, it thins under shear to a much greater extent that the epoxy with fumed silica. This results in a viscosity of 14,000 cp or almost as low as that of the epoxy with no thixotrope. This combination of high viscosity at low shear and low viscosity at high shear, we feel, is remarkable and certainly cost effective.

Up to this point, we have compared the merits of Kevlar® to those of fumed silica on an equal cost basis. We will now investigate how little Kevlar® is actually

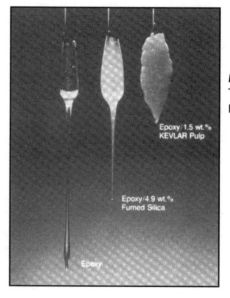

Figure 4
Thixotropy with Kevlar® Aramid Pulp

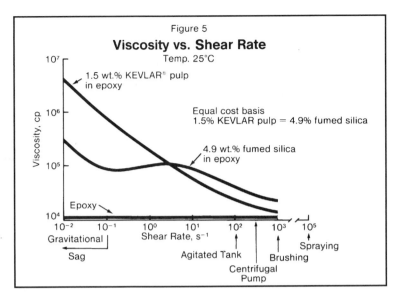

Figure 5
Viscosity vs. Shear Rate
Temp. 25°C

400°C. For this study, we investigated its effectiveness as a thixotrope in an epoxy from 5°C to 95°C. The results are very similar to those at 25°C.

The epoxy by itself is Newtonian at all temperatures with a viscosity as low as 25 cp at 95°C to just over 500,000 cp at 5°C. Both the Kevlar® pulp and fumed silica were shown to be more effective thixotropes at higher temperatures. Where the viscosity of the epoxy dropped rapidly with temperature, the drop was much less pronounced when filled with a thixotrope. Likewise, the shear thinning effect was more dramatic at high temperature as the viscosity of the reinforced epoxy always approached that of the pure epoxy which was, of course, lower at higher temperatures. However, for all the temperatures tested, 1.5% Kevlar® pulp was always more effective at building viscosity than the 4.9% fumed silica. Similarly, over the entire temperature range, the epoxy with Kevlar® thinned under shear to a greater extent than the corresponding sample with

needed (and therefore how cost effective it is) to match the performance imparted by the fumed silica. We again used the epoxy with 4.9% fumed silica and tried to match its viscosity at low shear with Kevlar® pulp. As shown in Figure 6, about 0.3% Kevlar® pulp will match the viscosity of the fumed silica. This translates to ~1/5 the cost, or an 80% savings, versus the fumed silica. To verify this, we tested these samples using the ASTM D-2202 Slump Test and found the epoxy with 0.3% Kevlar® pulp to actually sag less than the epoxy with 4.9% fumed silica. These findings are summarized in Table 1. Also, with only 0.3% Kevlar®, the epoxy's viscosity at high shear is as low as that of the pure epoxy (and considerably lower than that of the epoxy with fumed silica) which makes it very easy to pump or spray.

So far, all the data reported have been from samples run at 25°C. Certainly most applications are not run in controlled environments, but rather over a wide range of temperatures. Kevlar® itself has been shown to be unaffected at cryogenic temperatures and can perform as high as

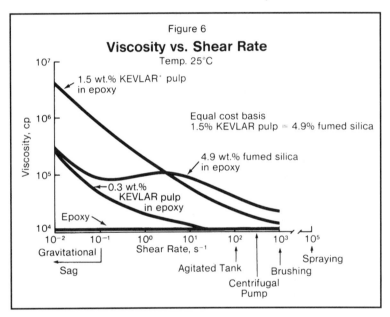

Figure 6
Viscosity vs. Shear Rate
Temp. 25°C

fumed silica. Viscosity versus shear rate curves have been generated over this temperature range and are similar to that of 25°C. To get a better perspective over this temperature range, we've plotted the viscosities at both low and high shear rates as a function of temperature. These are summarized in Figures 7 and 8.

We have also looked at Kevlar® pulp in various resins and found the results to be similar to epoxy. These included: neoprene, PVC plastisol, polyurethane, silicone, asphalt, and polybutadiene sealants and adhesives.

REINFORCEMENT

Kevlar® pulp is not a particulate thixotrope. Instead, it is a high performance engineered short fiber which reinforces the matrix in which it is compounded. Reinforcement in sealants and adhesives is an area where we are just

Table 1

Slump Test* for Epoxy with KEVLAR® Pulp and Fumed Silica

Time to Traverse 4 Inches

Sample	Min:Sec
100% epoxy	:10
Epoxy with 4.9% fumed silica	:23
Epoxy with 0.3% KEVLAR pulp	:28
Epoxy with 0.6% KEVLAR pulp	2:10
Epoxy with 0.9% KEVLAR pulp	8:30
Epoxy with 1.5% KEVLAR pulp	23:00

*ASTM D-2202

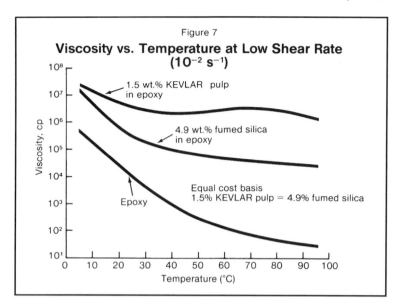

Figure 7

Viscosity vs. Temperature at Low Shear Rate
(10⁻² s⁻¹)

We began testing the effect of Kevlar® pulp on the bond strength in epoxy, plastisol, neoprene, and silicone adhesives to various substrates including: steel, aluminum, glass and plywood. The results were mixed and probably too early to detail, but generally, we concluded that the addition of Kevlar® can greatly improve the bond strength if the failure is cohesive (within the resin itself). However, if the failure is adhesive (at the interface between the adhesive and the substrate), the addition of Kevlar® will have no effect to a slight reduction in bond strength.

In summary, Kevlar® pulp can be used to reinforce a resin but care should be taken in designing the overall system. If the inherent strength of the adhesive is greater than that of the substrate it is bonding, or stronger than the adhesive forces between the substrate and resin, the addition of a reinforcement cannot help.

beginning to investigate the merits of Kevlar® pulp and will be the subject for a detailed study in the future. However, we have made some preliminary measurements to get an indication of what the addition of Kevlar® to a sealant or adhesive can offer in terms of reinforcement.

Kevlar® pulp was compounded into a PVC plastisol adhesive, a silicone sealant, and a castable polyurethane, and tested for reinforcement. We found that 2.5 wt. % Kevlar® pulp greatly improved the tensile and tear strengths of the silicone and plastisol and the magnitude of this improvement was generally more pronounced at elevated temperature. These results are summarized in Table 2. We also found that just 0.71% Kevlar® pulp added to a castable polyurethane about doubled its tear resistance and tripled its abrasion resistance. These results are given in Table 3. It is of particular interest that the wear resistance of urethanes can be improved by adding Kevlar®, since they are inherently wear resistant and used in many applications where wear is of concern.

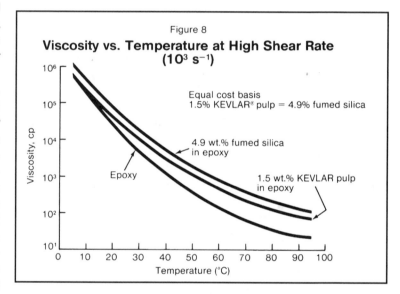

Figure 8

Viscosity vs. Temperature at High Shear Rate
(10³ s⁻¹)

PROCESSING TECHNIQUES

The final performance of a sealant or adhesive can vary with changes in processing depending upon the thixotrope used. Kevlar® pulp is extremely tough and will not break down or be reduced to dust by mixing. The thixotropic properties derived from Kevlar® pulp are dependent upon its physical structure. Consequently, the viscosity control Kevlar® pulp offers is not affected by the processing conditions, including shear, to which it is subjected. We feel this characteristic is important for product performance and quality control.

Asbestos, on the other hand, is reported to be a more brittle, inorganic fiber which can be broken down during processing. Any change in fiber length should result in a less effective thixotrope.

Likewise, the thixotropic nature of a resin filled with fumed silica is extremely dependent upon the amount

Table 2

Increased Tensile and Tear Strengths with KEVLAR® Pulp

Plastisol

% Pulp	Tensile 20°C	Tensile 75°C	Tear 20°C	Tear 75°C
0	1.0	1.0	1.0	1.0
2.5	2.6	4.3	4.6	3.1

Silicone

% Pulp	Tensile 20°C	Tensile 200°C	Tear 20°C	Tear 200°C
0	1.0	1.0	1.0	1.0
2.5	2.4	2.8	3.7	5.0

In all cases, the control was normalized to 1.0 and the test sample was calculated as a ratio to the control of shear that it sees. Apparently, the fumed silica particles will form branches which resist flow and therefore build viscosity. As these branches are broken under shear, the fluid will thin as shown earlier, in Figure 5. We find, however, that after the shear is removed, the thixotropic nature of the fluid does not return to its original state. This is depicted in Figure 9. Here we've taken the same epoxy samples reinforced with Kevlar® and fumed silica described in Figure 5, and subjected them to a relatively high shear rate by agitation in a "Waring" blender at 12,000 RPM for four and seven minutes. The viscosity curve for the epoxy with Kevlar® is unchanged, while there are dramatic changes for the epoxy/fumed silica curves. The viscosity enhancement offered by the fumed silica is greatly reduced after shear, which results in a fluid much more prone to "sag" or "slump."

Because Kevlar® pulp is so tough, however, it is more difficult to disperse than asbestos and fumed silica. High shear mixing or pre-opening of the fiber is usually required to obtain a uniform dispersion. We've found equipment typical to the industry, such as Double Planetary Change-Can Mixer*, to do a good job in dispersing the pulp. Likewise, good fiber dispersion can be obtained by mixing with an agitator in a tank, but this usually requires a high speed agitator with sharp blades. If the fiber is not uniformly dispersed, improvements can be obtained with a Fiber Processor**, which pre-opens and feeds pulp to a mixer which would not otherwise disperse pulp acceptably. This device is particularly well suited for in-line processing.

Table 3

Polyurethane Reinforcement with KEVLAR® Pulp

% Pulp	Tear Strength	Wear Resistance
0	1.0	1.0
0.71	1.8	2.9

The control was normalized to 1.0 and the test sample was calculated as a ratio to the control

Trouser tear strength and NBS Abrasion Index

SUMMARY AND CONCLUSIONS

We have introduced Kevlar® aramid pulp as a new high performance thixotrope. It is a safe alternative to asbestos, and costs less to use than fumed silica. It is exceptionally effective at building viscosity, yet shear thins to a viscosity almost as low as the resin with no thixotrope. Its rheological properties span a wide temperature range and are unaffected by processing conditions. This is also a product that can offer significant reinforcement to most resins.

ACKNOWLEDGEMENTS

The authors wish to thank their co-workers, R.H. Hayes and N.M. Gopez for technical and experimental assistance, and N.M. Banack for typing the manuscript.

Figure 9

Effect of Agitation on Viscosity
Temp. 25°C

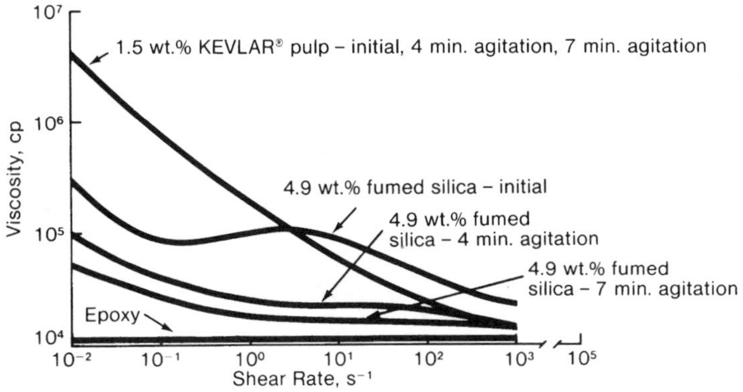

12,000 RPM in "Waring" 700 Blender

* Charles Ross & Son Company, P.O. Box 12308, Hauppage, NY 11788-0615 • 516-234-0500

**Fiber Technologies, Inc., 5710 Shadyhollow Lane, Cincinnati, OH 45230 • 513-232-4479

REFERENCE 6

PulPlus TA-12

POLYETHYLENE

TECHNICAL DATA

PulPlus TA-12 POLYETHYLENE PULP IS THE IDEAL REINFORCING THIXOTROPE

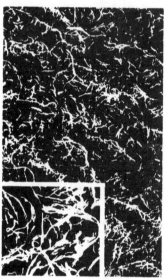

50x Magnification of PulPlus
(inset 200x Magnification)

Pulplus is an excellent thickener for paints, adhesives, mortars, mastics, caulks and coatings, but maintains an ease of application comparable to the un-thickened products. For example, at 0.5% incorporation of TA-12 into an epoxy mix, viscosity in the low shear "gravitational sag" region is increased substantially. In contrast, a competitive thixotrope, fumed silica, exhibited substantially less viscosity increase at double the incorporation.

In addition to acting as a thickening agent, Pulplus TA-12 has an especially engineered morphology that provides crack-stopping and reinforcement in the final cured products. Because TA-12 is an oleophilic material with a hydrophilic surface treatment, it disperses well in both aqueous and non-aqueous media. It is not recommended for high temperature applications.

YOU GET THE PROPERTIES YOU NEED:

- Better thixotropy
- Easy dispersion
- Good chemical resistance
- Increased tensile strength and modulus
- Increased tear strength
- Easily processed
- Environmentally safe
- Cost effective

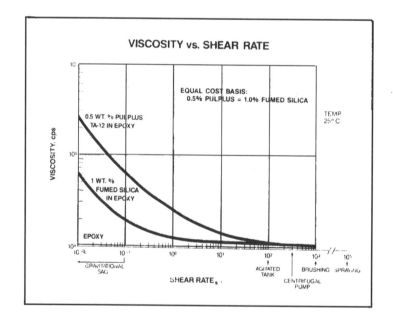

VISCOSITY vs. SHEAR RATE

EQUAL COST BASIS:
0.5% PULPLUS = 1.0% FUMED SILICA

TEMP 25° C

0.5 WT. % PULPLUS TA-12 IN EPOXY

1 WT. % FUMED SILICA IN EPOXY

EPOXY

GRAVITATIONAL SAG

AGITATED TANK

CENTRIFUGAL PUMP

BRUSHING SPRAYING

SHEAR RATE

Pulplus TA-12
POLYETHYLENE

Product Properties

BASE RESIN

Type	Linear High Density Polyethylene
Density, gm/cc	0.96
Melting Point, °C	134-138[1]
Chemical Reactivity	Inert[2]

PULP

Length, mm	0.8-1.0[3]
Diameter, Microns	1-20
Surface Area, M^2/gm (BET, N$_2$)	3-4
Surface Behavior	Hydrophilic[4]
Zero Span Strength, gm	22-25[5]

PROPERTY RETENTION[6]

	@ 80°C	@ 100°C
Tenacity	100%	75%
Modulus	56%	50%
Work-to-Break	380%	230%

[1] DSC peak at 10°C/min heating rate
[2] Swells in chlorinated hydrocarbons
[3] Tasman, TAPPI, Vol 55 #1, p. 136
[4] Treated for wettability and adhesion
[5] TAPPI 231 SU-70
[6] % of room temperature filament properties on yarns spun from the base resin.

OUTSIDE U.S.A.
Contact your local
Du Pont Representative

IN U.S.A.
Du Pont Company
Textile Fibers Department
Pulplus
Sealants & Adhesives Group
Fibers Marketing Center
Wilmington, DE 19898
1-800-441-2637

E-9?370-1

Printed in U.S.A.

REFERENCE 7

FIBERFRAX® ENGINEERED FIBERS

HS - 95C

Fiberfrax® HS-95C ceramic fiber has been specially engineered to be a thixotrope with structural benefits. HS-95C functions as a mechanical thixotrope which modifies the flow properties of the resin, producing similar viscosity properties to conventional thixotropes typically at equal or lower loading levels. HS-95C has been modified to improve its sprayability in unfiltered systems.

These ceramic fibers offer the following unique and outstanding properties:
- Excellent high temperature stability
- Good strength and high modulus
- Low coefficient of thermal expansion (9.3×10^{-7} in/in/°F)
- Superior chemical resistance
- Very low moisture absorption

The thixotropic properties of the HS-95C fiber in conjunction with the mechanical and physical properties it has to offer make it an excellent candidate for use in high performance coatings, caulks, sealants and adhesives. The fibrous nature of Fiberfrax® fibers impart improved strength to formulations. The reinforcement capabilities of the HS-95C fiber are maximized since the high fiber index significantly increases the number of fibers per pound. In applications such as thick film coatings, the reinforcement it offers can minimize or eliminate cracking.

TYPICAL PHYSICAL PROPERTIES

Color	White to Light Gray
Melting Point	3160°F (1738°C)
Fiber Index	95
Fiber Diameter	1.0 - 1.6 microns (mean)
Fiber Length	100 - 200 microns (Avg)
Specific Gravity	2.73 g/cu m
Tensile Strength	2.5×10^5 psi
Modulus	$13 - 15 \times 10^6$ psi

TYPICAL APPLICATIONS

Fiberfrax HS-95C ceramic fiber provides many advantages to compounders and formulators of high performance coatings, caulks, sealants and adhesives. The advantages of formulating with Fiberfrax® HS-95C include:

- High viscosity build at low loadings
- Reinforcement
- Superior wear resistance
- Superior corrosion resistance
- High temperature stability
- Good moisture resistance
- Improved sprayability

In addition in adhesives, Fiberfrax® HS-95C fiber offers:

- Improved peel strength
- Improved lap shear

CHEMICAL PROPERTIES

Fiberfrax® HS-95C fiber exhibits excellent resistance to attack from most corrosive agents. Its chemical resistance is superior to mineral fibers and many other reinforcements and fillers. Contact with hydrofluoric acid, phosphoric acid and strong alkalies should be avoided. Fiberfrax® HS-95C fiber contains very limited water of hydration and effectively resists oxidation and reduction.

CARBORUNDUM

The Carborundum Company
Fibers Division
P.O. Box 808
Niagara Falls, New York 14302-0808
Telephone 716 278-6221
Telex 68-54335
Cable (Foreign) Crboinuw

REFERENCE 8

PRIMARY AND SECONDARY INTER-LAMINAR BINDING

COMMENTARY

by John A. Wills

Three types of bonding occur between any two layers when laminating with reinforced resins.

1. A Primary Bond is generally thought to be a "chemical" one; *e.g.,* the resins from both surfaces are able to intermingle physically as if they were from the same batch. This is what is meant by the phrase, "wet-on-wet." Since this is rarely possible on large moldings, the next best primary bond is thought to be formed when a second layer of resin is applied just after the substrate resin surface had gelled and cooled past its exotherm.

2. A Secondary Bond is usually called a "mechanical" or "glued" bond between one chemically inactive surface — the substrate to which a chemically active layer is being applied — and the other. This is the type of bond most usually experienced, particularly with large moldings. This form of bond is generally considered inferior to a so-called primary bond. I do not completely agree with this concept; I will expand on this later.

3. There is a Gray Area between pure chemical bonding and mechanical bonding. The latter is by far the most common by the accepted definition of mechanical bonding. This is, of course, the process of laminating on top of an "air inhibited" surface. There is no way to avoid this on large moldings and, certainly under the right conditions, it is desired.

The expression "air inhibited" is misleading. Because air is usually the only gas above an open wet lay-up, it becomes the medium to which any volatile material will migrate. To be useful, all ester and acrylic resins contain volatile monomers. When an activator is added to an ester (acrylics are esters too) laminating resin, the amount used for a given temperature (hopefully in stoichiometric amount) on curing is for the correct resin-monomer mix. Because monomer is continuously lost on the air side of any laminate until resin gel, an imbalance of monomer and base resin will occur. If only a simple imbalance of base resin-to-monomer happened — as when the gas over the surface is inert, for example — and there was no chemical reaction which would be caused by the oxygen in the air, this would be ideal because sufficient extra monomer would be "donated" from the subsequent batch of resin to accomplish a near perfect chemical bond. Rarely does this condition occur in real practice.

The degree of successful inter-laminar bond will depend upon what is in the air surrounding the open lay-up, and the time between gel and next lay-up. The most serious offender to bonding (and later, hydrolytic attack) is moisture. Dr. Thomas Rockett, co-author of the URI Reports included in the text, claims that a polystyrene layer is formed from the reaction with styrene monomer and water vapor from the air.

He calls this the "X layer." In his earlier URI Report, he states that resin at the surface of a curing laminate reacts with "air" to form benzaldehyde. I have to assume he means the reaction to form benzaldehyde occurred between the resin and/or monomer and oxygen in the air. Benzaldehyde is only slightly soluble in water but enough so to be considered a contaminate which may contribute to osmosis.

The most accepted view of the reaction of oxygen and the resin or monomer is the production of a carbonate which is quite soluble in water and could contribute to osmosis.

Besides oxygen and moisture from the air, usually most shop particulates do not contribute to poor bond unless excessive amounts are deposited. They may, however, contribute to osmosis. Water (moisture vapor) is clearly the most serious culprit involved in poor inter-laminar bond. The scum formed by water may be polystyrene, a carbonate, or just a type of non-curable emulsion, but they will interfere with good adhesive bonding.

It would be difficult to control the presence of oxygen in the air surrounding the molding, but moisture vapor content is controllable. The problem can be reduced or eliminated if molding rooms are humidity controlled. If the factory is in Arizona in July the humidity problem is pretty well taken care of — some factories are in Arizona for this reason.

To achieve some sort of practical inter-laminar chemical bonding, cover sheets, wax additives, styrene suppressants, peel ply or film-forming mold releases must not be used. A quality-controlled imbalance of base resin to monomer must be allowed for at the air surface and in the least practical time.

Let's take another look at the term "secondary bonding." If all that is meant by this phrase is that two laminates are attached by mechanical means only, then the term must be re-defined. Even the term "gluing" is somehow inferred as inferior.

Mechanical Bonding. This is assumed to mean attachment of two surfaces by interlocking. Velcro is a good example.

Adhesive Bonding. This is a state where two surfaces are held together by inter-facial forces which may consist of valence (electron) forces. Besides mechanical surface preparation, the use of coupling agents (often called "primers") provide proper polarity orientation and result in chemisorption.

Secondary Bonding. By my definition, this implies laminating a liquid resin to a solid, properly prepared substrate. If we are talking about applying glass fabric and resin to a steel hull, the optimum would be a sandblasted metal surface to gray metal where temporarily, the steel surface is in a polar condition. A silane coupling agent (see text) would be applied followed by a coat of high elongation vinylester resin and, as soon as possible, an application of suitable resin and reinforcement. This will achieve a true adhesive bond as well as some mechanical interlocking at the metal-resin interface.

Where multiple laminations must be applied and the surface of each, of necessity, has been cured for a long period of time as in large hull construction, then we are dealing with a solid substrate (but non-polar) much like non-sandblasted metal. This is where the addition of a coupling agent to the resin which will be used next to the substrate is of great value in creating an adhesive bond.

There has been a lot of speculation about why some marine products have suffered osmotic and hydrolytic problems where others have not, even with things being apparently equal including workmanship and quality control of materials. My contention is that most of the problems can be traced to high air humidity at the time of molding and improper surface preparation of the substrate and non-use of coupling agents.

Inter-laminar bonding of epoxy resins are affected much in the same way as the esters. Though there is not an emission of monomer to the air, some epoxies (actually their hardeners) do react with air to form carbonates which usually can be removed with water. The same surface preparations — especially the use of couplers in the application of resin over a cured surface and the control of humidity must be followed.

Tie Coats. A tie coat is another term for adhesion. The term also infers the use of a substance acting as a mutually compatible ingredient.

It is accepted that an ester resin will not adhesively bond to an epoxy resin substrate, yet an epoxy resin will adhesively bond to an ester substrate. There are many other resin combinations where adhesive bonding is questionable. A liquid phenolic will not bond at all to a poly- or vinylester substrate and an attempted bond to an epoxy substrate is almost disastrous.

Futura Coatings, Inc.'s Ultrachrome 4000 *(MS 67)* produces a two-component hybrid urethane-polyester resin for use primarily as a substitute gel coat for polyester gel coat, but which works well as a means of bonding virtually any two dissimilar resin substrates — usually where a wet laminate is applied to another fully cured laminate, whether of the same or different resins.

The usual procedure is to spray or brush a thin (0.003–0.010-inch) coat of Ultracoat 4000 to the substrate. After a 25 to 45 minute cure (at 75°F), virtually any laminating resin may be applied over it. I have checked all possible bonds (tie coats) using the screwdriver test on resins such as phenolic, furane, epoxy, vinylester, polyester, and resorcinol formaldehyde. Futura also reports compatibility with polyurethane and hybrid polyester-urethane. (*See also Section III, Reference 35.*)

For further reading on secondary bonding, refer to an article by Bruce Pfund in *Professional Boatbuilder* magazine, page 37, December/January issue 1993.

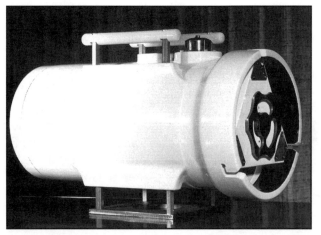

Undersea fiberglass battery housing (deep submergence). Built by author.

REFERENCE 9

REFERENCE 10

DERAKANE Vinyl Ester Resins Outperform Polyesters in Corrosion Resistant FRP

Historically, epoxy resins have demonstrated excellent strength, toughness, and chemical resistance in FRP pipe, but their relatively low reactivity and high viscosity made them difficult to fabricate. However, when an epoxy backbone was combined with vinyl groups (for high reactivity) and styrene monomer (for low viscosity) the chemical resistance and strength of the base epoxy resin was retained while the reactivity and basic handling characteristics were improved. Thus, vinyl ester resins were born.

Traditionally, polyester resins have been used in corrosion resistant (CR) FRP applications. The discussion that follows compares the properties and performance characteristics of the vinyl ester resin with those of two commonly used polyester materials.

This car load of 42" diameter duct, fabricated from DERAKANE 411-45, was installed in Dow's chlor-alkali plant at its Oyster Creek Division (Texas) in 1969 and has been in service ever since. The high chemical resistance of DERAKANE has withstood wet chlorine gas — a strong oxidizing agent — at 190°F temperature for 13 years.

Unique Resin Chemistry Yields Superior Chemical Resistance

Chemical attack on all ester-containing unsaturated resins, such as vinyl ester and polyester resins, will naturally occur at the most reactive sites of their chains — the ester linkages and unreacted (unsaturated) vinyl groups (carbon-to-carbon double bonds). Ester groups are subject to hydrolysis, whereas unreacted carbon-to-carbon double bonds can be split through reactions such as oxidation and halogenation.

In DERAKANE vinyl ester resins, both types of reactive sites are limited to the ends of the molecular chain as shown in Figure 1, p. 5. The absence of ester linkages in the epoxy backbone of DERAKANE vinyl ester resins make them **less susceptible than polyester resins to attack by strong acids such as hydrochloric acid and strong alkalies such as caustic soda.** Those ester linkages that do occur are shielded by methyl groups (see Figure 1) which hinder the hydrolysis of the esters. In comparison, the polyester resins commonly used in CR applications contain two or three times as many ester linkages because such linkages are a critical part of

their backbone. As a result, the **polyester molecule is more susceptible to breakdown through hydrolysis.**

Besides ester linkages, carbon-to-carbon double bonds also occur randomly throughout the bisphenol A-fumaric acid polyester and isophthalic polyester chains as can be seen in Figure 1, and not all of these double bonds react during polymerization. Thus, any unreacted vinyl groups in the finished polyester polymer remain susceptible to chemical attack, particularly through oxidation and halogenation. In DERAKANE vinyl ester resins the unreacted vinyl groups again are exposed only at the ends of the molecular chain where they react more completely on polymerization. The polymerized DERAKANE resin thus has fewer residual reactive sites and a much **more chemically resistant structure.**

This superior chemical resistance makes DERAKANE vinyl ester resins outstanding materials for use in FRP applications designed to handle corrosive environments. For more specific information on the limits of individual resins in specific environments, consult the bulletin, "DERAKANE Vinyl Ester Resins — Chemical Resistance Guide", Form No. 296-320.

DOW CHEMICAL U.S.A.
Midland, Michigan 48640
(MS 23)

Figure 1 — Comparative Molecular Structures

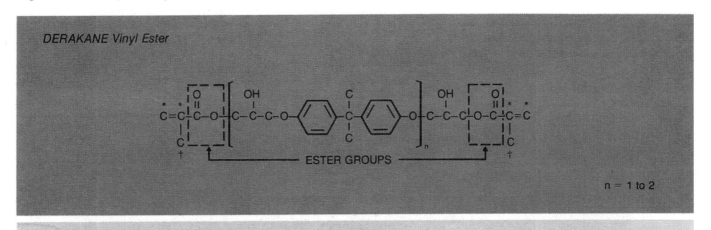

* Denotes reactive sites
† Shielding methyl groups

Outstanding Strength and Toughness

Superior chemical resistance of the resin does not, by itself, make the fabricated FRP composite a valuable construction material. The composite must also successfully contain the chemicals, bear process loads such as pressure and vacuum, and withstand occasional external loads such as wind and earthquake.

The most important fact to remember in designing a chemically resistant FRP structure is that it is a reinforced plastic. In general, the reinforcement provides the strength while the cured resin acts as a chemically resistant barrier for the less-resistant reinforcement. Consequently, the structure can fail when either the reinforcement breaks or the resin "barrier" is damaged by cracking.

continued page 6

Typically, in a glass-reinforced polyester or vinyl ester laminate under stress, the resin will crack before the glass breaks. This has important consequences:

1. The critical stress — maximum amount the laminate can bear without failure — is very dependent on the strength of the resin and its resistance to cracking.

2. Failures are rarely catastrophic. The contained chemical will gradually weep through the damaged resin and become visible on the exterior of the vessel, or cracks will appear on the interior, before the glass in the laminate is sufficiently stressed to break.

Resistance to Cracking Designed Into DERAKANE

Resistance to cracking has been designed into the chemistry of DERAKANE resins. With these resins, crosslinking is confined to the reactive groups located at the ends of the molecule (see Figure 1, p. 5). This leaves the entire length of the molecular chain free to elongate under stress, and thus to absorb mechanical and thermal stress or shocks. By comparison, in polyester resins, reactive vinyl groups are scattered throughout the molecular chain, resulting in more crosslinking and increased brittleness. The difference between these types of molecular chains is apparent in the strength and elongation of clear castings, shown in Table 1.

The combination of superior strength and elongation in DERAKANE vinyl ester resins has an even more dramatic effect on laminate properties. As discussed, ultimate laminate strength is dependent on the glass, but the critical strength is dependent on the resin. This is because, at some point before ultimate failure of an FRP vessel, the resin first develops microcracks, and then visible cracks. When the laminate reaches this critical point (measured in stress or corresponding strain) weeping and strain corrosion begin. This, then, is the true point of failure of an FRP vessel.

The first observation that resin failure occurs at some point before total laminate failure was made while testing 2″ diameter FRP pipe. Before reaching the theoretical burst point (calculated from the glass content and orientation), the pipes were observed to "weep". By using a tougher resin in the pipe, higher weep pressures were obtained. Hence the development of filament wound pipe made with DERAKANE vinyl ester resin — based on the resin's ability to contain chemicals under higher pressure than the typical polyester (see Table 2).

Table 1 — Comparative Properties of Clear Castings

	DERAKANE 411-45 Resin	Typical Bis A Fumarate Polyester Resin	Typical CR Isophthalic Polyester Resin
Tensile Strength, psi	11,000	10,000	9,300
Tensile Modulus	500,000	340,000	520,000
Tensile Elongation, %	4.5	2.5	2.4

Table 2 — Early Comparative Testing of 2″ Diameter Pipe

Resin	Weep (psi)	Burst (psi)	Wall Thickness (inches)
DERAKANE 412-45	2500	3100	.075
Bisphenol A Fumarate Polyester	1400	Did not burst due to excessive weeping	.085

REFERENCE 11

42nd Annual Conference, Composites Institute, The Society of the Plastics Industry, Inc. February 2-6, 1987

DAN A. RUGGEBERG*

A New High Performance Resin for the Marine Industry

ABSTRACT

A new marine laminating resin has been developed which combines a high degree of blister resistance with excellent laminate profile appearance. The performance of this product was compared against that of an isophthalic, an orthophthalic, and a vinyl ester resin.

The testing process involved the evaluation of these resins both with and without fiberglass reinforcement. The non-reinforced specimens were subjected to total immersion in boiling, distilled water for a period of 100 hours, the reinforced specimens to a one-side exposure under the same environment and time period. The test pieces were then examined visually for frequency and severity of blistering, as well as internal and external cracking. Physical testing was also used to characterize the effects of exposure. This included before and after-exposure evaluation of Barcol® hardness and tensile and flexural properties.

Surface profile evaluations were performed on one-quarter-inch thick black gel-coated RP panels exposed to the Florida sunlight for a period of one week. They were then scrutinized for surface smoothness with the aid of a special lightbox.

INTRODUCTION

Several papers have been written and presentations made addressing the subject of blister formation on the hulls of fiberglass boats. Most have focused on the chemical processes occurring at the gel-coat-to-resin interface. It is well known that the water molecule can and does penetrate the gel-coated surface and hydrolysis of the resin in that region is responsible for localized swelling to form blisters.

Although a number of factors are believed to contribute to blistering (fabricating technique, catalyst concentration, etc.), certainly the most important one is resin composition. The fewer the number of unprotected ester and ether linkages in the cured product, the less susceptible it will be to hydrolysis. Thus, water that has seeped into the gel-coat-to-resin interface region may attack the resin of the gel-coat, the back-up resin, or both. The use of a water-resistant gel-coat over a non-water-resistant laminating resin would not be expected to produce much less blistering than the reverse case. Keeping in mind that "water-resistant" primarily means "hydrolysis-resistant" and not "non-water-permeable," it is easy to see why even the use of a hydrolytically stable skincoat between the gel-coat and the back-up laminate may represent only a stop-gap measure. Ultimately, water will penetrate into the back-up laminate and the best protection against further blistering and/or possible structural damage is to fabricate throughout with a water-resistant resin product.

If hydrolytic stability was the only goal in designing a superior marine laminating resin, the job of the resin producer would indeed be easy. However, besides water-resistance, such a product must also take into account other performance objectives, among them surface cosmetics, or "profile."

In the course of attempts to maximize water resistance many resin producers have introduced products which severely compromise the profile appearance. Also true is the reverse case, whereby hydrolytic stability is compromised in favor of a smooth looking surface. The task then, was to design a superior marine resin which combines both of these good qualities into one product.

A newly developed marine resin, Hydrex® 33-250, has been evaluated against other products based on isophthalic acid, orthophthalic anhydride and methacrylated bisphenol-a diglycidyl ether (vinyl ester), which represent the bulk of marine compositions currently in use.

It must be mentioned here that all subject resins were fully promoted and thixed in the manner of conventional marine resins with the exception of the vinyl ester. It was properly promoted, but left unthixed. Vinyl ester resins do not take and hold a thix index with the use of conventional thixotropes at customary levels. Thixotropy is generally achieved through the use of alternative thixotropes which may adversely affect the water resistance and/or physical properties of the product. Thus, a neat vinyl ester was used as the control resin for water-resistance testing, representing the theoretical "best case."

HYDROLYTIC STABILITY

100-Hour Boil as Accelerated Test Method

The question of how one relates accelerated test results to "real life" exposure conditions is well beyond the scope of this paper. Many debate the legitimacy of data obtained using boiling water vs. water at 180°F, 150°F, and so on. As with any developmental program, test methods to be used are chosen based on accuracy and reproducibility combined with expectations of a reasonable data return time. As the water temperature is lowered, the return time lengthens to weeks, then to months. Boiling distilled water has proven to be a reliable and valuable screening tool in this development program in which scores of candidate resin compositions

*Reichhold Chemicals, Inc., 8540 Baycenter Road, Jacksonville, FL 32216.

®Trademark, Reichhold Chemicals, Inc.

had been evaluated, leading to the introduction of this new product.

100-Hour Boil Testing

PREPARATION OF 1/8" THICK CLEAR CASTINGS

The test resins were all promoted with cobalt and catalyzed using a methyl-ethyl-ketone-peroxide catalyst before being poured between glass plates. All were properly cured and post-cured, then cut into 2" × 5" coupons and physical testing specimens. These were vertically suspended in boiling, distilled water for a period of one hundred hours. Testing in this manner allowed for judgment of hydrolytic stability based solely upon resin composition, eliminating the fabricating variables (type of fiberglass, laminating technique, etc.) present in reinforced systems. Boiling distilled water was used as it represented the condition of maximum attack.

SUBJECTIVE EVALUATION, UNREINFORCED

The 2" × 5" coupons were then examined visually and rated for frequency of cracking and blistering. Throughout this paper the new high performance product is labeled "Resin A."

	Resin A	Isophthalic	Orthophthalic	Vinyl Ester
Blistering	0	1	3	0
Cracking	0	1	3	0

0) = none; 1 = slight; 2 = moderate; 3 = severe

Neither the new product, Resin A, nor the vinyl ester showed any signs of blistering or cracking after the exposure period. The isophthalic product did exhibit minor surface blistering and slight "glinting," internal cracking. The orthophthalic was so severely attacked as to be totally opaque, with extensive internal and surface cracking and blistering (Figure 1). All became somewhat cloudy, but this effect has not been related to any other category of performance.

Physical Testing, Unreinforced

The exposed (final) physical testing specimens were evaluated for Barcol hardness, tensile and flexural strength and compared against unexposed (initial) values so that strength-retention figures could be calculated. High retention values, of course, are reflective of minimal hydrolysis.

1/8" Casting Data[1]

	Resin A	Iso	Ortho	Vinyl Ester
Barcol hardness				
initial	34–36	33–35	31–33	34–36
final	33–35	29–31	17–19	33–35
% retention	97	88	56	97
Tensile strength (psi)				
initial	9,937	10,416	9,806	11,020
final	6,920	7,658	1,464	9,000
% retention	70	73	15	82

[1]Test results based on five specimens each.

Tensile modulus (psi × 10⁵)				
initial	5.5	5.6	5.4	5.2
final	4.7	4.9	2.8	4.7
% retention	85	88	52	90
Tensile elongation @ break (%)				
initial	2.6	2.7	2.4	6.2
final	1.5	1.7	0.5	2.2
% retention	58	63	21	35
Flexural strength (psi)				
initial	17,261	17,807	15,290	17,365
final	12,870	12,628	2,258	15,810
% retention	75	71	15	91
Flexural modulus (psi × 10⁵)				
initial	4.8	4.8	4.6	4.6
final	4.6	3.8	2.2	4.4
% retention	96	79	48	96

DISCUSSION OF PHYSICALS, UNREINFORCED

These data show a significant softening of the cured orthophthalic product after exposure. Its much lower retention values illustrate that resins of this composition are quite susceptible to hydrolytic attack, finally resulting in structural weakening.

Resin A, the isophthalic and the vinyl ester all performed admirably in this test, maintaining surface hardness and high strength retention values. The notable exception is the tensile elongation retention of the vinyl ester resin. Had all other retention values been low, this result would not be surprising. However, in this case the values are high, indicating very little hydrolytic attack. Therefore, this could be a result of a post-cure effect as the flexibility diminished over the one hundred hours of exposure to 212°F. This may also mean that this degree of cured resin toughness is a somewhat temporary property over a much greater period of time in actual service conditions.

100-Hour Boil Testing, Reinforced

As another check on hydrolytic stability, laminates of one-quarter-inch thickness were prepared against glass plates using the following laminating schedule:

1. 25 mils thick white gel-coat drawn over a waxed plate, cured at 77°F overnight
2. One ply of a synthetic glass veil laminated over gel-coat at 1:1 weight ratio to the test resin, allowed to gel
3. Fiberglass-to-resin ratio calculated at 40/60 before laminating
   (a) three plies 1.5-oz chopped strand mat
   (b) one ply 24-oz woven roving
   (c) one ply 1.5-oz chopped strand mat
   (d) one ply 24-oz woven roving

Again a MEKP catalyst was used, 2% for resin of the gel-coat, 1.25% for the resin of the laminate. All panels were post-cured before exposure of the gel-coat side to boiling in distilled water for 100 hours. They were then judged for frequency of surface blistering.

SUBJECTIVE EVALUATION, REINFORCED

Figures 2–5 show the effects of exposure on these panels. Below are the results of the subjective evaluation.

	Resin A	Iso	Ortho	Vinyl Ester
Blistering	0	0	3	0

132

Resin A. the isophthalic and the vinyl ester panels all endured the one-hundred-hour test period showing no blistering. The orthophthalic panel began blistering in under 24 hours. The blisters continued to grow and swell, reaching diameters as great as one inch.

Physical Testing, Reinforced

Following are the physical testing data obtained on the one-quarter-inch thick panels prepared as previously described:

1 4″ Laminate Data[1]

	Resin A	Iso	Ortho	Vinyl Ester
Barcol hardness (gel-coat side)				
initial	49–53	44–45	46–51	45–50
final	30–38	24–30	8–12	36–41
% retention	67	61	21	80
Tensile strength (psi)				
initial	19.900	18.300	20,680	20,650
final	13.140	14,880	11,480	13,540
% retention	66	81	55	65
Tensile modulus (psi $\times$ 10⁵)				
initial	20.6	17.1	18.6	20.3
final	16.8	18.9	15.2	17.8
% retention	82	110	82	88
Tensile elongation @ break (%)				
initial	1.6	1.5	1.6	1.5
final	0.8	0.8	0.6	0.9
% retention	50	53	38	60
Flexural strength (psi)				
initial	51,200	59,500	46,540	41,800
final	42,360	58,400	27,600	42,225
% retention	83	98	59	101
Flexural modulus (psi $\times$ 10⁵)				
initial	15.2	28.6	13.0	12.7
final	13.8	28.5	9.8	12.2
% retention	91	99	75	96
% Fiberglass	39	38.1	38.2	37.8

DISCUSSION OF PHYSICALS, REINFORCED

All panels suffered some surface softening as reflected in the Barcol hardness values. Resin A. the isophthalic and the control resin maintained generally high strength-retention values, indicating minor hydrolytic attack. The categorically lower retention values of the orthophthalic system are suggestive of greater structural weakening.

The isophthalic resin with its higher flexural strength value seemed to provide an inordinately high flexural modulus in this trial. The reason is not known.

The physical property-masking effect of the fiberglass reinforcement alluded to earlier is most evident in the tensile elongation figures. Comparing the values obtained on the clear casting specimens against those of the laminates, one sees that the effect of the reinforcement is virtually to equate all systems. This is due to the fact that the fiberglass itself has a tensile elongation of approximately 1.5 percent and therefore represents the weakest link in the system with respect to that particular property.

PROFILE

The term "profile" simply refers to the surface smoothness of a cured RP composite. Several fiberglass reinforcements, woven-roving chief among them, have a tendency to "telescope" their patterns up through the composite to its surface, creating a rough and undesirable appearance. This process is accelerated upon post-curing with heat and/or ultraviolet light. As with hydrolytic stability, resin composition is a major factor in controlling surface appearance.

Importance of Profile

This is a very critical resin property to boat manufacturers Unlike other resin properties. the surface quality that a fabricato achieves is not usually immediately apparent upon demolding o the hull or other part. Only after a period of exposure to the hea and sunlight can he finally judge its profile. A poor profile ma mean loss of sales and/or costly repairs.

Preparation of Profile Panels

In order to compare surface smoothness of panels made with the test resins the following procedure was used:

1. 25 mils-thick black gel-coat was applied to glass plate
2. 6″ × 12″ laminates were applied over the cured gel-coat using the same fiberglass schedule as was used in the boil testing mentioned earlier
3. all laminates were cured at 77°F for three days
4. all were placed on outdoor rack at a 45-degree angle to the horizon facing South into the Florida sun, in July, for a one week period

During the outdoor exposure, the average daily high temperature was 93°F. Black gel-coated panels thus exposed are known to reach surface temperatures in excess of 150°F.

Evaluation of Profile

Each was then subjectively evaluated with the aid of a special lightbox commonly used to judge surface smoothness on press-molded automotive test panels. The lightbox consists of a bank of fluorescent lights mounted at the back of a shallow wooden box whose face is covered by a glass plate. The outward face of the plate is cross-hatched with a series of parallel vertical and horizontal lines spaced one inch apart. When the light bank is turned on, the grid pattern of the glass plate is allowed to reflect from the surface of the panel. The surface profile is then subjectively judged by the sharpness of the reflected grid pattern. A panel of excellent profile would produce a reflection approaching that of a mirror-image of the grid, while one of poor profile would reflect a wavy or mottled image. This device has proven to be very valuable in the evaluation of the degree of fiberglass pattern transfer in the panels prepared for this study.

Discussion of Profile Results

Figures 6–9 illustrate the difference in profile between the exposed, "EXP," and control, "CONT," panels of each resin type. Those made with the isophthalic and orthophthalic resins show considerable pattern transfer of the woven-roving at the surface, the latter by far the worst. The vinyl ester resin panel shows a very mottled surface, clearly a poor profile performance although not of the usual surface pattern as described above. The new product Resin A has a very good profile as the reflected image from the lightbox remains relatively undistorted when compared to its control.

Figures 10–12 compare Resin A's exposed panel directly with that of each of the other three. Clearly, this high performance resin illustrates superior surface cosmetics over these other marine formulations.

SUMMARY OF PROPERTIES

This new marine resin has been compared against three typical marine resin compositions in two very important performance categories. The table below summarizes the results obtained:

	Resin A	Isophthalic	Orthophthalic	Vinyl Ester
Hydrolytic Stability	Good	Good	Poor	Good
Laminate Profile	Good	Poor	Poor	Poor

CONCLUSIONS

This new high-performance marine laminating resin has proven to possess a high degree of hydrolytic stability by means of its resistance to blistering and cracking and high strength retention values after 100-hour exposure to boiling distilled water.

It has shown its ability to resist fiberglass pattern print-through in one-quarter-inch gel-coated laminates after exposure to heat and ultraviolet light, thus providing improved surface appearance.

Furthermore, this product is the only one studied which combines both hydrolytic stability *and* smooth surface appearance in one resin.

FIELD TRIAL

A major fiberglass boat manufacturer has evaluated several drums of this product and has confirmed the findings stated above. Its own in-house testing confirmed its water resistance. The manufacturer is now building prototype boats with much improved surface appearance.

FIGURE 1. Effects of 100-hour boil on unreinforced specimens.

FIGURE 2. Gel-coated panel of Resin A, after boil.

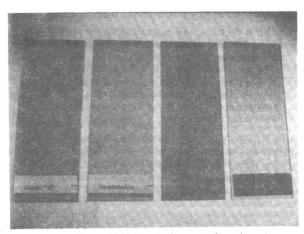

FIGURE 3. Gel-coated panel of Isophthalic, after boil.

FIGURE 4. Gel-coated panel of Orthophthalic, after boil.

REFERENCE 12

PHOTOINITIATORS
(*ULTRAVIOLET LIGHT*)

by John A. Wills

Polyester, polyesters containing dicyclopentadiene (DCPD), vinylester, epoxy, urethane, and acrylic resins along with their monomers or combinations may be cured with certain catalysts using different energy sources. These include ultraviolet light (UV), electron beam (EB), laser and, of course, sunlight.

UV-cured coatings, printing inks, and photo-polymer printing plates have been in commercial use for years. It is only recently that a serious attempt has been made to use photo-reactive catalysts for the purpose of curing resins for reinforced products.

End uses vary widely. A general purpose polyester fast wet-out resin might be specified by a plumbing fixture manufacturer using a chopper gun, while a resin for pre-preging for vacuum bag forming might be required by a skylight producer. Others may specify resins or monomers for casting. Still others may wish to laminate an epoxy or vinylester.

The marine industry could take advantage of the many features of this curing method providing the one important factor is recognized; the lay-up and sometimes the mold must be transparent to ultraviolet light in the wavelength range appropriate to the initiator. Medium pressure mercury vapor or low pressure mercury fluorescent lamps provide incident light in the range required. Additionally, direct or reflected sunlight could provide the UV light energy for curing using the appropriate photoinitiator. Opportunities offered by this system are:

1. The resin may be prepared as a one-component material ready to use with no required mixing of other activator.

2. Pot life is as long as the shelf life of the resin, which may be several months.

3. Useful molding ambient temperatures are from 10°-140°F. Heat does not affect gel time, only the viscosity, thus it is possible to produce any viscosity desired for wet-out simply by controlling temperature. This includes epoxy resins too!

4. Reinforcements may be pre-impregnated, rolled between barrier sheets, then stored within the shelf life of the resin at any temperature recommended by the resin manufacturer. Pre-impregnated material placed between ultraviolet transparent barrier films may be deep-drawn by vacuum forming, then in-place cured in a few minutes upon exposure to ultraviolet light.

A spool of roving may be pre-impregnated by resin bath re-wind or pressure-impregnating the entire spool without re-wind. The fact that the resin, though containing activator, may be heated to provide low viscosity for this type of impregnation without fear of premature curing is a tremendous advantage over conventional resin-activator impregnation.

5. VOC emissions are not reduced during impregnation or molding operations of wet lay-up products containing volatile monomer, but as soon as UV light is applied, the air side surface cures almost immediately. This forms a skin which traps and subsequently cures fumes that would otherwise escape to the surrounding atmosphere.

6. Cross linking of esters is virtually complete without post-cure. Some epoxy initiator-combinations are improved with post-cure. This improves inter-laminar bond and possible reduction of hydrolytic action. With a few exceptions, there is moderate exotherm with little shrinkage.

7. All unused resin may be recovered or simply left in the pot until needed. Covering the container if volatile monomers are present would be the only requirement. Epoxies would not even require covering. Trimmings may be saved providing they are covered to prevent loss of volatiles or exposure to reflected UV light.

8. Clean up of tools is required only at the end of the shift, if then. Even cleaning of clothes and washing of hands is made easier providing there has been no exposure to reflected UV light.

9. Any of the ester resins or blends or those containing DCPD already containing promoters and/or accelerators may be used with photoinitiators without effect.

10. Boatyard repairs, particularly where a laminate must be applied overhead, are made much easier. Pre-impregnated material contained on one side by a barrier sheet may be tailored in place with little mess. "Spot curing" at strategic points is possible with a UV gun and, providing the molding area is kept clear of direct or reflected UV light (ordinary shade is OK),

the molder has unlimited time to perform his work. Where objects must otherwise be molded outdoors uncovered or where there is only partial shade, night molding followed by sunlight or fill-in UV lamps might be considered.

Progressive molding is possible. Depending upon the UV transparency of the reinforcement, thinner lay-ups may be required. All-mat moldings are possible in one cure cycle up to 3/4-inch thickness. Inter-laminar bond between cures is about the same as where the resin is cured with promoted initiators. However, if the laminate has been cured for more than a few minutes, the air surface will cure hard faster than would be expected by other curing methods due to the skinning effect. This is because monomer is prevented from escaping to the atmosphere and moisture and oxygen are not able to react with the resin.

It will become immediately obvious that the skinning effect presents an opportunity to intentionally use an overlay of photoinitiated resin to lower VOCs from conventionally activated resins. Sunrez Corp. *(MS 29)* has patent numbers 4720392 and 4904536 covering this process.

From a practical standpoint, if thick sections are being cured, it may take from several minutes to an hour or two to accomplish through-cure. This means that the air surface will have achieved full or near-full cure before the rest of the laminate has cured. If no further plies are to be added, then it becomes a matter of waiting until mold release is possible before de-molding. Note: Until easy mold release is evident, the part has not completed curing. If further plies are to be added and the air side of the molding is no longer sticky, then sanding or grinding is absolutely required to provide adhesive bonding with additional plies. If the maximum thickness of a given laminate is known that can be cured in one lay-up by photoinitiating, then all other moldings up to this thickness should be laid up in a single impregnation to avoid grinding between thinner plies.

Cobalt-dimethylaniline or other promoted systems cured with conventional initiators often will not exotherm sufficiently or will have lost monomer. This often results in under-cure of thin laminates especially when attempting cure at low temperatures. Using a photoinitiated catalyst, a thin laminate — even a film of resin — will crosslink completely, even at low temperatures. Clear coatings may be applied over various substrates including the surface of fresh, conventionally catalyzed moldings to kill surface tack when required. Since a coating of this type has unlimited pot life, a pressure pot airless spray rig may be reserved in the shop for just this purpose.

Any honeycomb composed of ultraviolet light transparent material in thicknesses up to one-half inch can be laid-up on both sides and cured at the same time. For example, an inner skin, a UV transparent honeycomb core, and an outer skin using a transparent vacuum bag can be laid-up in large one-piece parts with unlimited processing time. A similar honeycomb and one face can be bonded to any substrate by this means also.

If for some reason an ester resin containing a photoinitiator only must be used as a conventional activated and/or promoted system, only the addition of the traditional activators would be required. Of course, this way it could be cured in or out of UV light.

A paste filler may be compounded using any UV transparent filler prepared in bulk or in tubes. Transparent fiber thickeners such as fumed silica, acrylic fibers, polyethylene pulp, ceramic fibers, or quartz powder may be used.

Photoinitiator curing is relatively new in the reinforced plastics industry. On-going tests will produce wet strength, barrier coat, and hydrolytic resistance data. The principal advantages of this system then appear to be unlimited lay-up time unaffected by temperature, along with wide viscosity control, lower toxicity, pre-preging and storage at room temperature, and low VOC emissions.

There are several photoinitiators which may be added to the resin of choice by the end-user. There are other systems where the manufacturer also supplies the resin as well as the initiator. Union Carbide Chemicals and Plastics Company, Inc. *(MS 5)*, and their Cyracure cycloaliphatic epoxides is one example.

On page 137 is a list of some commercially available photoinitiators.

Note: Marcel Dekker, Inc. has granted permission to reproduce this list. It is from "Handbook of Coating Additives," Volume 2 (CALBO), by Chia-Hu Chang, Andrew Mar, Ann Tiefenthaler, and Don Worstratzky.

continued on page 138

Photoinitiators: Mechanisms and Applications

VI. APPENDIX: LISTING OF COMMERCIALLY AVAILABLE PHOTOINITIATORS

Compound	CAS reg. No.	Trade name	Supplier
A. Alpha Cleavage Free Radical Photoinitiators			
Isobutyl benzoin ether	22499-12-3	Vicure 10	Akzo
2,4,6-Trimethylbenzoyldiphenyl- phosphene oxide	127090-72-6	Lucirin TPO	BASF
1-Hydroxycyclohexyl phenyl ketone	947-19-3	Irgacure 184	CIBA-GEIGY
2-Benzyl 2-dimethylamino-1- (4 morpholinophenyl)-butan- 1-one	119111-12 I	Irgacure 369	CIBA-GEIGY
Mixture of benzophenone and 1-hydroxycyclohexyl phenyl ketone	119-61-9 947-19-3	Irgacure 500	CIBA-GEIGY
2,2-Dimethoxy-2-phenylacteo- phenone	24650-42-8	Irgacure 651	CIBA-GEIGY
Perfluorinated diphenyl titanocene	Proprietary	Irgacure 784	CIBA-GEIGY
2-Methyl-1-(4-[methylthio]phenyl)- 2-(4-morpholinyl)-1 -propanone	71868-10-5	Irgacure 907	CIBA-GEIGY
2-Hydroxy-2-methyl-1-phenyl propan– 1-one	7473-98-5	Darocur 1173	CIBA-GEIGY
4-(2-Hydroxyethoxy) phenyl-2- hydroxy-2-propyl ketone	106797-53-9	Darocur 2959	CIBA-GEIGY
Blend of ketones and amines	Proprietary	Darocur 4043	CIBA-GEIGY
Blend of aromatic ketones	Proprietary	Darocur 4265	CIBA-GEIGY
2 2-Diethoxyacetophenone	6175-45-7	DEAP	First Chemical
B. Hydrogen Abstraction Free Radical Photoinitiators			
[4-(4-Methylphenylthio)phenyl] phenylmethanone 4-benzoyl-4'- methyldiphenyl sulfide	83846-85-9	Speedcure BMDS	Aceto Corp.
Ethyl-4-(dimethylamino)benzoate	10287-51-3	Speedcure EDB	Aceto Corp.
Mixture of 2-isopropyl thioxan- thone and 4-isopropyl thio- xanthone	5495-84-1	Speedcure ITX	Aceto Corp.
[4-(4-Methylphenylthio)phenyl] phenylmethatonone 4-benzoyl-4' methyldiphenyl sulfide	83846-85-9	Quantacure BMS	Biddle-Sawyer
2-(Dimethylamino)ethylbenzoate	2208-05-01	Quantacure DMB	Biddle-Sawyer
Ethyl-4-(dimethylamino)benzoate	10287-53-3	Quantacure EPD	Biddle-Sawyer
Mixture of 2-isopropyl thioxan- thone and 4-isopropyl thio- xanthone	5495 84-1	Quantacure ITX	Biddle-Sawyer
d,l-Camphoriquinone	10373-78-71	Camphorquinone	Epolin Inc.
Ethyl d,l-camphorquinone	10287-53-3	EDAB	Hampford Research Inc.
Mixture of benzophenone and 4-methylbenzophenone	119-61-9 134-84-9	Photocure 81	Henkel Corp.
Benzophenone	119-61-9 Benzophenone		Marlborough
4 4'-Bixdimethylamino benzo- phenone	90-94-8	Michler's ketone	RIT Chemical
4 4'-Bisdiethylamino benzo- phenone ethyl ketone	90-93-74	Michler's ethyl ketone	RIT Chemical
Benzophenone	119-61-9	Benzophenone	Velsicol
C. Cationic Photoinitiators			
(η^5-2,4-Cyclopentadien-1-yl) (η^6-isopropylbenzene)-iron(II) hexafluorophosphate	32760-80-8 Irgacure 261		CIBA-GEIGY
Triphenyl sulfonium hexa- fluorophosphate	57835-99-1	FX-512	3M
Mixed triphenyl sulfonium salts	98452-37-9 71449-78-0	Cyracure UVI-6974	Union Carbide
Mixed triphenyl sulfonium salts	74227-35-3 68156-13-9	Cyracure UVI-6990	Union Carbide

Chemical Abstract Service

You will notice three basic types of photoinitiating: alpha cleavage free radical, hydrogen abstraction free radical, and cationic. The alpha cleavage type is based on benzoin, benzoin ethers, and related compounds. Hydrogen abstraction free radical photoinitiators are based on benzophenone and related compounds with an amine acting as a hydrogen donor. These latter two are useful only with those resins which contain an acrylate double bond; *e.g.*, acrylic, polyester, and vinylester resins. Cationic photoinitiators will cure epoxides including bis-phenol A and bis-phenol F as well as cycloaliphatic epoxides.

Photoinitiators and Their Appropriate Resins

Type 1: Alpha Cleavage Free Radical

For Polyester, Vinylester, and Acrylates

1. Lucrin TPO by BASF *(MS 28)*. This is a fast activator and cures thick sections even in light sunlight. It should be pointed out that this particular activator may be available only under license from BASF.

2. Irgacure 184 by Ciba-Geigy *(MS 31)*. This is relatively fast-curing and will through-cure 1/8-inch UV transparent woven fabrics with as little as 1% addition of initiator in 30 to 40 minutes in direct sunlight.

3. Irgacure 369 by Ciba-Geigy works as well as Irgacure 184 with as little as 1/2% concentration of initiator.

4. Irgacure 500 by Ciba-Geigy works in thick laminates but even at 3% concentration may require several hours for through-cure in direct sunlight.

5. Darocur 4265 by Ciba-Geigy cures as rapidly as Lucrin TPO. It contains 50% TPO and 50% Darocur 1173, also by Ciba-Geigy. Again, there may be restrictions by BASF for certain end-uses such as reinforced laminating because of the presence of their TPO. Check with Ciba-Geigy for possible end-use restrictions.

6. Darocur 1173 by Ciba-Geigy works as well as Lucrin TPO or Darocur 4265. So to avoid any possible conflict, 1173 is recommended in place of Lucrin TPO or Darocur 4265. Note: Darocur 1173 is also used in hydrogen abstraction curing. See Type 2 below.

7. Henkel 51 by Henkel Corporation *(MS 36)* is benzophenone and will cure in direct sunlight at 1 to 3% concentration in 45 to 60 minutes in 1/8-inch laminate.

8. Velsicol Corp. *(MS 37)* and Marlborough Corp. *(MS 49)* both produce benzophenone.

Type 2: Hydrogen Abstraction Free Radical

These initiators are based on benzophenone (BP) or derivatives of benzophenone. Free radicals are generated upon imidization of BP in the presence of a tertiary amine such as dimethylanolamine (DMEA) or triethanolamine (TEA). *(See Dow Chemical Company, MS 23, for these.)*

Tertiary amine synergists that have proven to be most effective are Speedcure EDB by Aceto Corp. *(MS 38)* and Quantacure BMS by Biddle-Sawyer *(MS 39)*.

Typical resins (oligomers; *i.e.*, a monomer containing some polymer) are 3015, 3016, 4019, and 4028 by Henkel. The latter two are used to lower the viscosity of the higher-viscosity oligomers. These are epoxy or urethane acrylates.

Another typical oligomer is 15-1522 by Cargill *(MS 41)*. This is an acrylate functional aliphatic urethane. Cargill also supplies acrylated epoxy oligomers such as 15-1570 and acrylated unsaturated polyester oligomers.

All of the oligomers described above are used with hydrogen abstraction or alpha cleavage free radical initiators.

Type 3: Cationic

For epoxy type resins such as bis-phenol A (Shell's 828, *MS 30,* is a good example), use FX 512 by 3M Company *(MS 8)*. This is triphenyl sulfonium hexa flurophosphate. It will cure a 1/8-inch thick fiberglass laminate in direct sunlight in about one hour at 2% phr.

It is quite a change to be able to make a straight Shell 828 or 815 molding and have days to make the lay-up. It is hard to believe you can add as little as 1% 3M's FX 512 Epoxy UV Curing Agent, take all the time you want to set a vacuum bag or whatever, and as a bonus, have no strong odor and low toxicity. Just make sure the entire part "sees" UV light when you are ready to cure.

WARNING: Don't work under UV lights or walk out in the sun with resin on your skin!

Pleasant Advisory: I have some Shell 828 epoxy resin containing 2% 3M FX 512 epoxy curative which was catalyzed 3 years ago and kept in a light-tight container. It is still fluid and, when exposed to sunlight, cures to specification!

Curing Mechanism of Ultraviolet Light Cured Epoxy (Epoxide) Resins

Epoxides are a class of monomers which can be polymerized by either UV light or more conventional means by addition of hardeners such as amines or catalysts like borontrifluoride.

When polymerized with photoinitiator, an epoxide yields *ether* structures producing high thermal stability, mechanical strength, and chemical resistance.

Using the conventional method of curing epoxies by the addition-reaction of "hardeners" such as amines to produce ambient (room temperature) cure, results in lower physicals. If a true catalyst such as borontrifluoride is used with step-heat curing up to 350°F, then an ether linkage occurs similar to that produced by photoinitiation.

Two types of epoxies are used with photoinitiators. The first includes bis-phenol A with or without diluents such as Shell 828 or Dow 316 and bis-phenol F (fusion produced), such as Shell 862, which does not require a diluent.

The second type of epoxy is called cycloaliphatic. Union Carbide's Cyracure 6100 Series *(MS 5)* is one example.

Type 1

If a common epoxy resin such as Shell 828 is to be UV cured, I have found two catalysts that work well on thick fiberglass or polyethylene fiber laminates (up to 1/8 inch). The first and simplest to use is 3M's FX 512 *(MS 8)*. This catalyst produces H by photo-reaction and does not require heat for cure but is greatly accelerated by some infrared (sun) or the residual IR produced by UV lamps. This catalyst produces a tack-free surface and will through-cure a 1/8-inch fiberglass lay-up in about an hour in direct sunlight with as little as 2% phr catalyst. FX 512 is a clear liquid.

The second Type 1 catalyst which will cure a Shell 828 epoxy (a linear polymer) is based on a different principal. Irgacure 261 by Ciba-Geigy *(MS 31)* is an example. This is a yellow powder which must be pre-dissolved in a solvent such as acetone. Otherwise, if added directly to the resin, it will create a semi-opaque mixture but upon solution will eventually become clear. Without post-baking, this catalyst will only partially through-cure in sunlight. To accelerate cure or reduce post-baking, cumene hydroperoxide *(MS 7)* is added. This combination is very sensitive to any visible light — even ordinary fluorescent, incandescent, or incident light. Yellow filters must be used to provide enough light for molding operations. Irgacure 261 is expensive. The 2½ phr required per pound of resin can equal the cost of the resin itself. However, if high heat distortion temperature and high physical values are required, then the cost of this system may be justified.

Type 2: Cycloaliphatic Epoxy

These are made from polycyclic aliphatic compounds containing carbon-carbon double bonds. Characteristically, they are resistant to high temperature, water and chemicals. Cycloaliphatic epoxies are particularly useful when cured with cationic initiators.

Union Carbide with their Cyracure resin *(MS 5)* and Ciba-Geigy with their CY 179 resin *(MS 31)* offer cycloaliphatic epoxies. Union Carbide's resin is designed to be cured with their UVI 6974 initiator which is a mixed sulphonium salt. 6974 will also cure linear epoxy resins such as Shell 828.

Ciba-Geigy's CY 179 is designed to be used with their Irgacure 261 which is an iron arene complex. When used with cumene hydroperoxide this will cure linear epoxies also.

Some Guidelines for Laminating Reinforcements with Photoinitiated Resins

To serve as a *standard*, 10-ounce fiberglass cloth with Volan "A" coupling agent is used for all test panels. Moldings are made on glass plates to provide a uniform mold surface and to determine through-cure by observing ease of release from the plates.

Ester Resins

The catalysts Lucirin TPO *(MS 28)*, Irgacure 369 *(MS 31)*, and Darocur 1173 *(MS 31)* will through-cure five plies using polyester, vinylester, urethane-vinylester and some acrylic resins. Cure will be achieved almost instantly in bright sunlight at mix ratios as little as 1/2 phr catalyst. Low exotherm is produced and cures may be made ranging in air temperatures from 0° to 125°F. These catalysts are alpha cleavage types. There are many others also.

A low cost catalyst mixture consisting of equal parts, usually 2% phr of benzophenone (a hydrogen abstraction type) and Darocur 1173 along with triethanolamine, will cure the above esters as well. Most of these catalysts will cure polyester resins already containing dimethylaniline and/or cobalt napthenate.

Epoxy Acrylate (a Vinylester) and Urethane Acrylate Resins

Cargill Corp. *(MS 41)* and Henkel Corp. *(MS 36)* are two of several firms who produce these resins. Some specific catalyst curing systems using five plies of 10-ounce "boat" cloth as the reinforcement are:

1. Henkel 4028 epoxy acrylate with 1% Irgacure 369. This will through-cure five plies in bright sunlight in five seconds.

2. Henkel 15-1574 diluted with 30% HDODA *(MS 48)* at 1 phr. Irgacure 369 will cure five plies in ten seconds. This same resin with 3% benzophenone and 2% triethanolamine will through-cure five plies in about five minutes. Henkel 3016 plus 30% Henkel 3049 catalyzed with 2% benzophenone and 3% Darocur 1173 will cure five plies in bright sunlight almost instantly. All of these catalysts will cure epoxy acrylates, and urethane acrylates, with the same reinforcement lay-up in about the same length of time.

Many of the alpha cleavage and hydrogen abstraction catalysts cure their resins leaving a tacky surface on the air side due to the reaction of oxygen from the air. With time, the stickiness will disappear, but it may be removed with an acetone wipe. This is usually not any more of a problem than encountered with the air side using conventional initiator cured systems. You can eliminate the tacky surface by adding 1 to 2% of triethanolamine with benzophenone alone or along with Darocur 1173.

Linear and Cycloaliphatic Epoxy Resins

The catalysts used are the cationic type. Some resin-catalyst combinations are:

1. Minnesota Mining & Manufacturing (3M Company) Epoxy Curative FX 512 *(MS 33)* is the easiest and most forgiving for curing "regular" epoxy (linear) resins since the catalyst is a liquid, is tolerant of shop lighting or shade during lay-up operations, and is relatively low in cost.

2. For high structural strength and high heat distortion temperature, cycloaliphatic epoxy resin may be specified. Union Carbide's resin Cyracur UVR 610D series and their UVI 6900 photoinitiators *(MS 5)* blended with a cross-linking caprolacetone flexibilizer, Tone *(MS 5),* are used. A typical formulation is 70 parts UVR 6100 resin, 25 parts Tone polyol, and 2 to 4 parts UVI 6974 catalyst. This formulation will through-cure one to five plies of 10-ounce cloth laid concurrently in one to two hours in bright sunlight. You may substitute Ciba-Geigy's CY 179 cycloaliphatic epoxy resin for UVR 6100 in the above formula. Also, you may substitute 3M's FX 512 for UVI 6974 catalyst in the above formula.

3. Ciba-Geigy offers their cationic catalyst Irgacure 261. It is principally designed for use with their cycloaliphatic epoxy CY 179 but works equally well with the linear epoxies such as Dow 361, Shell 828, or Ciba-Geigy 6010. Irgacure 261 works best with cumene hydroperoxide added as an oxidizer to produce a tack-free surface and increased cure rate at ambient temperature. A typical formula is cycloaliphatic or linear epoxy 100 parts, cumene hydroperoxide 2 parts, Irgacure 261 2.5 parts. This formulation will not reliably through-cure more than one or two plies of 10-ounce cloth, so progressive lamination is recommended.

There are disadvantages to using the Irgacure 261 system. The catalyzed resin is very sensitive to any form of light except yellow or very subdued daylight. Florescent or incandescent lamps cannot be used or short pot life or premature gelling may occur. The catalyst is a powder and must be pre-dissolved with a solvent. Cost is high, often doubling the base cost of the resin. Thick lay-ups do not through-cure well, necessitating progressive laminating (which by itself would usually be acceptable). Finally, post-bake is required to achieve maximum physicals. Note: Over time, products will achieve high physicals without post-baking due to homo-curing.

There is a tremendous advantage to the use of Irgacure 261 where high heat distortion or glass transition temperatures are required in the range of 240°F. For most marine uses it is usually not necessary to have a high HDT or glass t.g. Items for marine use such as filament-wound or resin transfer molded products are well suited to the use of Irgacure 261.

Due to the "screening" effect of most UV catalysts — that is, the tendency of the air surface to cure or skin first — some blocking of UV light to the interior of the laminate will occur. If this becomes a problem, reduce the amount of catalyst in proportion to the thickness to be cured. Thus, FX 512 will through-cure five plies of 10-ounce cloth faster at 2 phr than at 4 phr.

Unlike most of the other curing systems previously discussed, cationic catalysts will cure the air side of a laminate or coating tack-free. However, because they do not through-cure rapidly, progressive lamination is suggested at least for the first ply. This insures thorough cure at the mold face, thus good mold release, which allows early stripping from the mold, even though the interior of the part may not be fully cured at the time. One or more

140

plies may be added progressively until the final plies are placed. This allows unlimited and variable thickness to be molded.

Resins cured with FX 512 will homo-cure also but low temperature post-cure is recommended.

Mold Releases and Parting Agents

While the prime function of a mold release is to provide parting from the mold, the ease with which actual parting takes place determines the degree of through-cure of photoinitiated resins. For insurance, when a non-film forming mold release may be questionable, most molders will first use a film-forming type parting agent designed to be removed with the part. Sprayable water solutions of polyvinyl alcohol or organic solvent solutions of cellulose acetate are examples.

Where used strictly as a coating, it is not necessary to know immediately when a photo-cured resin has reached complete through-cure at the interface between the substrate and the coating surface. Yet it is quite necessary that a molding is fully cured at the mold interface to ensure clean release.

To determine through-cure and mold release effectiveness, it is recommended that glass test plates be prepared with whatever release is to be used in production of a part. Freekote 400 or 700 *(MS 42)* are two examples of spray-on non-film formers which work very well. If a test laminate will release cleanly without effort, then through-cure will be assured on another mold for the same resin-catalyst mix and lay-up with the same UV source and exposure time. *NOTE*: If poor mold release is indicated or the mold is not ready in the time expected using a glass test plate, you will have the opportunity to turn the back side toward the UV source to eventually achieve a release in order to salvage the plate and possibly the part. This would apply to a mold as well, providing the mold is transparent to the UV source. If the part does not eventually release cleanly, then a film-forming release should be used.

Photoinitiated Resins as Coatings

The coatings industry has years of experience with paper, can coatings, printing inks, photo resists, and printing plates. This experience can be used to great advantage in many areas of the marine industry. The ability to maintain a spray system containing pre-catalyzed photo reactive resin which is immediately available for application of an epoxy, an acrylate, a polyester, a vinylester or an exotic urethane at will without gun clean-up should be of great value.

Sources of Ultraviolet Light

Manufacturers of marine products usually want to use sunlight whenever possible, but there will be situations where sunlight is neither practical nor desired. Ultraviolet lamps are often used. They are available in many forms usually designed for fast conveyor lines. These are high intensity arc or electron beam (microwave) units too dangerous for general boat shop use, so type "A" low pressure, low wattage bulbs or fluorescent tubes will be used for safety reasons. Panels containing UV tubes for "sun tanning" are often sufficient for small part production or small areas such as repairs. Banks of these may be assembled to cover more area. *(See MS 42, 43, 44, and 45.)*

Conclusion

During my more than 50 years in the plastics industry, I have been fortunate to run across a material, method, or process and become involved in developing and introducing it to some part of the reinforced plastics industry. The use of photoinitiating catalysts for curing the resin matrix used in reinforced plastics is certainly one of these. For more than 40 years, the coatings industry has constantly improved resin cure properties, but nearly always, these were directed to thin film end-uses or, at the most, printing plates and masks.

There are presently a few processors who use UV cured resins in filament winding, some surfboard producers, some manufacturers of pultruded products, and some working with resin injection. The big market yet to be exploited is in the production of multi-ply products of unlimited size.

Ultraviolet curing certainly has provided me with a new tool — one that you wonder how you ever did without. The producers of these very useful catalysts might do well to investigate not only the marine market, but the producers of all types of wet lay-up products. Here is an opportunity for the suppliers of photoinitiators to provide convenient packaging of these materials. An equal opportunity exists for those who wish to package ready-to-use pre-catalyzed resins. Sunrez Corp. *(MS 29)* is a pioneer in pre-packaged UV resins and pre-pregs. It is certain that others will follow. Above all, sound, simple-use instructions must be supplied.

REFERENCE 13

PHENOLIC RESINS

by John A. Wills

When most writers, including myself, come to the subject of phenolic resins, they recite the usual dialog about their use in some glues, distributor caps, brake linings, grinding wheels, light switches and pipe stems. Read about phenolics in any issue of *Modern Plastics Catalog* and you will find a description of the chemistry and physical data. You'll also learn that the phenolics come in resole or novolac form, and that high temperature and pressure are required. You may also be informed that phenolics have joined the ranks of so-called "engineering resins." Not one word is mentioned about liquid phenolics which can be processed like hand-laid polyesters and epoxies.

Sit back and be prepared for a longer-than-usual discussion about a resin. Because unlike the well known and accepted "big three" — polyester, vinylester and epoxy — the liquid phenolics are virtually unknown to the average marine producer.

It is my opinion that phenolic resin offers the only alternative to the many restrictions now imposed or to be imposed on the open mold process. This includes not only the marine industry but any manufacturing process involving open molding, especially when styrenic materials prevail. The use of suppressants, lower volatility monomers, higher solids, etc., will only mollify a situation where air quality control prevails, because these fixes apply only to those volatiles produced during the curing operation. The big issue is the potential of fire, smoke, and toxic fumes produced not only in the molding operation, but in the final product should it be subjected to fire.

Soon our "big brothers" — seven to nine government agencies in the United States alone, including the Coast Guard — will realize that the very serious, life-threatening potential of the big three resins can be dramatically reduced by informed use of phenolics. Then a new buzzword will be in, especially for the marine industry: "phenolic."

For the moment at least, accept the fact that all pure phenolics have high heat resistance; are virtually non-flammable (at least self-extinguishing); and produce very thin, low toxicity transparent smoke. Also, they are dimensionally stable.

History of Phenolics

Leo Bakeland, an American chemist, invented the first synthetic resin in 1909 by reacting carbolic acid (phenol) and embalming fluid (formaldehyde). In the next few years he and others perfected the chemistry and use of fillers to the point where high temperature and pressure moldings could be made. It was learned early that the condensation reaction could be delayed to allow impregnation of paper and fabrics (linen based Formica, for example) and to allow formulation of lacquers. Some clear and filled castings were produced, but until the mid-1930s almost all phenolic consumption was restricted to compounds for use in high heat and pressure molding.

Beginning in 1935-36, Durez Chemical Company, Baker Oil Tool, and some others generated small interest in specialized low temperature cured castings from the liquid form of phenolics. Baker Oil Tool's Dr. Leeg developed such a resin for an in-house need in this same time span and shortly after began looking for an outside market. Charles Wurdemann (later to establish Resolin Company) and I were probably Leeg's only customers. Both Wurdemann and I made various job-shop products, with Wurdemann taking the lead by far with his Resolin Company.

At that time we did not explore to any degree the use of this liquid form of phenolic resin for use in cloth laminates. When we tried we found that after cure, excessive brittleness and porosity were common. Since my interests were primarily in developing and using high solids solvent-carried resins as impregnants for woven fabrics, my interest in those phenolics of the day waned. I don't believe Chuck Wurdemann ever made any woven reinforced products using phenolic as the matrix resin at that time.

By 1940 a great deal of interest was developed in a flexible, tough, all-purpose phenolics lacquer paint. It was touted to be fireproof and chemically resistant to all solvents, acids and alkalines. While such products as keg drum and metal food container coating evolved from this era, very few of the other claimed virtues prevailed. There were practically no uses made of castings made of low pressure and temperature liquid phenolic resin during this period. There was, however, high use made of impregnated fabric stock which could be molded at nearly atmospheric pressure. Phenopreg, a semi-dry, phenolics impregnated, open weave cotton fabric, was one of those early products which could be bag molded or used in low pressure presses. However, relatively high cure temperatures were required.

Phenolics polymerize by condensation. They are, therefore, endothermic, meaning that continuous heat is required to provide full cure.

Polymers such as polyester are exothermic meaning that a small amount of heat usually with catalytic assist, will start polymerization which auto-ignites (that is, it self-cures without necessarily adding more heat). Room temperature-cured polyesters are examples.

Since phenolics require heat to cure, the reaction — which is continuous as long as heat is applied — can, however, be interrupted at any "stage." Thus, to make a liquid molding resin, a molding powder, a lacquer or a varnish, the reaction may be interrupted at any point up to full cure. This is called "staging." The foregoing description is somewhat simplistic and does not go into detail about the actual catalytic process involved.

Also during this same time period (1937-39), William Beech developed a "B" stage method of post-forming a pre-laminated, de-gassed, but semi-cured phenolic sheet molding, taking advantage of the three-step cure process typical of novolac phenolic. The first step is referred to as the "A" stage (resole); the second step is the "B" stage (resitol); and the third step is the "C" stage (recite). This won for Beech the prestigious John Wessley Hyatt[1] Award, which today is presented by the plastics industry annually to some individual for outstanding achievement.

From the early "B" staging technique, a method of coving phenolic impregnated paper sheet stock was developed. Post-forming of Formica, a paper impregnated with phenolic and over-laid with a melamine impregnated decorative sheet, is an example. Formed sink and deck tops were made very popular. This forming process was usually confined to single bends which were formed over heated mandrels. All operations had to be completed in a few seconds before the panel in the heated area of the bend cured. This process did not fare long in use, however, because something had been overlooked. Although the area in the cove may have been momentarily plasticized by heating, then subsequently cured while being formed, the rest of the sheet still remained in the "B" stage for months (in time it would have cured). So when the first hot frying pan was set on it, instant post-forming in the shape of the bottom of the pan resulted, not especially to the liking of the housewife. The popularity of this process lived on for a few more years by use of full heated dies which cured the entire panel. To a limited extent, post-formed melamine-phenolic sheet is still in use; of course, flat sheet molded in high pressure presses and fully cured is in wide use presently. Phenolic circuit board stock is an example.

By 1943 I confined my interests in phenolics to producing bag, plug, and matched metal die-molded pre-preg parts. All wet lay-up molding of other resins was still by the resin-solvent process, ethylcellulose being the principal resin used. About this time I was somewhat secretly brought a "new" resin to try out. This was a "war baby" called "polyester." The label on the drum said "Plastic Resin Glue." Fiberglas, the trademark of the new Owens Corning Fiberglass Corporation, had not yet been introduced.

Polyester-styrene resin showed promise as a wet lay-up impregnant even though the catalyst system (benzoyl peroxide) required a heat cure cycle around 250°F. Compared with our previous experience with heat curing wet-laid phenolic resin, this new polyester seemed the answer to the proverbial maiden's prayer. What little interest in wet lay-up phenolic still existed was definitely out the door at that time. The use of pre-preg phenolics also very quickly subsided because even press and bag molding of polyesters was far easier than using time-unstable "B" stage phenolic stock.

Over a period of time, some of us developed catalysts and promoters which made room temperature curing of polyesters possible. This, of course, completely eliminated the idea of using liquid phenolic for wet lay-up operations.

On the heels of room-temperature cured polyesters arrived the glamorous epoxies, bringing with them the era of the buzzwords such as "aerospace," "high tech," "composite," "syntactic," "synergistic" — you name it. The term phenolics was not one of the buzzwords.

On top of epoxies came vinylester, urethane, and so-called engineering plastics, when, in the novolac form, phenolics were considered at least a poor-mouse member. Until about 1989, U.S. producers of phenolic did not offer any appreciable amount of liquid phenolic resin for wet lay-up work including pultrusion, resin transfer, and cold or hot low pressure molding.

Meanwhile, Great Britain and some European countries began to make use of the virtues of phenolics, largely as a child of necessity. Underground transportation, mining, and some aircraft manufacturers were being pressured for safer materials, especially for the avoidance of fire and smoke propagation as well as toxic fumes. The British recognized early on the hazardous, life-threatening nature of burning esters, epoxies, urethanes, and vinylesters. The United States still had its head in the sand on this.

---

1. John Wessley Hyatt was a prolific inventor. His first claim-to-fame was having won in 1870 the enormous prize of $10,000 offered by Brunswick, Balke, and Collender (now Brunswick Corporation) for developing a substitute for ivory, then used exclusively for billiard balls, which he carved from cast nitrocellulose. Later, in 1872, he invented the first injection molding machine in which billiard balls and many other shapes ("Celluloid" collars, for example) could be molded. In appreciation of Hyatt's work, Brunswick started the annual awards of which Beech is one of the many recipients.

The licensing of passenger-carrying boats and vessels is performed in the United States by its Coast Guard. Some of the safety officers have realized for some time the life-threatening nature of the materials used in boat construction, even including wood. Had they had some magic product to hold under the nose of manufacturers which could realistically be substituted, I like to think they might have been willing to encourage its use. Such a material does exist and is an excellent candidate for substitution of, or co-use with, other resins. Of course, some learning adjustments will be required. I also would like to think the Coast Guard is generally aware of the potential of phenolic resins for marine use and, at last, should actively encourage the industry to investigate and promulgate their immediate use.

Great Britain and Europe are about 10 years ahead of the United States in this respect. Following is an excerpt from a paper presented to the Society of the Plastics Industry in 1988 by K. L. Forsdyke of BP Chemicals Ltd. It sums up the position of at least one firm's effort overseas.

The current worldwide increase in the use of composite materials has occurred at a time of increased technical and legislative requirements associated with an increased awareness of the need for public safety. Whilst traditional RP materials show excellent physical properties and moldability, making them ideal for a very wide range of applications, in general there are two limiting parameters for their use. The first is fire, smoke, and toxicity performance (FST); and the second is upper service temperature. As a major step to overcoming these limitations phenolic matrix resins have been developed which have excellent FST performance as well as raising the maximum service temperature available.

The acid cure of resol resins has been known as long as the resins themselves and much work was undertaken on the chemistry thereof in the 1940s to 1960s. However, no serious commercial effort appears to have been made to apply this chemistry to RP production until the early 1970s when a British company produced a resin and catalyst system which did not reach full commercialization. Whilst the system had problems of application such as relatively high viscosity and high free formaldehyde, these disadvantages could have been corrected. The main reason for the lack of success was almost total lack of safety awareness in the market place; in fact, the material was ahead of its time!

Having seen this development and its unfortunate demise, BP Chemicals Ltd. waited until the early 1980s before developing its own system. By that time safety was becoming the "in" word and the company's own experience in the manufacture of unsaturated polyester resin indicated that a need to improve smoke and toxicity performance would grow rapidly in importance. Traditional applications of phenolic resins in areas such as friction materials, foundry binders, and grinding and cutting equipment identified a possible bonus in the form of extra thermal stability.

So why choose phenolics as an RP matrix? Simply because an alternative organic matrix material, which can be handled by all existing RP conversion techniques, and which will better the FST properties of phenolic is not apparent. Add to this a service temperature of 200°C (392°F) and commercial interest results.

Producers of low-pressure, low-temperature, liquid resole (the British spell this resol) phenolic in the United States are very few. We have a number of manufacturers who make basic and compounded novolac phenolics which are high-temperature and high-pressure molding materials and some produce engineering phenolics. Even the second largest manufacturer of phenolic molding compounds in the United States either cannot or will not show itself in the production of wet lay-up phenolics.

Fortunately, we have BP Chemicals Ltd. *(MS 9)*, North American Resins (Borden) *(MS 15)*, and Georgia-Pacific *(MS 62)* who manufacture their liquid RP resins in the United States on the East coast. Up until 1993 we also had a French firm, Norold Composites, who provided an RP phenolic but because of lack of markets they have withdrawn their product from the United States. It is available in Canada and in Europe. Norold's product will be discussed later.

Occidental Chemical Corporation *(MS 55)*, now owner of Durez Chemical, does manufacture a liquid phenolic called Durez 7421A on special order only and therefore not presently readily available. I have not researched this resin as a candidate for wet lay-up work, but feel it is likely to perform competitively. Also, the Durez Division is an old timer in the phenolic business and is probably waiting to see the trend in acceptance of wet lay-up phenolics before jumping onto the band wagon.

Indspec Chemical Corporation *(MS 56)*, does manufacture in the United States a hybrid resorcinol-phenol resin which is discussed later. This resin system meets many of the criteria of pure phenolics, but it is not suitable for marine use if long-term immersion in water is required.

The re-introduction of "born again" phenolic resin has special appeal to me since it is the one over fifty years ago I cut my teeth on. Today this presents the exciting possibility of adapting an old resin for a new use.

In researching the few known liquid phenolic suppliers of record, I was discouraged at the lack of physical data available, especially as concerns the marine industry. I approached the six firms who at the time claimed to offer wet lay-up phenolic for the use I intended. These firms are BP Chemicals Ltd., Indspec Chemical Corporation, Norold Composites, Inc., North American Resins, Inc., Georgia Paific Resins, and Plastics Engineering Company *(MS 57)*. I suggested to them that structural panels be prepared using an identical reinforcement laminating schedule for each resin supplier. I also suggested that each make his own panels and test specimens, and that each use his own procedures. Five of the firms listed above preferred that I prepare the panels in my lab, but to field conditions, and they would see to the testing. Only Plastics Engineering Company, who at first were very enthusiastic about the program, suddenly declined to allow me to make their panels. They even refused to supply me with bench samples of their resin for evaluation; and further, for reasons of their own, declined participation in the test program.

Test results are now complete from the five suppliers who did participate. Following is a description of the test program and the individual results.

I asked each supplier to run physical tests on a panel made with Reichold's Dion 6631T *(MS 26)* iso polyester resin at the same time the supplier's phenolic panels were run. This, to provide control data because at present, most RP molders are familiar with poly and vinylesters and will compare any new resin to these.

To record test data I used a form I have developed called "Checklist for Evaluation of Resin," one I use for initial examination of almost any reactive resin. Note that there are two sections: "Non-Structual Information" and "First Structural Tests." These are arranged so that if an early failure is observed, time is saved by not pursuing further tests. The results of the four suppliers of liquid phenolic resins are reported as follows.

JOHN A. WILLS

Plastics _____ *Consultant*

Phone
(760) 742-3918

32776 VIA DEL VENADO
VALLEY CENTER, CALIFORNIA 92082

Fax
(760) 742-3167

CHECKLIST FOR EVALUATION OF RESIN

NON-STRUCTURAL INFORMATION ONLY

Resin Type: _____

Catalyst or Activator: _____

Typical Cure Schedule: _____

1. Cast activated resin on glass plate maintained at 72°F and observe for: usable viscosity, color, transparency, odor and changes during cure.

2. On glass plate as in (1.), make a 10-20 mil. glass veil and 1½ -2 oz. mat laminate, let r.t. cure 24 hrs. Check for binder, sizing, and coupling agent compatibility. Laminate 1½ -2 oz. mat with 7-10 oz. glass cloth over. Place 1/2- to 1-inch wide strip polyethylene film at one end between laminations to provide for interlamina bond check. R.t. cure for 24 hrs. then cut laminate in half. Post cure one half at 140°F for 2 hrs. Use screw driver to pry apart laminations to check for interlamina bond.

3. Check room temperature water Iimmersion. Make laminate as in (2.) but eliminate polyethylene film. Cut in half. Trim and sand all edges. Post cure one coupon at 140°F for 2 hrs. Keep the other at r.t. Seal all edges with wax or epoxy resin. Immerse both coupons in tap water. Check weight gain or loss at intervals for two weeks. Note stabilization point — if any.

4. Check laminate overlay bond to other resins. Use procedure as in (2.) at r.t. and post cure.

Polyester _____

Vinylester _____

Phenolic _____

Epoxy _____

Furfural _____

Polysulfide _____

If compatibility or poor bond is observed in (4.), re-check using "Poly Bond" or "Epoxy Bond" or other primer.

5. Check interlamina bond to various substrates. (Note: Make panel sizes at least 8x10 inches for No. 6 test following.) At room temperature, laminate two 1½ -2 oz. CSM with 18-24 oz. woven roving onto:

Plywood _____

Particle Board _____

2 lb/CF Expanded Styrene Bead Board _____

4 lb/CF Extruded Styrene Foam Board _____

4 lb/CF Vinyl Foam Board (Kleg-e-Cell) _____

4 lb/CF Vinyl Foam Board (Airex) _____

Vitreous Foamed Glass _____

Dry Cementious Concrete _____

Sandblasted Aluminum _____

Sandblasted Steel _____

6. Check fire characteristics by exposing laminate side of samples in (5.) to flame from gasoline or propane torch. It is suggested that a video be made.

7. Check individual fire characteristics in typical gasoline spill fire as follows: Construct a hemispheric female mold of suitable material (the bottom of a 6-inch round bottom glass flask works well as a form). Mold shells using one layer CSM and one ply of 18-24 oz. woven roving on the inside. Make as many shells as required for individual tests such as overlays, r.t. cure, post cure etc. Mount shells on a support or hold so that the plane at the equator is approximately 20° from the vertical to enable bowl to contain 25 cc. of gasoline.

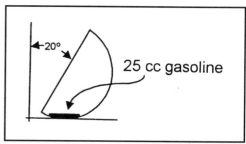

8. Ignite gasoline. Observe flame propagation, smoke, odor, and condition after gasoline has been consumed. It is suggested that a videotape also be made.

First Structural Test Requirements

Make 12 x 12-inch hand lay-up flat panels on glass plates starting with an 8-10 mil. glass or polyester veil followed by a 1½ -2 oz. CSM r.t. cured then followed by a layer of Style TVM 3408 (or equiv.) which is a zero degree, minus 45 degree, plus 45 degree, 3/4 ounce CSM stitched fabric assembly by Brunswick Technologies, Inc. This is a four ply unbound combo fabric which is non-woven and unidirectional. Their coupling agents are claimed to be universal. It is important to check on this and the veil mat as well. This first layer is to be room temperature cured and allowed to stand under shop conditions (approx. 72°F 50% RH) for at least 24 hrs. Add one or more plies of TVM 3408 to bring total laminate thickness to between 1/8-inch and 1/4-inch. Room temperature cure to specs. One panel which is cured at room temperature to be kept for dry tests and one panel for wet tests. Trim the edges on the wet test panels and seal the edges with wax or epoxy. Record original dry weight of all wet test panels.

Continuously immerse panels to be wet tested in tap water maintained at 150°F for two weeks. Surface dry wet panels with toweling then cut into standard structural test coupons and test ASAP. Before cutting wet panels into coupons, determine percent water absorption by weight. Dry sample testing may be run anytime after complete cure.

If the initial wet and dry tests appear favorable, more detailed tests will be performed.

Author's Note: I have produced a videotape of the comparative fire resistance of most major laminating resins in various configurations, *e.g.*, fiber reinforced panels, reinforced sandwich panels, etc. The phenolics won hands down! If you really want to see how dangerous, in terms of fire and smoke, all resins tested are except phenolic, then contact me (*see page 145 for address*) or Tiller Publishing, P.O. Box 447, St. Michaels, MD 21663; 1-800-6TILLER, for a copy of this tape. It is dramatic!

SUPPLIER NO. 1

BP CHEMICALS

CELLOBOND® RESINS J2027L
TECHNICAL DATA

PHENOLIC RESIN

FEATURES:

Easy to Process	Low Flame
Low Smoke	Low Smoke Toxicity

GENERAL DESCRIPTION:

J2027L is a low viscosity phenolic resin designed for use in filament winding, RTM, pultrusion and vacuum flow.

UNCURED PROPERTIES @ 77°F (TYPICAL)

Viscosity	300 cps	
Water Content	11.5%	
Specific Gravity	1.225	
pH	7.5	
Pot Life	4-8 minutes	(10 phr *Phencat 10*)
Stability @ 40°F	3 months	

MSDS #3156

APPLICATION:

Two acid catalysts are offered for use with J2027L. The choice of catalyst employed depends on the processing characteristics. Phencat 10 is a "slow" catalyst for use in filament winding and vacuum flow. Phencat 15 is a "fast" catalyst for use in RTM.

Recommended release agents are Frekote 700 & 750 (Dexter Hysol). Waxes may also be used but must be cleaned off prior to painting. PVA and other water soluble release agents should **not** be used.

Fillers that do not interfere with the acid cure can be used as extenders. China clay and glass microspheres can be incorporated up to 25% loading.

A post cure at 140°F is suggested to achieve optimum properties.

We believe this information is reliable, but we do not guarantee its accuracy and assume no liability arising out of its use. The user should thoroughly test any application before commercialization. Our recommendations should not be taken as inducements to infringe any patent or violate any law, safety code or insurance regulation.

For more information and samples contact:

Commercial Composites

3535 Latonia Ave., P.O. Box 15159
Fort Wright, KY 41015-0159
TEL: 606-292-7446
Customer Service - East

12335 S. Van Ness Ave., P.O. Box 5006
Hawthorne, CA 90251-5006
TEL: 213-241-5640
Customer Service - West

SUPPLIER NO. 1
CHECKLIST FOR EVALUATION OF RESIN
Non-Structural Information Only

BP Chemicals Corporation
Advanced Materials Division
Commercial Composites, Carborundum Building
P.O. Box 411, Keasbey, New Jersey 08832
Phone: 908-417-3099 • Fax: 908-738-5123

RESIN TYPE: Liquid phenol-formaldehyde.
         Product Name: "Cellobond J2018L"
CATALYST/ACTIVATOR: "Phencat 10" (p-toluene sulphonic acid) 6-8 phr.
TYPICAL CURE: At 6-8 phr, gel at 70°F approximately 30 minutes. Cure, 2 hours at 140°F.

1. Initial color, clear amber. Viscosity appears okay for hand lay-up. Mild odor of formaldehyde fumes. Breathing apparatus recommended. Turns white and non-transparent slowly, starting at about 45 minutes. Firm gel at 2 hours. At 24 hours rigid gel turns light pink. After 2 hours minimum at 140°F turns red, indicating cure.

2. Compatibility okay. Interlaminar bond (screwdriver test) good.

3. Room Temperature Water Immersion Check. Water pick-up in first 24 hours approximately 1%, then gradually increased to 3% at two weeks. At three months, stabilized at 4%.
   Oven Cure Water Immersion Check. Water pick-up in first 24 hours 0.9%, 2.5% at two weeks. At 3 months stabilized at 3%.

4. Overlay Bond.
   Room Temperature Cure: polyester, zero bond, complete release. Vinylester same as polyester. Phenolic, good bond. Epoxy, very poor bond, sticky inhibited mess. Furfural and polysulfide not checked.
   Oven Cure: Essentially same results as room temperature cure. Where incompatibility or poor or no bond was observed, "Poly bond" or "Epoxy bond" (a product of Revchem Plastics, Inc.) will act as a satisfactory "primer" and will provide good bond.

5. Bond to Various Substrates: Plywood, particle board, 2 pound/cubic foot expanded styrene bead board, 2 pound/cubic foot extruded styrene board, 4 pound/cubic foot vinyl foam board (Kleg-e-cell), 4 pound/cubic foot vinyl foam board (Airex), 2 pound/cubic foot rigid urethane board, vitreous glass foamed board all showed excellent bond with no distortion or solvency. Bond to dry cementious concrete and sandblasted aluminum and steel were good.

6. All showed excellent resistance to propagation of flame through the phenolic laminate overlay into the substrate. Charring or melting of some of the substrates was observed.

7. In this test, where the all-phenolic or phenolic overlaid shell was subjected to the gasoline fire, no ignition was observed and no structural damage was shown.

   NOTE to 6, 7, and 8: In all cases where J2018L was exposed to flame or burning gasoline, very little ignition of the resin was observed; and only slight, thin non-noxious smoke was produced.

First Structural Test Requirements Results

(See pages 149-150, Truesdail Laboratories report and BP Phencat 381 brochure.)

Comments

It will be observed that there is considerable drop in percentage of strength retention of the phenolic laminate after water immersion. The control panel with iso-phthalic polyester resin, Dion 6631T, indicates a higher strength after immersion due to the post-curing effect of the 125°F water.

Another consideration should be given to the actual values reported due to the method of testing. ASTM D638 and D749 are tests for isotropic materials where they use pounds per square inch in reporting certain tests, and specimen size is standardized. *(See Reference 18 for the author's arguments to this.)*

Because the considerable drop in structural values after a relatively short interval of water immersion, it is suggested that this product be further evaluated before specifying long-term immersion in, or containment of, water. Considering the chemistry of phenolic resin, it is not likely that resin hydrolysis problems will occur. However, because few if any coupling agents have been specifically developed for these resins, the lowering of structural values after immersion may be due to de-coupling or other breakdown of the resin-glass bond.

The outstanding resistance to fire, the low production of toxic smoke and the ease of fabrication make this product an excellent choice either as the sole structural resin, or as an over-lay to other materials not subject to long-term direct immersion.

BP Chemicals also offers a very new catalyst, "PHENCAT" 381. This is a delayed action catalyst which is described in the following pages. This is particularly useful where long lay-up time is required.

Another new product by BP is "QC-2130 Phenolic Sheet Molding Compound," which may be used for panels where long-term water immersion is not required but where fire resistance and thin, low toxic smoke qualities are required.

REPORT

TRUESDAIL LABORATORIES, INC.

CHEMISTS - MICROBIOLOGISTS - ENGINEERS

RESEARCH — DEVELOPMENT — TESTING

14201 FRANKLIN AVENUE
TUSTIN, CALIF. 92680
AREA CODE 714 • 730-6239
AREA CODE 213 • 225-1564
FAX 714 • 730-6462

CLIENT: BP Chemicals
12335 South Van Ness Avenue
Hawthorne, CA 90251-5006
Attention: Mathew G. Moreau

MATERIAL: Six Composite Panels

DATE: September 27, 1991

P.O. NO.: Moreau

LAB NO.: 51927A

SPECIFICATION: ASTM D638
ASTM D749

INVESTIGATION: Ultimate Tensile Strength, % Elongation, Tensile Modulus of Elasticity, Flexural Strength, Flexural Strain and Flexural Modulus of Elasticity

CORRECTED REPORT

BACKGROUND

On August --, 1991, Truesdail Laboratories, Inc. received for testing six composite panels for testing. They represented three different constructions, one set were conditioned and the others were control samples. The conditioned panels were subjected to 16-day immersion in 120-125°F tap water. The samples were identified as follows:

Room Temp. Cured - Dry   Room Temp. Cured - Wet
Oven Cured - Dry   Oven Cured - Wet
6631T - Dry   6631T - Wet

SUMMARY OF RESULTS

Determination	Sample I.D.	Dry	Wet
Tensile Strength (psi)	Room Temp.	19,000	13,600
	Oven Cured	20,700	16,300
	6631T	24,100	24,700
Elongation (% in 2.0")	Room Temp.	8.4	9.0
	Oven Cured	9.8	8.9
	6631T	9.3	10.7
Tensile Modulus of Elasticity (psi)	Room Temp.	390,000	325,000
	Oven Cured	418,000	388,000
	6631T	477,000	462,000

TRUESDAIL LABORATORIES, INC.

BP Chemicals
Laboratory No. 51927A
September 27, 1991
Page Two

Determination	Sample I.D.	Dry	Wet
Flexural Strength (psi)	Room Temp.	19,100	26,200
	Oven Cured	27,300	24,200
	6631T	44,000	45,500
Flexural Strain,r (in/in)	Room Temp.	0.029	0.024
	Oven Cured	0.025	0.026
	6631T	0.036	0.034
Flexural Modulus E_B (psi)	Room Temp.	1,140,000	1,230,000
	Oven Cured	1,160,000	1,060,000
	6631T	1,470,000	1,630,000

PHENCAT 381
Delayed Action Catalyst

Phentcat 381 is a recent addition to BP Chemicals' range of Cellobond FRP phenolic resins and catalysts for the manufacture of composites. It represents a major step forward in the technology of processing acid-set phenolic in that it is the first low temperature activated delayed-action catalyst to be available for these resins.

A range of potential advantages are now available, such as:

● Long pot/bath life (30 minutes - 5 hours)

● Reduced initial activity at elevated temperatures

● Similar cure times to conventional catalysts

● Improved health and safety in handling

● Reduced corrosivity

● Improvement of thixotropic systems

The main benefits to each composite manufacturing process may be summarized as follows:

Handlay

Long potlife; safer handling; improved thixotropy

RTM & VARI

Injection into isothermal elevated temperature tooling; reduced cycle times; longer tool life.

Press

Reduced exotherm risk in large components; faster cycling

Filament Winding & Pultrusion

Long bath life without forced cooling

Spray

Reduced exotherm risk; improved thixotropy

SUPPLIER NO. 2
CHECKLIST FOR EVALUATION OF RESIN
Non-Structural Information Only

Norold Composites, Inc.
4255 Sherwoodtowne Boulevard, Missisauaga, Ontario L4Z 1Y5
Phone: 416-279-2740 • Fax: 416-279-0050

RESIN TYPE: Liquid phenol-formaldehyde.
          Product Name: "Noracphen" NP-103
CATALYST/ACTIVATOR: p-toluene sulphonic acid, 5 phr
TYPICAL CURE: At 5 phr gel @ 70°F, approx. 45 minutes. Full cure 2 hours, min at 140°F. Eight hours recommended.

1. Initial color, clear amber. Viscosity appears okay for hand lay-up. Mild odor of formaldehyde fumes. (Norold reports as of August, 1991 formaldehyde emission is 1% or less.) Breathing apparatus and skin protection is still recommended. Turns ivory color in 35-60 minutes and becomes opaque. Slowly turns light pink to pink, 24-48 hours at room temperature.

2. Compatibility with reinforcement okay. Interlaminar bond (screwdriver test) okay.

3. Room Temperature Water Immersion Check: Water pick-up in first 24 hours 3%, stable at 2 weeks, 4% at three months.
   Oven Cured Room Temperature Water Immersion Check: Water pick-up first 24 hours 2%, stable at 2% for two weeks, then gradually increased to 3% at three months.

4. Overlay Bond.
   Room Temperature Cure: polyester zero bond — complete release. Vinylester same as polyester. Phenolic, good bond. Epoxy, no bond — inhibited. Furfural and polysulfide not checked.
   Oven Cure: Same results as room temperature observations. Where incompatibility or poor or no bond was observed, "Poly bond" or "Epoxy bond" will act as a satisfactory "primer" and will provide good bond.

5. Bond to Various Substrates: Plywood, particle board, 2 pound/cubic foot expanded styrene bead board, 4 pound/cubic foot extruded styrene board, 4 pound/cubic foot vinyl foam board (Kleg-e-cell), 4 pound/cubic foot vinyl foam board (Airex), 2 pound/cubic foot rigid urethane board, vitreous glass foamed board all showed excellent bond with no distortion or solvency. Bond to dry cementious concrete and sandblasted aluminum and steel were good.

6. All showed excellent resistance to propagation of flame through the phenolic laminate overlay into the substrate. Charring or melting of some of the substrate was observed.

7. This test, where the all-phenolic or phenolic overlaid shell was subjected to the gasoline fire, no ignition was observed and no structural damage was shown.

   NOTES to 6, 7, and 8: In all cases where NP103 was exposed to flame or burning gasoline, very little ignition of the resin was observed, and only a light, thin, non-noxious smoke was produced.

First Structural Test Requirements Results

(See pages 152-155, Norold NP-103 brochure and testing service report.)

Comments

It will be observed that there is considerable drop in percentage of strength retention of Norold's resin after water immersion (see structural strength wet data). The iso-phthalic polyester resin panels, 6631T indicates a higher strength after immersion due to the post-curing effect of the 125°F water.

Consideration should also be given to the actual values reported for the same reasons given for BP Chemical's phenolic resin. *(See Reference 18.)*

Because of the considerable drop in structural values after a relatively short interval of water immersion, it is suggested that this product be further evaluated before specifying long-term immersion in, or containment of, water. Considering the chemistry of the resin, it is not likely that resin hydrolysis problems will occur. However, because few if any coupling agents have been specifically developed for phenolic resins, the lowering of structural values after immersion may be due to de-coupling or other breakdown of the resin-glass bond.

The outstanding resistance to fire, the low production of toxic smoke and the ease of fabrication make this product an excellent choice either as the sole structural resin or as an over-lay to other materials where direct immersion in water is not required. *(See Reference 30.)*

1998 UPDATE ON NOROLD COMPOSITES, INC.

By the end of 1993, Norold was not able to generate sufficient market to justify distribution in the United States so operations were discontinued. Their products are available in Europe and Canada, however, and can be obtained from Canada for use in the United States. *(See Neste Resins North America, MS 58.)*

The loss of this supplier is most regrettable. The unwillingness of United States manufacturers to see the advantage of phenolic resins, particularly for wet lay-up molding, will be costly to them, as stiffer environmental requirements will eventually be imposed.

PRODUCT BULLETIN

NOROLD

NORSOPHEN NP-103

DESCRIPTION	Medium reactivity phenolic resole.
APPLICATIONS	• Developed for use in FRP applications.
FEATURES	• Low flammability. • Low smoke emission. • Superior heat resistance. • Excellent dimensional stability.

TYPICAL PROPERTIES

Viscosity @ 25°C (77°F) .... 500-700 cps
pH .... 6.5 - 7.0
Storage stability @15°C (60°F) .... 2 months
Pot life @ 20°C (68°F) (200p NP-103 and 12p NC-201) .. 14 - 16 min

PROCESSING

• Use molds and techniques generally used for FRP applications.

• The molds should be made of acid resistant material.

• The mold release can be any commercial release agent recommended for phenolics (Freekote, Axel and others)

• The glass reinforcement has to be checked for compatibility with the resin. The binder in some glass products will retard the curing.

• For cleaning, acetone or a mixture of 50/50 alcohol and water can be used.

SAFETY

Safely ventilate the working area. Handling the acidic catalyst requires care. The use of protective clothing, gloves and eye protection is recommended.

06/90-1

TOTAL

NOROLD COMPOSITES INC.

Head Office: 4255 Sherwoodtowne Blvd., Mississauga, Ontario, Canada L4Z 1Y5   Tel.: (416) 279-2740, 800-563-2089 Fax: (416) 279-0050
General Office: 217 Freeman Drive, P.O. Box 996, Port Washington, WI 53074   Tel: (414) 284-5541 Fax: (414) 284-7517

United States Testing Company, Inc.
Engineering Services Division
291 FAIRFIELD AVENUE • FAIRFIELD NEW JERSEY 07004-0000 • 201-575-5252

REPORT OF TEST

CLIENT: Norold Composites, Inc.
4255 Sherwoodtowne Boulevard
Mississauga, Ontario
Canada   L4Z 1Y5

NUMBER: 102011

October 22, 1991

SUBJECT: Physical Properties

REFERENCE:

Norold Composites, Inc., Purchase Order No. 000102.

SAMPLE IDENTIFICATION:

Four (4) samples of material were submitted and identified by the Client as follows:

Norsophen Phenolic Laminates -

1) Norsophen Room Temperature Set
2) Norsophen Post Cured
3) Norsophen Post Cured Immersed 14 Days in Water @ 145-150°F
4) ISO Polyester

TESTS PERFORMED:

The submitted samples were tested for the following properties in accordance with the procedures outlined in the ASTM Test Methods listed below:

1) Tensile Properties   ASTM D-638
2) Flexural Properties   ASTM D-790
3) Izod Impact Strength   ASTM D-256

Testing Supervised by:

Frank Savino

Frank Savino, Supervisor
Materials Engineering Section

SIGNED FOR THE COMPANY

By *[signature]*

Frank Pepe
Vice President

Page 1
of 4
njp

Form 804

A Member of the SGS Group

United States Testing Company, Inc.

CLIENT: *Norold Composites, Inc.*   **NUMBER:** *102011*

TEST RESULTS

Tensile Properties

Sample: *Norsophen Room Temperature Set*

Det.	Dimensions, IN		Modulus of Elasticity, PSI	Ultimate Tensile Strength, PSI	Elongation @ Break, %
	Width	Thickness			
1	0.499	0.226	1.70×10^6	27,200	2.01
2	0.498	0.221	1.56×10^6	26,200	1.96
3	0.498	0.220	1.26×10^6	22,400	1.97
4	0.504	0.218	1.35×10^6	21,300	1.26
5	0.507	0.229	1.27×10^6	23,300	2.24
Avg.			1.43×10^6	24,100	1.89

Sample: *Norsophen Post Cured*

Det.	Width	Thickness	Modulus	Ultimate	Elongation
1	0.503	0.234	1.67×10^6	25,600	2.10
2	0.502	0.236	1.57×10^6	23,200	1.91
3	0.503	0.235	1.49×10^6	21,800	2.34
4	0.501	0.239	1.44×10^6	19,500	1.26
5	0.501	0.233	1.50×10^6	24,200	2.24
Avg.			1.53×10^6	22,900	1.97

Sample: *Norsophen Post Cured Immersed 14 Days in Water at 145-150°F (1)*

Det.	Width	Thickness	Modulus	Ultimate	Elongation
1	0.507	0.246	1.55×10^6	23,600	1.72
2	0.505	0.238	1.52×10^6	23,300	1.87
3	0.506	0.232	1.47×10^6	22,800	1.93
4	0.506	0.233	1.34×10^6	23,200	1.82
5	0.497	0.244	1.38×10^6	20,700	1.47
Avg.			1.45×10^6	22,700	1.76

Sample: *ISO Polyester*

Det.	Width	Thickness	Modulus	Ultimate	Elongation
1	0.510	0.220	1.83×10^6	27,700	2.08
2	0.501	0.205	1.87×10^6	30,000	2.32
3	0.501	0.199	1.66×10^6	30,000	2.35
4	0.502	0.202	1.84×10^6	29,100	2.12
5	0.506	0.195	1.71×10^6	28,700	2.39
Avg.			1.78×10^6	29,100	2.25

NOTES: 1) This sample was kept in wet paper towels inside a plastic bag until it was tested.
2) Test date was September 6, 1991.
3) Crosshead speed was 0.2 inches per minute.

Page 2

United States Testing Company, Inc.

CLIENT: *Norold Composites, Inc.*　　　　　　　　　**NUMBER:** *102011*

TEST RESULTS

Flexural Properties

Sample: *Norsophen Room Temperature Set*

Det.	Dimensions, IN			Modulus of Elasticity, PSI	Flexural Strength, PSI	Deflection, Inches
	Width	*Depth*	*Span*			
1	0.541	0.217	4.00	1.61×10^6	43,600	0.41
2	0.539	0.227	4.00	1.61×10^6	35,600	0.32
3	0.539	0.219	4.00	1.60×10^6	40,400	0.35
4	0.538	0.224	4.00	1.48×10^6	31,800	0.30
5	0.547	0.222	4.00	1.62×10^6	37,400	0.32
Avg.				1.58×10^6	37,800	0.34

Sample: *Norsophen Post Cured*

Det.	Width	Depth	Span	Modulus of Elasticity, PSI	Flexural Strength, PSI	Deflection, Inches
1	0.541	0.236	4.00	1.73×10^6	39,400	0.31
2	0.529	0.225	4.00	1.92×10^6	39,700	0.28
3	0.542	0.227	4.00	1.61×10^6	40,400	0.32
4	0.538	0.230	4.00	1.85×10^6	43,400	0.28
5	0.543	0.231	4.00	1.67×10^6	38,300	0.31
Avg.				1.76×10^6	40,200	0.30

Sample: *Norsophen Post Cured Immersed 14 Days in Water @ 145-150°F (1)*

Det.	Width	Depth	Span	Modulus of Elasticity, PSI	Flexural Strength, PSI	Deflection, Inches
1	0.560	0.241	4.00	1.61×10^6	26,900	0.25
2	0.534	0.236	4.00	1.46×10^6	28,800	0.31
3	0.547	0.236	4.00	1.74×10^6	31,100	0.26
4	0.559	0.234	4.00	1.51×10^6	29,200	0.30
5	0.540	0.244	4.00	1.49×10^6	27,800	0.27
Avg.				1.56×10^6	28,800	0.28

Sample: *ISO Polyester*

Det.	Width	Depth	Span	Modulus of Elasticity, PSI	Flexural Strength, PSI	Deflection, Inches
1	0.543	0.199	4.00	2.14×10^6	57,500	0.47
2	0.540	0.203	4.00	1.95×10^6	53,100	0.47
3	0.535	0.198	4.00	2.07×10^6	52,900	0.45
4	0.547	0.194	4.00	2.04×10^6	49,500	0.44
5	0.547	0.201	4.00	2.08×10^6	54,800	0.46
Avg.				2.06×10^6	53,600	0.46

NOTES:
1) *This sample was kept in wet paper towels inside a plastic bag until it was tested.*
2) *Test date was September 9, 1991.*
3) *Crosshead speed was 0.1 inches per minute.*
4) *The rough surface of samples was face up.*

Page 3

SUPPLIER NO. 3

CHECKLIST FOR EVALUATION OF RESIN
Non-Structural Information Only

INDSPEC Chemical Corporation

411 Seventh Avenue, Suite 300, Pittsburgh, Pennsylvania 15219
Phone: 412-765-1200 • Fax: 412-765-0439

RESIN TYPE: Two components, precatalyzed phenol-resorcinol-formaldehyde. Product Name: PRF$_2$ 1000FM
CATALYST/ACTIVATOR: FIRE PRF$_2$ 1000 component — a base resin — is mixed with the curing agent, FIRE PRF$_2$ 100FM component B which also contains sodium hydroxide — the catalyst. Mix ratio: Component A, 45.7 parts wt.; component B, 34.4 part wt. filler, "Barytes" (barium sulphate) 20 parts wt. *Note*: Up to 3 parts phr (combined A and B) acetone may be added to lower viscosity. *Note:* Barium sulphate added to absorb some water but does not chemically react with the resin.

TYPICAL CURE: Initial gel (on laminate) begins at about 20 minutes at room temperature. Ultimate cure is very sensitive to time and temperature but will fully cure even at room temperature if given 2-4 weeks at 50% R.H. or less. Even when given a post cure of 131°F for one hour, laminate will require an additional 16-22 hours at room temperature to achieve full cure. A reading of 85 Shore D is required to attain full cure regardless of time-temperature schedule.

1. Initial color, dark purple, opaque liquid. Viscosity with or without acetone appears okay for hand lay-up, but opacity makes observation of air release difficult. Strong odor of formaldehyde and resorcinol; breathing apparatus and skin protection recommended. Laminate will gel in 20-45 minutes at room temperature, then will slowly develop hardness. Color will turn to nearly jet black.

2. Compatibility with reinforcements appears okay but impossible to detect visually due to opacity.

3. Room Temperature Water Immersion Check: Because this product is sensitive to water below a Shore B hardness of 75, laminate was held at room temperature for three weeks before immersion in tap water at room temperature. Water pick-up in first 24 hours 1%, at two weeks 3%, 5% at three months. During entire test immersion, water was not changed: much discoloration of water was observed due to exudation indicating that product had not reached full cure at time of immersion. After six weeks, severe surface blistering was observed. Oven Cure Water Immersion Check: Water pick-up first 24 hours 1%, at two weeks 3%, at 12 weeks 6%. Surface blisters were observed.

4. Overlay Bond. Results were the same as Suppliers 1 and 2.

5. Results were the same as Suppliers 1 and 2.

6. Results were the same as Suppliers 1 and 2.

7/8. In these observations where the all resorcinol phenol formaldehyde shell or overlay was subjected to the gasoline fire, some ignition was observed and was slow to self-extinguish. Strong fumes and some opaque smoke was observed.

Test Results From First Structural Test Requirement

Sample	% Glass	Flexural		Tensile	
		Strength ksi	Modulus	Strength ksi	Modulus
Dion 6631T	47.1	64.0	1818	32.44	2386
FIRE PRF$_2$ (Dry)	38.8	36.36	1110	22.28	1554
FIRE PRF$_2$ (Wet)	—	22.74	1173	15.50	1683

Comments

The product should not be used in applications where extended immersion in water is required. The INDSPEC people so advise and the physical tests reported so indicate.

The somewhat low fire resistance as reported in item 7 and 8 may have been due to undercure of the sample. Similar samples have been re-checked at 5 months at ambient temperature and after 4 hours bake at 140°F plus 5 months at ambient temperature. Fire resistance and smoke production appeared to be similar to the pure phenolic resins.

At the end of this commentary is a copy of a letter from INDSPEC regarding airborne emissions. Though this report indicates that the INDSPEC resin passed well below the OSHA limits, I strongly recommend use of gloves, full skin protection, use of a hood for small parts and SCBA for large parts. This suggestion applies to all open lay-up operations whether the resin is phenolic, furfural, urethane, or poly-vinylester. Those workers not necessarily occupied in direct application should be excluded from the molding area unless also protected. Ideally, the molding area should be a closed, atmospherically controlled room. In this regard the above statement may appear to be over-kill when applied to all resins. However, OSHA will get around to this requirement sooner or later, so the actual applicators might just as well get used to using protective equipment.

In regard to the physical test results, the wet strength retention of FIRE PRF$_2$ FM was about 70% in tensile strength and about 63% in flexural strength. In comparison to the 6631T iso-polyester control, dry strengths of INDSPEC are considerably lower due to the method of measurement, *i.e.*, use of ASTM test methods based on psi of sample rather than based on pounds-to-break. (*See Reference 18.*)

INDSPEC FIRE PRF$_2$ 1000FM resin has many applications as the total structural laminate or as cladding in composite construction where total immersion in water is not expected.

INDSPEC
Chemical Corporation
High Performance Resins

PRODUCT APPLICATION GUIDE

FIRE PRF$_2$™ RESINS
PATENT PENDING

FEBRUARY, 1990

APPLICATION GUIDE
FOR THE USE OF FIRE PRF$_2$™ 1000 FM
Thermoset Resin For Fabricating Factory Mutual Approved Fume and Smoke Exhaust Duct Systems

DESCRIPTION

FIRE PRF$_2$ 1000 FM is a two-component, pre-catalyzed phenol resorcinol-formaldehyde resin system for fabricating Factory Mutual approved fume and smoke exhaust duct systems.

Fire PRF$_2$ 1000 Component A base resin is mixed with the curing agent, Fire PRF$_2$ 1000 FM Component B. An inert filler is added to absorb water in the mix. Recommended fillers are barium sulfate or alumina trihydrate. Specific grades may be required to achieve published physical properties. See the mixing section for further details.

STORAGE CONDITIONS

The shelf life of Components A and B is 6 months when stored out of direct sunlight at temperatures of 70°F (21°C). Thickening may occur with storage temperatures exceeding 70°F (21°C). However this will not affect the physical properties of the laminate but will make reinforcement wet-out more difficult.

TO EXTEND SHELF LIFE EVEN LONGER:

1. Store the components in a cool area. Cold storage 40°F (5°C) would be best, but at the least, storage out of direct sunlight is necessary. Although freezing of the resins should be avoided, frozen resin should be stirred well after thawing to ensure uniformity before use.

2. Keep resin containers tightly closed when not in use to prevent evaporation of solvent.

3. For better wet-out, up to 3 parts acetone per 100 parts of mixed resin (10 parts per 100 parts of B Component) may be added to thin the resin mix with no negative effects. The added solvent will evaporate during the curing period. If adding solvent, give proper consideration to heated post-curing conditions as the concentration of flammable vapors will be increased.

SAFETY

Read and understand the Material Safety Data Sheet for these products prior to their use. Observe good industrial hygiene and safety practices when handling this product. Details of suggested personal protective equipment are available in the MSDS for these resins. **Use with adequate ventilation at all times. Keep out of the reach of children.**

MIXING INSTRUCTIONS

MIX TABLE
Component A
45.7 parts by weight or 4 parts by volume
Component B
34.3 parts by weight or 3 parts by volume
Filler
20 parts by weight or 1 part by volume

For optimum performance, the suggested ratio if mixing by weight is 45.7% Component A, 34.3% Component B and 20% filler. If mixing by volume is desired use 4 parts of Component A, 3 parts of Component B, and 1 part of filler.

Add component B to component A. Add the filler and stir to wet-out the powder, then mix with good mechanical agitation for 1 to 2 minutes until the filler is evenly dispersed. Then apply the resin to the reinforcement promptly, following normal procedures.

Automated mixing equipment designed for Fire PRF$_2$ Resins is available. Consult your technical representative for suggestions.

INDSPEC Chemical Corporation, Pittsburgh, Pennsylvania 15219

TECHNICAL DATA FOR FIRE PRF₂ 1000 FM

Description:
Pre-accelerated/pre-catalyzed, flame-retardant, low-smoke, phenol-resorcinol matrix resin.

General Characteristics:	
Form at 73°F (23°C)	Base Component A, amber liquid
	Component B, deep red liquid
Specific Gravity at 71.6°F (22°C)	Component A, 1.2 (approx.)
ASTM D 369	Component B, 1.2 (approx.)
Flash Point, Pensky-Martens	
Closed Cup	Component A, 150°F (65.5°C)
Closed Cup	Component B, 120°F (48.9°C)
Open Cup	Mix, No Flash Observed, Gelled
	at > 160°F (71°C)
Specifications:	
Total Solids, Abderhalden	Mix 90%
% Water	Mix 5%
Viscosity	Component A, 50-350 cps
cps at 73°F (23°C)	Component B, 500-3000 cps
	Mix 750-2000 cps
pH	Component A, 3.0-5.0
	Component B, 8.0-10.0
	Mix 8.0-9.5

Mix values given include 20 wt. % inert filler, barium sulfate.

PHYSICAL PROPERTIES FOR FIRE PRF₂ 1000 FM LAMINATES

Test Procedure	Glass Content, wt % 35
Flexural Strength, psi, – ASTM D 790	30,000
Flexural Modulus, psi, – ASTM D 790	1.1×10^6
Tensile Strength, psi, – ASTM D 638	16,000
Tensile Modulus, psi, – ASTM D 638	1.1×10^6
Tensile Elongation, %, – ASTM D 638	1.0–2.2
Shore D Hardness	75–85
Specific Gravity – ASTM D 369	1.9
Limiting Oxygen Index – ASTM D 229	52–55
Smoke Density per ASTM E-84 Tunnel Test	10–15
Heat Deflection Temp. at 264 psi, – ASTM D 648	About 400°F (202°C)
Coefficient of Expansion In./In./°C	22×10^{-6}
Izod Impact, Notched Ft. Lbs./In./In.	16.2
Flame Spread per ASTM E-84 Tunnel Test	10–15

Properties listed are for glass reinforcement as below:
    1 ply C-glass veil
    2 plies 2 oz. mat
    1 ply woven glass cloth

INDSPEC
Chemical Corporation

1010 William Pitt Way
Pittsburgh, PA 1523F

Telephone: 412-826-3666
FAX: 412-826-3699

Gentlemen:

Summarized below are results of tests commissioned by INDSPEC for formaldehyde and furfural airborne emissions during large scale hand lay-up fabrication using FIRE PRF$_2$® 1000 FM resin. Several workers were tested in each test. Results shown are the highest individual exposure in each test.

Maximum Formaldehyde Exposure	0.09 ppm CH$_2$O
OSHA 8 Hour Time Weighted Limit	1.0 ppm CH$_2$O
OSHA Short Term (15 Minute) Limit	2.0 ppm CH$_2$O
Maximum Furfural Exposure	0.28 ppm Furfural
OSHA 8 Hour Time Weighted Limit	2.0 ppm Furfural

In both cases, the worker with the maximum exposure was metering and mixing resin from an open-head container and then applying the resin by hand lay-up. Depending upon the application, local ventilation and temperature conditions, and the amount of direct contact with the resin, exposure may vary.

While these tests were conducted by an independent agency, following accepted test methods and procedures, for maximum protection, INDSPEC would advise that each site should conduct their own testing and document the results, as may be required by local regulations. Copies of the detailed test results are available upon request.

Very truly yours,

INDSPEC CHEMICAL CORPORATION

T. H. Dailey, Jr.
Group Leader
High Performance Resins

THD/vak

SUPPLIER NO. 4
GEORGIA PACIFIC RESINS, INC.

Georgia-Pacific Resins, Inc. produces several phenolic resins suitable for hand lay-up which may be ordered in different viscosities. I have used their GP-5111 "Resi-Set" Industrial Phenolic resin which has a viscosity range of 500-1000 cps. This provides fast wet-out of hand-laid fibrous reinforcements.

Although I have not run extensive physical structural tests on GP-5111, I expect these resins to perform on a par with those phenolic resins previously described.

Georgia-Pacific is a large producer of phenolic resins with 16 manufacturing facilities nationwide.

The following letter from Georgia-Pacific Resins quotes some physical values run on specimens run on their 5018 resin system with a post-cure of 30 minutes at 220°F. Note that the strength retention after a 60 day immersion in 10% salt water is reduced to 82%. This appears to be consistent with the other phenolic resins previously discussed.

The flexural strength data quoted is for samples post cured at 220°F and is for a higher viscosity resin.

GP-5111 with a lower viscosity and a post-cure (if at all) at a maximum of 140°F for 4 hours, would be realistic for hand lay-up operations.

Structural tests on GP-5111 made and tested by the same procedure as the four other producers discussed, may become available from Georgia Pacific. *(See pages 161-164 for Georgia Pacific technical data.)*

Georgia-Pacific Resins, Inc.

a wholly owned subsidiary of
Georgia-Pacific Corporation
2883 Miller Road
Decatur, Georgia 30035-4088
Telephone (404) 593-6800
Fax   (404) 593-6801

September 30, 1994

Mr. John A. Wills
32776 Via Del Venado
Valley Center, CA 92082

Dear Mr. Wills,

In response to your request, we have enclosed product brochures for two filament resins, GP5111 and GP5018. With this memo, we permit to reproduce the information for the Marine Reinforced Plastics Book.

Typical flexural properties for the glass fiber filament wound 5018 system are below:

Flex Strength   : 70,000 psi
Flex Modulus   : 2.30 msi
Resin Content   : 40-45%
Post Cure   : 30 minutes at 220^0 F

Regarding retention of flex strength in water and 10% salt solution, the composite specimens were soaked for 60 days at ambient temperature. After the soak, the flex strength retention was about 82% in water and salt solution.

This system offers excellent resistance to methylene chloride and ethylene dichloride solvents. The strength retention was 95% after one month soak in these solvents at room temperature.

Please let us know if you require additional data or have any questions.

Sincerely

Shahid P. Qureshi
Project Manager
Phenolic Composites

SPQ/kb
SPQ.wills.ltr

Georgia·Pacific

Georgia-Pacific Resins, Inc.

2883 Miller Road • Decatur, Georgia 30035 • Tel: (770) 593-6828 • Fax: (770) 322-9973

With the right chemistry, anything is possible.^sm

Product Information

GP-5111
RESI-SET® Industrial Resin

GP-5111 RESI-SET industrial resin is a phenolic resin developed for use in making fiber reinforced plastic products.

Specifically developed for filament winding, GP-5111 resin is also suitable for use in other FRP applications such as pultrusion, resin transfer molding and hand layup molding.

FRP products made with GP-5111 resin show superior flame resistance and low smoke generation while maintaining flexibility and toughness.

Uses and Application

The best performance of the finished plastic part is achieved when gelation and cure occur below 100°C.

Generally, cure time depends on the nature of the application, the mass of material, and the type and amount of catalyst. For non-volatile curing at atmospheric pressure the temperature of the resin during gelation must be maintained under 100°C. This prevents volatilization of the water in the resin as well as the water of condensation generated during cure.

Once the resin has gelled at the lower temperature, post curing at higher temperatures can be done, if desired, without void formation, bubbling or foaming.

Cure time can be decreased with an oven or other independent heating system.

Typical Properties

Type	phenol formaldehyde resole
Form supplied	liquid
Color	amber to brown
Solids, %	72 - 75
Viscosity, cps	500 - 1000
Specific gravity	1.19 - 1.21
Weight, lb/gal	10.0
pH	7.5 - 8.0
Flash point, °F	above 200
Storage life at 25°C	30 days

GP-5111 RESI-SET® Industrial Resin

Curing at temperatures under 100°C requires the use of an acid catalyst. A suggested acid catalyst suitable for use with GP-5111 resin is Witcat TXEG by Witco Chemical Co.

Cure rates with acid catalyzed phenolic resin systems are extremely sensitive and require careful attention to pot life.

Gel Time and Pot Life

Witcat TXEG (pph)	Gel Time at 90°C (sec)	Pot Life at 25°C (min)
8	35	300
10	26	25
12	20	14
15	16	7
18	14	5

The data in the table was generated using a resin mass of 50 grams. A larger mass will have a shorter pot life unless it can be kept cool by removing the exothermic heat generated.

Storage Stability GP-5111 Resin

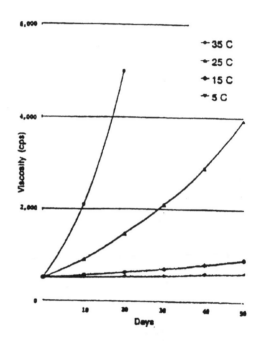

Other acid catalysts may be used but amounts and response times will vary from those reported here.

These catalyzed resin systems can be very exothermic and caution should be exercised when mixing and handling them.

High levels of catalyst generate greater exotherms, which can raise the temperatures of the mix above 100°C. This may cause volatilization of the water and undesirable subsequent foaming and void formation in the resin matrix.

Since the mechanism of curing is by condensation and not volatilization, actual use solids are in the 80% - 90% range.

Storage and Handling

GP-5111 resin should be stored at temperatures below 77°F and used in areas with good ventilation.

Stored GP-5111 resin should be transferred to the application area and brought to temperature prior to use.

As in any two part resin system, good mixing of the resin and catalyst is essential to achieve uniform cure and optimum quality.

Georgia-Pacific supplies GP-5111 RESI-SET industrial resin in drums and bulk quantities. More information on the safe handling of GP-5111 resin is in the Material Safety Data Sheet available from Georgia-Pacific.

92132(4/92)

Georgia-Pacific

Georgia-Pacific Resins, Inc.

2883 Miller Road • Decatur, Georgia 30035 • Tel: (770) 593-6828 • Fax: (770) 322-9973

*With the right chemistry, anything is possible.*sm

Product Information

GP® 5018/GP® 4839 RESI-SET® Industrial Resin System
For Fiber Reinforced Plastics

Description

GP® 5018/GP® 4839 RESI-SET® industrial resin system is a resin/catalyst system developed for use in the manufacture of fiber reinforced plastic (FRP) products. The GP-5018/GP-4839 resin system was specifically developed for filament winding, but is suitable for other FRP processes including pultrusion, resin transfer molding, and hand layup.

FRP products manufactured with the GP-5018/GP-4839 resin system demonstrate the superior flame resistance and low smoke generation required in many composite applications where fire and smoke are a concern; i.e., in the aerospace, construction, and mass transportation industries.

Uses and Application

The best performance of the finished FRP product is achieved when gelation and cure occur below 100°C. Curing at temperatures under 100°C requires the use of an acid catalyst. GP® 4839 catalyst was developed for use with GP® 5018 resin to provide extended working life and greater flexibility when processing.

Cure time generally depends on the nature of the application, the mass of the material, and the type and amount of catalyst. For non-volatile curing at atmospheric pressure, the temperature of the resin during gelation must be maintained under 100°C, thus preventing volatilization of the water in the resin as well as the water of condensation generated during cure.

Once the resin has gelled at the lower temperature, post-curing at higher temperatures can be accomplished, if desired, without void formation, bubbling, or foaming. Cure time can be decreased with an oven or other independent heating system.

Storage and Handling

GP-5018 resin and GP-4839 catalyst should be used in areas with good ventilation. Storage at temperatures below 50°F is recommended for the resin. The resin should be brought to room temperature prior to use.

As in any two-component resin system, thorough mixing of the resin and catalyst is essential to achieve uniform cure and optimum quality. Georgia-Pacific supplies GP-5018 and GP-4839 in drums and bulk quantities.

Additional information on the safe handling of GP-5018 and GP-4839 is in the Material Safety Data Sheets available from Georgia-Pacific.

Typical Properties

Type	phenol formaldehyde resole
Appearance	amber to brown liquid
Non-Volatiles, %	77 - 80
Viscosity, cps	1600 - 3000
pH	6.5 - 7.5
Specific Gravity at 25°C	1.22 - 1.24
Weight per gallon, lb.	10
Flash Point, °F	> 200
Storage Life at 25°C	30 days

(continued)

GP and RESI-SET are registered trademarks of Georgia-Pacific Resins, Inc. ©1995 Georgia-Pacific Resins, Inc. All rights reserved. Revised 10/95.

GP®5018/GP®4839 RESI-SET® Industrial Resin System

Storage Stability of GP®5018 Resin

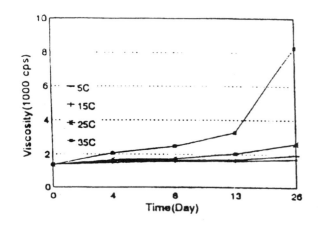

Stroke Cure and Pot Life

GP®4839 Catalyst (pph)	Stroke Cure at 90°C (sec)	Pot Life at 25°C (minutes)
8	10 - 13	>120
10	9 - 10	>90
12	7 - 8	60
14	6 - 7	40

Storage and Handling

GP®5018 and GP®4839 resins should be used in areas with good ventilation. Storage at temperatures below 77°F is recommended.

Prior to use the resins should be transferred to the application area and brought to temperature.

As in any two part resin system, good mixing of the resin and catalyst is essential to achieve uniform cure and optimum quality.

Georgia-Pacific supplied GP®5018 and GP®4839 resins in drums and bulk quantities.

More information on the safe handling of these resins is in the Material Safety Data Sheet available from Georgia-Pacific.

Fire and Smoke Properties

OSU heat release, kw-min-m^{-2}/kw-min^{-2} 2 minutes/peak	20/40
Flame spread index ASTM E-162	4
NBS smoke density ASTM F-814	<8
Flame spread index Tunnel Test ASTM E-84	15
Smoke generation Tunnel Test ASTM E-84	10

(rev 5/93)

SUPPLIER NO. 5
CHECKLIST FOR EVALUATION OF RESIN
Non-Structural Information Only

Borden, North American Resins Division

Liquid Phenolic Resin SL 414-B Lot # L5A-0478

Borden Laboratory, 6210 Campground Road, Louisville, KY 40216

Phone: (502) 449-6200 • Fax: (502) 447-4529

Attn: A.H. Gerber, PhD

RESIN TYPE: Liquid phenol-formaldehyde. Product name: SL 414-B

CATALYST/ACTIVATOR: Proprietary, triphenyl phosfite type

ACCELERATOR: Product name: Super Set BW 70, sulfonic acid type

PREPARATION OF TEST PANELS
RESIN

1. Initial color clear amber, slight formaldehyde odor (WARNING, FULL SCBA RECOMMENDED). Viscosity of neat resins @ 70°F approx. 1100 cps.

2. Manufacturer's instructions, quote:

    A suggested starting point is to use 13% hardener by weight on resin. To achieve 1-1½ hour mix life and curing in 4 to 5 hours @ 110°F (43°C) or at one day at room temperature, it is recommended to dilute the SL 414B 2% water and to pre-react the RC-901A hardener with either 3% water or 10% Super Set BW70 (*i.e.*, 10:1 weight ratio of RC-901A/BW). Pre-reaction is accomplished by simply agitating for 2-3 minutes. The solution can be used a half hour later an can then be stored indefinitely for future use. The BW leads to a more active hardener. Dilution of the SL 414B with 2% water will not only increase reactivity but will reduce resin viscosity to about 600 cps which will increase wetting of aggregate/filler, etc.

3. At approx. 600 cps mixed viscosity, wetting of reinforcement appears adequate.

REINFORCEMENT SCHEDULE

The following schedule is selected to represent most field practices for a relatively high structural strength product. This is the standard schedule to be used for all phenolic resin evaluations. Starting with the mold surface:

    1 ply fiberglass veil mat
    1 ply 18 ounce woven roving fiberglass (WR)
    1 ply 1 ounce chopped strand mat (csm)
    1 ply 18 oz. WR
    1 ply 1 oz. csm
    1 ply 18 oz. WR
    1 ply 1 oz. csm
    1 ply 18 oz. WR
    1 ply 1 oz. csm
    1 ply 18 oz. WR

CONSTRUCTION OF TEST PANELS

1. Apply mold release to glass plate. (Freekote 700NC recommended.)

2. Prepare catalyzed resin as follows: (300g batch) and 2% distilled water, 13% RC 901A which has been pre-reacted with 10% Sper Set BWW 90 (per instructions). Resultant viscosity approx. 500-600 cps.

3. Immediately start lay-up as follows:

    (A) Brush coat mold surface with resin (approx 14" x 14"). *Note:* Resin will not flow evenly on mold released surface due to nature of mold release.

    (B) All reinforcement plies are cut to approx 13" x 13". Apply 1st ply which is the veil mat. Use serrated roller to thoroughly wet reinforcement and to remove all air.

    (C) Apply 1st ply woven roving. Saturate with resin using brush. Remove air and complete saturation using serrated roller.

    (D) Apply 1st ply csm. Saturate and roll out air.

    (E) Repeat C and D until all plies are placed. A woven roving ply is the last on.

    Note: About halfway through, a second 300g batch of resin will be required. The resin must be used from its container within 10-15 minutes; otherwise it will likely exothermically react. Once applied to the lay-up, the resin may be manipulated for 1 to 2 hours.

OBSERVATIONS (from lab notes)

Total lay-up time 30 minutes. Viscosity of resin in lay-up slowly increased at 2½ hours to a non-firm gel when resin can no longer be manipulated. Note: Surplus resin from batch #2 in a 1" high x 3" diameter mass exothermed in approx. 45 minutes.

At 3¾ hrs., starts to turn white with a very soft gel. At 5¾ hrs., firm gel, pure white color. At 15½ hrs., laminate had achieved hard gel. De-molding appeared possible but was not attempted.

At 18½ hrs., with an average maintained temperature of 75°F, laminate was removed from glass plate. Excellent release observed. Panel was edge trimmed and weighed. Glass to resin ratio determined @ 4 glass to 5 resin (wt). Panel was cut in half. One half remains at room temperature for observation (starting date: 7/2/95). The other half was post cured @ 140°F for 6 hrs. Turned definite red-pink color. *Note*: No warpage observed in either half panel.

Comments

Use of this resin for typical open mold wet lay-up operations appears straightforward; *i.e.*, similar to polyester, vinylester or epoxy. Because of the mass effect, pot life appears to be less than desirable — more like epoxy wet lay-up resin than the esters. To avoid the nuisance of having to prepare endless small batches — especially making large moldings — a mixing head type roller-applicator will be required. These are already widely used in the marine industry. If a spray-up system is used, then there need not be a pot life problem.

TABLE 1

Phenolic: Laminate Maintained at 80°-90°F (44.9% Fiber Content) Without Post-Curing

Sample No.	Width (inches)	Thickness (inches)	Load (lbs)	Flexural Strength (psi)	Strength Normalized to Thickness (0.208 inch)	Strength Normalized to Fiber Content (51.6%)	Flexural Modulus (psi x 10⁶)	Modulus Normalized to Fiber Content (51.6%)
1	0.498	0.249	158	30,450	36,610	35,020	1.97	2.27
2	0.498	0.255	148	27,160	34,290	31,230	1.61	1.85
3	0.498	0.25	140	26,770	32,440	30,790	1.59	1.83
span: 3.968 inch for flexural modulus				Ave: 23,840	34,450	32,350	1.72	1.98

TABLE 2

Phenolic: Laminate Maintained at 140°F - 6 Hours (44.1% Fiber Content) Post-Curing

Sample No.	Width (inches)	Thickness (inches)	Load (lbs)	Flexural Strength (psi)	Strength Normalized to Thickness (0.208 inch)	Strength Normalized to Fiber Content (51.6%)	Flexural Modulus (psi x 10⁶)	Modulus Normalized to Fiber Content (51.6%)
4	0.499	0.245	163	32,300	37,690	37,790	1.78	2.08
5	0.499	0.244	153	30,670	35,380	35,880	1.72	2.01
6	0.500	0.245	153	30,430	35,310	35,600	1.76	2.06
span: 3.968 inch for flexural modulus				Ave: 31,130	36,130	36,420	1.75	2.05

TABLE 3

Polyester Lay-Up: Laminate Maintained at 80° - 90°F (51.6% Fiber Content) Without Post-Curing

Sample No.	Width (inches)	Thickness (inches)	Load (lbs)	Flexural Strength (psi)	Strength Normalized to Thickness (0.208 inch)	Strength Normalized to Fiber Content (51.6%)	Flexural Modulus (psi x 10⁶)	Modulus Normalized to Fiber Content (51.6%)
7	1.002	0.213	323	35,470	35,470	35,470	1.62	1.62
8	1.002	0.203	307	37,120	37,120	37,120	1.82	1.82
9	1.001	0.208	312	35,960	35,960	35,960	1.72	1.72
span: 3.328 inch for flexural modulus				Ave: 36,180	36,180	36,180	1.72	1.72

TABLE 4

Phenolic: Laminate Maintained at 80° - 90°F (44.9% Fiber Content) Without Post-Curing

Sample No.	Width (inches)	Thickness (inches)	Load (lbs)	Tensile Strength (psi)	Strength Normalized to Thickness (0.196 inch)	Strength Normalized to Fiber Content (51.6%)	Flexural Modulus (psi x 10⁶)	Modulus Normalized to Fiber Content (51.6%)
10	0.487	0.251	2,895	23,690	30,330	27,240	1.56	1.83
11	0.510	0.245	3,156	25,250	31,570	29,040	1.69	1.98
12	0.497	0.247	2,773	22,580	28,470	25,970	1.47	1.72
				Ave: 23,840	30,120	27,420	1.57	1.81

The polyester was INTERPLASTIC 75-200-319 isophthalic acid based polyester (manufactured by Interplastic Corp., Vadnais Heights, Minnesota). The polyester laminate underwent cure for one day at 75°F, followed by several days at about 80° to about 90°F without post-curing at a higher temperature.

TABLE 5

Phenolic: Laminate Maintained at 140°F (44.1% Fiber Content) Post-Curing

Sample No.	Width (inches)	Thickness (inches)	Load (lbs)	Flexural Strength (psi)	Strength Normalized to Thickness (0.208 inch)	Strength Normalized to Fiber Content (51.6%)	Flexural Modulus (psi x 10⁶)	Modulus Normalized to Fiber Content (51.6%)
13	0.492	0.245	2,827	23,460	29,320	27,450	1.81	2.12
14	0.474	0.244	2,961	25,590	31,870	29,940	1.7	1.99
15	0.501	0.246	2,965	24,040	30,190	28,130	1.56	1.83
				Ave: 24,370	30,460	28,510	1.68	1.97

TABLE 6

Polyester Lay-Up: Laminate Maintained at 80° - 90°F (51.6% Fiber Content) Without Post-Curing

Sample No.	Width (inches)	Thickness (inches)	Load (lbs)	Tensile Strength (psi)	Strength Normalized to Thickness (0.196 inch)	Strength Normalized to Fiber Content (51.6%)	Flexural Modulus (psi x 10⁶)	Modulus Normalized to Fiber Content (51.6%)
16	0.502	0.197	3,201	32,370	35,530	32,530	2.05	2.05
17	0.503	0.199	3,318	33,150	33,660	33,660	2.31	2.31
18	0.503	0.192	3,167	32,790	32,120	32,120	2.18	2.18
				Ave: 32,770	32,770	32,770	2.18	2.18

NORTH AMERICAN RESINS
WORLDWIDE PACKAGING and INDUSTRIAL PRODUCTS
DIVISION OF BORDEN, INC.
520 112TH AVENUE, NE, BELLEVUE, WASHINGTON 98004
TELEPHONE: 206-455-4400   FAX: 206-462-5487

DURITE® Phenolic Resin
SL-414B

Description and Applications

SL-414B is a phenolic resole resin designed for low temperature cure with latent acid hardeners. Applications include Resin Transfer Molding (RTM), filament winding, hand lay-up and syntactic foams.

Certified Physical Properties		**Mechanical Properties**	
Viscosity @ 25°C (cPs)	1050-1400	Tensile Strength (psi)	24,400
Solids @ 135°C (%)	71.0-75.0	Tensile Modulus (Msi)	1.68
pH, @ 25°C	5.0-6.0	Flexural Strength (psi)	31,100
Water Content (%)	6.5-7.7	Flexural Strength (Msi)	1.75

Packaging

SL-414B is available in standard 55-gallon, non-returnable drums containing approximately 500 pounds net.

Storage

The viscosity and cure characteristics of SL-414B will change based on storage conditions (time-temperature). For optimum product performance we recommend storage at lowest available temperature (50°F or below) and controlled stock usage.

Phyiscal Properties

The physical properties were tested in accordance with the current Borden Standard Test methods.

Mechanical Properties

Mechanical properties are an average of three measurements determined on laminates of 0.25 inch thickness with 55% glass reinforcement. Laminates were made by hand lay-up at 80-90°F. Test specimens were post-cured at a temperature of 140°F (60°C) for six hours.

3/96   Page 1 of 1

REFERENCE 14

FURFURYL ALCOHOL RESINS
by John A. Wills

Furfural resins, particularly furfuryl alcohol, is another group of materials overlooked by many in the reinforced plastics industry and, in particular, the marine industry. It is bad enough that *Modern Plastics Catalog* barely mentions liquid phenolics, and then only as a liquid casting resin; for this catalog to not even mention the furfurals as construction resins is a disservice to the plastics industry.

To those who at least know of its existence, furfural alcohol resin in particular is considered useful only for its outstanding chemical resistance and for use in making sand cores for the foundry industry. Some also recognize its fire resistance, which is comparable to the phenolics. Few realize the value of furfuryl alcohol as a marine construction resin.

Although fabrication techniques are similar to epoxy, phenolic and polyester resins, so far the marine industry has made little use of furfuryl alcohol resins for the same reason that phenolics are not yet accepted: unfamiliarity and a concern that new or modified techniques may be required. Again, necessity may change this attitude when regulatory agencies begin to set emission, smoke, toxicity, and fire propagation standards.

Furfural alcohol is a member of the furan family and is produced by the catalytic hydrogenation of furfural, which is an aldehyde of furan. Furfural is obtained from pentosan-containing agricultural products. Pentosan is a complex carbohydrate which is present in several woody plant tissues such as cereal straws, corn cobs, oat hulls, sugar cane bagasse, cotton seed hulls, and rice hulls.

Furfuryl alcohol resin is produced by homopolymerization of primary (water liquid-like) furfuryl alcohol. When the polymerization reaction is carried to a predetermined viscosity of 350–400 cps at 77°F and then stopped, it produces a useful viscosity for wet lay-up operations at room temperature.

In the following evaluation, furfural alcohol resin is offered as another candidate for use as a marine construction resin as against the inevitable time when imposition of stringent standards by government agencies as well as voluntary industry standards will be imposed. Environmental and life-threatening conditions beginning with the actual manufacture of marine products involving VOCs (emissions) and ending with consumer use of the product will require further investigation of available materials.

Manufacturers of Furfuryl Alcohol Resins

The QO Chemicals Division of Quaker Oats Company has been cooperative in supplying technical and physical data for the following Checklist for Evaluation of Resin. They are not to be considered in any way, however, to be sponsors or endorsers of my views or the work I have performed with their materials. (Their legal counsel has rather emphatically informed me of this!) QO Chemicals is not the only producer of furan resins, but they are a principal supplier for the general market and the only company I know of that produces the resin at useful viscosities (400 cps range) along with a practical catalyst system designed specifically for wet lay-up molding.

The Durez Division of Occidental Chemical Corporation offers Durez 16470 and Durez 18719 — both furfuryl alcohol resins in the 170 cps range.

Ashland Chemicals produces two furfuryl alcohol resins: Chem-Rez 244 and Chem-Rez 489, also of low viscosity in the 110-200 cps range.

The Occidental and Ashland resins are used primarily as binders for sand cores in the foundry industry where a low viscosity resin appears to be required. As such, these are not suitable for use in conventional wet lay-up operations. However, it is a matter of simple chemistry to produce these at higher viscosities as evidenced by the present fact that one of the above suppliers produces high viscosity furfuryl alcohol resins for another, yet does not produce this product for the open market. If sufficient market becomes evident in the reinforced plastics industry, including the marine market, then these two firms could become strong competitors to QO Chemicals which, at present, enjoys a monopoly.

Furfuryl Alcohol Resin Supplier
CHECKLIST FOR EVALUATION OF RESIN
Author's Laboratory Report

Evaluation of QO Chemicals' Furfuryl Alcohol Resin

QO Chemicals, Inc.
2801 Kent Avenue, West Lafayette, IN 47906
RESIN TYPE: Furfuryl Alcohol Resin
             Product Name: QuaCorr 1000
CATALYST/ACTIVATOR: Proprietary
TYPICAL CURE: 30 minutes, 3.5% cat 500 g 75°F.

1. Cast activated resin on glass plate maintained at 72°F and observe for: usable viscosity, color, transparency, odor and changes during cure.
   RESULTS: Dark color, transparent in thin film, mild stringent odor (SCBA recommended).

2. On glass plate as in (1), make a 10–20 mil glass veil and 1½–2 oz mat laminate. Let room temperature cure 24 hours. Check for binder, sizing, and coupling agent compatibility. Laminate 1½–2 oz mat with 7–10 oz. glass cloth over. Place 1/2–1" wide strip polyethylene film at one end between laminations to provide for intermediate bond check. Let room temperature cure 24 hours. Cut laminate in half vertically. Post cure one-half at 140°F for two hours. Use screwdriver to pry apart laminations to check for interlamina bond.
RESULTS: Good interlamina bond observed.

3. Room Temperature Water Immersion Check. Make laminate as in (2), but eliminate polyethylene film. Cut in half vertically. Trim, sand, and seal all edges with resin. Post-cure one coupon at 140°F for two hours. Keep the other at room temperature. Seal all edges with wax or epoxy resin. Immerse both coupons in tap water at room temperature. Check weight gain or loss at intervals for two weeks. Note stabilization point, if any.

4. Check Laminate Overlay Bond to other resins. Use procedure as in (2) at room temperature and post cure.

Polyester	Good
Vinylester	Good
Phenolic	Not Checked
Epoxy	Good
Furfural	Good
Polysulfide	Not Checked

If compatibility or poor bond is observed in (4), re-check using "Poly Bond" or "Epoxy Bond" or other primer.

5. Bond check of Other Resins to QO 1000:

Polyester	Poor Bond
Vinylester	Poor Bond
Epoxy	Poor Bond

If incompatibility or poor bond is observed in (5), re-check using "Poly Bond" or "Epoxy Bond" or other primer.
RESULTS: No improvement was observed.

6. Check iInterlamina bond to various substrates. (Note: make panel sizes at 8"x10" for No. 7 test following.)
At room temperature, laminate two 1½–2 oz chopped strand mat with 18–24 oz. woven roving onto and check for compatibility and bond to:

Plywood	Good Bond
Particle Board	Good Bond
2 lb/CF Expanded Styrene Bead Board	Good Bond
4 lb/CF Extruded Styrene Foam Board	Good Bond
4 lb/CF Vinyl Foam Board (Klege-Cell)	Good Bond
4 lb/CF Vinyl Foam Board (Airex)	Good Bond
Vitreous Foamed Glass	Good Bond
Dry Cementious Concrete	Good Bond
Sandblasted Aluminum	Good Bond
Sandblasted Steel	Good Bond

7. Check fire characteristics by exposing laminate side of samples in (6) to flame from gasoline or propane torch. It is suggested that a video be made.
RESULTS: In all panels, QO 1000 ignited slowly with production of considerable smoke and slightly irritating fumes. After approximately one minute, QO resin continued to support combustion slowly. This is usually an indication of under cure which at room temperature may require several weeks to show an improvement in fire resistance and reduction of smoke production.

8. Check individual fire characteristics in typical gasoline spill fire as follows: construct a hemispheric female mold of suitable material (the bottom of a 6" round bottom glass flask works well as a form). Mold shells using one layer chopped strand mat and one ply of 18–24 ounce woven roving on the inside. This will represent the typical inside surface of a boat hull. Make one shell and leave at room temperature for four weeks. Post cure another shell at 140°F for four hours.
Mount shells on a support or hold so the equator is approximately 20° from the vertical to enable bowl to contain 25 cc of gasoline. Ignite gasoline.
RESULTS: Room temperature cured shell was ignited by gasoline in approximately one minute by which time total combustion of shell had occurred. Considerable dense smoke was produced. Post cured shell required approximately 10 minutes to ignite shell after which time flame was self-supporting after gasoline had been consumed. Flame extinguished itself in 15 minutes. Considerable structural integrity of the shell remained. There was mild smoke production.

Test Results from First Structural Test Requirement

STRUCTURAL TEST PANEL CONSTRUCTION: QuaCorr 1000

Make 12"x 2" hand lay-up flat panels on glass plates starting with an 0.008-inch to 0.010-inch glass veil, followed by one assembly ply of Brunswick Technologies fabric, Style TVM 3408, which is a zero degree, minus 45 degree, plus 45 degree unidirectional roving plus one layer of chopped strand mat. This is a four ply stitched together unbound assembly whose dry weight is 40.75 ounces per square yard. The coupling agent on the glass is claimed to be compatible with all resins. It is important to check on this and the veil mat as well. I observed no incompatibility.

Completely saturate this first layer using firm roller pressure. Allow to room temperature cure for 24 hours at approximately 72°F at 50% humidity. Add a second and third ply of TVM 3408, each layer being allowed to cure at room temperature 24 hours. This process will make panels approximately 0.200-inch thick. Make four panels.

Two panels cured at room temperature are to be kept, one for wet and one for dry tests. Cure 2 panels at 140°F for 8 hours, one panel for wet and one panel for dry tests. Trim the edges of all panels. Seal the edges of those to be used for wet tests with QuaCorr 1000 or epoxy resin. Record original dry weight of all wet test panels.

Continuously immerse panels to be wet tested in tap water maintained at 140°F for two weeks. Surface dry wet panels with toweling, then cut into standard structural test coupons and test as soon as possible. Before cutting wet panels into coupons, determine percent loss or gain in weight. Dry sample testing may be run any time after complete cure.

NOTE: Room temperature wet panel gained 3% in two weeks. Post cured panel gained 2% in two weeks.

The following test data were submitted by QO Chemicals test lab to us. We made and conditioned the test panels. QO Chemicals prepared the test coupon, and performed the structural tests.

Sample Description	Heat Cured		Room Temp	
	Dry	Wet	Dry	Wet
TENSILE LOAD AT BREAK LBS.	2071	2093	2308	2324
TENSILE STRENGTH PSI	19334	19542	21549	21696
TENSILE ELONGATION	6	5	6	4
FLEXURAL LOAD AT	425	471	204	296
FLEXURAL STRENGTH	30363	29112	12578	18264
FLEXURAL MODULUS				
10KS psi BREAK LBS.	13.2	11.7	10.9	10.8

The following is typical laminate property as stated in QO Chemicals sales brochure:

A 32% glass laminate consisting of one ply of veil, 3 plies chopped strand mat, 1 ply woven roving, 1 ply mat, 1 ply woven roving, 1 ply mat, and 1 ply of veil. The cure schedule is: 1 hr. at 140°F, 2 hrs. at 180°F. and 1 hr. at 200°F. Structural values for this particular laminate are quoted as follows:

FLEXURAL STRENGTH, psi	(D-790)	20,000
FLEXURAL MODULUS, psi	(D-790)	800,000
TENSILE STRENGTH, psi	(D-638)	12,000
TENSILE MODULUS, psi	(D638)	1,000,000

Comments

From the foregoing Structural Testing Results of QO Samples constructed with TVM 3408 unidirectional glass fabrics, the heat-cured panels tested higher in tensile loads after water immersion than those that were tested dry! Flexural measurements for heat-cured samples both wet and dry showed little loss of strength.

Flexural measurements for samples cured at room temperature appear to be quite low. The indicated increase

in flexural strength for the room-temperature wet sample is due to some post-cure effect from two weeks of immersion in 140°F water.

It is curious to note that tensile strength measurements are reported higher for room temperature-cured specimens both wet and dry than those which were post-cured.

Fire resistance of QuaCorr 1001 is considerably less than the phenolic resins tested, but it appears to be self-extinguishing, at least if post-cured long enough.

Conclusions

For marine structural purposes, this resin appears to be satisfactory, particularly where high chemical resistance is required, and especially when used as an overlay. Hydrolysis does not appear to be a problem though long-term testing should be performed.

Although fire resistance without additives is considerably less than phenolics, it is much better than conventional epoxy or ester resins.

The main advantage of furfuryl alcohol resins over phenolics is their relatively long shelf life of uncatalyzed resin at ambient temperatures. Their odor is perhaps milder to some people than the phenolics, but SCBA is advised for either resin. Chemical resistance of fully cured furfuryl alcohol resin is high and could be of advantage for some end uses.

One disadvantage as of this writing is that only one principal supplier is available for a practical FA lay-up resin, which often leaves the user at the whim and fancy of a single source.

Structural Note

The phenolics, modified phenolics, and furfural resins have low tensile elongation; and in structures where dynamic loading is likely, they may not be suitable as the total structural resin.

When used as an overlay for fire and chemical resistance, some additional structural value will be gained. However, for hulls, the main structural resin should be one or a combination of esters or epoxies.

Note Regarding Non-Structural Foams

BP Chemicals, and possibly other producers of phenolics and furfurals, has a non-structural foam which is valuable when used as a fire barrier. This foam is friable (brittle) and will absorb water; but when injected into a cable duct or sprayed onto fire walls of ships, it will prevent the propagation of fire from one compartment to another. This happened to the British Navy during the Falklands war when one of their ships hit by a missile took four days to sink as no one could stop the fire propagation. Phenolic foam is now widely used by the British Navy!

REFERENCE 15

PROVISIONAL DATA SHEET

RP 6401-1 Resin and Hardener
REN:C:O-THANE® Polyurethane Elastomer
A Tough Resilient Shore 65 ± 10A Elastomer for Flexible Molds

DESCRIPTION: REN® RP 6401-1R/H is an off-white, two-component polyurethane elastomer that develops superior physical strengths without containing MOCA[1] or TDI[2]. The low viscosity liquids are easily mixed and cast with a minimum of air entrapment to produce surfaces with fine detail reproduction. Physical properties are excellent compared to RTV silicone. The flexibility of RP 6401-1R/H allows easy removal of complex parts. This product is an unpigmented version of RP 6401.

APPLICATIONS: Flexible molds
Resilient parts
Rollers
Strippers and pads

MIXING INSTRUCTIONS: Reaction Ratio   25R to 100H (by wt.)

Mixing: Stir each component thoroughly before use. Weigh each component accurately (± 5%) into clean containers. Thoroughly mix resin and hardener together (minimum 3 minutes) scraping container sidewalls, bottom and mixing stick several times to assure a uniform mix.

TYPICAL MIXED PROPERTIES:

Property		ASTM Test Method	Test Values[3]
		Time (min.)	Viscosity (cP)
Gel time and		5	1,000
Viscosity Profile (125g)		10	1,200
		15	2,200
		20	gelled
Color	Resin	Visual	Amber
	Hardener		Off-white
Viscosity	Resin	D-2393	50 cP
	Hardener		1,300 cP
Demold time (for most applications)			24 hrs.
Cure time (for ultimate properties)			7 days

[1]MOCA - 4,4'methylene bis(2-chloroaniline)
[2]TDI - toluene diisocyanate
[3]Tested @ 77°F (25°C)

(continued)

Page 2
RP 6401-1R/H

TYPICAL CURED PROPERTIES: Property	ASTM Test Method	Test Values[1]	Test Values[2]
Density (g/cc)	D-792	1.07	1.07
Hardness (Shore A)	D-2240	65 ± 10	65 ± 10
Ultimate Tensile Strength (psi)	D-638 @ 20"/min.	1,820 (12,548 kPa)	2,410 (16,616 kPa)
Ultimate Elongation (%)	D-638 @ 20"/min.	338	443
Tear Strength (ppi)	D-624 @ 20"/min. DIE C	171 (29.9 kN/m)	212 (37.1 kN/m)
Compression set[3] (%)	D-395 B	6.7	10.7
Linear shrinkage (in/in)	D-2566 Mold #1	0.0005	0.006

[1]Cure Schedule - 7 days @ 77°F (25°C), tested @ 77°F

[2]Cure Schedule - 24 hrs. @ 77°F (25°C), + 16 hrs. @ 176°F (80°C)

[3]Compression set, ASTM D-395, Method B.
The percent of permanent deformation resulting from constant deflection/pressure required to compress samples 25%.

Note: <u>Typical Properties</u> - These physical properties are reported as typical test values obtained by our test laboratory. If assistance is needed in establishing product specifications, please consult with our Quality Control Department.

CURING INSTRUCTIONS:

Although room temperature polyurethanes will normally set up to a rigid, demoldable state within 24 hours at room temperature (75°F ± 5°F), these systems reach their full cure after seven days at room temperature. A full cure can be accelerated by applying heat after the part has set rigid. We recommend a postcure of 176°F for a minimum of 16 hours. (Add to this adequate time to bring the part to the postcure temperature.) After cure, the part should be cooled at a slow rate so as not to shock the part thermally.

Uniform heat distribution is also required during postcure; concentrated heat, such as that directed from a lamp, can cause warp. An elevated temperature cure will increase the shrinkage compared to a room temperature cure.

(continued)

PROVISIONAL DATA SHEET

RP 6401-1 Resin and Hardener
REN:C:O-THANE® Polyurethane Elastomer
A Tough Resilient Shore 65 ± 10A Elastomer for Flexible Molds

---

DESCRIPTION: REN® RP 6401-1R/H is an off-white, two-component polyurethane elastomer that develops superior physical strengths without containing MOCA[1] or TDI[2]. The low viscosity liquids are easily mixed and cast with a minimum of air entrapment to produce surfaces with fine detail reproduction. Physical properties are excellent compared to RTV silicone. The flexibility of RP 6401-1R/H allows easy removal of complex parts. This product is an unpigmented version of RP 6401.

APPLICATIONS: Flexible molds
Resilient parts
Rollers
Strippers and pads

MIXING INSTRUCTIONS: Reaction Ratio   25R to 100H (by wt.)

Mixing: Stir each component thoroughly before use. Weigh each component accurately (± 5%) into clean containers. Thoroughly mix resin and hardener together (minimum 3 minutes) scraping container sidewalls, bottom and mixing stick several times to assure a uniform mix.

TYPICAL MIXED PROPERTIES:

Property		ASTM Test Method	Test Values[3]
		Time (min.)	Viscosity (cP)
Gel time and		5	1,000
Viscosity Profile (125g)		10	1,200
		15	2,200
		20	gelled
Color	Resin	Visual	Amber
	Hardener		Off-white
Viscosity	Resin	D-2393	50 cP
	Hardener		1,300 cP
Demold time (for most applications)			24 hrs.
Cure time (for ultimate properties)			7 days

[1]MOCA - 4,4'methylene bis(2-chloroaniline)
[2]TDI - toluene diisocyanate
[3]Tested @ 77°F (25°C)

REFERENCE 16

COMMENT ON DURATEC VINYLESTER PRIMER-SURFACER

by John A. Wills

In terms of the paint manufacturing craft, this is a high quality coating. By virtue of sound paint-making practice using modern grinding equipment, grinding and dispersing aids to produce pigment grinds around 7 on the fineness-of-grind scale along with air releases and surfacing agents, this product exhibits outstanding low moisture vapor transmission even at elevated temperatures.

While Durall and its distributors, Hawkeye Industries, Inc. (*MS 34*) and Revchem Plastics, Inc. (*MS 34*), do not warrant or claim this primer to be a "blister preventer." I suggest you make tests for your own decision for its use for hydrolytic protection. One graphic test would be to devote a square yard of surface clearly located on a hull bottom where Duratec primer will be coated. Over this and the rest of the bottom you would apply one of the commercial epoxy barrier resins. When required, apply anti-fouling paint overall. At the next haul-out, inspect for blisters. If any are found, I predict none will appear in the area coated with Duratec Vinylester Primer.

(See page 175 for Duratec data sheet.)

REFERENCE 17

CYCOM NICKEL COATED GRAPHITE FIBERS

COMPOSITE MATERIALS, L.L.C.

700 Waverly Street, Mamaroneck, NY 10543
914-381-4848 Fax: 914-381-4897

Cloth that has been woven from CYCOM nickel coated (NCG) fiber is an electrically conductive fabric suitable for various resistance heating applications When laminated into a composite tool and connected to a low voltage power supply, CYCOM nickel coated graphite cloth can provide the following advantages:

Controllable Heating Rate - Use of a suitable microprocessor enables the heat-up rates and cycle times to be controlled very accurately. The cloth is capable of being heated at a rate of 100°F/min. or faster if necessary.

Good Temperature Control - Very even heating across the tool surface is possible. With proper tool construction, temperature variation can be controlled to within 5°F across the surface.

High Temperature Capability - The service temperature of the cloth is limited only by the temperature capability of the resin. Tools can be constructed of epoxy, bis-maliemide, or polyimide resins. Prolonged use above 750°F is not recommended.

Cost Effectiveness - The use of nickel coated graphite cloth in tooling can be cost effective in several ways. When compared to the use of heating tubes in conventional integrally heated tools, the use of the cloth can substantially reduce tool fabrication costs. In use, a tool constructed with nickel coated graphite cloth can dramatically reduce the energy required for processing composite parts. For example, during autoclave processing only the tool needs to be heated, not the entire autoclave.

APPLICATIONS

Nickel coated graphite cloth can be used in tools for foam molding, resin transfer molding, and vacuum forming. Other non-tooling applications include heating blankets and field repair of composites. With CYCOM nickel coated graphite the applications are limited only by the imagination. Some fundamental technical information on the use of CYCOM nickel coated graphite fiber is contained in the following figures and notes. A typical arrangement of CYCOM NCG cloth for use as a heating element is shown in Figure 1*(see page 176)*.

ELECTRICAL PROPERTIES

Some preliminary electrical measurements have been made on Nickel Coated Graphite fiber 3k70PW plain weave fabric woven to 11.5x11.5 picks/inch. Other weave patterns and densities will be likely to perform somewhat differently. All measurements were made with the bare cloth in air at 70°F ambient temperature.

(continued on page 176)

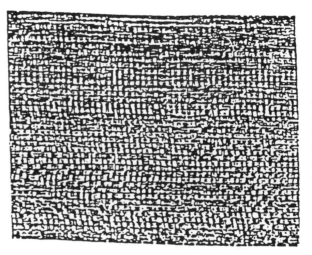

Cycom® Nickel Coated Graphite Fiber for integrally heated tooling applications.

DURATEC VINYL ESTER PRIMER

FOR OSMOSIS & BLISTER REPAIRS
OF COMPOSITE & METAL BOAT BOTTOMS

DURATEC Vinyl Ester Primer is a high quality primer manufactured from the finest corrosion-resistant vinyl ester resin system available today. This unique, high-build (up to two millimeters, wet on wet), easily sandable, porosity-free primer can be sprayed, rolled or brushed onto peeled or sandblasted composite and metal surfaces.

DURATEC Vinyl Ester Primer has been exposed to boiling water for 1000 hours with no evidence of blistering. Substrates are manufactured from orthophthalic and isophthalic polyester, vinyl ester and epoxy resins. Extensive testing has also been performed on actual repaired boat bottom cut-out pieces.

DURATEC Vinyl Ester Primer is used in conjunction with available anti-fouling paint systems.

For Hi-Build Fairing

DURATEC Vinyl Ester Primer is available with a low viscosity formulation that allows for the introduction of low density fillers, either pre-blended or sprayed dry into the primer when applied. This allows for very rapid build-up (up to 5 milimeters wet-on-wet), and creates an exceptionally easily sandable fairing compound.

Applications include: Composite and metal boat fairing; vacuum-forming mold surfacing, RTM mold surfacing; concrete mold surfacing, and plug & pattern surfacing.

Osmosis Damaged Hull

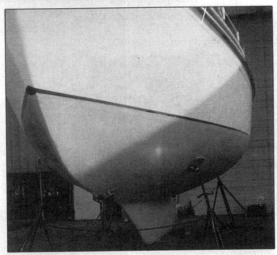

Same boat hull showing DURATEC Vinyl Ester Primer sanded to an 80-grit finish.

Also available from Hawkeye Industries:

DURATEC POLYESTER PRIMERS & COATINGS

Full Range of:
HI-BUILD PRIMERS, HI-GLOSS PIGMENTED & CLEAR COATINGS

HAWKEYE INDUSTRIES, INC.

3050 BROOKVIEW DRIVE
MARIETTA, GA 30068 USA
PHN: (404) 977-3336
FAX: (404) 565-5094

★ MOLD REPAIRS
★ MOLD RESURFACING
★ GEL COAT REPAIRS
★ PATTERN SURFACING
★ WOOD FINISHES

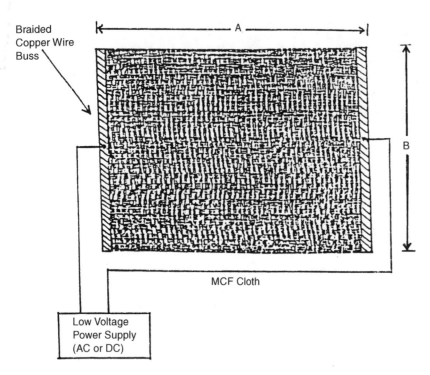

Braided
Copper Wire
Buss

A

B

MCF Cloth

Low Voltage
Power Supply
(AC or DC)

Figure 1

● Power dissipated as watts/sq. in. of NCG fiber fabric to achieve a desired temperature.

● Voltage drop/inch of NCG fiber fabric between the buss bars as a function of temperature.

● Current requirements/inch of NCG fiber fabric along the buss bar as a function of temperature.

(Note: The information contained in the preceding three notes provides guidelines for sizing a power supply. Additional information to help you more accurately size a power supply for a specific application is available from the firm which assisted American Cyanamid in developing the data included in this bulletin: Rectifier Systems Corporation, 338 Ferry Street, Newark, NJ 07015; 201-589-7910, attn. Mr. Chris Boyhan.

TERMINATIONS

We have found that a number of methods of making electrical termination to the NCG fiber fabric provide satisfactory results.

● Soldering a buss bar directly to the NCG fiber fabric provides a strong connection and is easily done. Simply brush the flux into the fabric first.

● Easiest of all methods we've tried in our labs is to lay up a flat braided copper wire cable as part of the laminate. Placed directly beneath the NCG fiber fabric ply, the wire braid requires no soldering. It is simply co-cured in place in direct contact with the NCG fiber fabric. Painting the NCG fiber fabric with a silver conductive paint where it will make

contact with the wire braid seems to eliminate all chances of hot spots. Other conductive paints may work as well. Electrical service is then connected to the ends of the wire braid that protrude from the cured laminate.

● Overlaps and joints of NCG fiber fabrics are treated similarly. Simply co-curing the overlapped fabric under vacuum pressure appears to be adequate. Very close tolerances may be achieved by applying a small bead of conductive paint between the layers of fabric to insure even and low resistance.

LAMINATE FABRICATION

No special construction techniques are required other than good toolmaking skills. We believe that vacuum bagging the prepregged tool during its own cure cycle is necessary for achieving and maintaining consistent electrical and thermal performance.

REFERENCE 18

COMMENTARY ON TESTING PROCEDURES FOR LAMINATES

by John A. Wills

The method of measuring tensile and flexural properties of composites using such procedures as ASTM D-638 and D-790 is misleading and not representative of true strength conditions. Flexural and tensile measurements are meaningful, generally when screening a composite, but unfortunately they are based on pounds per square inch of the sample. This is particularly a problem when the product is open-molded (single male or female molds) where thickness cannot be controlled. While the reinforcement, schedule in an open-molded composite laminate (*i.e.*, number of layers, lay and direction of the reinforcement and its style) can be accurately controlled, the laminate thickness can only be approximately controlled.

Any open molding containing reinforcement must be thoroughly saturated with the impregnating resin. This means that regardless of viscosity, 100% saturation is required. A high viscosity resin will always produce a thicker part, while low viscosity will produce a thinner part, assuming in both cases that full saturation is obtained and that the same amount of compaction is achieved.

If thin or thick panels both containing the same amount and type of reinforcement are structurally tested on a psi basis, the thicker one will always test lower — assuming the reinforcement alone has higher structural values (tensile) than the matrix resin. The result is that structural measurements made on a square inch basis will vary widely depending upon resin content, which is determined by the amount of compaction, even though the reinforcement is known exactly.

A method of obtaining meaningful structural values, particularly tensile strength, is to use test specimens dimensioned appropriate to the physical reinforcement schedule specified. For example, the reinforcement schedule for the foregoing phenolic panels called for layers of unidirectional rovings, each layer placed at 0°, plus 45°, and minus 45°. Three such layers were used which produced a finished nominal thickness of approximately 1/4 inch. Each individual continuous roving occupied about 1/4 inch of width, so depending upon how the test coupons were cut. ASTM D-638, which allows coupons

only 1/2 inch in width, does not provide true values because a wider coupon would be required to represent the actual lay of the reinforcement. Thus, coupon width in this case should have been at least 1 inch wide. The actual (nominal) thickness turns out to be approximately 1/4 inch, but this dimension is only useful for reference in design considerations. To break a coupon of this reinforcement configuration, *i.e.*, 1 to 2 inches in width by 1/4 inch nominal thickness, will require powerful test equipment, especially in tensile measurements.

Reports from testing laboratories often do not give pounds-force-to-break data in conventional tensile measurements. From a practical standpoint, if the design requires an open mold process, all the designer needs to know is the reinforcement schedule. He will assume that full saturation of these reinforcements will have been accomplished regardless of viscosity, compaction, and laminating schedule. He will also realize that resultant "thickness" of the product is somewhat irrelevant because "you takes what you gets." Also on most large moldings, several laminates are laid and cured separately on top of each other. Compared to the method of impregnating all plies at the same time, this always increases net thickness because more resin must be used to provide complete saturation of each layer. To take a coupon from an open-molded product and measure structural values on a pounds-per square-inch basis is inaccurate, to say the least.

I remind you that this discussion so far refers to those products whose principal reinforcements are constructed from uni-directional continuous strand materials, whether they be glass or other materials. Random laid fibers such as veil or chopped strand mat often are combined with uni-directional strands, but contribute little strength other than bonding of strands, some compressive strength, and some stiffness. Very little tensile strength is contributed.

Testing for Design Considerations

Press-molded, filament-wound, vacuum bag, pressure bag, and plug-molded products — unlike open-molded products — can be tested structurally by classic means (psi). Thickness can be closely controlled, thus allowing pre-determination of percent reinforcement content by weight and/or volume.

If structural tests are run on coupons made from a flat plate containing directionally laid reinforcements where the exact amount of reinforcement in terms of volume or weight is known, then any ultimate resin to reinforcement ratio may be accomplished simply by adjusting the thickness. Of course, reinforcement content per unit area determines ultimate strength. If thickness is fixed, then adjustment of weight or volume of reinforcement will determine resin-reinforcement ratio which, in turn, will determine the final strength figures. Thickness makes very little difference in the ultimate strength of a laminate as long as the exact amount and placement of reinforcement is known and saturation (elimination of air or gas voids) is complete.

Stiffness is another matter. Consider two panels, each made with a given reinforcement weight of one pound per square foot. Make one panel with a 25:75 resin-to-reinforcement ratio and the other with a 75:25 resin-to-reinforcement ratio. Both will develop about the same pounds-force-to-break in tensile loading per unit width, which of course, is not measured on a psi basis. The 25:75 panel will be about half as thick as the other. The 75:25 panel will be much stiffer due to the high volume resin content. From a practical standpoint, most boat hull skins, whether single or cored, will have approximately a 70:30 resin-to-reinforcement ratio, which provides a desirably stiff panel for a given amount of reinforcement.

To determine the useful strength of filament-wound pipe is to determine the number of strands (volume) which can be wound per unit thickness. This is done by tensioning the fibers (rovings) by a known amount. Viscosity variations of the matrix resin will not affect ultimate thickness if the tensioning is relatively high. Viscosity is of more concern in pre-impregnation of fibers prior to reaching the mandrel.

Pressure testing to burst is the usual way of determining structural values for pressure vessels, especially pipe.

The test results, of course, relate to the amount and lay of the reinforcement per unit thickness which also relates to the tensioning pressure for round or near-round wound structures, and closing pressure for dies, bags and plugs. All of these methods determine reinforcement content per square inch of section.

What this boils down to in terms of providing useful structural information for products manufactured by open mold technique is this: It is necessary to select appropriate test specimen width in the order of 1 to 2 inches and often 1/4 inch or more in thickness when testing state-of-the-art high strength structures. Net thicknesses of more than 1/4 inch and 1 to 2 inches wide would require excessively strong test equipment.

Finally, if the exact amount (weight and/or volume) of reinforcement is specified per unit width of laminate, and if resin saturation is complete, the final thickness will depend solely on the method of compaction. For open mold lay-up, this in turn depends on the true viscosity, thixotropy, and wetting ability of the matrix resin and the technique of the molder.

Conventional structural test results should not only report observed psi data, but more important, the actual pounds-force-to-break information. You will find that as long as you know the exact width of the test sample and the amount of directional reinforcement, measurements of pounds-force-to-break will be close regardless of thickness or resin content.

Remember, you can never determine the strength of an open molded laminate by measuring its thickness.

Camera housing and battery case molded in matched molds from boat grade fiberglass and polyester resin. Used by scuba divers to 300 feet and by astronauts on outer space. Fisrt camera used on the moon by Neil Armstrong. Produced by the author for D.B. Milliken Co.

REFERENCE 19

Chapter 1

Introduction

According to a 1987 survey conducted by *Practical Sailor* magazine among 1,852 of its readers, on average, 27% of all boats have developed osmotic gelcoat blistering. That figure varies by geographic region; from 10% in the northeast, soaring to nearly 50% in the gulf states. Based on the survey, *Practical Sailor* also estimated that in areas where a boat will remain in the water a major portion of the year, there is a 50-50 risk of developing blisters.

Obviously, gelcoat blistering is no longer an occasional occurrence; but, rather an epidemic which has shaken the entire fiberglass boat industry. And there is additional evidence that blisters are not only cosmetic, but can also lead to critical structural failure as well. Builders, resin manufacturers, repair yards, and owners have suddenly found themselves dealing with a problem which presents more questions than answers.

In 1985, the University of Rhode Island, through the U.S. Coast Guard and the American Boat Builders and Repairers Association, began a $60,000 research program to investigate and document the causes of osmotic blistering. Under the direction of

Dr. Thomas Rockett and Dr. Vincent Rose, the final report was released in late 1986: the first scientifically-based, impartial look into the fiberglass osmosis/laminate deterioration problem.

Although the study presented the most comprehensive and detailed explanation of the osmosis problem to date, it did little to tell the boat owner or repair facility what course of action might be taken to remedy or

prevent blistering. Furthermore, little was done in terms of determining the long-term effectiveness of some of the popular repair methods and procedures being advocated by a variety of credible and not-so-credible sources.

Gougeon Brothers first became actively involved in the blister phenomenon approximately 10 years ago, when Morgan Yachts began experiencing fiberglass laminate problems. Morgan was

Figure 1 *Gougeon Brothers' modern laboratory includes two MTS, servo-hydraulic test machines. The lab has also conducted material test programs for NASA, General Electric and Westinghouse.*

the first company to recognize blistering as an industry-wide problem; and came to Gougeon Brothers for a solution. WEST SYSTEM® Brand products were used to successfully repair these early cases of blistering.

Thousands of boats have since been repaired or protected using WEST SYSTEM epoxy along with the Gougeon Brothers' techniques and procedures. Gougeon Brothers has worked closely on a daily basis with individuals and yards, striving for a better understanding of the gelcoat blister problems in an effort to develop better solutions.

Several years ago, the Gougeon laboratory initiated a comprehensive osmosis research program. We are now testing laminates with a variety of commercially available coatings and finishes for blister prevention effectiveness. Beyond coating analysis, we're also subjecting these same samples to fatigue testing--in effect, speeding up time to determine how a particular material and repair procedure will hold up over an extended period of real-world service. Using sophisticated test equipment, we can compress the millions of load cycles a sample would normally experience over many years into a day or two of testing. *(Figures 1 & 2)*

Meade and Jan Gougeon have now led a team of chemists, engineers, builders and technicians in producing the first truly comprehensive guide to effectively diagnosis, repair and prevent gelcoat blistering. In this manual, we will explain the physical and chemical changes that take place in a fiberglass structure over the years, and how to diagnose and repair gelcoat blistering.

There is still a great deal to learn about this very serious problem, with answers that will require many years of exhaustive research and a commitment of capital and resources; a commitment that Gougeon Brothers, Inc. has made. For now, we offer you the best possible solution available, based on our laboratory research and more than ten years of in-the-field experience, along with unmatched technical support.

If, after reading this material, you still have specific questions, please call one of our Technical Staff. There is no charge for this service, and these highly-experienced technicians will be happy to discuss your problem in detail with you.

To keep our data base as comprehensive as possible, we also encourage you to write or call with your experiences involving osmosis, blistering and repair materials and techniques.

Figure 2 *Various epoxy formulations are cast into cylindrical annular shear samples and tested on the MTS machines for physical properties. Other tests include moisture exclusion ability and fatigue resistance.*

TECHNICAL ASSISTANCE

Telephone: (517) 684-7286
FAX: (517) 684-1374

Chapter 2

Why are Fiberglass Composites Susceptible to Osmosis and Gelcoat Blistering?

Gelcoat blistering occurs when moisture is allowed between the gelcoat and the laminate, or within the laminate itself. Moisture can enter the laminate from the inside or outside of the hull, passing through the gelcoat or via cracks or other structural flaws. The moisture begins reacting with water-soluble materials remaining within the laminate from the curing process, creating a caustic fluid and osmotic pressure. To understand this phenomenon, you need to understand how a typical fiberglass laminate is built, and the materials that are used in the construction process.

A fiberglass boat is a composite structure, made of many layers of various reinforcing fabrics and core materials, bonded together with a polyester resin. There are as many lay-up schedules as there are boats. A typical hull section might consist of a layer of polyester gelcoat, several alternating layers of mat and woven roving, and in many cases a core material such as end-grain balsa or foam, followed by several more alternating layers of mat and woven roving. *(Figures 3 & 4)*

Figure 3 *A solid fiberglass laminate is made up of various reinforcing fabrics, all bonded together with polyester resin.*

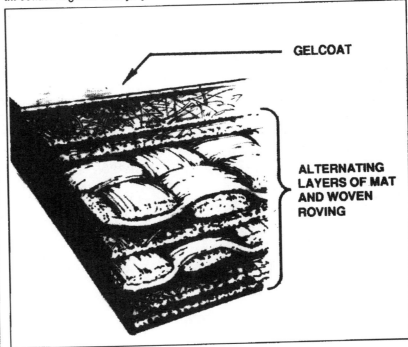

GELCOAT

ALTERNATING LAYERS OF MAT AND WOVEN ROVING

Gelcoat Blisters: Diagnosis, Repair & Prevention 3

The gelcoat may be anywhere from 12 to 22 mils thick. It is a pigmented, unsaturated polyester resin designed to act as a moisture barrier for the underlying laminate, as well as a cosmetic finish.

Generally, production fiberglass boats are built in a female mold. A release agent is first applied to the bonding surface of the mold, over which the gelcoat is applied. Subsequent layers of the laminate are laid up over the gelcoat.

Hull thickness may vary from boat to boat. Older boats were often laid up with a solid laminate hull thickness of 1 1/2" (3.8cm) to as much as 5" (12.7cm) in the keel areas of some of the more heavily-built boats. Today, however, the trend is toward thinner, lighter laminates; a fact that makes the structural integrity of each of the laminate components all the more critical.

Modern unsaturated polyesters used in boat construction are made up of three basic components: glycol, organic acid and reactive diluents (usually styrene).

If you were to look at uncured polyester resin under an electron microscope, you would see what appears to be thousands of chains made up of alternating glycol and acid. Adding a peroxide catalyst, typically MEKP, to the polyester resin mixture initiates a cross-linking reaction; in effect, creating bridges which link adjacent chains together. As the mixture cures, more and more bridges are established, and the free-moving glycol/acid chains begin to gel becoming a solid mass. Eventually, enough bridges are built to form a rigid, three-dimensional grid—the mixture has become a solid thermoset.

Many different types and combinations of glycols, acids and reactive diluents can be used by the resin manufacturer when developing a formulation. Each ingredient alters the basic physical characteristics of the cured resin, including hydrolytic stability, strength and elongation. The mixing proportions can also have an impact, leaving unreacted glycols trapped in the resin after cure.

As a building material, the unsaturated polyesters seem to be a logical choice. They offer relative ease of handling, reasonable cost and, what appears to be, an acceptable working lifetime. Unfortunately, there are two other important characteristics that we now know are working against the polyester structures.

First, the unsaturated polyesters used in laminating resins and gelcoats are not waterproof. In fact, they are quite permeable and will allow water to migrate through the cured resin at a consistent, predictable rate. We also know that the warmer the ambient temperature, the higher the rate of permeation. *(Figure 5)*

Second, the polyester resin decomposes when exposed to water under the right conditions; a process called hydrolysis. As the resin breaks down, many contaminants may be present in a heavy solution containing water, unreacted glycols, metals and acids.

Figure 4 *A cored laminate, in addition to alternating layers of synthetic fabrics, utilizes end-grain balsa or foam to provide strength with less weight.*

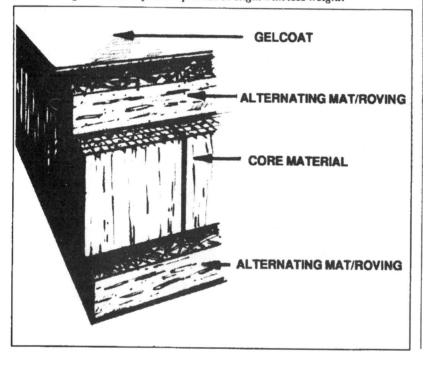

GELCOAT

ALTERNATING MAT/ROVING

CORE MATERIAL

ALTERNATING MAT/ROVING

Very simply, this aqueous solution is made up of chemicals with primarily large molecules, trapped between the laminates, or between the laminate and the gelcoat. Your boat, meanwhile, is sitting in a relatively clean solution of water—a substance made of much smaller molecules. The gelcoat becomes a semi-permeable membrane which will allow water molecules to pass through the resin without allowing the contaminated solutes to pass out.

Water passing through the gelcoat into voids and resin-starved pockets helps break down more of the unsaturated polyester molecule chains, which allow more water to pass into the laminate. This one-sided movement of water into the laminate is known as osmotic pressure. And research has shown that osmotic pressure increases in

Figure 5 *Ambient temperature can play an important role in a laminate's susceptibility to moisture permeation. Permeation tends to increase with higher temperatures.*

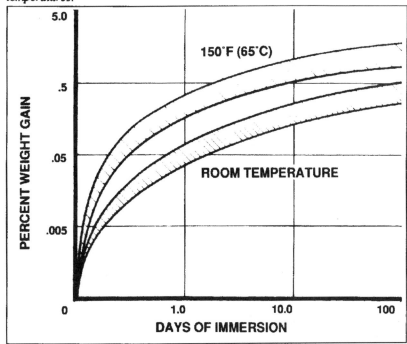

Figure 6 *A relatively sound laminate (1) will experience less moisture migration than a structure with interlaminate voids containing solutes (2). As the level of solute increases, the rate of permeation accelerates.*

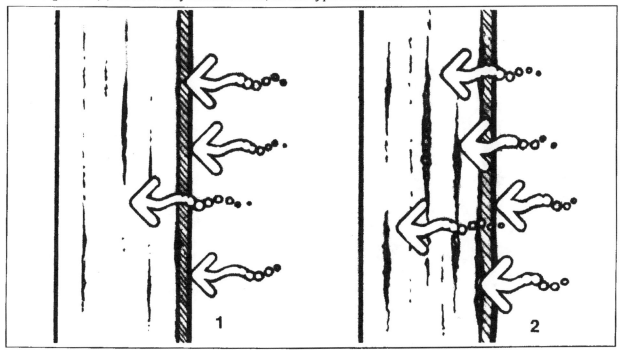

direct proportion to the level of solute (excess glycols, acids, metals, etc.) in the water within the laminate. *(Figure 6)* The process, in effect, feeds on itself, creating pressure between the gelcoat and laminate, or the laminates themselves and results in a gelcoat blister. *(Figure 7)*

It is important to understand that this whole process is happening even in an absolutely perfect fiberglass laminate. Imagine what's going on in a laminate where the manufacturer might have been less than conscientious, leaving resin-starved pockets, gaps, voids or contaminants. Areas where gelcoat thickness wasn't properly monitored can result in unscheduled thin areas and therefore, areas with even less resis-tance to the migration of water into the laminate. (For a more detailed explanation of the blistering problem, see Appendix A: Variables Influencing Blister Formation)

Figure 7 *As osmotic pressure increases, gelcoat blisters between the laminate and polyester gelcoat begin to appear.*

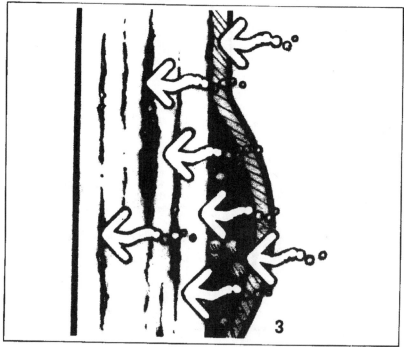

APPENDIX A
Variables Influencing Blister Formation

Experts throughout the marine and coating industries agree that blistering of polyester resin matrices is a complex question offering few easy answers. The broad range of variables affecting the formation of blisters runs from the formulation of the resin for specific applications to manufacturing quality assurance to the service environment. The common thread is the ease with which moisture can enter the laminate and alter the chemistry of the resin matrix. The presence of water in concert with resident components can provide an acid condition which can cause a breakdown in the susceptible ester linkages. The chemical stability of the polymer and the permeability of the matrix are the key items affecting the durability of the fiberglass hull.

Formulation

A large number of formulation variables influence the susceptibility or resistance of cured polyester laminates to degradation and blistering. The use of unsaturated polyester resin and the choice of promoter and catalyst can act as blister initiators in poorly mixed or incompletely reacted matrices. Theoretically, a wide variety of additives (air-release agents, leveling additives, UV-resistant additives, surfactants, abrasion-resistant additives, fire retardants, anti-oxidants and co-monomers) have the potential to affect blister resistance in the cured laminate. Thixotropic agents, hydrophilic fillers, pigment, color paste vehicle, and the use of solvents as a diluent can change the sensitivity to moisture and aid in the formation of blisters. The inclusion of any moisture-sensitive materials could stimulate hydrolysis of the matrix materials and promote the osmotic pressure which causes blisters.

Permeability

The permeability of polyester and epoxy polymer matrices involves a number of factors.

A primary consideration is the distribution of free volume (voids) in the matrix. In any polymer, the free volume can be everything from the gaps (in angstroms) between and within the molecules to manufacturing artifacts such as entrapped air bubbles and cracks. The solidification (cure) rate, degree of cross-linking and the crystallinity variation of the cured matrix all affect this void distribution while also contributing to the overall chemical stability of the finished laminate.

Thickness of the gelcoat/membrane is an important element in diffusion of water through the membrane (all the physical laws of diffusion use thickness as a variable). A thick coating of a stable polymer is a very capable moisture barrier, while a thick layer of an unstable polymer contains more of the elements that will facilitate its own breakdown.

The overall chemical stability of the matrix involves the formulation considerations outlined above. With any particular formulation, the polarity of the polymer can affect how freely water will pass through the matrix by assisting or hindering the hydrogen bonding of the water molecule. An increase in the service temperature can boost the rate of permeation through an unstable matrix by intensifying the molecular motion of both the polyester and the water. When water is present in the laminate, the higher temperatures can cause increased sensitivity to degradation in the ester linkages, additional swelling of the matrix and accelerate hydrolysis where it is already occurring in the laminate. In addition, surface oxidation can increase the wetability (and moisture content) of the polyester.

The hydrolysis potential of the thermoset matrix can vary by the material. In general, when comparing epoxy to polyester, the structure of the cured epoxy's ether linkage is more stable than the structure of the polyester's ester linkage. This means that the epoxy matrix will not break down by water hydrolysis as easily as the polyester matrix.

Interfacial adhesion between the polyester and fiber reinforcement in the laminate is an area vulnerable to poor quality manufacturing practices, material limitations and the rigors of the service environment. Beyond poor wet-out during fabrication, high stress or strain in the laminate during use can cause a loss of adhesion or the initiation of micro-cracking at the interface. Micro-bubbles and multiphase interfaces within the matrix (due to differential cure and shrinkage rates) are all stress concentrations and as such, are areas vulnerable to loss of adhesion or cohesion. The resulting voids are sites for water migration, the concentration of any soluble materials in the laminate and hydrolysis.

With all these variables, defining a laminate schedule, polyester matrix formulation and manufacturing plan that is impervious to attack is probably impossible. Epoxy has a service history unmarred by blistering problems but does incur a processing penalty when used in large-scale production boat building. For the custom boat builder, high-end production facility or marine repair yard, the high mechanical and chemical stability, coupled with the excellent moisture resistance properties of epoxy, offer reassurance in the choice of materials to battle gelcoat blistering.

REFERENCE 20

HOW THE U.S. NAVY NEARLY SHOT DOWN THE BOAT INDUSTRY

by John A. Wills

Having been a manufacturer of reinforced plastics since the first gleam, I had the questionable privilege, along with others, of fighting the "Plastics Battle of the U.S. Navy."

When fiberglass boats were first rubbed under the noses of the mighty naval specifiers, we were simply snubbed flat for several years. How could a few "pepper tree" shops provide the quality control and workmanship so necessary to deliver any product to the U.S. Navy? How could we possibly adhere to any MIL spec? At first there weren't any specs that we could adhere to until the all-knowing Navy engineers produced their version of "how-to" fiberglass production "techniques." Almost all of us pepper tree artists steered clear of the Navy and concentrated on going broke more slowly by staying in the civilian recreational boat market.

In the early '50s, in the Bellingham area of the state of Washington, a large shipyard, who will best be unnamed, had been producing wood hulled mine sweepers during and after World War II. By the late 1940s to early 1950s, the Navy had finally recognized reinforced plastics for boats as a possible replacement for cost-intensive wood construction (Navy style).

One way or another, the Navy convinced the Bellingham firm to produce a prototype RP mine sweeper *à la* Navy specifications including strict Navy manufacturing methods. It was fortunate for the Bellingham firm that the contract was cost-plus because any domestic boat builder would have gone broke by the time the first lay-up had gelled. Not many of these mine sweepers were built but they did perform well for several years. They also showed that large RP boats up to about 100 feet could be built even if they cost four times as much as wood construction. Of course, because of their size, these boats had to be left in the water all of the time. The Navy had become quite exuberant over fiberglass construction by this time. So much so that all Navy craft (boats) under 85 feet in length, including all life boats and other small support craft, were to be constructed of fiberglass and fire-resistant polyester resin.

The same shipyard that produced these mine sweepers became interested in manufacturing boats for the local recreation market. The owners also wanted to free themselves from the rigid naval specifications and almost ridiculous manufacturing procedures they had been required to follow.

I spent quite a bit of time "re-educating" them in pepper tree techniques, particularly in mold construction.

Unfortunately, I could not wean them from using Navy style fire-retardant resins and fillers. Their argument was that they could boast over competitors that theirs was fireproof and made to Navy specifications. The competitors did not suffer much. We had very few serious fires in 14 foot open boats at the time!

As it has turned out today, few if any of these small boats have shown any problems caused by fire retardants as have their later brothers of larger civilian craft where these materials were used, simply because they were almost always hauled out after each use.

This same firm was very successful in producing boats and, as was expected, they were conditioned to think large. Sizes from all producers increased rapidly and trailering became impossible as lengths approached 30 feet. Even after some acquisitions and inevitable name changes, this same firm continued to use fire retardants in some form until a short time ago.

I must add that the use of fire retardants by this company and its descendants, as well as other manufacturers, was done in some innocence. After all, weren't they thinking of their customer's safety? And, if it was good enough for our Navy, shouldn't it be good enough for you?

Have you ever seen a fire-retardant polyester resin laminate burn — especially a real boat? Get a gasoline fire started, and you will get an RP laminate to burn brightly with deadly smoke no matter what's in the resin. Usually, by the time enough flame is produced to react the fire retardant, the fun is over. The fumes from the burning fire retardant are often more toxic than those from the resin.

After all its fanfare, the Navy for a long time had ceased to specify RP for most small boats that could not be hauled out after use. The use of fire retardants, whether active or additive, is generally recognized to be poor practice if used in any polyester resin for the construction of marine products because of possible hydrolytic reaction. As it stands today, the failure or near-collapse of some large boat manufacturers is a direct cause of the use of fire retardants.

REFERENCE 21

COMMENTARY ON MOISTURE METERS

by John A. Wills

I am not a great believer in moisture meters because of the widespread misuse and misunderstanding of their readings.

If you are a buyer of a used boat and your surveyor reports a "high" reading somewhere on the hull, you could be deterred from buying what may be a sound boat. At least, you should ask for a second independent reading by another person with another meter. If the same area shows a similarly high reading by both observers, then further investigation should be made.

A low reading on a survey in no way assures a sound boat; it only indicates a low reading or one similar to the "dry control" somewhere on the hull. This can mean only a relatively low moisture content at the time of reading. Only in the process of lowering the moisture content of a fiberglass product is a moisture meter useful in monitoring drying progress. The drying and/or repair process will determine the necessity of using one of these instruments.

It is important to note that a dry control number be established in the part of the world where and when the meter will be used. A piece of supposedly dry window glass may not read zero in your area. A reading greater than zero would be expected on a hot day in the middle of the Gobi Desert. It is necessary to establish one dry number somewhere on the hull (it will rarely be zero) which stabilizes after several readings days apart. The area selected should be above the waterline and protected from the weather. This number must be established before readings in other areas are meaningful. It is also important that readings be taken as close as possible each day to the same time of day, same temperature, same relative humidity and same surface dryness as for the first readings (the control readings). It is against these control readings that suspected wetter areas are measured and logged.

This all presupposes that the hull is out of the water and that natural lowering of moisture content will be expected. Even if the relative humidity is 100%, some drop in moisture meter reading would be expected if the meter is used correctly. Only when the meter shows a general drop in readings is the drying process proceeding, no matter how induced. This procedure is used to measure loss over a period of time.

An assessment of degree of damage is somewhat dependent on *true percentage* moisture content, which only destructive testing can provide. The moisture meter can show areas where the moisture content is higher than another. As stated before, a high reading does not always mean problems. A dry reading — one approaching the dry control number — does not always mean no problems. Actual physical testing of core samples is the only way to provide accurate, at-the-moment information about the condition of the hull, and then only at the area where the core was taken. If structural test data are available from samples run on the hull at the time of manufacture, test data run from wet samples taken later will provide actual percentage structural loss information. All of these data should be entered in the boat's log.

There are several manufacturers of moisture meters. I will describe two which I have used.

The Sovereign Moisture Meter

The following is a quote from the Sovereign data sheet: "High frequency radio waves penetrate the material being checked and they identify, both visually on a meter and aurally with a speaker, where water is and shouldn't be."

The Tramex "Skipper" Moisture Meter

The following is a quote from the Tramex data sheet: "with the two rubber electrodes on the base of the Skipper held against the surface, low frequency AC signals are transmitted into the material being tested. A meter provides the reading."

REFERENCE 22

UPDATE ON VACUUM ASSISTED DRYING OF BOAT HULLS

Gougeon Brothers, Inc.

2/10/89

The enthusiasm at Gougeon Brothers, Inc. for vacuum-assisted hull drying is based on lengthy history of drying wood and composites. For years, we have sought the effects of vacuum drying and felt that the process could be used to assist in the drying of FRP boat hulls during blister repair procedures. Early successes by yards in Florida and California fed our enthusiasm.

As part of our overall gelcoat blister test program, we took 24 panels from an aged fiberglass boat and soaked them at 120°F for 14 days. We then vacuum-dried the panels and saw a measurable drop in all instances and significant drop (=50%) in the moisture content of others.

While proficient in using vacuum procedures, we are not a marine service yard and we felt it necessary to test vacuum drying on a full-size boat. We obtained a damaged Seidelman 30 from a local yard and, after soaking the boat in a slip for two months, conducted full-size vacuum drying tests. We found that the moisture content in the 1/4"-thick hull laminate dropped by 5% over a 24 hour period. Additional panels were removed from the Seidelman 30 and soak/vacuum tested, confirming the original testing. While not exhaustive, we felt the tests suggested that vacuum drying was an attractive and aggressive method for accelerating the drying process in FRP hulls. We outlined the procedure in our Gelcoat Blister and Vacuum Bagging manuals.

Results from the field by several service yards employing vacuum drying systems have been mixed. We feel that the large number of variables affecting the drying process, along with the difficulty in establishing criteria for success, has resulted in confusion and ambivalence over the drying system.

As removing water is the objective of the drying process, it is important to understand that different forms of water can be physically or chemically bonded, absorbed, suspended, trapped or dissolved in the hull. To evaporate or diffuse through the FRP hull, each of the physical and chemical forms of water requires a different level of thermodynamic energy input. Furthermore, these variables are affected by the physical (and chemical) nature of the hull structure itself.

The type of moisture (chemically bonded, absorbed, trapped, etc.) is very important to the rate of drying. In general, the mechanics of the drying are that sufficient energy must be supplied to water to convert liquid water to vapor at the substrate surface. A portion of the energy will be used to promote water migration through diffusion (or capillary action in cracks).

There are two periods during the drying process. One is the "constant rate period" when free water and moisture diffused or flowing from the interior are removed. The other is the "falling rate period" when the rate changes as the moisture content of the solids decreases. Plotted, the combined drying rate will look asymptotic.

The moisture content of the solid material at the transition from the constant rate period to the falling rate period is called the critical moisture content. This moisture content can be considered chemically, tightly-bound or diffused water. The energy required to convert or remove this water must increase, or the time required for drying will increase. While this energy/time equation can be calculated, the considerable number of variables outlined above determine the energy levels required and are difficult to model.

In field conditions, vacuum drying will initially show a rapid decrease in the moisture content as the surface and free water are removed, then the rate will slow as it reaches the critical moisture content. It is at this point, as the energy requirements begin to go up, that the extra heat and vacuum may not be warranted as the extra wear on the equipment and the time required to monitor the process may not make the vacuum drying economically justifiable.

Establishing the technical and economic criteria for success is not easy. A yard may find that the cost balance is not appropriate for their circumstances. The private owner with access to vacuum and heating systems may feel the trade-offs are justified. We feel that vacuum drying will find its own level of acceptance as local conditions, costs and boat specifics are better understood.

Several key factors which affect the transfer of the water through the polymer composite are built into the hull or occur during operation. These include:

1) The hydrophilicity of the basic composite material (the hydrate form of certain materials and impurities fit into this category).

2) The distribution of voids or porosity in the laminate. Matrix type, cure and dimensional stability, fiber type and orientation, manufacturing defects, matrix strain rates and fatigue damage can all determine the degree of voids, porosity and cracking. Whether the voids or damage occur as molecular, micro or macro phenomena will also determine their effect on the drying process.

3) Contamination within the laminate (including unreacted resins and additive components identified as contributing to the blistering phenomena). This will affect dispersion of the moisture through the laminate.

Beyond the physical and chemical factors determining the nature of the water in the laminate and the composite itself, temperature, pressure and time are the main variables which the end-user has control over. As temperature is a key factor in drying the boat, optimization of the temperature, commensurate with safety and the structural tolerance of the hull, is desirable. Lowering the pressure, *i.e.*, vacuum, is the other complimentary approach in drying the boat.

The key function of the lower pressure is to remove the free water from the laminate. However, to accelerate the evaporation of water from the hull surface, energy has to be supplied. For the most efficient drying under vacuum, a heat source and the rate of the heat transfer to the surface water must be considered. A change in the laminate temperature from 60°F to 100°F will increase the water vapor pressure about 4.5 times at 1 atmosphere, greatly accelerating the drying process. The best results from vacuum drying have been seen in Florida and southern California because of the higher ambient temperatures in those areas. Yards in the north, who have heated the boats to aid the drying process, have met with mixed results.

REFERENCE 23

UNIVERSITY OF RHODE ISLAND REPORT #1

This first report, released in May of 1987, is reproduced here for your evaluation. Please realize that this first report describes the CAUSES of blisters only and intentionally does not offer repair options as many at the time expected, to their disappointment. A second report, "The Prevention and Repair of Gel Coat Blisters," follows *(Reference 24)*.

I will leave the judgement of the value of these reports to the reader. Certainly, there is some valuable information offered. There are some eyebrow-raising data presented, too!

THE CAUSES OF BOAT HULL BLISTERS

by

Thomas J. Rockett, Ph.D. and
Vincent Rose, Ph.D.
Department of Chemical Engineering
University of Rhode Island
Kingston, Rhode Island
This report is the product of work accomplished under
U. S. Coast Guard Grant #l501.83

FOREWORD

The problem of fiberglass gel coat blistering has plagued the boat business, both recreational and commercial, for the past 15 to 20 years, reaching significant importance within the past decade. Boat owners, especially those who had paid huge sums for highly competitive racing sailboats, were incensed when their $200,000 yacht developed a severe case of "boat pox." Other owners of less expensive craft — be they lobster boats or sport fishermen — were similarly horrified when they discovered what it cost to repair a blistered boat bottom. Boat owners pointed to their dealers who pointed to the boat manufacturers who pointed to their raw material suppliers. In the middle were the boat repair and service yards who were faced with repairing a problem that was entirely new to them, the causes of which they did not understand, and for which methods of repair ranged from slap dash to almost absurdly inefficient, impractical, and prohibitively expensive. The writer can testify to the above from firsthand experience in his New England repair yard.

Other considerations aside, however, the matter of structural integrity and, in the final analysis, the ultimate safety of the individual boat concerned many in this industry, and the U. S. Coast Guard in particular. Numerous well-intentioned studies had been undertaken by many factions in the boat building and material manufacturing industries, both in this country and especially in the United Kingdom, and the size of the bibliography of relevant printed reports is impressive. Many of these studies, however well-intentioned, had been made by interested parties or focused on perhaps only one part of the problem. Many concerned persons felt that an in-depth and exhaustive study by a highly qualified yet completely impartial laboratory was necessary to establish once and for all the causes, prevention, and cure for the problem of osmotic blistering, as the disease is now more accurately called. The American Boat Builders and Repairers Association (which is a national association of boat building, repair and service yards), taking the bull by the horns, made a small grant to the University of Rhode Island to undertake an initial study of the problems in 1984, hoping that other sectors would come forward to support this research. Unfortunately, and for reasons best known to them, such support was not forthcoming — and to tell the truth the suggestion was turned aside by some in distinctly antagonistic terms. By this time, however, the Coast Guard was very anxious to determine the true severity of the problem (or the lack of severity for that matter), and in 1985 approved a grant to the ABBRA in the amount of $60,600 to pursue an in-depth study of Phase I of the problem — the causes of blistering. The Association, in turn, contracted with the University of Rhode Island to do the research and to write a report on the findings of the research team.

This study was undertaken by Drs. Thomas Rockett and Vincent Rose of the U.R.I. Graduate School of Chemical Engineering, ably assisted by several graduate students, and was completed in the fall of 1986. The report itself, highly technical, is difficult if not impossible for the average layman to understand, but this highly-readable and condensed summary has been prepared for the interested public. We firmly believe that the $60,600 of tax payers' money has been well spent, and that an enormous amount of hitherto-unknown information has been discovered. Some theories have been discounted and others reinforced by scientific enquiry, and the net result is a solid base of information upon which boat builders, manufacturers, suppliers and the basic synthetic materials industry can rely.

Phase 11, the implications and techniques of blister repair and surface reconstruction, has been funded by a further Coast Guard grant of $78,500, and the necessary research is currently underway, also at the University of Rhode Island. A full report on this phase will be completed, hopefully, by the fall of 1987.

The American Boat Builders and Repairers Association would like to express its thanks to those in the Coast Guard in Washington who have been instrumental in helping us to obtain the necessary funding and to the members of the staff at the University of Rhode Island, especially Messrs. Rockett and Rose, who have so skillfully conducted this intricate research project to date.

Thomas Hale
American Boat Builders & Repairers Association, Inc.
715 Boylston Street, Boston, MA 02116
May 1987

INTRODUCTION

Fiberglass reinforced polyester (FRP) composites, the structural material of many boats, are subject to a degradation phenomenon known as blistering. The surface blister is a bump that appears on the hull surface, usually under the water line. It grows because a pocket of acidic fluid develops within the hull. Blisters range in size from a few millimeters to several inches in diameter and normally occur near the gel coat- laminate interface but have been observed deeper in the hull. Blisters are very rarely seen in the gel coat material itself. Only in one case, where two layers of gel coat were used, were blisters observed to form at the interface within the gel coat.

Good statistical information on the occurrence and severity of blisters on boats does not exist. While we have seen over 100 cases of boat blisters, there is no statistically established correlation between boat age and blister onset, severity or depth into hull. The influence of the cycle of dry land storage to immersion is not known. Reports from warmer water locations suggest the problem is more severe than in northern areas. We have seen three cases in which the hull is severely delaminated and in which decomposed resin is found more than half way through the hull. These were boats which were more than 10 years old. Estimates of the number of boats showing blisters in given localities range from 1% to 90%. There is a belief among many marina personnel that the problem is more widespread now among newer boats than it was ten years ago. Again, this is unsubstantiated by reliable statistics but has been reported to us by many marina operators. Indeed, one manufacturer stated that prior to about 1980, they had never had a reported blister but since then, hundreds of complaints have been filed.

The cost of repair is significant to boat owners, ranging from $10 to $200 per foot of boat, and several boats have been declared unseaworthy because of structural damage associated with blistering. A solution to the problem must be found to restore consumer faith in glass-polyester boats. The University of Rhode Island and the American Boat Builders and Repairers Association undertook a research project on the blister problem which was sponsored by the United States Coast Guard. Through laboratory research, field observations and interviews, and a thorough review of past research work, the causes of blistering have been defined. The application of this knowledge will prevent many cases of blistering and direct future work toward minimizing the problem in new boats and permitting the successful repair of older boats. A technical report has been submitted to the Coast Guard which presents tabulated data and experimental details. This report, drawn on those findings, discusses the causes of blistering.

HOW BLISTERS FORM

The first step in blister formation involves the movement of water into the gel coat material of a boat hull and then into the laminate material. All polymeric materials are subject to some degree of water permeation. Details of how the water moves through the laminate and the way the different materials and other factors effect the water movement will be discussed later. This water movement, by itself, is not harmful. It is a necessary step for blistering but this step alone is not sufficient to cause blistering without other contributing factors.

The second necessary feature of blister formation is the presence of small clusters of water soluble material (WSM) within the hull. These clusters are harmless and remain dormant until the permeating water molecules reach them and react with them to form tiny droplets of water and WSM locked into the laminate.

The minute droplet of solution is separated from the surrounding water by the semi-permeable polymer membrane which consists of a gel coat and usually a thin layer of laminating resin. Water molecules can pass through this layer, but the WSM molecules cannot. Since the outside water and the solution are of different concentrations, water will permeate through the gel coat, attempting to dilute the droplet of solution trapped in the laminate. This process is known as osmosis. During this process, more water enters the droplet causing it to expand and create a pressure on the surrounding hull-material. It takes place whenever two solutions of different concentrations are separated by a semi-permeable membrane. This increased pressure is referred to as osmotic pressure. Theoretically, the osmotic flow of water into the droplet should continue until the solution has the same concentration as the water outside the hull. As water is drawn into the droplet, an outward force is exerted on the laminate and gel coat surrounding the growing solution. When the pressure exceeds the deformation point of the hull material it begins to flow or crack. This decreases the pressure and allows more space for water to be drawn into the solution. As the pressure grows, a blister forms on the surface.

The solution inside the blister is acidic because many of the WSM compounds react with water to form acids. Because the solution is under pressure, if the blister is punctured, the blister liquid will squirt out of the opening, sometimes at high velocity. Furthermore, if the boat is removed from the water, the hull will begin to dry causing water to permeate outward. Water will leave the blister solution as well and eventually the blister disappears. During this stage the WSM still remains and stays dormant until the boat is launched again at which time blister growth will begin again. This phenomenon has been observed by many boat yard owners.

This brief look at blistering brings up many questions which were addressed during the study, and which are also discussed in this report. Some of the questions which will be considered are the following:

- How do the WSM materials get into the hull?

- What controls water movement through the gel coat?

- How do different plastic materials affect water movement?

- What types of reactions take place between WSM and diffusing water molecules?

- What kinds of damage does blistering do to hull materials?

- Is there more than one type of blister?

- and finally, how can blisters be prevented?

THE HULL MATERIAL

To fully understand blistering, it is necessary to have a working knowledge of the components of gel coats and fiber reinforced composites. In the currently used materials, which are the best polymer boat building materials ever developed, there are many components each one of which is added to contribute an essential property to the final structure.

The unsaturated polyester resin liquid is made up of short chains of polyester molecules dissolved in styrene. The styrene units can be considered as tiny ball bearings the same size as each link in the polyester chain. The chains are made up by joining three types of links together. The properties of the chain, such as strength, flexibility, and water resistance, depend on the properties of each link, the number of each kind of link in each chain and the length of each chain. The links are glycols, phthallic acids and unsaturated acids. In altering the properties of a polyester, trade-offs must be made to optimize their use for boat building. A chain must contain a certain number of unsaturated units to give a strong polyester, but too many will yield a brittle material which will crack during use. A typical general purpose polyester liquid resin will have chains containing 16 links. Eight of these will be glycol units occupying every other link in the chain. Four of the links will be phthallic units (isophthalic, orthophthalic or terephthalic) and four will be unsaturated units. For each one of these chains there will be eight spherical units of styrene.

When the proper catalyst package or hardener is added, the unsaturated units in the chain form bonds with the styrene units or with short chains of polystyrene. The polystyrene chains join the polyester chains together at the unsaturated links, hardening or curing the liquid into a three-dimensional network.

This setting reaction is called cross-linking or curing and produces heat which is extremely important in obtaining a complete cure since the heat involved promotes further cross-linking.

The catalyst package for hardening the polymer contains several types of compounds. Only one of these compounds will become part of the polymer network. The others will remain in the free space between the chain units of the polymerized network. Table 1 lists the components of a polyester resin-glass composite. Also shown in the table are the constituents which do not become part of the network but reside in the free space. Those units which are water soluble can contribute to the blister problem under circumstances discussed below. From one to five percent of a completely cured resin can consist of water soluble material (WSM).

The second source of WSM units comes from the network formers as a result of incomplete cure of the resin. In Table 1, all the polyester groups should be bound into a three-dimensional network. Three things can convert network molecules into WSM units. First, incomplete cure, caused by poor mixing, low lay-up temperature, decomposed or aged peroxide, reaction of styrene with air, or improper catalyst package selection will mean that a certain fraction of the network formers will remain as WSM in the free space of the network. Second, in "cooking" the polyester, a certain fraction of material either does not react to form chains or forms short saturated chains that become WSM units. Thirdly, chemical reactions with water or acids can break down the network and convert parts of it to WSM units. All three of the above mechanisms can produce WSM in a resin. An example of this is the formation of free glycol which has been shown to cause blisters.

In making a gel coat material, a polyester resin is used for the base. To obtain the color and the hiding power desired, a pigment powder is blended into the resin. The resin is thickened to prevent run off by the addition of extremely fine silica powder. Certain clays can also be added to help the flow properties. Finally, extenders or fillers can be added to reduce the amount of resin needed in the gel coat and which in some cases add strength. During our study, four hull materials were analyzed for the content of metal atoms. As shown in Table 2 the materials are chemically quite complex because of the variety of additives used to optimize properties.

An unanswered question which bears on WSM concentration concerns the curing mechanism of the hull material. We have assumed that during cure, all WSM units are trapped within the growing network. If, during the lay-up, polymerization begins at the mold surface and moves outward, the WSM units could be pushed ahead of the moving gel boundary and concentrated at the free surface. These might be dissolved in the next layer of resin and upset the distribution of WSM units locally. Evidence of this type of segregation has been discovered during this program. The full implications of this type of separation are not clearly understood at this time.

TABLE I

Some Common Constituents in a Polyester Glass Composite Marine Material

Materials are classified as network formers (NET), water soluble units in the network (WSM) and stable additives (STAB).

1. Polyester Groups

Orthophthalic acid or anhydride	(NET)
Isophthalic acid or anhydride	(NET)
Ethylene glycol	(NET)
Propylene glycol	(NET)
Neopentyl glycol	(NET)
Maleic acid or anhydride (unsaturated)	(NET)
Fumaric acid (unsaturated)	(NET)

A phthalic acid, a glycol and a maleic are reacted to form the unsaturated polyester. The ratios can vary from 2p:1m:3g for a low reactive polyester to 1p:1m:2g to make a moderately reactive polyester to 1p:2m:3g for a highly reactive polyester. Ordinarily, a slight excess of glycol (1:1:2.1) is added to ensure termination of the chains by glycol units. Excess glycol or un-cured components will contribute to WSM fraction.
(WSM)

2. Cross-linking Agent or Vinyl Molecule   (NET)

Styrene (40 to 50 weight percent) (unsaturated vinyl molecule) (Added styrene will yield a total ratio of 1p:1m:2g:4 styrene. The viscosity of the resin is largely controlled by the amount of styrene.)

3. Inhibitor: (0.1 - 0.5%) added to increase shelf life.

Quinones	(WSM)
Amines	(WSM)

4. Ultraviolet Stabilizer- (in gel coats 0.1 - 1%)

Benzophenones	(WSM)
Hindered amines	(WSM)

5. Colorants (in gel coat materials)

Inorganic pigments (1 - 5%)	(STAB)
Organic pigments (1 - 5%)	(WSM)
Carriers (phthalate plasticizers) (0 - 3%)	(WSM)

6. Catalyst (initiators - added to react with unsaturated bonds and cause cross-linking and become part of network)

Azo-compounds	
Methyl ethylketone peroxide (1 - 2%)	(NET)
Benzoyl peroxide	(NET)
Phthalate carriers	(WSM)

7. Promoter (the true catalyst which activates the initiator)

Cobalt salts (octoates, napthenates, alsynates)	(WSM)
Anilines (dimethyl)	(WSM)
Mineral spirit carriers (toluene)	(WSM)

8. Reinforcement (mats, woven fabrics, chopped fibers)

Glass surface ions leached through long-term acid exposure	(WSM)
Fiberglass Silicate network w/calcium, sodium	(STAB)
Magnesium and aluminum	(WSM)
Aramid Fibers - Carbon Fibers	(STAB)

9. Coupling Agents

(bond formers between the polymer and the glass)

Various silane compounds	(STAB)
Titanates, Mordants (chromium compounds)	(STAB)
Reaction products from long-term acid exposure	
	(WSM)

10. Sizing (lubricants and handling agents added during fiber-glass manufacture)

Starches and emulsions	(WSM)
Most are burned off before composite manufacture.	

11. Binders (added to hold mats & filaments together)

Polyvinylacetate emulsions	(WSM)
Polyester powder	(STAB)

12. Thixotropes (added to prevent runoff of resin)

Ultrafine SiO_2	(STAB)
Clays	(STAB)
Acid leachate from clays	(WSM)

13. Fillers (added to reduce cost)

Clay	(STAB)
Talc	(STAB)
Limestone	(STAB)
Ions leached from fillers	(WSM)

14. Waxes   (STAB)

(added to prevent air inhibition and as mold release agents)

Cause localized low strength zones

15. Wetting Agents (added to lower interfacial energy and enhance resin wetting of glass)

Oleates, stearates, emulsifiers, surfactant	(WSM)

16. Flame Retardants

Halogenated compounds	(WSM)
Aluminum hydrates	(STAB)

17. Impurities (can enter at any stage in which new materials are added)

Water, Benzene, Aldehydes, Ketones, etc.	(WSM)
Dirt, dust	

TABLE 2

Qualitative X-Ray Fluorescent Analysis of Typical Polyester Resins and Gel Coat Materials

Element	Isophthalic (Neopentyl Glycol) Gel Coat A	Gel Coat B	Orthophthalic (Neopentyl Glycol) Gel Coat	Orthophthalic (Propylene Glycol) Resin	Vinyl Gel Coat	Possible Sources
Al	Moderate	Moderate	Moderate	None	Moderate	Fillers (clays) or Flame Retardants
As	Trace	Trace	Trace	None	None	Fillers (clays)
Br	Trace	Trace	None	None	None	Fillers (clays)
Ca	High	Moderate	High	Low	None	Fillers ($CaCO_3$ or clays)
Co	Low	Low	Low	High	None	Promoter
Cu	Low	Low	Low	Trace	None	Promoter
Fe	Moderate	High	Moderate	Low	High	Fillers (clays)
K	Low	None	Low	None	Moderate	Fillers (clays)
Mg	Moderate	High	High	None	Moderate	Fillers ($MgCO_3$ or clays)
Mn	Low	None	Low	None	Low	Fillers (clays)
Rb	Trace	Trace	None	None	None	Fillers (clays)
S	Moderate	Low	Low	None	Low	Resin
Si	High	High	High	High	High	Thixotrope and Clays
Sr	Low	Low	Low	None	None	Fillers (clays)
Ti	High	High	High	Low	High	Pigment

A certain level of WSM is essential to a well designed resin. Their presence does not result in a composite of low blister resistance. However, if they are concentrated beyond normal limits or if they are concentrated at a given zone, blistering will result.

Resin manufacturers continue to develop these polyester materials to improve the properties. Table 1 gives some idea of resin complexity. Changes in formulation to improve one property could decrease another property. Boat builders must test all incoming materials for blister resistance. A simple 100 hour boil test will warn of potential problems. This test can be performed by placing a 4"x4" test laminate in boiling water for 100 hours. New materials must be certified by the boat builder and familiar materials must be tested to guarantee the quality is maintained from batch to batch.

MANUFACTURING PROCESSES

Boat hulls are usually made from the outside in by applying the gel coat to a waxed mold and then adding the layers of glass reinforcement and polyester to complete the hull. The gel coat, the pigmented and filled polyester, is used to hide the underlying glass composite structure, to color the hull, to produce a flexible surface which acts as a shock absorber and to help keep water from diffusing into the composite. It is usually sprayed onto the mold to a thickness of 20 mil (0.020") which, as curing takes place, will shrink to a thickness of 14 to 18 mils. The gel coat can be cured by mixing the catalyst and spraying or rolling this "hot" mix onto the mold within the 10 to 20 minutes available until setting. It can also be applied by co-spraying the catalyst and resin using a variety of commercially available spray guns. In both cases good mixing is critical. A clogged or partially clogged nozzle will give an under-cured resin which will have little blister resistance because constituents which should be in the network remain unpolymerized as WSM. Also, the peroxide catalysts have limited shelf life. They should be stored cold, kept well sealed, used at temperatures above 60°F, and never used beyond the manufacturers' expiration date. The gel coat should be applied as one continuous layer. If it is put on in several layers, with a cure cycle between layers, blistering can take place at these interfaces. The gel coat should be applied as thickly as possible since added mass increases the cross-link heating which aids curing. A thicker gel coat also acts as a more effective water barrier. In practice, a 35 mil, wet, gel coat is about the maximum which can be achieved without run-off from the mold.

An air inhibited layer produced at this point in manufacture can lead to blistering. Styrene, the cross-linking units, can react with air to form benzaldehydes which are water soluble. If the styrene is consumed near the surface by reaction with air, the surface polyester will not cross-link and will remain tacky even after the bulk has completely cured. The surface layer will be enriched in WSM and blistering will be promoted. Several things have been done in our laboratory to minimize this problem. Some are impractical in manufacture. They are listed below:

1. A thicker coating gives a hotter, faster set which reduces the time the styrene can react with air. At least 30 mils, wet, should be applied.

2. The air inhibited layer can be stripped off with acetone. However, if this is not done with care, it could exacerbate the problem by producing localized areas of concentrated WSM.

3. A wax can be added to the resin which floats to the surface during cure and keeps air out but this also introduces problems. The wax must be removed before continuation of lay-up.

4. A wax paper barrier can be applied to the surface after the lay-up to keep air out during curing. However, this is difficult because the pressure of applying the wax paper to the wet gel coat destroys its uniform thickness.

5. A water-soluble barrier layer, such as P.V.A., which is applied and washed off after the cure, has been tried. While this technique looks promising, further tests must be performed to prove its effectiveness. Thorough removal is critical since the P.V.A. left behind will be dissolved in the next layer of resin and, by becoming a source of WSM, will cause blistering.

6. The gel coat can be heated in the spray gun or on the mold with a moving bank of lamps or other heat source. This will help reduce the air inhibited layer by increasing both the rate and degree of cure.

Removal of the air inhibited layer by sanding produced severe blisters because the sticky material was not removed but was repacked into the surface. In practice, the best way to avoid an air inhibited layer under the gel coat is to use a thick layer, heat it, and continue lay-up as soon as possible. It will be obvious to the reader that many of the suggestions made here with regard to gel coats are also applicable to resin lay-up interfaces.

Once the gel coat has become tacky to the touch, laminating resin is sprayed onto the gel coat and a reinforcing mat is applied with serrated rollers. This is done to squeeze out entrapped air, to obtain thorough wetting of the glass by the resin and to keep high glass to resin ratio. Some entrapped air bubbles are inevitable and do not themselves cause blistering. Densification should be as complete as possible because air bubbles greatly reduce composite strength.

For a variety of reasons associated with matching coefficients of expansion, moduli of elasticity and swelling stresses associated with water pickup, it is accepted practice to put a resin-rich layer between the gel coat and the first structural layer. A veil mat or light chopped glass layer is placed between the gel coat and the laminate.

The selection of glass in this layer and in the underlying laminate must be chosen with a binder which is not water soluble. Water soluble binders cause blistering because they are WSM. Some of the roving used in chopper guns is emulsion bound and burn-out tests show one to five weight percent of binder can be removed from chopper glass. This concentration of WSM under the gel could result in blisters.

There have been some major changes in manufacturing processes since the early fifties. Some of these changes were the result of design changes, some the result of material changes, and some the result of regulatory changes. The use of spray-gun equipment increased drastically in the 1970s. Catalyst compositions were altered by the Department of Transportation Shipping regulations in the late 1970s. These regulations reduced the percent of active oxygen in the MEKP catalyst from 11% to 9%. OSHA regulations issued in the early 1980s may affect resin compositions. Oil prices also could alter the source of resin and the percent of fillers used. If statistical information on blister frequency were available, these data could be correlated with such changes to isolate cause and effect relationships.

WATER DIFFUSION IN HULL MATERIALS

Once a fiberglass boat is put in water, water diffusion through the gel coat begins. All polymers (plastics) exhibit some degree of water diffusion. Diffusion is the site to site jumping of single water molecules through the gel coat. The water molecule enters the free space between the chains in the polymer network and jumps to the next open site. This differs in many important ways from the flow of water through pin holes.

Molecular diffusion controls the permeation rate or rate of water movement through the hull. Water diffusion through polymers is related to the following factors:

1. The ease with which the water molecule can jump from one site to the next. This is expressed by the diffusion coefficient and is related to the strength of the forces acting on the water molecule by the atoms in the polymer network.

2. The difference in water concentration at any two points in the hull. As the concentration difference increases, water moves faster. When the concentration at the two points becomes the same, water movement stops.

3. The amount of water which the polymer can hold which is known as the saturation level. This controls the concentration difference and is different for each polymer. It is essentially the number of sites in the network available for occupation by a water molecule. The degree of cross-linking can affect this greatly.

4. The temperature of the polymer. The rate of water movement increases with temperature so that an 18°F temperature increase will cause water to move twice as fast.

5. The amount of filler or glass in a polymer reduces the sites available for water and reduces water transport.

This movement of water through the hull structure can be expressed mathematically by a series of laws known as Fick's laws. Using these equations, a computer model was constructed during this study. The model was used to predict the water concentration throughout the hull structure at any given time for a range of different polyester materials.

194

The major finding from these results indicate that if the resin composition changes at an interface, a discontinuity in water concentration will result. This discontinuity has some implications to blister formation because it affects the stress at the interface. In general, the rate at which water moves through the gel coat in a composite which will blister determines the time at which blistering begins. Water diffusion does not cause blistering but is is an important step in the sequence of events which lead to blistering.

STRESSES IN HULL MATERIALS

Corrosion and degradation processes are greatly affected by localized stress. This is true for all materials and is particularly true of polymers. There are four sources of localized stress in a boat hull all of which can influence blister formation and growth. The four are:

1. Stresses are produced by polymer shrinkage during curing. After the gel coats are cured on a mold, the resin is applied. It bonds to the gel coat before it cures. The resin near the gel coat interface goes into tension as the resin away from the interface cures and shrinks.

2. Stresses are produced by swelling of the resin due to water diffusion. The amount of water present causes swelling of the polymer. Our measurements and literature values show the resin can swell as much as 10 percent by volume and this is greatly affected by the degree of cross linking. Stresses are generated by differential swelling. If the entire hull swells uniformly, no differential stress will result. However, if one layer swells and the adjacent layer does not, the adjacent layer will be pulled apart (put in tension) by the swelled layer. The level of differential stress generated will be determined by the water gradient and discontinuities in the gradient and not by the absolute amount of water present.

Figure I shows the relationship between water concentration and stress development. Note that the maximum tensile stress will develop under the surface and ahead of the diffusing water. If the tensile strength of the polymer is exceeded at the maximum tensile stress position, disk cracking will take place.

The stress is transient. The maximum tension will move inward and decrease in magnitude as water diffuses. If the resin has high strength, that is, it is well-cured, highly cross-linked, and reinforced with glass, it can survive the passing stress field and not crack. If a disk crack forms, it constitutes a vacuum. Any local WSM units will be drawn toward the crack to increase the pressure. This is a mechanism for concentration of WSM units

in the vicinity of the crack. Our conclusion is that stress cracks can create blister centers.

The stress build-up can have an effect on water transport and lead to concentration gradients which would not be predicted by Fick's Law. As the resin network goes into tension, the free sites are opened and water advances faster than anticipated. This can lead to a diffusion profile with a sudden drop, A water front moves through the polymer. Behind it the polymer is close to saturated; in front of it the polymer is dry. To establish the shape of the water profile, water concentration measurements at different depths at given times must be measured.

3. Stresses are produced during boat use. Peak stress is produced by wave action, rigging stresses, impact stresses and buoyancy stress.

4. Internal cracks produce stress concentration sites at the crack tips which can lead to further cracking or accelerated chemical attack. Strictly speaking, the crack does not produce a new stress but intensifies one of the above three stresses. Cracks can magnify a stress by hundreds of times.

Two or more of the above four types of stress can interact at a particular point in time and space. For example, if a modest shrinkage stress combines with a small water swelling stress and at the same time, severe wave impact flexes the hull, localized disk cracking can take place. Furthermore, the reaction of the polyester resin to the stresses applied is dependent on the

Figure I. Sketch of a laminate cross-section. The amount of water absorbed by the polymer is plotted with the dashed line. The absorbed water generates swelling stresses which are indicated by the solid line.

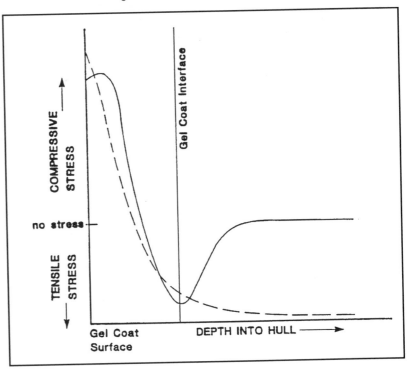

flexibility and toughness, *i.e.* resistance to cracking, of the resin. If the resin is brittle cracking will occur. A flexible resin can deform under peak stress loads without cracking. Resin flexibility depends on the type and number of links in the polyester chain and, very importantly, on the number of cross-links between the chains.

TESTING FOR BLISTER RESISTANCE

In order to decide which materials are best for hull manufacture and which parameters reduce blister susceptibility, 168 sample laminates were made and tested during this study.

Gel coated test laminates were made by hand lay-up techniques, using both brushed and sprayed resins, following standard manufacturing techniques. The typical panel, made on a waxed glass mold, was 2'x2'x¼". Table 3 lists the materials used. Polymerization was initiated using methyl ethyl ketone peroxide according to manufacturer's instructions. The fiberglass reinforcement was three layers of woven roving. Various types of resin rich construction were used between the gel coat and the roving. This included one or two layers or combination of layers of 3/4 oz. veil, 1½ oz. mat and approximately 20% by weight chopped gun roving. The panels were made and post cured to constant Barcol hardness values at the same temperatures. Most were made and post-cured at 75°F but a series were made and post-cured at 50, 70, 90, 100°F to test the effects of manufacturing temperature.

Samples were tested for blister resistance by immersion in a 65°C (149°F) constant temperature water bath. Samples were examined on a routine basis for blistering. The longest exposure time was 24 months. Blister initiation time, the time at which blisters are first observed, and blister severity (number and size of blister per cm²) were measured. Representative samples were cross-sectioned for polarized light microscopic examination and measurement of gel coat thickness. Two sets of each laminate were fabricated and tested.

In general, the test panels fall into five categories:

1. A series of NPG-isophthalic gel coated TMPD-isophthalic laminates, in which gel coats were obtained from three different suppliers.

2. A series using NPG-orthophthalic, NPG-isophthalic and vinyl gel coats and PC-orthophthalic and NPG/EG isophthalic laminating resins.

3. A series of NPG-isophthalic gel coated, PC-orthophthalic laminates made up and post-cured at 50, 75, 90 and 100°F.

4. A series of NPG-isophthalic gel coated, PG-orthophthalic laminates in which various types of glass were used in the resin rich layer beneath the gel coat, and

5. A series of NPG-orthophthalic gel coated, PG-orthophthalic laminates in which the effect of air inhibition of the gel coat was tested.

TABLE 3

Chemical composition of polyester gel coat and laminating resins
(Stars designate presence of constituent material.)

GEL COATS

MATERIAL SUPPLIER	IPA (NPG)	OPA (NPG)	VINYL
1	★		
2	★		
3		★	
4	★		
5			★
6	★		
7	★		
8	★		
9	★		

LAMINATING RESINS

MATERIAL SUPPLIER	IPA	OPA	NPG	EG	PG	TMPD
1	★		★	★		
2		★		★		
3		★			★	
4	★					★
5		★			★	

IPA - ISOPHTHALIC ACID
PG - PROPYLENE GLYCOL
OPA - ORTHOPHTHALIC ACID
VINYL - URETHANE BASED POLYESTER RESIN
NPG - NEOPENTYL GLYCOL
TMPD - 2, 2, 4 - TRIMETHYL - 1, 3 PENTANE DIOL
EG - ETHYLENE GLYCOL

Figure 5 presents the results for blister initiation time on various samples. Other factors aside, the initiation time is a function of gel coat thickness as discussed in the section on water permeation. Comparisons of different laminates for blister initiation are meaningless unless gel coat thickness is either constant or the initiation time is corrected for thickness variations. A dry 30 mil gel coat will not show blistering for at least twice the time that a 15 mil gel coated laminate begins to blister.

Figure 5 shows that blister initiation time is also a function of both the laminating resin and the gel coat formulation. In rating the laminating resins for initiation time, orthophthalic resin was best in all cases. For the gel coat, the rating depended on the laminating resin. The NPG-orthophthalic gel coat was better than NPG-isophthalic which was better than vinyl when used with PG-orthophthalic laminating resins. When these same gel coats are used with isophthalic laminating resins the order becomes NPG-isophthalic was best, vinyl was intermediate and NPG-orthophthalic blistered most quickly. It appears from the

TABLE 5 - BLISTER INITIATION TIME
(Normalized to a 14 mil thick gel coat)

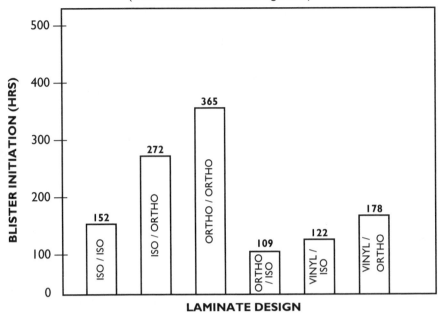

birefringence, which is an optical effect caused by stress and is observed using a polarized microscope, that residual stresses created during lay-up and stresses produced by water diffusion related swelling account for some of these differences.

The severity of blistering, as measured by the density and size of the blisters, was a function of the laminating resin used if all other factors are kept constant. The orthophthalic resin resulted in fewer but larger blisters while isophthalic resin produced more, but smaller, blisters. In both cases, the total area affected was about the same. However, when vinyl gel coats were used, orthophthalic and isophthalic laminates produced small blisters, in both cases, and approximately the same number of blisters per square centimeter.

The blister initiation time was approximately the same for similar gel coat materials regardless of the supplier. However, the severity of blistering varied greatly among similar gel coats from different suppliers. One reason for this could be the difference in filler and extender contents in different gel coats made from the same base resin. While other gel coated orthophthalic laminate panels showed the best blister resistance, there is reason to believe that prolonged exposure to water may deteriorate the strength of these laminates faster than isophthalic laminates. Our studies on this aspect are continuing.

The series of experiments made to test the effects of laminating and post cure temperature showed that a lay-up temperature between 50° and 90°F did not have a major influence on blister resistance. These NPG-isophthalic gel coated orthophthalic laminates did show an effect of temperature at 100°F. The high temperature post cured laminates showed a high density of blisters sooner than the 90°F laminate and the blisters were very small (less than 0.4 mm² surface area). No significant

difference could be found in the blister initiation time for the 50°, 60°, 70° or 90°F laminates. With these samples, as well as all the other samples, there was considerable variation between samples.

In addition, the blister initiation time was not an indicator of blister severity. Samples which blistered early may or may not develop a severe case of blisters.

As reported previously, glass binders can play a significant role in promoting blister severity. Samples made with a chopped gun roving, resin rich backup layer showed early and severe blistering. The gun roving was found to contain a binder which was applied as an emulsion. The amount depended on the supplier. Samples made with veil mats showed intermediate blistering while a 1½ oz. of powder bound mat used in the resin rich backup layer showed superior blister resistance. Other studies are continuing using a variety of reinforcement glasses.

Preliminary results on the importance of an air inhibition layer at the gel coat-laminate interface show that exposure of the gel coat to air severely decreases blister resistance. It appears that the air inhibited layer dissolves in the laminating resin and promotes blistering. The nature of this air inhibited material and its role as a WSM is discussed above in the section on manufacturing.

TYPES OF BLISTERS

Our findings indicate that there are at least two and perhaps three types of blisters.

The first type we call WSM concentration blisters. Using red dye, tiny colored grains of pressed sorbitol, a WSM, were placed into the laminate under the gel coat during construction. The exact location of the sorbitol could easily be seen when the panels were viewed from the glass/resin side. These panels were placed in the water test tank and in less than 24 hours blisters began to form at the exact location of the red particles. The remainder of the panel was unblistered.

This experiment confirmed the long held belief that pockets of concentrated WSM will cause blistering. The speed at which they formed was unexpected. This corresponds to blister formation in a month in water at 60°F. To have WSM concentration blisters, a local zone of WSM must be introduced into the gel coat or laminate at some time during manufacture. Poor attention to good housekeeping practices during lay-up can result in this type of blister. Our microscopic examinations have shown debris and wood particles at gel coat interfaces that have caused blisters. Excess catalyst, accidently sprayed onto or placed in the laminate, can also create such blisters. A clogged spray nozzle which does not deliver catalyst to an area or delivers an improper amount and leaves a zone of uncured resin will also act as WSM and result in a zone of blistering. Improper triggering of a spray gun also can lead to undercured resin or zones that are over-saturated with catalyst. A large zone of air inhibited resin is a concentrated zone of WSM and will result in blistering. A thick coating of water soluble binder on glass reinforcement is a WSM concentration and, as soon as water soluble material reaches it, osmotic pressure will begin to grow. It is possible that a particular resin could contain inordinate amounts of WSM because of an additive or water soluble filler. Boat builders may recognize other sources of WSM that are not listed here. The size of blisters will be related to the size of the WSM concentration sites. The extent of blistering on a hull will depend on the number of WSM sites and can vary from one to many. The time that the blister begins to form will depend on the depth of the WSM in the laminate, the permeation rate of water through the gel coat and the length of time of continuous immersion of the hull. In severe cases, WSM concentration blisters can form above the water line. In a humid environment the hull will pick up water from the air. If the WSM is close to the surface, it can build a high enough osmotic pressure to draw in water and cause blisters from the humidity in the air.

There is a second type of blister to which a well made hull with no built in WSM pockets is susceptible. We call these stress induced blisters. In these blisters the WSM concentration is formed during the immersion of the boat. The mechanism for formation is the following:

1. When gel coat material is applied to the mold, the surface away from the mold is cured in the presence of air which produces an air inhibited layer containing water soluble benzaldehydes.

2. When the laminating resin is applied, this water soluble material is dissolved in the first layer of the laminate.

3. As the laminating resin cures it bonds to the solid gel coat and then shrinks on curing producing a tensile stress in the laminate near the gel coat interface.

4. Upon immersion of a polyester laminate, water begins to diffuse into the polymer network.

5. This water absorption produces a swelling of the gel coat.

6. As the swollen layer tries to expand it produces tension in the underlying dry layer to which it is bonded.

7. This tensile field which lies ahead of the advancing water front produces stress or disk cracks in weak or brittle resin. The stress field is maximized by combination with the polymerization stressed zone.

8. When the disk cracks open, they create a localized vacuum into which adjacent water soluble molecules can diffuse. The water soluble material produced by air inhibition is already present in this zone.

9. Diffusing water molecules reach the cracked zone and interact with the now concentrated water soluble material forming a concentrated solution.

10. At this point, the osmotic process begins. Water is drawn into the zone producing osmotic pressure which builds until the creep stress of the polymer is exceeded and a bubble appears in the gel coat. From this process, stress induced blisters form just below the gel coat-laminate interface and stress plays a role in their nucleation. Our microscopic examination of many samples obtained from blistered boats show this to be the most common site for blisters to be located.

Finally, if a boat is made so that no WSM concentration blisters form and the hull material resists cracking during water diffusion so that no stress induced blisters form, will the boat last forever without blistering? Perhaps not. There may be a third type of blister, known as long term blisters, that could form and these are discussed below.

LEACHING OF SUBSTANCES FROM HULL MATERIAL

There is a process that prevents blistering which must now be discussed. Some WSM units are absorbed on to the chains inside the polymer network when water begins to diffuse inward. Table 1 lists many of the possibilities. These are not harmful unless they are concentrated.

A phenomenon known as leaching or extraction of WSM from the gel coat and laminate during water immersion plays an important role in blistering. When one makes coffee or tea he makes use of the leaching process. The hot water extracts from the bean or leaf the soluble flavor-producing chemicals, leaving behind the spent grounds or leaves. By the same process water can extract certain WSM from the hull.

WSM units are held onto the polymer chains by weak forces. These forces can be eliminated by water molecules. When water diffuses into the hull, it dislodges WSM from the polymer chains, surrounds it with water and aids in the outward movement of the WSM. Figure 8 shows the weight change of two composite samples made in this study. The initial weight gain of the samples is due to water molecules moving into the polyester network. At 600 hours of immersion time, the sample begins to lose weight. This weight loss is caused by leaching and extraction of WSM from the resin. After a very long time, more than 4000 hours, parts of the network and some of the glass can also be attacked and leached out of the hull. The point at which weight loss overcomes water pick-up corresponds to about one year of continuous immersion in warm waters (76°F) and about three years of continuous immersion in cold water at a temperature of 55°F.

Leaching can cause crazing or cracking of gel coat materials. As leaching takes place, polyesters shrink in size. As the surface shrinks, small cracks form. As leaching continues, the cracks spread and intersect to form a crazing pattern. Currently available gel coats are remarkably free of excessive leaching. Of the eight gel coats examined in this study, only one showed severe crazing and this was an experimental material.

Excessive leaching will prevent blistering. In order to form blisters, the WSM must remain trapped inside the laminate.

The inward movement of water, coupled with the inability of WSM to move outward, are required to generate osmotic pressure which causes blister growth. If WSM can move out as water moves in, blisters can not form. Many of the older polyester boats which did not blister, but showed crazing, probably were made of highly leachable polyesters. The group at the University of Rhode Island has developed a method for increasing the leachability of WSM from composites and thereby preventing blister formation. What is not known, at this point, is the effect of the porous gel coat on the long term strength properties of the polyester. This is a subject on which research is continuing.

LONG TERM EFFECTS OF WATER UP-TAKE

We have seen that diffusing water can form internal solutions with WSM to form blisters and that diffusing water can leach WSM from the polyester. There are some additional types of water/polymer interactions that can influence the long term strength of hull materials and possibly lead to a third type of blistering. Concentration of WSM creates the first type of blister. Stress induced blistering is the second type. The third type, long term blistering, is proposed but has not been established in the laboratory. Long term blisters would form only after the hull material is saturated with water. Field observations suggest this type of blister may form. Work is continuing to prove or disprove their existence.

In addition to the interactions of WSM with diffusing water molecules discussed above, water molecules also can react with certain WSM to form acid solutions. After very long immersion times, small zones in the polymer network contain acid solution. While the acid may not be concentrated enough to form a blister at this stage, it can attack the polymer chains and break off links which are then dissolved in the liquid. This reaction is known as ester hydrolysis. It is self perpetuating because the addition of the broken link to the solution creates additional acid which leads to more attack. Furthermore, as this solution becomes concentrated by dissolving more links it can generate osmotic pressure. Hence, this slow acid attack converts some of the polymer network into WSM. The process is slow but it could yield long term or the third type of blisters.

There are certain types of fire retardant components used in some resins which make up links in the polyester. A brominated phthalic group is one such material. These units react with water to form stronger acids than phthalic acid. This acid can attack the polyester at a greater rate than normal and cause long-term blistering.

The acid solution which forms inside the first and second type of blisters can also attack the polymer around the blisters by ester hydrolysis. This results in polymer network attack. Links that are removed from the network become WSM units and continue the growth of the blister. The exact extent to which blister solution corrodes the surrounding polymer is not known and more work is required on this problem.

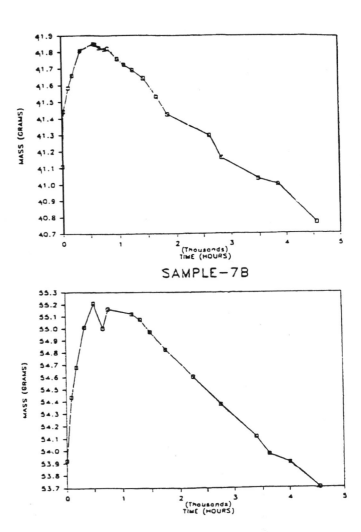

SAMPLE-7B

Figure 8. *Observed net weight changes for typical polyester composites. Samples were exposed to 65°C distilled water on all surfaces.*

SUMMARY

Listed below are the major findings of the American Boat Builders and Repairers Association/University of Rhode Island research project. The reader is urged to consider the implications only after a thoughtful reading of the text.

1. Currently used glass reinforced polyester laminates are excellent materials for boat building, but under some circumstances, can exhibit blisters.

2. All resins contain some water soluble material (WSM). Only if that material is concentrated at a point in the hull will it cause blistering.

3. All blisters are caused by water diffusing into the hull and reacting with water soluble material to form a droplet of solution which, because of osmotic pressure, grows in volume and creates a force which results in a blister.

4. Three types of blisters are discussed. Water soluble material concentration blisters are formed from clusters of materials present in the hull when the boat is built. Stress induced blisters form because water soluble material is concentrated by water diffusion and stresses. Long term blisters form because of ester hydrolysis of the polyester molecules.

5. Other factors being equal, gel coat thickness determines when blisters will begin to form.

6. Laminate lay-up and post-cure temperatures did not have a major effect on initiation time or severity for temperatures between 50°F and 90°F. Higher temperature post-cure should improve laminate stability. The degree of cross-linking is a critical parameter in determining the properties of a resin.

7. Design of the resin-rich region between the gel coat and laminate is important in minimizing blisters.

8. Control of air inhibition during lay-up can improve blister resistance.

9. Microscopic examination of blisters indicated presence of sawdust, disk cracks, promoter and internal stresses in the blister region. Without such examination it is impossible to pinpoint the exact cause of blistering in a particular boat.

10. Leaching of material from gel coats will cause surface crazing of the material.

11. The blister initiation time and the severity of the blisters formed during this study was a function of both the laminating resin and the gel coat used. However, the area affected by the blisters was similar in all cases. The size of the blisters depended on the laminating resin used. The chemistry of the materials are complex and variations were seen among generic types from different manufacturers.

12. It is recommended that boat manufacturers institute programs of quality control and quality assurance, with specification for their supplies, to minimize the blister problem.

BIBLIOGRAPHY

1. Abeysinghe, H. P. W., Edwards, G. Pritchard, and G. J Swampillai. "Degradation of cross-linked resins in water and electrolyte solutions." *Polymer*, 23, 1982, p. 1785.

2. Abeysinghe, H. P., J. S. Ghortra, and C. Pritchard. "Substances contributing to the generation of osmotic pressure in resins and laminates." *Composites,* 1983, p. 57.

3. Adams, R. C., "Variables influencing the blister resistance of marine laminates.'" 37th Annual Conference, SPI Reinforced Plastics/Composites Institute, Paper 2T-B, 1982.

4. Bireley, A. W., J. V. Dawkins and H. E. Strauss, "Blistering in Glass Fibre Reinforced Polyester Laminates." British Plastics Federation, 14th Reinforced Plastics Congress, 1985.

5. Brueggman, W. H., and S. D. Denoms. "Blistering in coated reinforced plastic laminates exposed to water." 38th Annual Conference, SPI Reinforced Plastics/Composites Institute, Paper 17-C, 1983.

6. Crump, Scott, "A Study of Blister Formation in Gel Coated Laminates." 41st Annual Conference, Reinforced Plastics/Composites Institute, SPI, Paper 13-C, 1986.

7. Davis, R., J. S. Ghortra, T. R. Halhi, and G. Pritchard. "Blister formation in RP: the origin of the osmotic process." 38th Annual Conference, SPI Reinforced Plastics/Composites Institute, Paper 17-B, 1983.

8. Edwards, H. R., "Variables influencing the performance of a gel coated laminate." 34th Annual Conference, SPI Reinforced Plastics/Composites Institute, Paper 4-D, 1979.

9. Florio, John. Master of Science Thesis, University of Rhode Island, Kingston, RI, 1986.

10. Fraser-Harris, A. B. F., and J. H. Kyle. "FRP bottom blistering." Paper presented at the Chesapeake Sailing Yacht Symposium, Annapolis, MD, January 15, 1983.

11. Marino, Rachel, Thomas Rockett and Vincent Rose. "Blistering of Glass Reinforced Plastic Marine Materials: A Review." NOAA/Sea Grant, Marine Technical Report 88. Marine Advisory Service, University of Rhode Island.

12. Norwood, L. S., "Recent developments in Polyester Matrices and Reinforcement for Marine Applications, in particular polyester/Kevlar composites." Paper 6, Port and Coast Services Conference, U. K., 1980.

Reference 24

University of Rhode Island Report #2

The Prevention and Repair of Gel Coat Blisters

by

Thomas J. Rockett, Ph.D.,
Vincent Rose, Ph.D.,
and Andra Kirsteins
Department of Chemical Engineering
University of Rhode Island
Kingston, Rhode Island

This report is the product of work accomplished under
U.S. Coast Guard Grant #1601.82

Foreword

The following is a brief summary in layman's language of an in-depth, impartial, scientific study to determine the best methods of repairing blister damage to fiberglass boats. Our association, the American Boat Builders and Repairers Association, Inc., has long been concerned with the lack of knowledge regarding a problem that has numerous serious ramifications for our industry, the prevention and cure of which were both unknown. The Coast Guard was concerned because of the potential for life threatening structural failures. The research grant provided by the directors of ABBRA and the two provided by the Coast Guard, we feel, have gone a long way in answering the questions which have plagued numerous members of our industry as well as the boating public.

ABBRA wishes to express its deep appreciation to the U.S. Coast Guard for the financial grants that made the research possible and to the members of the Department of Chemical Engineering at the University of Rhode Island for their dedication in pursuing all aspects of this most perplexing and serious problem.

Thomas Hale
American Boat Builders & Repairers Association, Inc.
715 Boylston Street, Boston, MA
October 1988

Introduction

These recommendations, prepared by Dr. Thomas Rockett, Dr. Vincent Rose and Miss Andra Kirsteins of the University of Rhode Island, are based on five years of research work conducted for ABBRA under the sponsorship of the United States Coast Guard. The work was overseen by Mr. Donald Ellison of the Coast Guard Office of Recreational Boating Product Assurance Branch and Mr. Thomas Hale of ABBRA. While no guarantees are implied or intended, the recommendations are based on the most current knowledge of the blister problem. The detailed technical description and results of all experiments conducted are available at the Coast Guard Headquarters, Washington, D.C.

Preventative Maintenance

Most fiberglass boat hulls are susceptible to blistering or internal water damage after long periods of immersion. To prevent or greatly delay the onset of blistering, the following two procedures are recommended.

1. The below water portion of the hull should be sanded and coated every one to three years depending on the extent of use and water temperature. Any previously applied antifouling or marine paint should first be removed, and then fresh antifouling paint should be applied over the new coating. Between sanding and coating, allow two or three days of air drying to reduce moisture in the gel coat. If a boat is land stored in the winter the best procedure is to sand to the gel coat in the fall and coat in the spring. For this application, two coats of a modern alkyd marine paint is not only sufficient but protects better than an equal thickness of some epoxies. Best results were obtained with an alkyd-urethane-silicone blended marine paint. Sand lightly between layers. A major source of protection comes, not from the paint layer itself, but rather because a constituent of the paint interacts with the gel coat polyester making the gel coat a more effective water barrier. Small paint blisters may develop on the paint surfaces but these will not destroy the protective effect of the paint. Also, for the preventative purpose a high build epoxy may be used and at least a 10 mil coating should be applied. Epoxies reduce blisters because of their barrier properties — not because of their interaction with polyester.

2. The bilge of the boat MUST be kept as dry as possible. A totally dry bilge is impossible, but one should never leave the boat sitting for long periods with water in the bilge. When storing the boat, dry the bilge by sponging the water not removed by the bilge pumps or by using a forced air dehumidifier system to dry the bilge area. Deep seated blistering and delamination of the hull can not take place unless the polymer in the hull is saturated. Saturation can only occur if the inside of the hull is in contact with water or 100% relative humidity air which results if free water is allowed to remain in the bilge. Since there is normally no inside gel coat protection, a wet interior surface will combine with normal water diffusion from the gel coat to produce a disastrous saturation, which can lead to deep blistering, delamination and deterioration of inner hull strength.

Normally, water diffuses slowly through a fiberglass hull, and can not be stopped. As long as the bilge side is dry, saturation is reached only in material near the gel coat and the blistering process begins. Deep seated damage is highly unlikely with a dry bilge. This is because saturation in the polymer is controlled by saturated conditions outside the polymer. If one side of the hull is in contact with water it becomes saturated. If the other side is in contact with water, the entire hull thickness becomes saturated and subject to blistering. However, if the bilge side is dry, the material near it is well below saturation. Across the thickness of the hull the water concentration will fall from saturated to below saturation in a linear manner. Normally hull material below saturation will not blister. Obviously all bilges become wet. A soaked bilge for several days probably presents no problem. However, prolonged stagnation of bilgewater is the surest method for destroying hull integrity. Boat designers and builders should consider bilge dryness in new boats, and an interior gel coat or paint coating will add protection.

BLISTER REPAIRS

For repair of fiberglass polyester hulls which show blisters, the following steps are recommended. The good news is that acceptable techniques can be recommended, but the bad news is that all the methods of repair described may be only temporary. The repair will stop the process only until water re-enters the hull, which will happen sooner or later depending largely upon water temperature and the length of continuous immersion.

Assessment of Damage

A core plug sample must be taken in a representative area. This plug may then be sectioned by making two parallel cuts, one to two millimeters apart, so that a thin cross-section of the hull can be obtained for microscopic study. While this is the best method, an alternative is to cut the plug in half and sand the plug perpendicular to the hull surface to expose a flat cross-section. *(See Figure 1.)* After sanding, a red dye penetrant (such as Spotcheck, Magnaflux Corporation, Chicago) should be sprayed on the surface. Let the surface dry and sand to remove superficial red dye. Observe the cross-section and the damage (blisters, osmotic disk cracks, delaminations, and extensive glass debonding) will be strongly marked in red.

The hull damage can now be classified into three types. Type I damage is near surface blistering. Type II damage will show deeper blisters and cracks extending through resin rich surface layers but not reaching half the hull thickness. Type III damage is severe deep seated blistering, cracking and delamination which extends through most of the hull thickness and jeopardizes the structural integrity of the hull. Each of these classes requires different repair procedures and therefore classification of the damage is essential to repair. The damage may be uniform or it may be localized in one or more areas. The following repair procedures apply to both situations, but in the case of localized damage only the affected area should be repaired.

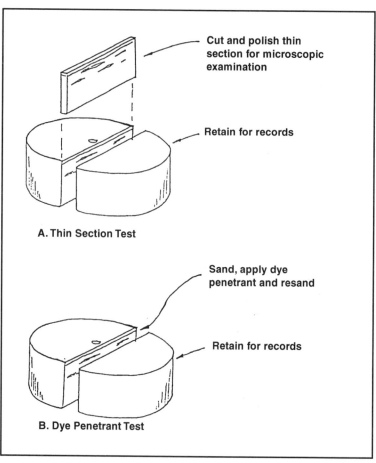

Figure 1. *Preparation of core samples for damage evaluation.*

Repair of Type I Damage

Step 1: Remove gel coat and all damaged material. Existing blisters MUST be opened and adjacent damaged material removed or reblistering will be rapid. A power sander using 20 grit aluminum oxide or silicone carbide paper works well. Sand blasting is an alternative, but the nozzle must be kept at a low angle to the surface (less than 30 degrees) to prevent damage of the underlying fiber glass. This procedure should be attempted only by an experienced operator.

Step 2: Rinsing and cleaning. The purpose of this operation is to remove loose debris and wash off blister fluid. Rinse well with fresh water from a hose and scrub surface with a stiff nylon brush. A mild detergent may be used but be certain the hull is well rinsed after use. Examine the surface with a 10x magnifying lens to be sure debris has been dislodged from the air bubbles in the resin.

Step 3: Drying. Allow the hull to air dry for 48 hours and check for weeping. If a sticky liquid is seen to weep from the hull, the blisters have not been removed and the sanding step must be repeated. Continue the drying process. All water will not be removed by this treatment, but the degree of saturation of the hull will be below 50% which is well in the safe zone for the hull. Use the following table for a guide for drying.

**Drying Time in Days for Various Air Temperatures
and Relative Humidities to Reach an
Acceptable Water Level for Repair**

Temperature	50% Relative Humidity	25% Relative Humidity
100 degrees F	16 days	9 days
83 degrees F	32 days	18 days
65 degrees F	64 days	36 days
47 degrees F	128 days	72 days

This table is based on extensive experimentation with 1/4" hull sections and is only applicable if both sides of the hull are exposed to the drying air. The bilge must be completely dried. Since the bilge must be examined thoroughly at this point, recommendations to the owner regarding future bilge dryness should be made. A perfect repair job can be ruined if, after relaunching, stagnant bilgewater is allowed to resaturate the hull.

Step 4: Recoating of the fiberglass/polyester hull. The repairer must choose between three different coating methods. The repairer may opt for a thick marine epoxy which will keep water out of the hull for a longer period but may result in more severe blistering once it starts. The second choice is a thinner coating of marine paint which may reblister sooner, but which will not make blistering more severe. Finally, one could choose to repair the hull using a gel coat designed to cure in air. All give good protection. Since different hulls have different blister characteristics, the only certain way of selecting the best repair method is to test the coatings over a repaired plug section. This is both time consuming and expensive. Thus a calculated risk will usually be taken. Both paints and epoxies introduce a constituent from the uncured coating into the polyester/glass hull materials. In the case of almost all paints tested, this interaction protects the hull material and is largely responsible for the protective role of paints. The interaction of the epoxy with the hull material makes the hull material more susceptible to blistering but keeps the water away from the blister site longer because of good water diffusion properties and because epoxy coating can be applied thicker than paint.

If fairing is necessary and the epoxy coating will be used, fair the surface with layers of high-build epoxy. If using paint or gel coat, add to a polyester laminating resin, chopped glass and colloidal silica to make a thick fairing material. Catalyze and spread with a non-stick roller or spatula. Since sanding is difficult, fair in the liquid state as much as possible. Avoid using any hollow type of filler for the fairing compound.

The Epoxy Method

Of the six epoxies tested, good results were obtained with the four pure epoxy systems (as opposed to blends). A filled and pigmented epoxy gave slightly better results than a clear unfilled epoxy. A two layer system with clear epoxy on the hull and filled epoxy over it also gave good results. Follow the manufacturers' instructions for application. If more than two hours elapse between adding layers during the build up, be certain to sand the surface to remove any tacky blush. Aim for at least 10 mils of cured coating or the manufacturers' recommended thickness if that is greater. This can be achieved with two or three coats of a high build epoxy but may require five or more layers of the thinner materials.

Marine Paints

All paints protected much better than expected. Several modern alkyds performed as well as epoxies on the samples tested. Best results were obtained using an alkyd-urethane-silicon blend, and a two-part marine polyurethane paint also performed well. In both cases, these were applied directly to the fiberglass-resin without a primer coat. Three layers are recommended with light sanding and washing to remove sanding debris between layers. After immersion, some small paint blisters can be expected, but these do not stop the protection of the hull material. Some of these coating blisters formed because the paint does not stick well to exposed glass. Apply antifouling paint over the marine paint. This technique will not give as smooth a finish as a gel coat and the sanding job will largely determine the smoothness.

Gel Coat Method

Our test on gel coats gave excellent results if at least 20 mils of the dry gel coat was applied. Use as rapid a curing method as possible. If the manufacturer recommends one to two percent catalyst, go with the higher value. Manufacturers will recommend formulations for use in air curing. If no air inhibition additive is used, a thin tacky water-soluble layer will remain on the surface and this must be removed. Wet sand to a hard surface. If wax additives are used to prevent surface tackiness, the wax must be sanded off. Wet sanding is best but change the paper often to prevent clogging. After sanding, apply two coats of marine paint and then add antifouling coating.

Step 5: Inspection. These methods should give one to three years of protection if all previously blistered material has been removed. Inspection should take place annually. At the first sign of blistering, repair should be repeated because the repair of surface blisters is much less expensive than the repair of Type 11 damage. In the absence of blisters, the maintenance step of repainting every other year will make the repair last longer. The boat must be hauled for proper inspection and pressure hose cleaning is recommended. Lighting is extremely important. A high intensity light must be used at a very low angle to make the blisters visible by shadowing.

Repair of Type 11 Damage

Step 1: Remove gel coat and affected area as for Type 1 damage. The amount of material removed will be far greater.

Step 2: Rinse and clean as for Type 1 damage.

Step 3: Drying. Follow recommendations for Type 1 damage.

Step 4: Restoration of hull strength and resin-rich zone. On the clean, dry, prepared surface apply at least 1/8" of glass reinforced polyester. The reason the layer must be this thick is that water can cause debonding of a new fiberglass layer over an old one. If the layer is too thin, diffusing water could reach the interface, saturate the area and cause debonding. The layer can be applied by spraying (use airless gun) or rolling an isophthalic polyester resin or a high quality orthophthalic resin on one or two layers of veil mat or using a chopper gun to apply chopped glass with the resin. There may be other materials, such as vinylesters, which may be acceptable, but we cannot recommend them at this time because we have not produced or seen data to prove their efficacy. If the airless spray gun is used the resin must still be rolled into the surface and glass. The layer must be added in one continuous operation. Do not allow part of the thickness of the layer to cure completely before adding a second layer to it. Additional resin can be added up to half an hour after the first application, but if part of the layer cures completely before more resin is placed on top of it, an interface is introduced which could cause problems.

The type of glass used is critical. It must be E-glass or a corrosion resistant glass, and it must be free of a soluble binder. Veil mats must be lightly powder bound and chopped glass must be clean. If there is any question don't use the glass without having tested it. It is often helpful to use a chopped glass with red fibers in the bundle to aid in applying a uniform coat.

Step 5: Preparation of new fiberglass for surface coat. When the polyester added has a wax added to prevent air inhibition or is allowed to cure with an air inhibited tacky surface or is sprayed after roll on with a water soluble PVA layer to prevent air inhibition, the surface must now be sanded into the hard and well-cured polyester. This step is difficult and requires care, patience and lots of sand paper. If any of the PVA, the wax or the air inhibited material is left on the repaired surface it will blister at this interface in a matter of months. First, use a nylon brush and scrub the surface with lots of water. Then sand, replacing the sand paper as it fills. Don't redistribute the water solubles or the wax on the surface. Get it off. Finish by scrubbing with water and a mild detergent to remove all loose debris. Let repaired area dry thoroughly.

Step 6: Recoating of the hull. Follow step 4 for Type I damage. Apply three coats of marine paint, the thick epoxy coating, or re-gel coat.

Repair of Type III Damage

In this situation the hull is virtually useless. The following recommendations are aimed at removing as much of the hull as is possible without having the boat collapse. The remnant shell is then used as a male mold for construction of a new hull. The collapse possibility is a real one and care must be taken when placing the bilge post or poppets during the removal of the damaged hull material. This procedure should only be attempted by experienced boat builders and repairers.

Step 1: Removal of damaged zone. This step should be done by sand blasting. It is virtually certain that areas of the hull will be penetrated. Care must be taken to protect the equipment inside the hull.

Step 2: Wash and scrub the surface.

Step 3: Reconstruction of the hull. Follow recommendations in step 4 of damage Type II. Rebuild hull to at least the original thickness. Three layers of heavy woven roving (E-glass powder bound) with a veil mat or a chopped glass layer will give approximately 1/4" of hull thickness. Without a veil or chop glass layer, four layers are necessary to yield 1/4" of thickness. Finish with the veil mat or a light chop layer or both. Again (see step 4, Type II) the fewer interruptions in the build-up, the better. Never interrupt the resin rich surface layers. Sanding is a must between interrupted layers.

Step 4: Preparation of the surface for coating. Follow the instructions for step 5, Type II.

Step 5: Surface coating. Again the repairer must choose paint, epoxy or gel coat as described in step 4 of Type I damage.

These procedures for repairing blister-damaged hulls, if followed carefully, should give added life to blistered fiberglass boats.

REFERENCE 25

COMMENTARY ON THE UNIVERSITY OF RHODE ISLAND REPORT #2

by John A. Wills

Preventative Maintenance

Page 201, Item 1: Everyone will want to know at least one trade name of this magic paint. As indicated, this silicone-based paint will not last long as a water barrier. This has been experienced with most silicone-based paints. Removal of an anti-fouling paint sufficiently enough to allow a 10 mil coating of epoxy or two coats of marine paint on an average of every two years is not likely to be performed by most boat owners. If a paint or epoxy coating is to be applied every two years, then it might be well to increase bottom cleaning service and eliminate anti-fouling paint altogether since removal of an anti-foulant can equal the cost of all other operations.

I would like to see proof that the alkyd-urethane-silicone coating actually does "react" with gel coat and what the resulting compound is.

Page 201, Item 2: I agree that bilges must be kept free of standing water which is often produced by rain or wash-down rather than leakage. This would be relatively fresh water, and as stated before, fresh water is several times more chemically reactive than that containing salt or other contaminates.

Unless a de-humidifier is constantly used in the bilge throughout the life of the boat, a high humidity will always exist, so the same care in slowing water penetration into the hull from the outside should be used in the bilge as well. The bilge appears to be a great place for the magic silicone paint since there will be little exposure to ultraviolet light — the main cause of silicone-based paint deterioration — and standing water can be controlled.

Blister Repairs

Page 202, Assessments of Damage: I agree that a core sample should be taken. It is nice to observe what has happened under a microscope — but certainly, short beam structural tests should be run on this sample to determine structural strength retention. Absolutely no mention of this in the URI Report!

Page 202, Type I Damage: The narration of repair Type I Damage in Steps 1 through 3 is informative. The Drying Time Table is interesting, but how many boats have hulls only 1/4" thick? Not mine.

Page 203, Step 4: Re-coating the Fiberglass Hull. The comment about fairing with chopped glass and colloidal silica is a bit comical. Ever try applying chopped glass with a spatula? The statement, "Avoid using any hollow type (microballoons) or filler for the fairing compound" is misleading and the authors should give their reasons for not using such things as glass or ceramic microballoons. A fairing compound, in my opinion, is just that. If the authors mean that hollow fillers should not be used for structural repairs, then they would be correct but should so state this opinion. Properly selected microballoons are successfully used in fairing and filling compounds.

Page 203, The Epoxy Method: Again, why not at least state some trade names? If the authors want you to "follow the manufacturers' instructions" they should, at least, tell who the manufacturers are.

Page 203, Gel Coat Method: Once more, some manufacturers should be named. Effective wet (or dry) sanding air-inhibited gel coat is nearly impossible without re-contamination. Wax additives should never be used except for the very last spray coat which is intended to be

the final application of any further material including anti-fouling paint, since wax would prevent adhesion. If further coating is intended, use a water soluble PVA mold release as an anti-air inhibitor. Thorough scrubbing and washing will prepare the surface for further coatings. Sanding, though preferable, is usually not necessary.

Page 204, Repair of Type II Damage, Step 4: This is a very nebulous narrative. It is obvious that the authors have not had much shop experience. To imply that the "restoration layer" must be at least 1/8" thick to avoid de-bonding is misleading. A thickness of properly scheduled reinforcements determined by structural strength loss tests should be applied, and de-bonding should be expected to some extent. No mention of the use of coupling agents is made for the first layer of new skin to improve bonding, but this is absolutely necessary.

Page 204, Repair of Type III Damage, Step 1: This statement does not include the very real probability that there is considerable distortion of the hull. These areas are not very well prepared for repair by sandblasting! Sections may have to be removed, thus requiring temporary molds be installed on the inside of the hull.

At the point where sandblasting has been completed and the required temporary molds installed, a thorough saturation of the repaired area should be made using only catalyzed resin containing a coupling agent on the first saturation coat to improve resin bonding to the now raw glass fibers.

Page 204, Repair of Type III Damage, Step 3: This paragraph is poorly stated. There is no such thing as "E glass powder bound woven roving." What I hope is meant here would be restated as follows: "Three layers of woven or uni-directional roving whose binders and/or coupling agents are compatible with the resin to be used will be applied. Each layer of roving shall have laid between it a veil mat, or preferably, chopped strand or chopped strand mat with compatible binders. The finish over the last layer of roving should be either veil or chopped strand. Ideally for cosmetic purposes, this last layer would be veil or chopped strand mat rolled out but before gelation, a final ply of 10-ounce boat cloth would be squeegeed on, followed by coats of the laminating resin, then reverse gel coated."

For a hull which is considered to be in Type III condition, little or no consideration should be given to the retained structural strength of the wetted portion of the old hull.

Now is the opportunity to "redesign" the structurals on the new hull. A re-hulled boat should be provided with a laminating schedule as if it were a new factory hull built today.

REFERENCE 26

Following is a reproduction of "A Position Paper on the ABBRA/URI Gelcoat Report" by the Gougeon Brothers, Inc. I believe this well-presented and diplomatic response provides a public service and reflects the feeling of all of us associated with the problem of hydrolytic damage in fiberglass structures. — JW

A POSITION PAPER ON THE ABBRA / URI GELCOAT REPORT

by Gougeon Brothers, Inc.
© Copyright February 1989

The January issue of *Practical Sailor* featured the cover story "*The Blister Chronicles: Good News, Bad News.*" This article was based on a recently released report by the American Boat Builders and Repair Association (ABBRA), entitled "*The Prevention and Repair of Gelcoat Blisters.*" The investigative work for this report was done at the University of Rhode Island under sponsorship of the U.S. Coast Guard, Grant #1601.82.

This brief summary draws a number of conclusions and makes recommendations that are surprising to us and others in the marine industry who have long been connected with the blister problem. Among the more significant disclosures are:

1. Some marine paints, especially alkyd/urethane/silicon blends with two-coat applications, appeared to form a positive chemical interaction with polyester resin, creating barrier properties on test samples "that protect better than an equal thickness of some epoxies."

2. They found that some epoxies, when applied to polyester gelcoat surfaces, can have a detrimental chemical reaction with the polyester surface. This reaction appeared to have a definite effect on the blister process in some samples.

All test products were purposely not identified as to brand name or manufacturer. The report only provided a general description of generic type. We believe that WEST SYSTEM epoxy was one of the six brands of epoxy tested, but we, like other manufacturers whose products might be involved, cannot be sure. *Of more concern is the fact that a detailed report on testing methods, procedures and results is unavailable at this time.*[1] While some of the test methods and procedures have been communicated to us with some general conclusions by Dr. Rose of URI, we have not been able to evaluate the data on the actual results of the individual test samples and their performance.

The purpose of our own in-house gelcoat blister testing program has been to evaluate the effect of coating thickness on blister resistance and to compare our products against other competitive products that have been promoted in the market place. We have achieved excellent results with this program, showing our product as one of the most effective barriers in preventing blistering. Certainly we have not seen the adverse chemical reaction with our epoxies such as is briefly described in the URI summary report.

In the spring of 1987, the University of Rhode Island published the first phase of this research, the "*Cause of Gelcoat Blisters*" (Coast Guard Grant #1501.83). We found this report to be both definitive and well documented. Its 29 pages covered the key elements of the testing procedure used, together with some detailed results on the various resin systems evaluated. Unfortunately, the most recent URI report, "*The Prevention and Repair of Gelcoat Blisters,*" is only seven pages long and raises more questions than it answers. Certainly it is not the complete and detailed document that is its predecessor, and serves only to confuse boat owners, professional repairers and material suppliers, as to what should now be the proper response to the gelcoat blister problem in light of this new knowledge.

EPOXY AS A PREVENTATIVE COATING

Our main concern is with the URI conclusion that there is a general inclination of some epoxy formulations to aggravate the tendency of an F.R.P. hull to blister. Without seeing the test data, we can only speculate on the test methodology that has led to this conclusion.

First, it is important to recognize that all laboratory testing (including our own) is not an exact reproduction of what actually may occur in a typical marine environment. The major departure is temperature. Because chemical reactivity is known to increase dramatically with increase of temperature (it can roughly double every 10°C), most testing is accomplished at elevated temperatures.

There is a great incentive for researchers to test at high temperatures since years of chemical activity can be compressed into weeks or months to speed up results. The down side to this economy is that all polymer materials have physical performance curves that are very much dependent on temperature. Some polymers are much more temperamental to heat than others, and the researcher has to be mindful not to test materials at temperatures beyond their performance limits.

Much of the original gelcoat blister testing was done at boiling temperatures (212°F), until it was discovered that the heat distortion temperature (HDT) limit for most polyester resins is well below 212°F. Rightfully, the researchers at URI chose 149°F (65°C) which is substantially below polyester's HDT — to perform their work with polyester laminate samples to understand the cause of gelcoat blisters.

Unfortunately, they have used the same temperatures to test the various candidate coating materials as a solution to the gelcoat blister problem. The HDT of room-temperature-cure epoxy systems is not very high, with most being under 130°F. Any test results accomplished at higher temperatures are likely to be compromised as representative of actual product performance under normal circumstances where most water temperatures range from 50°F to 85°F.

The HDT of WEST SYSTEM® 105/206 epoxy is about 125°F. Because of this, we have conducted all of our gelcoat blister testing in 120°F water baths. Even at this lower temperature, we have some concern that we are not properly characterizing the true performance of our products.

Three other factors may be contributing to this URI reported phenomena:

1. URI made up their own test panels using a single brand of polyester resin system for all the samples. While this approach is proper test procedure to reduce the number of variables, the fact is, boats are built with many different resin systems. The question is: *would they have seen the same results if they had evaluated the same epoxies on other brands of polyester resin systems?*

2. Polyester resins and gelcoats are known to be chemically active for some time before a full cure takes place. Typically, styrene monomers are given off in smellable quantities for many months after the initial cure. URI manufactured samples were reportedly cured for 30 days before testing. *Is this enough cure time to represent a typical boat hull's chemical interaction with a protective coating?*

In comparison, the test panels used in the Gougeon blister testing program have been taken from actual fiberglass boat hulls. Not only are these actual hull panels naturally aged, but they have been stressed under load, which we consider an important issue when addressing permeation. (Micro-cracking due to stress greatly increases the permeability of a laminate.) While the disadvantage of this approach is that the exact make-up of the laminate is not known, a statistical sampling population from each hull with adequate controls can be developed with ease at low cost.

3. We are also concerned that all of the protective coating materials that were evaluated were not allowed adequate, proper cure times before testing. This is a crucial issue having significant impact on the performance of WEST SYSTEM epoxy products and, we suspect, many others. Two weeks at room temperature is necessary to achieve a full cure with our 105/206 epoxy. Even then, there is minor chemical activity that continues for some time before full physical properties develop.

Could it be that an incompletely cured polyester laminate, coated with an incompletely cured epoxy system, and then submerged in 149°F water, may cause the noted adverse chemical reaction, whereas properly cured polyesters and epoxies in water below epoxy's HDT may not? Our chemists and engineers, along with others within the industry, are concerned that this is a very real potential. Without further testing and/or evaluation of the ABBRA/URI data, we can not fairly and accurately evaluate these factors which may be influencing a coating product's performance.

SECONDARY BONDING FOR STRUCTURAL REPAIRS

We strongly disagree with the ABBRA/URI report on repairing fiberglass laminates suffering from internal blistering. They refer to a Type II and Type III repair where anywhere from 1/8"-thickness to almost all of the laminate needs to be replaced. In all cases, the report recommends the use of polyester resin with the proper E-glass material to re-laminate the hull. It doesn't make sense to us to replace blistered polyester with the same material that might likely blister again. They carefully point out (Step 5 on Page 6 of the report) how difficult it can be to get good bonding with fresh polyester to cured polyester surfaces. They totally ignore epoxies as a possible structural repair material. We view this as a major oversight, considering the far superior bonding capabilities of a quality epoxy over polyesters.

CONCLUSION

In the coming months we hope to duplicate URI test data to see if we can detect any negative reactions with our epoxies and, if so, determine whether or not the cause is related to any of the possibilities previously mentioned. At the same time, we will add paints (especially the alkyd/urethane/silicon blends) to our test program to see if the URI results can be duplicated with these products.

It is important to clearly state at this point that we feel the work done by the University of Rhode Island needs to be taken seriously and evaluated in depth. It is the only independent, government-funded effort undertaken in this country. Dr. Rose and Dr. Rockett, who headed this program, are well-regarded in their fields and are, we believe, sincere in their desire to produce only accurate and competent results. But the world of chemistry and physics with regard to the gelcoat blister problem is immensely complex.

The fact is that several thousands of boats have been coated with WEST SYSTEM products over the past ten years and to date, there have been surprisingly few reports of polyester blister re-occurrence on those boats. We feel that our product has been performing well, substantiated by many case histories where boats repaired and coated with WEST SYSTEM products have not re-blistered after long periods of immersion.[2]

We have been involved with gelcoat blister repair and prevention longer than anyone, and firmly believe our products are the best response to the problem. But we intend to be open minded as we carefully evaluate this new URI data. We will publish the results of our continuing investigations as they become available. In the meantime, we would like to get all the feedback we can from the field, especially on any reported coating failures with any coating product, not only our own.

1. Although the *Practical Sailor* article states "For members of the industry, full details of the report are available at Coast Guard Headquarters in Washington . . ." and Dr. Rockett's report states "The detailed technical description and results of all experiments conducted are available at the Coast Guard Headquarters, Washington, D.C.", after six weeks of exhaustive efforts, neither Gougeon Brothers, Inc. personnel or consultants, nor anyone else within the industry, to the best of our knowledge, have been able to obtain this "full" report.

2. WEST SYSTEM epoxy has never been known to blister when properly mixed and applied to wood, fiberglass or metal surfaces.

Gougeon Brothers, Inc. P.O. Box X908, Bay City, MI 48707
Telephone: (517) 684-7286 • Fax: (517) 684-1374

REFERENCE 27

A Study of Permeation Barriers to Prevent Blisters in Marine Composites and a New Technique for Evaluating Blister Formation

By Paul P. Burrell, David J. Herzog, R. Terrance McCabe
INTERPLASTIC CORPORATION

Reprinted from: 42nd Annual, 1987, SPI Conference
Section Marine Session 15-E

ABSTRACT

Blistering of gel coated surfaces below the water line is a major problem in the marine craft and swimming pool industries. Some causes of this problem can be attributed to manufacturing technique, but many can be reduced or eliminated by changing the type of raw materials such as the polyester resins utilized in constructing the composites.

This paper presents an alternative method for evaluating blister resistance in castings and prototype marine laminates without the stresses normally found in a boiling water bath test. A wide variety of gel coated back-up composites were tested by a submersed laminate evaluation procedure. Testing emphasis is on comparison of orthophthalic laminating resins, which are these industries' norm, to vinylester skin coats and laminates. The test program showed that a vinylester cladding system can significantly delay blister formation utilizing these same orthophthalic laminating resins.

INTRODUCTION

During the life of a polyester boat hull or swimming pool laminate, the gel coat has some degree of permeability and thus over time allows water to pass through to the resin-glass substrate. If the polyester component of the laminate is an orthophthalic resin, the composite structure at best is subject to gradual degradation by hydrolysis which can result in eventual blister formation over time. A scrape, crack, or chip in the gel coat surface allowing direct water contact with the laminate will, at the worst, eventually lead to reduced composite strength.

In the "World of Composites" orthophthalic general purpose marine laminating resins have generally been the boat builders' choice primarily due to cost considerations. Use of premium resins such as vinylester resin and isophthalic polyester resin has, for the same reason, been limited to high performance applications where low weight, high strength, or corrosion resistance is of greater importance. Both the isophthalic and the vinylester resins have been known in the polyester industry for many years for their superior corrosion resistance (*References 1 and 2*) which include their superior hydrolytic stability. vinylester resins are also noted particularly for their excellent physical properties including impact and fatigue resistance (*Reference 3*). The incorporation of these properties in a reinforced fiberglass composite should lead to major improvements in the overall quality and capabilities of products manufactured by the marine and swimming pool industries.

The introduction of a vinylester barrier skin coat or cladding layer between the gel coat and the laminate interface, as pictured in Figure 1, has been investigated in the Commercial Resins' laboratories as a means of decreasing water absorption. This reinforced marine "gel coat/skin coat" water permeation barrier potentially has similar structural strength relative to the underlying reinforced composite. As we change the all-resin

Figure 1. Structure Description for a Skin Coated Composite

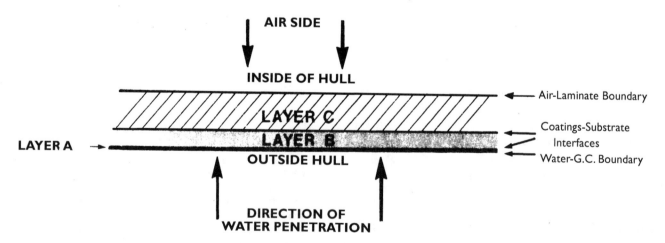

Layer A: A 20 mils wet drawdown of neopentyl glycol isophthalic gel coat as the standard protective polyester coating on the outside.
Layer B: A 20 mils interlayer or a 60 mils interlaminate made from vinylester.
Layer C: A standard laminate substrate made from two-parts of unsaturated polyester laminating resin and one-part glass to a ¼-½ inch thickness.

vinylester skin coat in a fiberglass reinforced vinylester skin coat, the reduced capabilities of an all resin system in impact can be minimized.

THEORETICAL

The gel coat layer has been described in the literature as a semipermeable membrane that allows diffusion of fluids; *i.e.*, mass transfer of liquids through the membrane *(Reference 4)* to the laminate. After water diffuses into a polyester laminate, it can attack the polymer matrix by a hydrolysis reaction. The hydrolytic cleavage of an orthophthalic polymer molecule presumably occurs both at the gel coat-resin interface and in a reaction zone beneath the laminate surface *(Reference 5)*. Blistering results from residual gel coat surface stresses, either compressive or tensile, originating from a point in the substrate microstructure. The stresses could be induced by osmotic pressures, microencapsulation of air bubbles and non-reactants in the polyester, bonding imperfections in the interface, and many other factors *(Reference 5 and 6)*.

An accepted test to evaluating blister resistance of composites has been the boiling water test. This accelerated test of blister resistance sometimes gives unreliable results since the boiling water and the clamps utilized for a tight seal induce additional stresses in the test specimen other than the typical hydrostatic forces that a marine or swimming pool laminate would be exposed to. In the normal test a 4-inch by 4-inch gel coated composite is clamped, by its corners and supported with a back plate, to a porthole in a test box and then exposed to 212°F boiling water. The boil test induces three stresses in addition to the hydrostatic forces exerted on the composite. These stresses are the action of boiling water, thermal expansion/contraction of the resin or resin-fiberglass matrixes, and stresses from obtaining a tight seal. The cumulative effects of these stresses can cause premature failure. While the boiling water test can show relative differences between structures, it does not simulate the actual product use conditions.

Another accepted test for evaluating various plastic materials Is ASTM D570 ("Water Absorption of Plastics") and shown in Figure 2a is a non-coated all resin casting that does not have a gel coat/skin coat barrier. Figure 2b illustrates the water concentration gradient within an unsaturated polyester resin clear casting. Initially, there is minimum resistance to water penetration at the surface of the polyester casting. The water diffuses through the polymer and over time its concentration varies with depth *(Reference 7)*. Experimentally we observe the following stages in ASTM D570 testing of clear castings:

Stage	Mechanism	Weight Gain Graph Comments
1	Absorption	Logarithmic Increase Initially
2	Saturation Point	Asymptote -Time/Weight Gain Slowdown
3	Equilibrium	Maximum - % H₂O Gain Plateau
4	Hydrolysis/Solubilize	Decrease after Saturation

Figure 2. Diffusion of Water Into a Solid

a.) Penetration over time

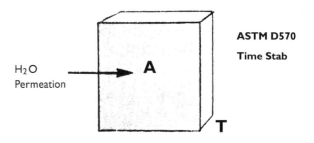

W_T = weight of solid specimen in grams at time t

W_O = original weight of solid specimen in grams

X = T/2 = one half of the thickness

T = 2/X = thickness of solid = 0.125 inches

A = surface area of solid face, 2 faces, 2 inches by 2 inches

V = volume of solid = (A x 2X)

d = density in gm/in^3 = W/V

C(t) = mass fraction concentration of H_2O at time t in the composite =

$$\frac{W_T - W_2}{W_1}$$

b.) Penetration depth versus concentration gradient

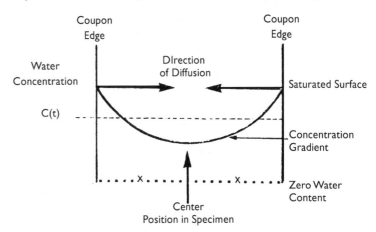

Initially the water penetration at the surface is very quick and we observe a logarithmic rate of increase. However, the rate of water absorption gradually decreases until it reaches the maximum water gain value or saturation point of the test coupons. If the resin matrix is inert to water, we have reached an equilibrium; but if the polymer can be chemically broken down and solubilized, the weight of the composite will decrease as portions of the heavier matrix are broken down, leached out, and replaced with water. We know we have achieved a good "Gel Coat/Skin Coat/Back-up Composite" system design in a reinforced laminate when the water weight gain reaches a maximum value and stays there indefinitely.

ASTM D570 is a useful screening tool to determine the relative merits of various polyester resins for use in improving the composite structure. Clear castings of a wide variety of unsaturated polyester resins were scanned by this test at room temperature, 150°F, and 200°F for water absorption rate, approximate saturation point, and percent solubles; a summary is tabulated in Table 1 *(Reference 8)*. The vinylester resin, which has low water absorption and minimal solubles, the excellent physical properties shown in Table 2, and superior fatigue resistance *(Reference 3)* made it an excellent resin choice for marine and swimming pool composites. These outstanding qualities of vinylester resins further show that a vinylester would be an excellent candidate for a skin coat barrier labeled as Layer B in Figure 1. Figures 3 and 4 compare the vinylester resin water absorption over time and temperature to a neopentyl glycol based gel coat and to other polyester resins in Figure 5 including a typical orthophthalic polyester laminating resin. The vinylester resins will reach point of saturation and maintain it while the less capable orthophthalic resins continue to absorb water and degrade over the test period and test temperatures.

We set out to remove two sources of stresses from the boil test so the conditions of the accelerated test will more closely relate to actual use conditions. In order to remove the stress induced by the clamps the whole coupon is immersed in water. This created a special problem, so the laminate is constructed with two gel coated surfaces to eliminate a non-gel coated surface being exposed to water. The edges of the test panels were sealed with vinylester resin to protect the orthophthalic laminating resin and glass fibers exposed during trimming to prevent wicking of water into the laminate and hydrolysis of the polymer.

Figure 3: ASTM D570 Water Absorption of vinylester Resins versus Time and Tempertaure (1/8 inch Clear Castings)

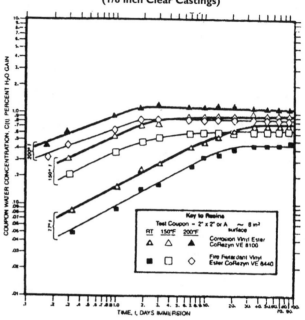

EXPERIMENTAL

The purpose of the outlined test is to obtain and analyze water diffusion data through several gel coat/skin coat barriers using various back-up resin castings and laminates. These composites were tested under ambient conditions as well as at 150°F to accelerate water contact exposure. The test procedure that we are using is a modified ASTM D570 ("Water Absorption of Plastics") where the weight gain of a standard composite specimen is recorded at set increments of time.

Figure 4: ASTM D570 Water Absorption of Gel Coat and Skin Coat Resins versus Time and Tempertaure (1/8 inch Clear Castings)

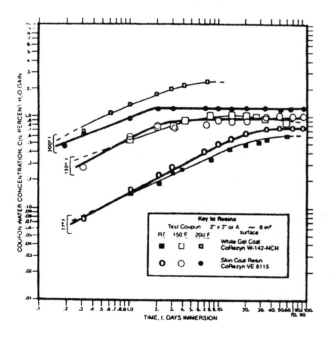

Figure 5: ASTM D570 Water Absorption of Laminating Resins versus Time and Tempertaure (1/8 inch Clear Castings)

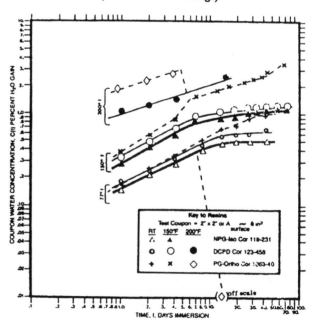

TABLE 1: VARIATION OF ASTM D570 WATER ABSORPTION WITH RESIN CASTING TYPE OVER TIME AND TEMPERATURE

CoRezyn	1063-40	253	393	119-231	123-458	8115	W142
Generic Type	PG/Ortho	PG/Ortho	PG/Iso	NPG/Iso	DCPD	Thixo/VE	NPG/Iso
Reactivity	Low	High	Medium	Medium	High	Medium	Medium
Application	General Purpose	Tooling	Laminating	Laminating	Laminating	SkinCoat & Lam	Gel Coat
5 Weeks Dwell in 77°F Water*							
Saturation, percent	.99	1.20	.85	.50	.65	.57	.62
Solubles, percent	.16	.13	.25	.19	.04	.06	.18
7 Day Fit, a	.14	.20	.18	.13	15	.13	.13
b	.16	.22	.18	.12	.14	.10	.10
r^2	.97	.98	.98	.99	.99	.98	.99
10 Weeks Dwell in 150°F Water*							
Saturation, percent	3.55	2.82	1.05	1.16	1.19	.92	1.05
Solubles, percent	.69	.46	.35	.62	.19	.21	.36
3 Day Fit, a	.36	.46	.35	.28	.34	.33	.56
b	.30	.36	.24	.19	.21	.20	.25
r^2	1.00	1.00	1.00	1.00	1.00	1.00	1.00
14 Days Dwell in 200°F Water*							
Saturation, percent	—	2.88	2.30	—	2.37	1.15	2.40
Solubles, percent	4.29	3.84	.35	—	.24	.37	—
3 Day Fit, a	1.84	1.94	1.20	—	1.00	1.00	1.37
b	.64	.67	.20	—	.31	.10	.57
r^2	1.00	1.00	.98	—	1.00	.97	.99

*Equation for a Logarithmic Curve Fit is: $C(t) = a + b \ln t$
where $C(t)$ = mass fraction of water in percent, t = time in days,
a & b = regression coefficients,
and r^2 = coefficient of determination or quality of curve fit.

TABLE 2: LAMINATING RESIN MECHANICAL/LIQUID CHARACTERISTICS

CoRezyn Product	Cor 1063-40	Cor 9595	VE 8100	VE 8440
Generic Formula Type	All-PG/ Ortho	All-PG/ Iso	Bis A-Epoxy	Brom Bis A-Epoxy
Typical Application	General Purpose	Polyester Laminating	Corrosion Vinyl Ester	VE Fire Retardant
LIQUID PROPERTIES:				
Viscosity, cps	1400/436	950/450	125	520
Percent Non-Volatile	52,3	56.2	50.5	60.5
Weight per Gallon, lb	8.99	9.00	8.60	9.66
Specific Gravity[2]	1.0816	1.0828	1.0346	1.1626
CURED 1/8 INCH CASTING PROPERTIES[1]				
Flexural Strength, psi ASTM D790	16,300	18,500	16,900	18,500
Flexural Modulus, psi x 10^5	5.45	5.18	4.38	4.53
Tensile Strength, psi ASTM D638	8,600	10,300	11,500	11,200
Tensile Modulus, psi x 10^5	6.32	5.65	4.46	4.61
Elongation, %	1.5	2.0	6.0	4.3
Heat Distortion, °C ASTM D648	73	87	106	116
Barcol Hardness, 934-1 ASTM D2583	39	46	36	35
Apparent Density, (lb/ft³)[3]	74.346	73.972	70.225	77.607
Specific Gravity ASTM D792	1.1945	1.1885	1.1283	1.2469
Volumetric Shrink, %[4]	9.45	8.90	8.30	6.76
Glass Transition, DSC, °C	63/66/69	94/97/100	111/115/119	111/113/116
Specific Heat, via DSC @50°C	1.50	1.50	—	1.42
J/(gm °C) @70/90°C	1.75/1.82	1.63/1.74	1.71/1.81	1.36/1.44
@110/130°C	1.80/1.80	1.88/1.94	—	1.59/1.78
@150/170°C	1.80/1.81	1.94/1.96	—	1.79/1.80
@120/140°C	1.81/1.81	—	2.31/2.26	1.80/1.76

1. All were catalyzed with 1% MEKP; N.P. V.E.'s promoted with 0.20%, 12% Cobalt and 0.05% DMA.
2. As compared to H_2O @ 77°F, 8.31212 lb/gal.
3. As compared to H_2O @ 77°F, 62.24 lb/ft³
4. % Shrink = $[(1/SG_S) - (1/SG_L)]/(1/SG_L)$

The first step in test panel construction is to prepare the gel coat/skin coat barrier. The gel coat is catalyzed with 2.0% of Lupersol DDM-9 methyl ethyl ketone peroxide (MEKP) and drawn down using a wet film applicator on two glass plates. When a vinylester resin interlayer is used, the same basic drawn down technique is used at an increased mil thickness setting. The CoRezyn VE 8115 skin coat resin used in the study is a prepromoted thixotropic CoRezyn VE 8110-type series catalyzed with 2.0% Witco Hipoint 90 MEKP. The resin/glass interlaminate barrier is approximately 30 mils in thickness and constructed using a 2:1 ratio of resin to glass mat consisting of two layers of 3/4 ounce Owens Corning M722.

To prepare the all-resin back-up castings, two barrier coated plates are assembled together into a mold with U-shaped metal stop edges and rubber gaskets to prevent leakage. Five mil thick strips of DuPont Mylar were added as needed to offset the thickness of the gel coat/skin coat barriers and control the all-resin casting cores at ⅛" thickness. The laminate cores are constructed using a 2:1 ratio of resin to glass mat and layed-up using 7 and 8 layers respectively of ¾ ounce mat on each plate for laminate core sandwiches. Before gelation occurs the plates are pressed together to fuse into a double mold surface laminate having a ¼" core.

The laminates and castings are post cured and then cut into test coupons. An exploded view of the 5½ inch by 5½ inch test coupons is in Figure 6. To evaluate the effects of the barrier design on water absorption rates we chose the orthophthalic, CoRezyn 1063-40, all-resin casting core to assure a homogeneous substrate back-up. Several resins are studied in laminate cores to determine the influence of each resin matrix on the blister resistance of the gel coated composite. The moisture content at ambient and 150°F is monitored over time and related to blister formation due to the differences in the barrier structure.

OBSERVATIONS/RESULTS

A compilation of the mechanical and liquid characteristics of the four resins utilized in the study for back-up resins in the composite's core are in Table 2. The physical properties of a composite manufactured from any of these resins will have similar composite strength (*Reference 9*). Any differences noted in the blistering or relative absorption rates should then be due to the chemical resistance or hydrolytic stability of the back-up resin utilized in the laminate substrate underlying the barrier (*Reference 10*).

The initial boil test data on the resins in this study are discussed below. Table 3 shows the water weight gained and time to blister during the boil test for several different composite structures. The 212°F test temperature used is well above the heat distortion point of most orthophthalic resins. This test shows relative differences and that the vinylester resins do perform well under the severe conditions of the boil test.

The diffusivity of the various barriers is difficult to predict and is generally measured on the membrane material under the actual desired conditions. Table 4 shows the experimental data derived for an orthophthalic resin casting core with different barrier constructions immersed at room temperature through 29 weeks. To more readily compare the initial water permeation rates, a logarithmic curve fit has been computed via the least squares method for the data through 7 weeks exposure. Several curves are plotted in Figure 7. The initial slope of the curve is denoted by the regression coefficient "b" and the values indicate that the relative permeation rates at room temperature are essentially the same for all barriers except the gel coat backed-up with the inter-laminate VE 8115 vinylester skin coat. The measured rate of water gain was essentially the same (b=0.16) for samples prepared without a gel coat, 20 mils gel coat, 35 mils gel coat, and for 20 mils of gel coat plus 15 mils of an interlayer of vinylester skin coat. The coefficient of

Figure 6. Exploded View of "Submersed Boat" Coupon

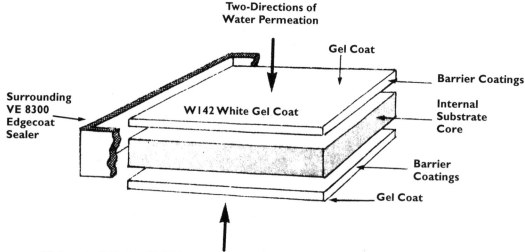

Two-Directions of Water Permeation

Gel Coat

Barrier Coatings

Internal Substrate Core

Surrounding VE 8300 Edgecoat Sealer

W142 White Gel Coat

Barrier Coatings

Gel Coat

"Submarine" Shell or Hull: The outer envelope consists of a top and bottom cosmetic coating of white gel coat backed up with a vinylester skin coat interlayer or interlaminate. All four edges are dipped and sealed with a vinylester resin to prevent wicking.
Internal Structure: The center core is usually a standard orthophthalic resin and glass laminate composite or an all-resin clear casting.
Boat Dimensions: 5½" x 5½" x T Coupons

determination, "r^2," indicates that we have a good curve fit and can have confidence that the permeation rate is initially unaffected by the thickness of the gel coat or a barrier coat 15 mils in thickness. The resins used to construct the core of the laminates is the key variable that is controlling the rate of diffusion. This is shown by the data on the casting without a gel coated surface, which has the same rate of diffusion as the gel coated castings.

Coupons with the same barrier coating construction used in the ambient testing described above were immersed in a 150°F water bath in order to accelerate the blistering process. A plot of these values in Figure 7 indicates that the initial slope is similar for the addition of the interlaminate skin coat significantly decreases the absorption rate. No blistering was visible at 150°F through 29 weeks suggesting the vinylester skin coat barrier removed the reaction zone beneath the gel coat surface.

The data collected for the accelerated test were run at 150°F and are compiled in Table 7. Note that the calculated absorption rate, "b", is the lowest and the

TABLE 3: GRAMS WATER WEIGHT GAIN IN BOIL TESTS					
Composite Structures		**Hours Total Boiling Water Exposure #**			
Barrier Coating	**Back-Up Laminate**	**50**	**100**	**200**	**300**
None (Control)	Orthophthalic	.39	.49	—	—
20 mils Gel Coat	Orthophthalic	.33*	.49	—	—
20 mils Gel Coat	Isophthalic	—	.31*	.49	.55
20 mils Gel Coat	Vinyl Ester	—	—	.10*	.07
20 mils Gel Coat	Brom. VE	—	—	—	.09*
20 mils Gel Coat with VE Interlaminate Skincoat (30 mils)	Orthophthalic	—	.15	.28	.42*

#Coupon exposure is 2¾" x 2¾" = 7.56 in² water contact surface area.
*Blistering started, weight gain in grams of water weighed hot on removal.

TABLE 4: WEIGHT GAIN OVER TIME ON AMBIENT CASTINGS				
Immersion Conditions				
Composite = All Resin Clear Casting				
Core = General Purpose Orthophthalic Laminating Resin, Cor 1063-40				
Temperature = Ambient				
Barrier Structure Composition				
VE 8115 Skin	0	0	0	15 mils	Laminate
GC 142, mils	0	20	35	20	20
Coupon Specifics (5½" x 5½")					
A, in²	29.86 ± .45	30.12 ± .22	30.18 ± .22	30.10 ± .19	30.16 ± .13
T, inches	.131 ± .005	.178 ± .006	.216 ± .006	.227 ± .007	.238 ± .017
d, gm/in³	19.63 ± .31	20.10 ± .09	20.46 ± .08	19.93 ± .10	21.22 ± .24
Water Weight Gain Over Time in Grams					
1 Day	.06 ± .02	.06 ± .03	.07 ± .02	.06 ± .02	.08 ± .02
2 Days	.15 ± .03	.15 ± .03	.17 ± .01	.16 ± .02	.18 ± .01
3 Days	.19 ± .03	.18 ± .02	.19 ± .02	.19 ± .02	.21 ± .02
7 days	.27 ± .02	.27 ± .02	.27 ± .01	.26 ± .02	.27 ± .02
2 Weeks	.40 ± .03	.37 ± .04	.36 ± .03	.37 ± .02	.32 ± .01
3 Weeks	.50 ± .03	.50 ± .03	.48 ± .03	.47 ± .04	.45 ± .02
5 Weeks	.60 ± .02	.62 ± .04	.61 ± .01	.61 ± .02	.52 ± .02
7 Weeks	.67 ± .06	.73 ± .03	.73 ± .02	.71 ± .03	.60 ± .03
10 Weeks	.86 ± .02	.93 ± .07	.96 ± .03	.93 ± .02	.81 ± .02
14 Weeks	.82 ± .02	.99 ± .04	1.03 ± .02	1.02 ± .03	.84 ± .03
20 Weeks	.88 ± .02	1.11 ± .05	1.16 ± .03	1.12 ± .05	.99 ± .03
29 Weeks	.92 ± .03	1.18 ± .09	1.33 ± .03	1.31 ± .04	1.19 ± .05
Logarithmic Curve Fit*					
a	.02669	.01199	.02682	.02101	.06625
b	.15571	.16505	.15801	.15781	.12450
r^2	.976	.951	.937	.948	.953

*y = a + b ln x where x = time in days through 7 weeks and y = H₂O gain in grams

correlation coefficient, "r^2", is the highest for the vinylester resins VE 8100 and VE 8440. These two panels did not exhibit blisters through 20 weeks of exposure. The low absorption rate and high correlation coefficient is an indication of the excellent hydrolytic stability of the composite attributable to vinylester resin. The composite with a skin coated interlaminate barrier made of CoRezyn VE 8110-type series vinylester resin with the orthophthalic back-up laminate exhibited no blisters through 29 weeks but had a higher absorption rate. The isophthalic back-up resin had approximately the same absorption rate as the vinylester skin coat but exhibited significant blistering after 10 weeks of immersion.

One panel of each construction was removed at 10 and 29 weeks and dried in an oven. The results showing the weight loss due to hydrolysis and the leaching out of water soluble compounds are compiled in Table 8. The incorporation of the vinylester as a skin coat interlayer barrier or as the entire back-up laminate into the composite significantly decreased the amount of solubles and dramatically increased the time to blister. Substantial reduction of blister formation is obtained through the use of the CoRezyn vinylester VE 8110 series resins.

TABLE 5: WEIGHT GAIN OVER TIME ON 150°F CASTINGS

Immersion Conditions

Composite = All Resin Clear Casting
Core = General Purpose Orthophthalic Laminating Resin, Cor 1063-40
Temperature = 150°F

Barrier Structure Composition					
VE 8115 Skin	0	0	0	15 mils	Laminate
GC 142, mils	0	20	35	20	20
Coupon Specifics (5½" x 5½")					
A, in^2	29.52 ± .44	30.14 ± .21	30.04 ± .17	30.10 ± .12	30.12 ± .44
T, inches	.130 ± .004	.185 ± .003	.201 ± .013	.228 ± .006	.234 ± .010
d, gm/in^3	19.47 ± .14	20.06 ± .10	20.55 ± .15	19.93 ± .05	21.11 ± .28
Water Weight Gain Over Time in Grams					
8 Hours	.28 ± .01	.23 ± .03	.22 ± .02	.23 ± .02	.23 ± .02
16 Hours	.44 ± .01	.40 ± .03	.35 ± .02	.36 ± .01	.33 ± .02
1 Day	.55 ± .01	.52 ± .02	.45 ± .03	.46 ± .02	.41 ± .04
2 days	.87 ± .03	.87 ± .04	.78 ± .02	.74 ± .04	.61 ± .03
3 Days	1.04 ± .03	1.08 ± .09	1.04 ± .04	.93 ± .04	.77 ± .04
7 Days	1.42 ± .05	1.74 ± .03	1.73 ± .04	1.48 ± .06	1.16 ± .03
10 Days	1.56 ± .05	2.05 ± .05	2.06 ± .07	1.74 ± .07	1.37 ± .05
15 Days	1.60 ± .05	2.21 ± .05	2.17 ± .07	1.94 ± .07	1.48 ± .05
3 Weeks	1.83 ± .07	2.82 ± .09	2.72 ± .10	2.28 ± .09	1.81 ± .05
5 Weeks	2.52 ± .07	4.60 ± .12	3.90 ± .13	2.82 ± .16	2.21 ± .09
7 Weeks	1.37 ± .55	5.80 ± .30	4.64 ± .12	3.22 ± .20	2.46 ± .11
10 Weeks	− .01 ± .09	7.49 ± .72	4.40 ± .40	3.73 ± .27	2.77 ± .13
14 Weeks	− .12 ± .16	9.63 ± 1.86	7.63 ± .94	4.64 ± .55	3.28 ± .15
20 Weeks	−2 35 ± .04	11.55 ± 4.42	9.74 ± 1.52	4.31 ± 1.48	3.63 ± .20
29 Weeks	−3.65 ± .16	11.10 ± 6.08	7.62 ± 2.05	2.61 ± 1.86	1.59 ± .10
Logarithmic Curve Fit*					
a	.60600	.55983	.47170	.53353	.45878
b	.43702	.78893	.96594	.55222	.41841
r^2	.952	.847	.815	.956	.951

*$y = a + b \ln x$ where x = time in days through 5 weeks and y = H_2O gain in grams

TABLE 6: WEIGHT GAIN OVER TIME ON AMBIENT LAMINATES

Immersion Conditions

Composite = Laminate = 2/1 of Resin/Glass Mat
Resin = Various Types as Noted
Temperature = Ambient

Panel Structure Description					
Backup Resin	GP	GP	Laminating	Vinyl	GP
Type	Ortho	Ortho	Iso	Ester	Ortho
CoRezyn Num.	1063-40	1063-40	9595	8100	1063-40
Barrier Structure Composition					
VE 8115 Skin	0	0	0	0	Laminate
GC 142, mils	0	20	20	20	20
Coupon Specifics (5½" x 5½")					
A, in^2	30.14 ± .42	30.60 ± .84	30.30 ± .28	30.38 ± .30	30.42 ± .36
T, inches	.273 ± .008	.295 ± .007	.292 ± .033	.289 ± .023	.316 ± .017
d, gm/in^3	23.87 ± .17	24.00 ± .19	23.80 ± .45	23.50 ± .77	23.89 ± .24
Water Weight Gain Over Time in Grams					
1 Day	.05 ± .02	.06 ± .02	.10 ± .03	.22 ± .05	.11 ± .03
2 Days	.13 ± .03	.17 ± .02	.16 ± .07	.31 ± .02	.15 ± .03
3 Days	.16 ± .03	.20 ± .02	.19 ± .07	.33 ± .02	.19 ± .03
7 Days	.23 ± .03	.26 ± .02	.30 ± .06	.38 ± .03	.29 ± .04
2 Weeks	.31 ± .03	.34 ± .02	.34 ± .07	.48 ± .03	.28 ± .05
3 Weeks	.36 ± .03	.44 ± .02	.44 ± .10	.53 ± .04	.37 ± .04
5 Weeks	.44 ± .03	.53 ± .02	.55 ± .09	.60 ± .04	.51 ± .03
7 Weeks	.50 ± .03	.59 ± 02	.61 ± .10	.65 ± .06	.50 ± .02
10 Weeks	.71 ± .05	.84 ± .05	−	.83 ± .06	.50 ± .02
14 Weeks	.74 ± .04	.86 ± .02	1.05 ± .13	.81 ± .07	.96 ± .04
20 Weeks	.86 ± .07	1.02 ± .04	1.05 ± .13	.95 ± .07	.98 ± .02
29 Weeks	1.31 ± .39	1.26 ± .03	1.25 ± .18	1.10 ± .08	1.19 ± .08
Logarithmic Curve Fit*					
a	.03915	.05126	.06406	.21340	.08182
b	.11067	.12923	.12909	.10628	.10348
r^2	.985	.970	.963	.981	.931

*$y = a + b \ln x$ where x = time in days through 7 weeks and y = H_2O gain in grams

TABLE 7: WEIGHT GAIN OVER TIME ON 150°F LAMINATES

Immersion Conditions

Composite = Laminate = 2/1 of Resin/Glass Mat
Resin = Various Types as Noted
Temperature = 150°F

Panel Structure Description

Backup Resin, Type and, CoRezyn Number	General Purpose Orthophthalic 1063-40	General Purpose Orthophthalic 1063-40	Laminating Isophthalic 9595	Vinyl Ester 8100	Brominated Vinyl Ester 8440	General Purpose Orthophthalic 1063-40
Barrier Structure Composition						
VE 8115 Skin	0	0	0	0	0	Laminate
GC 142, mils	0	20	20	20	20	20
Coupon Specifics (5½″ x 5½″)						
A, in²	30.20 ± .60	30.02 ± .08	30.40 ± .14	30.26 ± .28	30.34 ± .18	30.34 ± .15
T, inches	.263 ± .012	.293 ± .009	.291 ± .018	.296 ± .023	.268 ± .022	.326 ± .007
d, gm/in³	23.96 ± .60	24.09 ± .12	23.64 ± .18	25.02 ± .32	24.75 ± .46	23.87 ± .17
Water Weight Gain Over Time in Grams						
8 Hours	.18 ± .01	.18 ± .02	.18 ± .03	.31 ± .04	.28 ± .07	.21 ± .02
16 Hours	.26 ± .01	.29 ± .01	.28 ± .02	.36 ± .03	.33 ± .08	.31 ± .02
1 Day	.37 ± .04	.44 ± .01	.38 ± .04	.40 ± .04	.41 ± .08	.37 ± .02
2 Days	.56 ± .02	.67 ± .02	.57 ± .03	.54 ± .03	.50 ± .07	.57 ± .04
3 Days	.73 ± .01	.85 ± .03	.68 ± .03	.59 ± .03	.57 ± .06	.66 ± .04
7 Days	1.26 ± .04	1.41 ± .03	1.10 ± .04	.84 ± .02	.74 ± .07	1.02 ± .04
10 Days	1.67 ± .05	2.31 ± .04	1.83 ± .05	.93 ± .02	.76 ± .12	1.18 ± .03
15 Days	1.99 ± .07	2.14 ± .05	1.44 ± .06	1.02 ± .02	.84 ± .07	1.40 ± .03
3 Weeks	2.78 ± .09	2.90 ± .05	1.72 ± .06	1.17 ± .04	.95 ± .08	1.83 ± .04
5 Weeks	4.28 ± .16	4.63 ± .06	2.18 ± .10	1.26 ± .07	1.17 ± .07	2.62 ± .08
7 Weeks	5.23 ± .13	5.74 ± .40	2.69 ± .19	1.31 ± .07	1.04 ± .10	3.15 ± .11
10 Weeks	5.78 ± .09	7.08 ± .27	3.33 ± .17	1.29 ± .09	1.02 ± .11	3.77 ± .14
14 Weeks	4.27 ± 1.51	8.24 ± 1.13	4.88 ± .20	1.21 ± .10	.98 ± .04	4.81 ± .21
20 Weeks	3.61 ± .22	8.87 ± 2.16	6.43 ± .22	1.15 ± .11	1.03 ± .05	5.36 ± .23
29 Weeks	.04 ± .11	6.46 ± 4.67	8.41 ± .30	1.25 ± .32	1.26 ± .06	5.21 ± .65
Logarithmic Curve Fit*						
a	.36405	.44035	.43001	.44032	.40709	.39018
b	.75411	.82468	.43774	.21792	.17908	45279
r²	.808	.830	.915	.971	.960	.860

*y = a + b ln x where x = time in days through 5 weeks and y = H₂O gain in grams

---

TABLE 8: 150°F COUPON WEIGHT LOSS AND TIME TO BLISTER FORMATION

Coupon Descriptions	Weight Loss of Matrix*		Time To Blister
Exposure Time, t Panel Dried	10 Weeks Coupon 5	29 Weeks Coupon 4	Exposure @ 150°F
ORTHOPHTHALIC ALL-RESIN CASTINGS WITH VARIOUS BARRIERS			
	Wt. /%	Wt. /%	Days
No Barrier	−2.55/−3.21	−5.65/−7.98	15
20 mils GC	−0.49/−0.44	+1.21/+1.06	35
35 mils GC	−0.77/−0.60	−21.65/−16.79#	49
20 mils GC/15 mils VE Layer Skincoat	−0.29/−0.21	−4.80/−3.49	>203
20 mils GC/VE Interlaminate Skincoat (30 mils)	−0.18/−0.12	−2.46/−1.67	203
LAMINATE STRUCTURES			
None (Control) Orthophthalic	−0.99/−0.55	−6.87/−3.68	15
20 mils Gel Coat Orthophthalic	−0.61/−0.29	−5.99/−2.86	15
20 mils Gel Coat Isophthalic	−0.33/−0.16	+0.09/+0.04	21
20 mils Gel Coat Vinyl Ester	−0.13/−0.07	−0.26/−0.12	>203
20 mils Gel Coat Brom. VE	−0.30/−0.16	−0.24/−0.12	>203
20 mils Gel Coat Orthophthalic with VE Interlaminate Skincoat (30 mils)	−0.10/−0.04	−1.16/−0.50	>203

*Dehydrated for 1 day @150°F, 2 days @ 180°F, and 5 days @ 220°F; for laminate core sandwiches the observed Weight Loss/Gain = −/+ in grams and C(t) as a percent of W.

#Gel coat surface broken.

Figure 7: Water Absorption of Coated Orthophthalic Resin Castings with Time and Temperaure

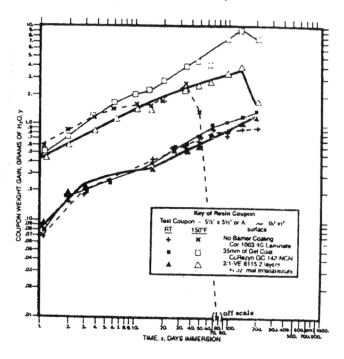

CONCLUSIONS

The polymer membranes studied were unsaturated polyester barriers. One of the membranes was constructed of a premium neopentyl glycol gel coat with a vinylester resin "skin coat" and the other was a premium neopentyl glycol gel coat. They both had an orthophthalic laminating resin back-up. The permeation and diffusion rates of water through the polymer membranes were measured, tabulated, and graphed. A vinylester cladding applied on an orthophthalic laminating resin reinforced composite substantially reduced the blistering caused by water permeation and matrix solubility for immersion at 150°F. Further evaluation of the coupons immersed at room temperature will reveal the degree of correlation between the elevated temperature and the room temperature studies. The increased hydrophobicity of the gel coat/skin coat membrane, as compared to only gel coat, improved the composite's hydrolytic stability thus reducing water absorption rates and increased its blister resistance. The vinylester skin coat barrier, when applied to a boat hull or swimming pool, should result in increased product durability and lifetime in the "World of Composites".

REFERENCES

1. "CoRezyn Vinyl Ester Resins", Interplastic Corporation, 1986.

2. "CoRezyn Isopolyesters", Interplastic Corporation.

3. P. Burrell, T. McCabe, R. de la Rosa, "Cycle Test Evaluation of Various Polyester Types and a Mathematical Model for Projecting Flexural Fatigue Endurance", Paper 7-D, 41st Annual Conference, SPI Reinforced Plastics/Composites Institute (1986).

4. Ghotra, J. S., and Pritchard, G. *Developments in Reinforced Plastics-3*. Editor, G. Pritchard. New York: Elsevier Science Publishing Co. Inc., 1984.

5. H. R. Edwards, "Variables Influencing the Performance of a Gel Coated Laminate," 34th Annual Technical Conference, Reinforced Plastics/Composites Institute, The Society of the Plastics Industry, Session 4D (1979).

6. S. Crump, "A Study of Blister Formation in Gel Coated Laminates", Paper 13-C, 41st Annual Conference, SPI Reinforced Plastics/Composites Institute (1986).

7. J. M. Marshall, G. P. Marshall, R. F Pinzelli, "The Diffusion of Liquids into Resins and Composites," 37th Annual Conference, SPI Reinforced Plastics/Composites Institute, (1982).

8. P. Burrell, unpublished work.

9. D. S. Knoebel, "Mechanical Property and Performance Characterization of Marine Laminates and the Effect of Matrix Resin", Paper 12-C, 40th Annual Conference, SPI Reinforced Plastics/Composites Institute (1985).

10. R. C. Adams, "Variables Influencing the Blister Resistance of Marine Laminates", Paper 21-B, 37th Annual Conference, SPI Reinforced Plastics/Composites Institute (1982).

BIOGRAPHIES

Paul Burrell graduated from the University of Minnesota Institute of Technology with a B.S. in Chemical Engineering. He has been employed by the Commercial Resins Division of Interplastic Corporation since 1971 and is presently the Engineering Resins Group Leader.

David Herzog received a B.A. in chemistry from Carelton College in 1980 and graduated from the University of Minnesota, Duluth, with an M.S. in Chemistry with emphasis in Analytical. He has been employed by the Commercial Resins Division of Interplastic Corporation since 1983 and is currently the Group Leader in charge of Vinylester Resins and Analytical Testing.

Terry McCabe has been employed by Interplastic Corporation since 1968. He was the Technical Director for 14 years and is currently a Vice-President of Interplastic Corporation and the Marketing Director of Commercial Resins Division.

Reference 28

For presentation at the Atlantic Marine Surveyors Conference on "Newest Developments in Boatbuilding and Repairing" Annapolis, Md. October 9-10, 1990

Correct Core Installation, Bonding Techniques, and a Repair Case History of a 56' Sailboat and a 47' Sportfishing Yacht

by

Thomas J. Johannsen
Torin Inc., Waldwick, N. J. 07463

Cored composite construction in the marine industry aims mainly at a reduction in weight with a corresponding increase in stiffness. Careful consideration is normally given to the design of the skins and the selection of the core. Yet the bondline between the core and the skins is a highly stressed area. Designers and builders are now becoming increasingly aware of examining this area more closely. This paper states the required criteria of the bondline, describes problems resulting from faulty shop practices, and offers guidelines for a core installation system using a syntactic foam adhesive. It also suggests a repair procedure using the syntactic foam adhesive system for bonding cured laminates to a new core.

INTRODUCTION

Sandwich construction in the marine industry, or "cored composites," have been very successful. As their use becomes more widespread, as the type of core materials are more varied than ever before, and as shop practices vary considerably due to the different building methods used, much experience originating from problems encountered in the shop and the field is being gained.

A young industry has to learn from its problems, and the majority of these problems in sandwich construction can be traced back to improper shop practices and lack of understanding of the important criteria during core installation.

This paper examines these criteria, relates some of the problems, describes a syntactic foam bonding system [Torin(2)(3)], outlines core installation procedures that are practical and that conform with current shop capabilities, and also describes a hull repair method.

CRITERIA OF THE BONDLINE

Some sandwich structures in the marine industry are produced by the lay-up of both skins directly to each side of the core material. Maximum bond strength is therefore readily assured. Most core installations, however, are performed in a female mold, or where the core is bonded to a cured FRP (fibre reinforced plastic) skin. In this application, the sandwich core bonding system is a critical component of the structure and must satisfy the following requirements:

- Low weight
- Low styrene emission
- No sag on a vertical surface
- Low shrinkage
- Elasticity of the bondline (non brittle behaviour)
- Cost effectiveness
- Adhesive strength to a cured FRP laminate
- Maximum prevention of core pattern/core joint print-through
- Ease of application within current boatbuilding/shop practices

TYPICAL PROBLEMS

Voids in Cored Laminates

A major problem that has concerned boat owners and surveyors is water trickling out of the core when a hole has to be drilled into the hull. It absolutely shatters a boat owner's confidence in sandwich construction. It raises major questions: the resistance of the core to sea or freshwater, the structural integrity under impacts, the effect of freezing and thawing cycles, and the possibility of spreading delamination.

There is no excuse for voids being left during the core installation process which are then covered up by the inside skin. Such voids occur under the core (lack of bond), between the core (lack of fit), and in transition areas from the core to single skin lay-up. The vast majority of builders are conscientious during the construction sequence and check this carefully. But some instances have been found, both with imported and domestically produced boats, where voids have been left between the inside and outside skin and which have required a major repair.

It is a law of nature that water will collect in any void. In any larger boat the temperature conditions inside and outside vary. This causes water vapour pressure in a void and water will collect there. Laminates are not completely impervious to water vapour pressure. This is a major reason why honeycomb cores should not be used in the hull, deck and superstructure (outside surfaces) of larger boats.

Voids Occurring in Chopped Strand Mat Installations

Resin-rich mat has been the industry's traditional core bedding material. Even though many good boats have been produced in this manner, there are still a number of drawbacks which can lead to voids, and in some cases, to severe structural problems.

Resin drainage. A common cause for voids is resin drainage on a vertical surface, where dry areas can occur before and after core installation. Extra resin for bonding the core is required, and the mat may not hold the extra amount beyond that required for the mat itself.

Excess roller pressure. Another common cause of creating a void is excess roller pressure to get the core "down" into the mat. This often happens where laminate overlaps cause thickness irregularities in the outside skin and in hull curvatures. Too much roller pressure squeezes out the resin from under the core, and the core will want to "lift," thereby creating a dry spot. The chopped strand mat laminate, due to the roller pressure, and therefore a lack of resin (not enough resin-mass and exotherm), doesn't cure in this area, and releases styrene fumes into the foam or into the endgrain balsawood core. Therefore, a cure is further inhibited and a void remains under the core.

Lack of bonding resin. Very often, the amount of resin required to obtain a good bond is underestimated. The extra resin required becomes the "glue." Saving weight or resin by assuming that the laminating resin can also be the bonding resin will lead to voids, poor bonds, and structural problems.

Lack of gel-time control. More frightening than the physical causes of voids are the countless variables that can lead to chemical causes. Sudden changes in temperature, humidity, catalyst levels, improper resin mixing, variance in production cycles, and undetected changes in resin specifications can affect resin gel-times. Excessive geltimes can cause styrene evaporation and migration into cores. The result is an under-cured resin in the bonding layer, a tacky laminate, and a void.

Excess vacuum-bag pressure. In vacuum bagging, too much resin can sometimes squeeze out between the core blocks if a contoured core version is used. This leaves an insufficient amount of resin under the core for a good cure and a void-free bond.

Voids with "Contoured" Cores (core blocks on a scrim)

Most cores used in the industry today are "contoured" core materials. Grooves are cut to create core blocks, and these blocks are attached to a scrimcloth. These grooves rarely fill with resin in a chopped strand mat installation system, especially not on a curved surface (see Fig. I) where the groove opens up into a "V."

More desirable is a knife-cut where no void is left between the core blocks. When the sheet is flat, no gaps between

the core blocks are visible. However, in compound hull mold curvatures, the gaps open up, especially when core thicknesses increase, making it difficult for the resin to reach all the way up between the core blocks, and creating the potential for a void. This kind of void creates a series of channels in the entire cored laminate through which water will travel. These voids are also stress risers, and can be the cause of shear failure in the core, especially with the more brittle foams.

Undercured Skins

In addition to the correct core installation techniques and systems, much more consideration has to be given to the quality of the skins (as there is less skin to do the work). Traditionally, FRP single skin composites in boatbuilding were heavy since weight was not a major design criteria. The degree of cure, the glass/resin content, and the mechanical properties were not as critical, since most laminates were overdesigned. Mostly, the mass of the layup itself assured sufficient exothermic reaction for sufficient cure in marginally promoted and catalyzed laminates. Even with variances in resin performance, and with varying shop temperatures and humidity conditions, satisfactory laminates were normally achieved.

However, as lower weights are desired, the skins become thinner, and achievement of the mechanical properties — a high glass content and a full cure of the resin — is much more critical. In the more precisely engineered sandwich laminate the skins must perform right up to their expected properties, or the required factors of safety are not achieved and the structure can fail. The same properties as those achieved with thicker laminates cannot automatically be expected. Therefore, builders are advised to have the skins of the sandwich laminate tested separately to assure that expected mechanical properties are achieved.

TABLE I

Flexural Moduli, psi, Vinylester - Kevlar/E-glass Laminates

	0°	90°
Top Skin, 2.84mm	.475[6]	.335[6]
Bottom Skin, 2.62mm	.743[6]	.460[6]

Table I shows one example of a "hi-tech" laminate produced under normal "shop-level" conditions in an offshore racing yacht. It shows that the flexural moduli are far below those to

Figure I

30 mm

25 mm

saw-cut width = .040" (1mm)

2° angle = 30% gap-volume increase

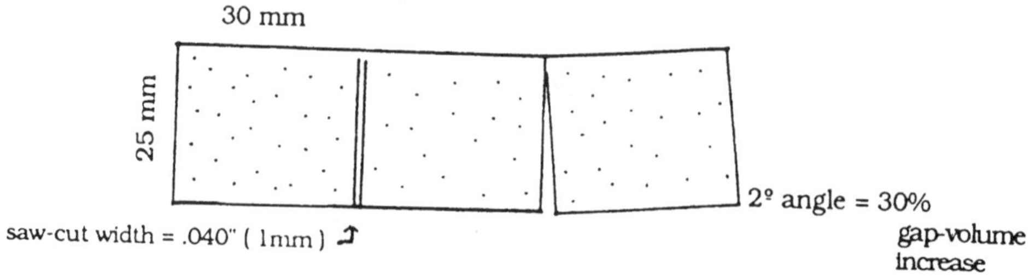

be expected if one considers the expensive fibers and resins used. Much higher moduli can be achieved with "ground level tech" reinforcements and resins. The resins in these relatively thin laminates, that are now typical for higher-tech boats, harden, but often do not develop their full cure and their expected performance in conventional hand-layup shop procedures.

The flexural moduli in Table 1 are extremely low, are only 30% of those that should be expected, and hopefully present an isolated case. It is absolutely necessary to monitor resin performance more closely, and to consider postcure methods with some resin systems.

Directional Variation of Skin Flexural Moduli

Design of a sandwich panel skin must take the directional properties of the reinforcements into account. Directional reinforcements, when tested in an "off-axis" direction, can show significant variances in mechanical properties. When designing with such reinforcements, it is assumed that the designer knows from which direction the load is induced, and in which direction higher stiffness criteria exist. However, this is extremely difficult to predict. Table 2 below shows an extreme case of the directional variance in moduli using carbon unidirectional fibres in one direction.

TABLE 2

Flexural Moduli, psi, Carbon Uni/S-Glass + misc. Resins

	0°	45°	90°
AME 4000	$.769^6$	1.558^6	3.052^6
Aristech VE	$.714^6$	1.794^6	3.669^6
Atlac VE	$.824^6$	1.636^6	3.183^6
Epoxy W	1.284^6	1.940^6	3.437^6

Tables 3, 4 and 5 following show a series of laminates, produced under normal shop level conditions, that our industry considers to be "hi-tech". These laminates were provided to us by several builders. Tests for the flexural moduli in the directions of 0°, 45°, 90° were conducted at the materials testing laboratory of Airex AG, Switzerland. The results listed are not to be interpreted as a measure of resin performance.

According to the fiberglass manufacturers' data, flexural moduli achieved in higher glass content woven E-glass/chopped strand mat laminates using conventional polyester resins are in the same range, with probably less directional variance. In one test, in a laminate with multiple layers of cloth and a glass content of 50%+, flexural moduli of 2.5^6 psi were achieved (6). Although the principle of unidirectional fibers is a logical approach to design, we need to learn more how to maximize the use of these fibers.

TABLE 3

Flexural Moduli, psi, Triax 1808/Hydrex

	0°	45°	90°
2 layers 0/90	2.12^6	1.51^6	1.15^6
3 layers 0/90	2.10^6	1.78^6	1.21^6
4 layers 0/90	1.81^6	1.63^6	1.11^6
1 layer 45/45	1.35^6	1.17^6	2.16^6
2 layers 45/45	1.13^6	1.08^6	1.44^6
3 layers 45/45	1.40^6	1.32^6	1.90^6
4 layers 45/45	1.23^6	1.25^6	1.89^6

TABLE 4

Flexural Moduli, psi, Triax + Mat 3/4oz./Hydrex

	0°	45°	90°
1 layer 0/90	1.76^6	$.76^6$	$.84^6$
2 layers 0/90	1.80^6	1.59^6	1.12^6
3 layers 0/90	1.95^6	1.75^6	1.24^6
4 layers 0/90	2.05^6	1.79^6	1.18^6

TABLE 5

Flexural Moduli, psi, 4 Layers Triax 1208 + misc. resins

	0°	45°	90°
AME 4000	1.218^6	1.295^6	$.950^6$
Aristech VE	1.198^6	1.574^6	1.160^6
Hydrex	1.211^6	1.727^6	1.164^6
Atlac VE	1.138^6	1.574^6	1.294^6
Atlac VE (vac-bag)	1.376^6	1.525^6	1.200^6
Epoxy W	1.248^6	1.547^6	1.155^6
Epoxy T	$.723^6$	$.820^6$	$.709^6$

Much more testing of the laminate skins by the builders is required so that high quality laminates can be produced using current production/shop level procedures. Not only proper design, but the production of laminates with the aim of developing their full properties is essential and must be considered an integral part of the overall performance of the sandwich.

The core installation method must follow the same high quality design objective — maximum strength and adhesion at the least weight. This is integral to the overall performance of the sandwich.

Resin Rich Skins and Bondlines

The basic design principle for skins in a sandwich is sometimes overlooked when using established laminating materials and procedures successful with heavier single skin laminates. A case that demonstrates this point is a laminate used by a builder for a deck house. The skins in this case consisted of an all chopped strand mat laminate, with an additional layer of resin-rich synthetic fiber felt containing hollow microspheres between the layers of mat in the outside skin. The mat under the core was well saturated with resin — no voids. The outside skin had almost three times the thickness of the inside skin.

When the laminate was exposed to southern sun temperatures, the skin postcured and wrinkled. In a burn-out test, the outside skin showed an extremely high resin content, well above that expected even in a normal chopped strand mat laminate, even taking the synthetic fiber content in the laminate into account. The heavy resin content skin thereby postcured in the sun, and backed by the insulation properties of the foam core, "collected" the heat in the outside skin. Consequently, the skin, in postcuring, lost its flatness and buckled, sufficiently enough for re-fairing to be necessary. This occurrence can even be accentuated by dark colors, dark stripes or dark color decorative areas.

This shows that the basic design principles of a sandwich — balanced skin thicknesses; sufficient core thickness in proportion to the skins; a high glass or fiber content in the skins; good resin cure; and desirability of light colors in southern climes should not be overlooked.

USING A SYNTACTIC FOAM ADHESIVE (*E.G.* TORIN/CORE-BOND™ SYSTEM)

Because of the variables and the drawbacks of any resin-rich system, the industry long ago recognized the advantages of a syntactic foam adhesive compound in core installation. Table 6 below compares values and costs between a syntactic foam adhesive, a conventional chopped strand mat laminate, and a resin rich synthetic fiber felt for use in core installation systems.

TABLE 6

Comparison of Different Core Installation Systems Syntactic Foam Chopped Strand Synthetic Fiber

	Adhesive	Mat	Felt
Bond Line Thickness	.025"	.060" - .080"	.090" - .128"
Density, g/cm³	.66	1.45	1.2
lb/ft³	42	93	75
Bond Line Weight	3 oz./sf.	7-9 oz./sf.	8.6 - 12.2 oz./sf.
Cost, appr.	$.47/sf.	$.40 -.55/sf.	$.65 -.81/sf.
Resin Usage	2.25 oz./sf	5.6 -7.2 oz./sf.	8-11 oz./sf.*
Styrene Emission	20%	50 - 65%	75 - 100%*

(*max. 11 oz = 100%)

A syntactic foam adhesive system must be cost effective, simple to use under normal shop conditions, have low styrene emission, have a thorough and predictable cure in a thin bondline, be light in weight, achieve a good bond to a cured

FRP skin, maintain the degree of elasticity required by the core to skin interface — even after aging — have low shrinkage to prevent print-through, and not sag on a vertical surface.

Such criteria are not easy to attain, but are possible. Good shop and field results have been achieved with such a system (2) (3) over several years, and a variety of boats have withstood extremely demanding offshore service conditions without bond failure.

Hand-Layup Installation

Hand-layup(2) core installations almost exclusively use "contoured cores" — small blocks of foam or a balsawood core bonded to a scrimcloth. In this form of supply, the core conforms to the hull shape, and drapes easily into the laminate curvature. This method is used predominantly in the industry today. It is more practical with smaller craft and cores up to appr. 5/8" or 3/4". Thicker cores, in this form of supply, need a considerable amount of bonding resin between the core blocks, especially In hull curvatures. Therefore, syntactic foam adhesives are becoming increasingly popular due to their ease of application and their low styrene emission levels.

As the size of cored composite boats has increased (now up to appr. 140' LOA), vacuum bagging and thicker cores, primarily in plain foam sheets, have become more common. As the requirements for low styrene emission become more critical in most parts of this country, the syntactic foam adhesive system will become a widely accepted method of core installation. The use of vacuum-bagging with plain foam sheets will further contribute towards achieving lower styrene emission levels.

Vacuum-Bag Installation

Vacuum-bag installations [Brandl(4)] use plain sheets, and syntactic foam adhesives, and therefore less resin. Gaps between foam blocks do not exist to the extent they do in the contoured/scrim version. If they do, in core sheet joints, the distance must be kept to a minimum [Zenkert et al(1)], and sufficient resin must come up between the foam joints so that voids are eliminated. Thermoforming of the core material is the more advanced approach to seamless core installation. Peel-ply and a bleeder cloth should be used if bagging of contoured foam is necessary so that no bonding resin remains attached to the inside surface of the foam.

QUALITY CONTROL

Gel-Time Control of the Bondline. The insulating properties of the core, especially the foams, can influence the gel-time of the resin in the bonding system. Therefore, we have developed a simple test (2) to determine the gel-time of the bonding layer for the Torin/Core-Bond System™ which can also be used for CSM/resin systems. Small core blocks (appr. 1.25"x1.25") are put separately into a control laminate. After some time, f.i. 20 minutes, rotate the first core block. If it moves, the resin has not gelled. After 5 more minutes, try the next core block, and try to rotate it again. Proceed in this manner until the core blocks don't move anymore, and the geltime under the core is thereby determined.

Quality Control of the Bond. After the core is installed, and before the inner skin is layed up, a thorough check for the quality of the bond, and the presence of voids under the core, is necessary. This is normally achieved by the "quarter method" — a coin is dragged over the core and a distinct "hollow sound" signals a void. This is more audible with foams than with balsa, where this test is mostly performed by tapping the core. The appearance of resin between the foam blocks in a contoured version is a sign of a good bond in most cases, but not always. Excess roller pressure could still have caused a void under the core. In vacuum-bagging of plain foam sheets (3), small holes punched into the foam allow excess resin to appear. This is a good sign of a consistent bond.

REPAIR OF HULLS WITH CORE FAILURES

56' Cruising Sailboat

The hull laminate of a cruising sailboat was designed to ABS scantlings which were subsequently plan-approved. The core used was a dark green cross-linked PVC, 1". with sufficient shear strength to meet the rules. The foam was supplied as blocks on a scrim. The cuts between the foam blocks were made by a saw, and the gap between the blocks was appr. .040". The core was installed on a 1.5 oz. chopped strand mat.

The boat, while under power at maximum speed, suffered an impact on the starboard bow which, judging by the core failure later, must have damaged the core and caused a localized foam shear failure. Subsequently, in a severe storm offshore, the whole boat dropped off several waves, causing considerable impact loading in the hull side area where the previous impact had occurred. Bulkheads, secondary bonds, and joinerwork were starting to break loose, and severe oilcanning of the hull was observed.

The boat was later hauled and a survey was conducted. Large area delaminations — the outer skin was loose — were detected. An outside skin section, appr. 2-3 sq. ft., was removed from the starboard side of the hull. No bond existed, the panel fell away without any effort to pry it loose. Portions of the foam core were still bonded to the outside skin.

It was concluded that:

1. the core material did not have sufficient impact strength capability to have withstood the initial impact without core damage, that

2. an insufficient amount of resin was used in the bonding process under the core blocks, and that

3. the gaps between the foam blocks were left unfilled in many areas and that water had collected there (see Figure 1: if one assumes a 2° curvature for the 56' boathull, it would have taken appr. one drum of resin to fill all the gaps).

A core having insufficient impact strength (being too brittle), and installed with improper workmanship (lacking the proper quality control procedures), combined to cause this structural failure.

The boat was repaired by the builder in the following manner:

1. Outside skin sections, appr. 15-30 sq. ft. per section, were removed.

2. The foam was then ground from the outside skin and from the remaining inside skin.

3. A new core (Airex R63.80, with higher impact strength) was vacuum-bagged to the inner skin with Core-Bond™, a syntactic foam adhesive (3). It was carefully checked for voids and bonds.

4. Small holes, at appr. 4" centers, were drilled into the outside skin. The skin sections, and some new skin sections layed up in the existing mold, were used. The thickness next to the butt joints was reduced on the outside skin.

5. The outside skin sections were then vacuum-bagged with Core-Bond™, a syntactic foam adhesive(3) to the core.

6. The butt joints were taped with additional laminate.

7. The boat was sanded, faired, and refinished/painted.

Since then, the boat has again been in severe offshore weather conditions several times, and is absolutely solid. No stress cracks have been found anywhere in the outside skin after 1½ years, and no hull movement or oilcanning has been detected. The insurance companies, both of the owner and the yard, were satisfied and closely supervised the repair through a marine surveyor. The builder has, at some expense, learned a new repair procedure.

47' Sportfishing Yacht

In this case, the same repair procedure in the aft 2/3 bottom of a 47' sportfishing yacht as described above was used. However, the cause was assumed to be different, and could be traced back primarily to shop/core installation procedures.

In a survey, the moisture meter detected high levels in the bottom of the boat, primarily in the aft section. Upon cutting out a one sq. ft section, the outside skin removed easily. The balsawood core was dark and wet, and had only bonded in small areas. The inside of the outside skin, that facing the core, showed a cured layer of mat, and only spotty contact with the core. It looked as if a void had existed all along — the mat had cured before core contact had occurred. In addition, all bottom through-hull fittings were bolted through the balsawood core, and moisture meter readings were high in these areas.

The repair procedure followed was identical to the one described previously, with the exception that an epoxy based adhesive was used to re-bond an Airex foam core (with high impact strength) to the inner skin. An Airex high density foam core was used under the through-hull fittings. A new outside skin, with pre-drilled bleeder holes, in appr. 30 sq. ft. sections, was then vacuum-bagged to the core with Core-Bond™, a syntactic foam adhesive. Instead of using a full skin thickness with a thinner edge for taping, two outside skins can be bonded with staggered overlaps to avoid excessive taping.

This repair procedure demonstrates that a sound repair method for cored hulls is indeed possible, and at less cost than previously assumed. As the skin tensile stress [Torin(7)] in cored FRP hulls is relatively low (normally below 10,000 psi) due to the overall hull shell stiffness and absence of oilcanning, the tensile stress in the secondary bond of a sandwich skin is much lower than in a single skin laminate. In addition, improved resins with good adhesive strength and a syntactic foam adhesive system make this repair procedure practical.

CONCLUSION

Composite core construction in the marine industry is becoming much more accepted by boat owners, designers and builders, and is used increasingly in larger vessels and even small ships. Syntactic foam adhesive systems that conform to present shop level process conditions, have a low weight, have low styrene emission, and are cost effective, will become a major factor in designing optimized cored structures.

REFERENCES

(1) D. Zenkert and H. L. Groth "THE INFLUENCE OF FLAWED BUTTJOINTS IN FOAM CORE SANDWICH BEAMS". First International Conference on Sandwich Constructions, Stockholm, 1989

(2) Torin Inc. "CORE-BOND SYSTEM, HAND-LAYUP", 1989

(3) Torin Inc. "CORE-BOND SYSTEM, VACUUM-BAGGING", 1989

(4) Karl Brandl "CELLULAR PLASTICS OF PURE PVC AS A SANDWICH CORE FOR LARGE FRP BOATHULLS", Conference on Fishing Vessel Construction Materials, Montreal, Canada, 1968

(5) H. J. Baumann, Materials Testing Laboratory, AIREX AG, Switzerland

(6) Detroit Testing Laboratory Inc., Report 306056 H

(7) Torin Inc., Small Craft Engineering, Factors of Safety, Tertiary Stress Panel Analysis

ATC Corporation

1051 Clinton Street, Buffalo, NY 14206

Tel: (716) 836-1943 • Fax: (716) 836-2362

REFERENCE 29

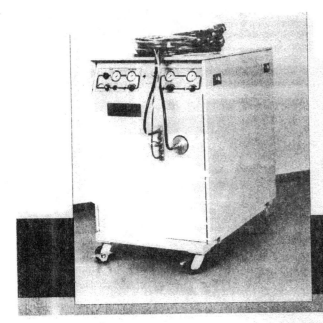

Mechanically Blended Foam™ Processing from Venus-Gusmer

Unique system reduces costs and VOCs, boosts productivity and quality

Polyester foam processing has always required reactive chemicals to actually cause the foaming of resin. That is, until now.

Venus-Gusmer's new Mechanically Blended Foam™ system provides a revolutionary method to create foam. The first and only system to use gas instead of chemicals to foam polyester resin, the MBF-01™ unit minimizes exothermic reactions and high temperatures that have caused other polyester foam systems to yield rejects or fail altogether.

The Secret: Stabilizing Additives and a Special Mixer

The Venus-Gusmer Mechanically Blended Foam System is the culmination of 15 years of research into a better way to produce resin foam. Basically, the MBF-01 uses compressed gas to create foam. The gas is blended into the resin by our specially designed mixer, which is built into the MBF-01

Normally, compressed gas would not have a lasting foaming effect on resin and bubbles would immediately begin to burst. But another special ingredient,

called the MBA-100™, actually stabilizes the resin until curing takes effect to set the the bubbles permanently. This MBA-100 Mechanical Blending Additive™, manufactured by Venus-Gusmer, is a non-reactive chemical compound that is premixed into the resin. Compressed gas then mixes into the resin at the machine to create foam. In effect, the treated resin "captures" the gas in its own bubbles.

Bubbles created by the MBF-0 system are uniform in size and shape. Uniformity is especially important when you want to make strong parts with smooth surfaces. Depending on the gas used, it is possible to vary the density of the resin foam. Less dense foam with relatively large cells provides excellent compressive strength while small-cell foam is ideal for use as a print-through barrier. The MBF-01, used with our special MBA-100 additive, will foam a wide variety of resins successfully if processed according to Venus-Gusmer guidelines.

Reduce VOC Emissions, Improve Production

Polyester foam emits far fewer volatile organic compounds (VOCs) than unfoamed resin. That's because the resin is sprayed at much lower pressure than in an atomized spray fan. This inherent advantage, combined with Venus-Gusmer's airless Hydraulic Injection

pumping system, helps make the MBF-01 the ideal choice to help comply with environmental and safety regulations.

Minimize Heat Reactions, Maximize Performance

Compressed gas is an excellent choice for foaming because it is non-reactive. By contrast, chemical foaming agents create exothermic reactions that, in turn, cause temperature variations. This can hinder the control of material density. In addition, excessive heat often causes thermo cracks. By reducing heat, the MBF-01 also reduces processing odors which are a by-product of other polyester foam systems.

No Rollout, Stronger Bonding

In chop-and-spray applications, the MBF-01 delivers additional labor and time savings because glass fiber, sprayed directly with polyester foam, requires no roll-out. This feature offers maximum savings when the MBF-01 is used with robot automation.

Fiberglass panels made by the MBF-01 can be made as thick as desired by "sandwiching" foam between fiberglass skins. Depending on the catalyst and promoters used, it is also possible to build thick cores quickly without waiting for curing of incremental layers. Moreover, panels made with the MBF-01 deliver superior strength. That's because the

polyester foam and polyester laminate form a chemical bond, which is stronger than the simple mechanical bond of urethane, PCV or other core materials.

Double Slave-Arm Configuration

For even greater time savings, Venus-Gusmer offers the MBF-02 Mechanical Foam Unit featuring a double slave-arm. The second slave arm on this unit meters and mixes MBA-100 additive into the resin at the machine. This system avoids pre-mixing and speeds up operations. With the MBF-02, you can also disconnect the second slave pump to laminate without foam since the foaming additive is metered in separately.

Either way, both Mechanically Blended Foam systems replace labor-intensive, time-consuming processes. We encourage you to use your imagination to see just how many ways polyester foam and the MBF System™ can be used to your advantage. For example, use it in place of honeycomb and cardboard cores. (It's ideal because foam penetrates honeycomb cells.) Use the MBF System to avoid cutting, placing and vacuum-bagging of foam sheets with polyester putty. (It's a tremendous time-saver!) In fact, the user-friendly Venus-Gusmer Mechanical Foam Processing System lets virtually any FRP shop enjoy increased

productivity and savings in numerous manufacturing applications:

- Marine
- Transportation
- Tub and spa
- Corrosion
- Construction/structural panels
- Cavity fill flotation
- Cavity filling of blow and rotational molded parts

Your Venus-Gusmer distributor is:

 **VENUS-GUSMER**
A DIVISION OF PMC, INC.

1862 Ives Avenue
Kent, WA 98032 U.S.A.
Phone: (206) 854-2660
FAX: (206) 854-1666

Specifications

Air Consumption
Chopper: 10 CFM
P21 Pump: 14 CFM
Optional Air Amplifier

Electrical Requirements
Heater: 230 volts, 10 amp single-phase, 50/60 cycle
Mix Motor: 230 volts, 10 amp, 3-phase, 60 cycle

Outputs:
Density of Foam: 0.25 to 0.60 specific gravity, depending on type of gas used for processing.

Printed on recycled paper

MBA-100™
Mechanical Blending Additive™

The key agent in the revolutionary new Mechanically Blended Foam™ processing system from Venus-Gusmer.

In the past, polyester foam processing always required reactive chemicals to actually cause the foaming of resin. But now there is Venus-Gusmer's new MBF-01™ Mechanically Blended Foam system featuring the MBA-100 Mechanical Blending Additive. This the first and only polyester system to use compressed gas instead of chemicals to create foam. In operation, the system forces gas into the machine. There, our specially designed mixer blends the gas into the resin, forming bubbles.

MBA-100: The Stabilizer

Normally, compressed gas would not have a lasting foaming effect on resin and bubbles would immediately begin to burst. But our MBA-100 actually stabilizes the resin until curing takes effect to set the the bubbles permanently. This Mechanical Blending Additive is a non-reactive chemical compound that is premixed into the resin before gas is blended into it. Compressed gas then mixes into the resin to create foam. In effect, the treated resin "captures" the gas in its own bubbles.

Note: The MBA-100 Mechanical Blending Additive should be used only with MBF-01 Mechanically Blended Foam equipment from Venus-Gusmer.

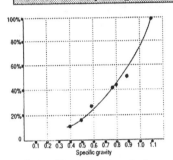

Mechanically Blended Foam™ processing:
- Reduces VOC emissions
- Saves materials and labor
- Makes uniform foam bubbles for strong parts, smooth surfaces
- Is compatible with various gases and resins
- Minimizes heat reactions and processing odors

Enjoy increased productivity and savings in numerous manufacturing applications:
- Marine
- Transportation
- Tub and spa
- Corrosion
- Construction/structural panels
- Cavity filling

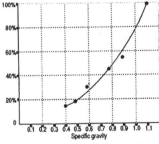

Fig. 1- Unreinforced polyester foams. Tensile strength vs. density

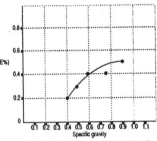

Fig. 3-Unreinforced polyester foams - elongation in tensile vs. density

Fig. 2-Unreinforced polyester foams - tensile modulus vs. density

Your Venus-Gusmer distributor is:

VENUS-GUSMER
1862 Ives Avenue, Kent, WA 98032 U.S.A.
(206) 854-2660 Fax: (206) 854-1666

225

REFERENCE 29 *continued*

UNIQUE SPRAYED LOW-DENSITY CORING AND LAMINATING SYSTEM

by John Raymer and Claire Niland
VENUS-GUSMER

INTRODUCTION

For more than 20 years the RP industry has sought to reduce labor and material expenses through an improved method of applying resin and consolidating it with glass. In an increasingly competitive world, the time-honored method of spray-up followed by rollout makes decreasing sense. Spray-up, as a single application method, is fairly reasonable since it can achieve throughput rates as high as 25 lbs./min. The critical bottleneck however, has always been rollout because labor requirements are often three times as great as those for operating a chop-and-spray gun.

Polyester foam, in one form or another, has often been used to solve this problem because of several advantages. Namely, polyester foam processing promised a rapid method of applying resin to open molds without the need to roll out the laminate. In addition to saving costs associated with rollout labor, the process offered the benefits of reduced laminate weight and increased laminate thickness, which in turn yielded greater laminate stiffness.

Despite its promise, polyester foam processing introduced technical stumbling blocks that prevented its widespread use. The most severe of these were excessive exotherm, expense, hard-to-handle fillers, poorly controlled densities, and sensitivity to shop temperatures. Most of these difficulties originated with the chemistry needed to create the gas within the resin. It required highly reactive additives that induced excess exotherm and created poorly controlled cell structures. In addition, catalyst reacted with additives and with resin. The two competing reactions were controlled by temperature. Polyester simply did not lend itself to being expanded as other plastic resins do.

The problems associated with the chemical method of creating gas prompted research into methods that bypassed reactive chemistry. It seemed a reasonable venture; there are thousands of substances that are foamed in commercial applications without using chemistry. Consider whipped cream, light butter, shaving cream, ice cream and foam rubber, to name just a few. These commercial products are all foamed mechanically through the use of a mechanism that blends air or gas into the unfoamed product. This proven technology, incorporated into standard resin application equipment, has made it possible to create a highly controllable polyester foam.

PROCESS ADVANTAGES

In this mechanical process, gas is whipped into the resin between the pump and gun, and so creates foam. Thus, resin leaves the gun or pour head in a fully expanded, frothed state. The foam's cell structure is uniform and its gel-time can be varied according to convenience for processing. Chemically foamed resins generally create exotherm heat during the process of foaming and have very quick gel-times. By extending the gel-time with mechanically blended foam it becomes possible to limit exotherm and create thick cores or castings. Additionally, it then becomes practical to post-form the foam by enclosing it in a vacuum-formed thermoplastic part, or rotationally molding it with centrifugal force.

PROCESS DESCRIPTION

Most processors prefer to meter-mix polyester resins with MEKP catalyst. MEKP offers reasonable cost, some tolerance for error, and easy-to-use application equipment. This polyester foam system is based on conventional slave-arm internal-mix pumping equipment, with modifications that allow injection of compressed gas that is then blended into the resin between the pump and mixhead.

Compressed gas in the form of carbon dioxide or nitrogen is loaded in bottles into the machine where it is then pumped to operating pressure before being injected into the resin stream. The mixture of gas and resin then enters a rapidly rotating blending mechanism where it is sheared into a homogeneous mixture. The size of the cells is a function of the type of gas used and the pressure under which it is injected.

Because the resin is foamed before being catalyzed, the foamed resin can remain in the hoses indefinitely until it is needed. The foamed resin mixes in a conventional internal mixing gun head, where it can be applied as a chopper gun laminate or sprayed alone as a core material. Internal-mix gun heads can easily be converted to a casting and pouring type operation by adding a static mixer.

The gas is blended into the resin with equipment not much different from that used to make whipped food products. The equipment is easy to operate and repair; it includes an impeller that rotates between sets of pins and imparts enough shear to divide the gas cells into small, equal units.

ADDITIVE

While the equipment is easy to operate and the concept is familiar, the key to the process is a proprietary complex additive. Its unique formulation allows formation of uniform cells and then holds them in place until the resin gels. The additive is processed as a liquid and is mixed at approximately 1.5% by volume. It is possible to premix the additive in the resin batch, or use an additional slave arm pump to meter in the correct amount of the additive and preblend it at the resin pump. Unlike additives used for chemical foams, this agent is a very stable and safe material. The MSDS rating shows a very low hazard rating and the shipping classification is not in the "flammable liquid" category.

BLOWING GASES

This system can inject virtually any gas, except flammable gas. Different gases produce different cell structures. Nitrogen and carbon dioxide are low-cost, commonly available gases, and so have been developed as the primary gases for the process. Carbon dioxide-foamed resin can achieve a specific gravity as low as 0.2 (typical resin = 1.2) and the cells are relatively large. Nitrogen is used for higher densities (greater than 0.6) and finer cell structure. Gas consumption is equal to the volume of the bubbles formed in the resin. To avoid partial emptying of gas bottles and to closely regulate flow, the system uses a pneumatically powered gas pump to amplify gas pressure to the desired level. As the gas pressure increases to exceed resin pressure, the gas flow will increase and density will decrease.

RESIN PARAMETERS

Physical properties of polyester foam will be entirely determined by the resin selected and foam density. We have examined various polyester resins of various composition with successful results. To date, tests have been conducted with conventional ortho GP resins and determined that the following characteristics are important for maintaining the foam cells in suspension and controlling exotherm.

1. Where possible, styrene content should be 28–30%. This helps control the cells and keep them in suspension. Lower viscosity can affect the foam's ability to hold the cells.

2. No anti-foaming agents may be used in the resin production process.

3. Conventional cobalt napthanate additives cause problems due to the naptha solvent. Substitution with cobalt octoate is a good solution; other promoters may be used as well.

It should be stressed that virtually every polyester resin company can easily supply these characteristics in a resin. Cold-press molding resin with these specifications is already available.

It is possible to vary the physical properties of the foam by selecting and processing different resins, and by blending flexible resins for toughness. It is also expected that many other thermoset resins, including epoxies, phenolics, vinylesters and hybrids, will be processable.

APPLICATIONS

Almost every RP product can benefit from a processing method that increases thickness while reducing weight. Indeed, weight is usually an overriding concern in RP product design and lightweight cores are therefore common. Typical core materials are PVC foam, polyurethane foam, balsa wood, cardboard, pipes, plywood, wood, metal and other materials that create thickness. The primary obstacle to using a core is the labor required to install it. Moreover, some cores (such as plywood) are difficult to shape and they lose strength when cut into small pieces. A sprayed core material with good adhesion to polyester allows quick installation and easy coring of complex forms without resorting to cutting and piecing the core material.

MARINE

One of the largest RP markets — and the greatest market for core material use — is the marine industry. Boats are often built with cores in the hull, deck and cabin. The premium cores for boats have been PVC foam and balsa. Because of their high cost, these materials are used almost exclusively in the high-end leisure market and the commercial work-boat market. Polyester foam, thanks to its low material and processing labor costs, should allow production of low-end, high-volume boats with cores. The products will weigh less, use less resin, and offer stiffer hull construction than those made heretofore. In those cases where the special physical properties of PVC foam are needed, sprayed foam may be used in place of manually trowelled putties for bonding to the laminate. Sprayed foam offers excellent adhesion due to its ability to penetrate porous surfaces with minimal material volume. Sprayed foam should also perform well when bonded to honeycomb cores since honeycomb cells can be filled partially with a stable foamed resin that is sprayed against the laminate.

Polyester foam may also be used to prevent gelcoat fiber print-through. Boat laminates often show a fiber pattern in the gelcoat because the resin shrinks around the glass fibers and sinks to expose the glass fibers beneath the surface. If a layer of polyester foam is first cured against the gelcoat, the fiber pattern cannot push through to the gelcoat. The result is a nearly perfect gelcoat surface. Furthermore, proper selection of densities reduces damage caused by impact because stress is localized to the impact point.

Another marine application for foam is the mass production of small boats using chopper guns. Strong laminates can be built up quickly by chopping short (1/4-in or 6.3 mm) fibers and spraying them along with the foam. The surface can then be skinned with standard resin, or sprayed with a high-density foam.

TUB/SHOWER

In this sizable, highly competitive industry, polyester foam has long helped efforts to reduce labor and material costs, and make lightweight products. Unfortunately, many of the foams that have been used are temperature-sensitive and given to wide variations in density. They also tend to overheat with exotherm, and they release more styrene than resin that is not chemically blown.

In the absence of sprayed polyester foam, most tub and shower manufacturers resort to low-cost cores such as cardboard and sheet polyurethane. These materials add processing steps, and require manual cutting and sizing for installation. Moreover, they bond poorly with polyester and are prone to moisture absorption. Sheet goods are also expensive to ship and store, and they introduce potentially costly inventory control problems. They usually require extra resin for bonding, which effectively negates the benefits of material savings that are inherent to polyester foam processing.

Resin that is prefoamed by the new mechanical method allows density to be set the moment the foam hits the mold, instead of after a sensitive chemical reaction occurs. Its use as a core material also avoids the problems introduced by sheet goods.

CASTING AND POURING

It is possible to cast very large shapes with foamed polyester resin. This opens a range of applications, from casting of figurines to plaster replacement to cavity filling of structural parts. Many years ago, water-extended polyesters (WEP) were used with little success for replacing plaster. Reducing the density of polyester to a specific gravity of 0.2 and 0.6 makes it competitive with plaster and eliminates the problems of WEP. The material is self-skinning and can be cast into complex open molds for forming wood-scroll work substitutes. Molding of small figurines is yet another popular application that lends itself well to polyester foam processing.

Rotational molding of polyester foam is yet another option with the extended gel-time that is possible with mechanically foamed resin. Large shapes such as figurines, mannequins, taxidermy forms, columns and decorative architectural forms are often molded with filled resins that may be replaced by foam.

Cavity filling of structural parts can be easily accomplished as well. Blow-molded or rotationally molded thermoplastic parts often require structural backing. Toys and marine devices can be filled easily with polyester foam without the expansion problems associated with urethane foams. In such processes, it is possible to tailor the density to the required compression strength.

CORROSION

The corrosion business often relies on cores to develop stiffness in pipes, tanks and panels. Plywood is frequently used as a core because of its strength and resistance to moisture. However, a properly designed foam-core laminate can exceed the stiffness of plywood and retain integrity under chemical corrosion. Research has shown potential with vinylester resin foam core, as well, and a foaming system should soon be available for vinylester processing.

To achieve a smooth foam core between laminates, it is possible to integrate foam spraying with filament winding to apply foam automatically. Similarly, an automatic reciprocator can be used to build foam core panels for use in corrosion applications as well as the truck-trailer business.

MARBLE AND POLYMER CONCRETE

Cultured marble is a highly competitive business with low retail costs and strict quality requirements, especially regarding the control of resin properties. Thermal cycling is a severe problem that can hinder control. Foaming the marble resin relieves resin thermal stress in the marble matrix. Resin expansion can be accommodated within the foam cells to minimize internal stress during thermal expansion and contraction. This effect will likely allow the use of many more casting resins for this process. Marble products will also be lighter and easier to sand and grind, and their resin consumption is likely to decrease to a very competitive level.

Polymer concrete processing requires efficient filler wetting and low resin content. By its nature, foam is a better wetting agent than polymer concrete. Lower percentages of polyester, epoxy and vinylester will reduce material costs and improve the strength-to-weight performance of products.

TOOLING

Almost every RP tool incorporates some type of core to increase stiffness. Good dimensional stability is critical to tooling, and fabricators invest considerable time and expense to maintain tool shape and surface. A thick tool is ideal for meeting these criteria; however, tools must be built up layer by layer to avoid distortion from heat and shrinkage.

Polyester foam allows a low distortion laminate to be built quickly with minimal exotherm. Additionally, thicker laminates can be built from polyester foam without excessive weight and with lower cost. Labor is saved due to rapid application rates, and material weight is typically reduced to between 25% and 50%. Much larger boat tools can be built with less structural steel and less weight distortion.

By spraying a foam layer between the tooling gelcoat and laminate, it is also possible to restrict fiber print through and therefore improve critical tool surface. Tools made with foam cores are also likely to age better, without post-shrinkage and fiber print-through caused by heat exposure.

VOC REDUCTION

There is little doubt that polyester foam processing, with low exotherm, creates far fewer VOCs than the typical laminate. A number of factors support this claim, particularly the large drops of resin-gas that are created at the gun nozzle. VOC generation is a function of drop size: exposed drop surface area increases as the size of the drop decreases. The worst case is a drop that is so small it becomes airborne. Resin mixed with gas tends to cling together rather than burst off into discreet drops. The result is a web-like pattern that clings to itself.

Another factor which supports foam processing in VOC reduction is the greater buildup in thickness relative to weight. The foam cells act as a barrier to migration of styrene to the laminate surface where it becomes a problem. That is, styrene must travel a greater distance to reach the surface.

A more obvious benefit to fume control is the reduction in total resin weight needed to accomplish a given structural task. Every unit of resin eliminated from a part results in a proportional reduction in VOC fumes generated. This is perhaps the easiest concept to demonstrate to regulatory agency inspectors. With the government and public examining every industry regarding its VOC emission levels, the time is right for the RP industry to move toward new ways to reduce emissions. Mechanical foam processing is an excellent example.

CONCLUSIONS

Polyester foam is now economically feasible and technically practical. The simplicity of its application with a chopper gun now allows processing of material with less than half the weight of unformed polyester. This reduces density and is repeatable. Because the necessary additive is blended at just 1.5%, the economics of mechanically blended foam are very attractive. Other material costs are reduced by half, with very little additional expense that is unique to this system and process. Processing is simplified to resemble a typical meter-mix pumping operation. The additional gas injection equipment has been proven highly reliable and easy to trouble-shoot, keeping operation and maintenance costs low. Finally, VOC reduction is perhaps the most significant benefit to the molder. It is now possible to demonstrate to regulatory agencies the true technological advancement of this process that reduces styrene emissions significantly without introducing economic drawbacks.

ECONOMICS
Foamed Laminate vs. Compact Laminate

Assumptions: Typical tub of 100 lbs. laminate, 25% fiberglass, burdened labor at $20/hour

LABOR	FOAMED		UNFOAMED	
Chopper	1 man @ $20/hr. x 0.2 hr.	= $ 4.00	1 man @ $20/hr. x 0.2 hr.	= $ 4.00
Rollout	none	= $ 0.00	3 men @ $20/hr. x 0.2 hr.	= $12.00
Gelcoater	1 man @ $20/hr. x 0.2 hr.	= $ 4.00	1 man @ $20/hr. x 0.2 hr.	= $ 4.00
MATERIAL				
Resin	37.5 lbs. @ $0.65	= $24.38	75 lbs. @ $0.65	= $48.75
Fiberglass	25 lbs. @ $1.20	= $30.00	25 lbs. @ $1.20	= $30.00
Total Per Unit	$62.38		$98.75	
50 units/day	$3,119.00		$4,937.50	
10,000 units/year	$623,800.00		$987,500.00	

Annual savings: $363,700.00

REFERENCE 30

THE APPLICATION OF PHENOLIC RESINS IN FRP COMPOSITES

by

Aram Mekjian

INTRODUCTION

The increasing use of FRP composites in aerospace, automotive, marine, construction, mass transit, mining and tunneling needs no elaboration.

Of increasing concern is the Fire, Smoke and Smoke Toxicity (FST) properties of composites in case of fire in enclosed areas.

The inherently excellent FST properties of phenolic are well known. However, until recently, the difficult processability of phenolic resins and the costly use of phenolic prepreg have prevented the widespread usage of phenolic composites.

The recent availability of low viscosity phenolic resins that make them suitable for RTM, hand lay-up, spray-up, filament winding, pultrusion, and press molding has sparked new interest in phenolics in heretofore impractical applications.

This paper will review the processability of the new phenolic resins, the properties of phenolic composites and show examples of phenolic usage.

MATERIALS

Table I illustrates the various resins available from BP Chemicals for the different processes. Most of the processes require an acid catalyst and a post cure to achieve optimum properties. For pultrusion and press molding there is a heat curable resin, J2041L which does not require any catalyst, a postcure, or any modification on equipment currently used for polyester.

Physical properties of phenolics (Table 2) are comparable to polyester with one notable advantage of 310°F HDT on a clear casting.

ADVANTAGES

The advantages of phenolic composites compared to the other FRP's are:

High temperature resistance
Does not burn readily
Low smoke
Low smoke toxicity

The high temperature resistance of phenolic composites is demonstrated in Fig. 1[1]. The excellent long term heat aging properties of phenolic makes it ideal for the automotive industry for under the hood applications and for heat shields around catalytic converters and exhaust systems.

Because phenolics are inherently fire resistant, there is no need to add fillers such as alumina trihydrate (ATH) to obtain fire retardance of Class 1 rating. This provides composites with a low specific gravity of 1.3–1.4.

The low smoke and smoke toxicity properties of phenolics are illustrated in Figures 2[1], 3 and 4. These excellent properties obviously make phenolic composites the ideal choice of material for aerospace, mass transit, construction, tunneling and mining where the risk of death due to exposure to smoke is very high.

Although phenolic prepreg can be used in many of these applications, the high cost of material and processing (tooling) has been prohibitive for its wide usage. The low material cost and easy processing of these 'wet' systems leave no excuse for not using the optimum material for maximum safety.

DISADVANTAGES OF PHENOLICS

The disadvantages of using phenolics compared to other FRP's are:

Shelf life
Not pigmentable
Acid cure
Cycle time/post cure

The resin has to be stored at 50°F for a shelf life of at least 3 months. Phenolics are not pigmentable unless brown or black are the desired colors. Parts need to be painted to obtain the desired color. Polyester gel coats should not be used in conjunction with phenolics because the difference in the thermal coefficient of linear expansion can cause stress cracks in the gel coat.

The acid catalyst is corrosive. Therefore, aluminum or soft steel tooling or processing equipment cannot be used. Polyester, epoxy or stainless steel (or plated) tooling are required. Spray-up or RTM injection equipment needs to be stainless steel (they are available).

Although processing such as hand lay-up, spray-up (rolling, wetting) does not require more time than does polyester. Phenolic parts need to be post cured for 1–4 hours (depending on thickness) at 140–180°F.

Although these processing parameters are different and may sound impractical for those fabricators used to working with polyester, they are not insurmountable, to achieve the product performance that phenolics provide.

HEALTH AND SAFETY

Health and safety issues for phenolics are quite manageable. Any well ventilated shop that meets styrene emission standards will have no problem with phenolics. Precautions in handling peroxides are adequate for handling the acid catalyst. When handling the acid catalyst, goggles should be worn. In the US, the maximum 8 hour TWA is 1 ppm for formaldehyde. Much lower levels have been measured in well ventilated shops.

CORROSION RESISTANCE

The corrosion resistance of phenolics are quite good except for strong acids and bases. Tables 3, 4 and 5 illustrate the retention of Flexural Strength and Modulus of laminates immersed in various solutions at 77°F. As predicted, strong acids and bases should be avoided although the excellent resistance to organic solvents makes phenolics suitable for many applications.

Table 6[2] a shows the retention of physicals of laminates using 42 oz/yd[2] unidirectional roving (not woven) immersed in water at 125°F .

Table 7[3] shows the tensile and compressive properties of RTM panels in a variety of exposure conditions.

PHENOLIC-FRP USAGE

Phenolic FRP are very prominently used in mass transit such as the London Underground — both exterior and interior of most of the trains, the Eurotunnel Locomotive, Baltimore RR, Dallas Fort Worth people movers, ducting for coal mines and tunnels, various chemical treatment plants where Factory Mutual Approved ducting is required, roof and wall panels for subways, automotive heat shields, submarines, surface ships and many other applications where the high temperature resistance and FST properties of phenolics are desirable.

SUMMARY

With the availability of low viscosity phenolic resins that are easily processable via:

    RTM
    Hand lay-up
    Spray-up
    Filament winding
    Pultrusion
    Press molding,

there is no reason why the superior properties of phenolic FRP should not be utilized for maximum safety in many areas where until now they were not considered because of processing limitations or cost.

The driving forces for using phenolic FRP today, are:

    FST
    High temperature resistance
    Low specific gravity
    Readily available
    Easy processing
    Reasonable cost

REFERENCES

1. Forsdyke, K.L. "Phenolic GRP and Its Application in Mass Transit." 44th Annual Conference, SPI Composites Institute (February, 1989).

2. Wills, John A., Plastics Consultant. Valley Center, CA..

3. Houston, Daniel, Q. Ford Motor Co. Dearborn, MI.

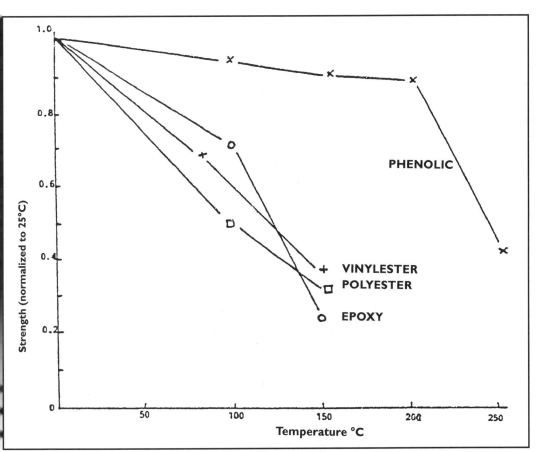

Figure 1.

Flexural strength at elevated temperature.

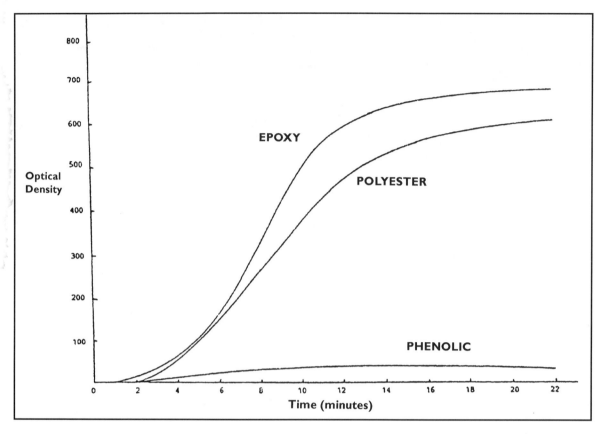

Figure 2. NBS smoke chamber (smoldering).

Figure 3
FIRE/SMOKE TEST RESULTS ON
CELLOBOND PHENOLIC LAMINATES

E-84 TUNNEL TEST

	FLAME SPREAD	SMOKE DENSITY
UNPAINTED	5	5
PAINTED	20	10

PITTSBURGH TOXICITY TEST
LC 50 = 61

35% GLASS   HAND LAY-UP

Figure 4
FIRE/SMOKE TEST RESULTS
CELLOBOND PHENOLIC LAMINATES*

UL 94	CLASSIFICATION		94 Vo
ASTM E 162	FLAME SPREAD INDEX		2.8
ASTM E 662		Flaming	Non Flaming
	OPTICAL DENSITY	23	7
OSU		Result	FAA Requirement
	TOTAL HEAT RELEASE	26	<65
	PEAK HEAT RELEASE	48	<65

35% GLASS LAMINATE

Table 1
CELLOBOND PHENOLIC RESINS

PROCESS	RESIN	VISCOSITY	CATALYST
RTM &	J2027L	300	P10 or
FILAMENT	J2018L	700	P15
WINDING			
HAND LAY-UP &	J2027L	300	PIO
SPRAY-UP	J2018L	700	or
	J2042L	1400/3800	P15
PULTRUSION	J2041L	4800	NONE
PRESS MOLDING	J2041L	4800	NONE
	J2033L	2000	P15
SURFACE PASTE	J26/053L	15,000/45,000	P15

Table 2
PHYSICAL PROPERTIES CELLOBOND J2018L

	Clear Casting	35% CSM Laminate
FLEX STR (psi)	12,600	27,000
FLEX MOD (psi)	500,000	890,000
TENSILE STR (psi)	7,400	16,000
TENSILE MOD (psi)	-	980,000
ELONGATION (Z)	1.8	2.3
NOTCHED IZOD (ft lb/in)	-	12
HDT (°F)	310	>400

Table 3
35% CLASS PHENOLIC LAY-UP
IMMERSED IN SOLVENT AT 77°F
% RETENTION

	6 mos		12 mos	
	F	M	F	M
1% SULFURIC ACID	66	87	60	75
10% SULPHURIC ACID	40	63	36	53
1% PHOSPHORIC ACID	72	85	67	77
10% PHOSPHPORIC ACID	66	84	65	80
WATER (DEIONIZED)	84	88	72	81

F = FLEX STR   *M = FLEX MOD*

Table 4
35% CLASS PHENOLIC LAY-UP
IMMERSED IN SOLVENT AT 77°F
% RETENTION

	6 mos		12 mos	
	F	M	F	M
25% ACETIC ACID	82	82	78	77
1% HYDROCHLORIC ACID	70	85	65	79
10% HYDROCHLORIC ACID	59	75	66	73
1% NITRIC ACID	67	79	69	75
10% NITRIC ACID	65	67	53	55

F = FLEX STR   *M = FLEX MOD*

Table 5
35% CLASS PHENOLIC LAY-UP
IMMERSED IN SOLVENT AT 77°F
% RETENTION

	6 mos		12 mos	
	F	M	F	M
1% AMMONIUM HYDROXIDE	61	73	57	70
SAT. SODIUM CHLORIDE	86	90	79	90
FUEL OIL	95	93	97	94
KEROSENE	105	106	94	91

F = FLEX STR   *M = FLEX MOD*

Table 6
35% CLASS PHENOLIC LAY-UP
SOAKED 16 DAYS IN 125°F WATER

	Control	% Retention
TENSILE STR	20,000 psi	79
TENSILE MOD	0.42×10^6 psi	93
ELONGATION	9.8%	96
FLEXURAL STR	27,000 psi	89
FLEXURAL MOD	1.16×10^6 psi	91

Table 7
50% CLASS PHENOLIC RTM

Control	
TENSILE STRENGTH	28,000 psi
TENSILE MODULUS	2.26×10^6 psi
COMPRESSIVE STRENGTH	25,800 psi
COMPRESSIVE MODULUS	2.21×10^6 psi

REFERENCE 31

FIRE RESISTANCE OF LAMINATE RESINS (VIDEOTAPE)

I have produced a videotape of the comparative fire resistance of most major laminating resins in various configurations, *e.g.*, fiber reinforced panels, reinforced sandwich panels, etc. The phenolics won hands down!

If you really want to see how dangerous in terms of fire and smoke all resins tested are, except phenolics, then contact me or Tiller Publishing for a copy of this tape. It is very dramatic!

JOHN A. WILLS, Plastics Consultant
32776 Via Del Venado, Valley Center, CA 92082
Phone: (760) 742-3918 • Fax: (760) 742-3167

TILLER PUBLISHING
P.O. Box 447, St. Michaels, MD 21663
Phone: 1-800-6TILLER • Fax: (410) 745-9743

REFERENCE 32

CORE-CEL PVC STRUCTURAL FOAM

ATC Chemical Corporation (Canada) is a major Producer of linear polyvinyl chloride structural foam, using the trade name Core-Cell. The product is available in several sheet thicknesses and densities are 3, 4, 5, and 6 pounds per cubic foot.

The name ATC Chemical Corporation is relatively new in the PVC foam business, but Thomas J. Johannsen, president, is not. You will notice several references to Torin Inc. in the text. Between 1981 and 1991 Torin, which was owned by Mr. Johannsen, represented in the United States AIREX — the PVC foam product of Airex/ Switzerland. When his contract with them terminated, Al Horsmon, who was Torin's technical representative at the time, became the US agent for Airex.

During 1991 Mr. Johannsen began producing linear PVC structural foam with the trade name Core-Cell. The product meets or exceeds the specifications of Airex. ATC's product sheet and distributor list follows on the next page.

Thomas Johannsen has written several technical papers which are available. Write to him at the Oakville, Ontario, address for copies.

ATC   Structural Foams, Bonding and Fairing Compounds

July 1994

CORE-CELL® - CORE-BOND® - POLY-BOND™ - POLY-FAIR™ - POLY-FILL™

CORE-CELL® is a linear polymer foam that is non-friable, tough, rigid, and has a closed-cell structure. Core-Cell has good heat distortion temperature in the ambient range, good impact strength, and is used primarily in the marine industry for coring hulls, decks and superstructures. Core-Cell is supplied in densities of 3, 4, 5, and 6 pcf, and in plain and contoured sheets.

CORE-BOND® is a light weight polyester-based core installation compound developed for both handlayup and vacuum-bag installation. Core-Bond is supplied with its own paste catalyst, and is formulated to the degree of elasticity required for the core-skin interface. Core-Bond can also be supplied as a sprayable version.

POLY-BOND™ B46F is a glassfiber reinforced, non-brittle, low-exotherm, waterproof adhesive for general bonding applications such as hull/deck joints, bonding of interior liners and engine stringers, rudders and keels. Poly-Bond can also be supplied in a version for pump dispension.

POLY-FAIR™ F26 is a waterproof polyester-based fairing compound used for plugs and molds, and for fairing one-off hulls and decks. Poly-Fair has good sandability and inherent toughness and impact resistance. Poly-Fair is often covered with our sanding primer Poly-Fill.

POLY-FILL™ is a sprayable (HVLP gun) polyester sanding primer. Poly-Fill provides an easy to sand base before using the primers for the various paint systems and surface finishes. Poly-Fill has a tough and damage resistant surface. Poly-Fill can be dry to the touch within 45-60 minutes depending on the thickness sprayed, and can be sanded within 2 hours at 70ºF. Poly-Fill can be polished to obtain a glossy surface.

Representatives:

Florida: Jef Benkelman, 716 Lagoon Drive, North Palm Beach, FL 33408 Tel: (407)622-6706, Fax: (407) 624-0637
Midwest: Albert W. Horsmon Jr.*, 59940 Knevels Court, Three Rivers, MI 49093 Tel: (616) 244-5541, Fax:(616) 244-8573
California: Alex Kozloff *, 18021-J Skypark Circle, Irvine, CA 92714 Tel: (714) 786-7742, Fax: (714) 786-3936

Distributors:
* Compounds only

New England
RP Associates, Inc.
Minturn Farm Road
Bristol, RI 02809
Tel : (401) 253-4800
Fax: (401) 253-4720

Mid-Atlantic
Oceana Inc.
18111 Virginia Street
Annapolis, MD 21401
Tel: (800) 523-8890
Fax: (410) 268-6528

Clark-Schwebel Distr. Corp.*
698 Bryant Blvd.
Rock Hill, SC 29732
Tel: (800) 327-9058
Fax: (803) 327-8089

Florida
Clark Schwebel Distr.Corp.*
150 N.W. 176th Street
Miami, FL 33169
Tel: (305) 652-4100
Fax: (305) 652-0933

Florida, cont.
Clark Schwebel Distr.Corp.*
733 Kraft Road
Lakeland, FL 33801
Tel: (813) 687-8111
Fax: (813) 687-3902

South
Seemann Fiberglass Inc.
6117 River Road
Harahan, LA 70123
Tel: (800) 358-1666
Fax: (504) 738-0032

Seemann Fiberglass Inc.
5880 1-10 Industrial Pkwy.
Theodore, AL 36582
Tel: (205) 653-5066
Fax: (205) 653-5249

California
Diversified Materials Co.
8250 Commercial Street
La Mesa, CA 92042
Tel: (619) 464-4111
Fax: (619) 464-4186

Pacific Northwest
Tacoma Fiberglass
2406 Port of Tacoma Road
Tacoma, WA 98421
Tel: (206) 272-1258
Fax: (206) 272-2148

Canada
Plastics Maritime Ltd.
180 Chain Lake Drive
Halifax, NS B3S 1B9
Tel: (902) 450-5777
Fax: (902) 450-5660

East Coast Fibre Glass Inc.
1 Highland Heights Road
South Side, NS BOW 1PO
Tel: (902) 745-2855
Fax: (902) 745-2778

Armkem, Inc.
2400 Canadian Street
Drummondville, Que.J 2B 8A9
Tel: (819) 477-1146
Fax: (819) 474-5000

Canada, cont.
Queen City Distributors Ltd.
49 Toro Road
Downsview, Ont. M3J 2A4
Tel: (416) 630-2110
Fax: (416) 630-0667

Gwil Industries Inc.
6888 Burlington Ave.
Burnaby, BC V5J 4H1
Tel: (604) 438-1341
Fax: (604) 438-7347

ATC CHEMICAL CORPORATION
1051 Clinton Street, Buffalo, NY 14206
Tel: (716) 836-1943 Fax: (716) 836-2362

ATC CHEMICALS INC.
96 Forsythe Street, Oakville, Ontario L6K 3J9
Tel: (905) 842-2338 Fax; (905) 842-1514

REFERENCE 33

COMMENTARY: THE PATENT GAME

by

John A. Wills

You have a good idea and you made it work. You have spent a lot of time and money to get this far so you don't want any one to steal it from you. You can:

A. Keep it a secret. Do not tell anyone how it works — just reap all the profits! Coca-Cola got away with this for years.

B. Sell licenses to use your idea, but be sure to get lots of nondisclosure agreements, then hire a staff of attorneys.

C. Get a *PATENT*. Be sure to make it as confusing as possible, then no one will try to copy what you have invented. Be sure you have a good supply of lawyers.

D. Get a patent, so no one else can file on your claims. Then, you the hero, can donate your work to the public domain.

E. You don't have a good idea but if you look around, maybe you can steal one. Published articles and books serve them up. The Patent Office lists over five million of them. If you want to be legit, maybe you can gain by filing your own patent on someone else's claim as an improvement.

Let's take another look at A through E.

A. If your product is a witch's brew and you can make it in your basement without telling your mother-in-law and you don't have suppliers who might snitch on you, then you may be able to get away with it. The little farming community where I live is known as "The Methamphetamine Capitol of the World." The formulators use the "secret" system to protect their invention but they smell bad and often blow themselves up. This is not always good for business.

B. You can sell licenses for any un-patented idea even if you know you could patent it. Patent laws do require that you make a full disclosure of your art to the point where "anyone skilled in the art" can reproduce what you claim. Your only protection in licensing is in a nondisclosure contract agreement which guarantees that no licensee will ever release your secrets. No way!

C. Go ahead and get a patent. When it's issued be sure to hire as many attorneys as possible to protect your rights, then you can make your brew on the first floor, sell licenses, go to court, and hire some spies to see who's infringing. Hire some more lawyers.

D. Patent your idea so no one else will be able to when you disclose it. You might be surprised how cost effective this can be and, you may not be aware of the large number of producers ranging from ingredients to finished goods or processes who follow this procedure. This is not benevolence. It is good business practice.

Another way I have found that will work for you for years is to publish your work — and let it be known that the information is for the public domain. Write some "how-tos" or shop manuals which are truly hands-on meaningful. These will sell for years and you automatically become a fee consultant, if you wish. A copyright at present costs 20 bucks. I use the copyright to encourage my readers to quote any of my books. Certainly, I impose no restriction on the information. I find it far more satisfying to endorse checks received than sign mine to pay someone for protection.

E. If you can improve on an existing patent, you can do so legally. You can find out how — ask a patent attorney or the Patent Office.

Conclusion

Today, we label our segment of the plastics industry "composites." Not long ago, we used the words, "reinforced plastics." We even added some acronyms such as: "RP" or "FRP." Go back a little further and we carried the label "laminator." We even used "molder" at times.

When you do look back 50 years in the "composite" industry — if you will — you should see why our industry developed so rapidly and freely, especially at first. Any idea, good or bad, was shared. When we all had mold release problems and something finally seemed to work, we learned about it freely. I remember that quince seed jelly was *the* mold release item for a time (it didn't work).

As soon as we were presented with polyester resin early in World War II, we started to look for some means of curing this marvelous new resin at room temperature. Early on, someone discovered that benzoin (a photographic chemical) would cure polymers if given enough sun (ultraviolet light). It was not very good but we all shared its use. Dr. Muscat, an early pioneer in the use of polymer resin, added organic metal salts to pre-catalyzed resin, which would produce a room temperature cure of poor quality with limited use. *Note:* This is a good example of someone trying to capture a mediocre process. Had Dr. Muscat fully disclosed his discovery immediately, others would have quickly corrected his primary mistake and the industry would have been advanced several years.

A couple of years after Dr. Muscat came out with his process, I improved upon his work and developed a reliable, very efficient method of room temperature curing of polyester resin. This is still the basic process used today.

In an another area, at first, most hand laid moldings were made on male plaster-of-paris molds. The usual lay-up was one or more layers of chopped strand mat over which a ply of open weave glass cloth was placed in order to act as a kind of screen through which we could saturate the unruly mat underneath with a large brush. One of my employees, an old plasterer, "Pappy" Reed, found that a postcard size, half inch thick, soft gum rubber "paddle" worked magic on forcing resin through this fiberglass screen to impregnate the mat below. Thus, the "squeegee" was born. Sheet rubber suppliers were soon run out of stock. Within days, every molder and his brother freely had this new tool.

We needed some better mold material than plaster. We also needed usable female molds. Yes, we had female plaster molds, but any female mold was difficult to use until "Pappy" came up with the squeegee idea. Then, they were a piece of cake. I finally realized that when we made a fiberglass part over a male mold, we also were making a candidate female mold. It did not take much brain work to figure out how to make female molds from then on. This was a happy development, especially for the small boat builder at the time.

I had nothing to do with the resin-glass chopper gun. This gun produced an opportunity for many to start up a special industry. One benefit from users of chopper guns was the development of the serrated roller. A technician in the Marion, Virginia, plastics plant of Brunswick Corporation assembled an alternating series of two different diameters of flat washers onto a shaft, attached a handle, and out came a "roller." Lighter weight versions were turned on a lathe using solid aluminum. Brunswick tried to keep this art to themselves. I heard they did — for exactly one week.

Now that we had a room temperature cure system, the rubber squeegee, the serrated roller and fiberglass female tooling with very smooth surfaces, I began to look for some way we could create a "paint job" in these smooth female molds to avoid the requirement for painting parts. Having experience as a paint chemist, I began to experiment with grinding pigments into our resin. With the help of Glidden Paint Company doing the grinding, we eventually came up with a good coating later dubbed "gel coat."

NONE OF THESE DEVELOPMENTS WERE EVER RESTRAINED BY PATENTS OR LICENSES.

My point to reviewing these past experiences is to state by example the value of sharing information without the payment of a pound of flesh. Recently, our industry has become so patent happy that the slightest little development seems to require protection. Except for those seeking patents to be placed in the public domain, much of the value of "captive" is dissipated in a rapidly growing industry, patent infringement law.

If you, the inventor, don't ultimately wish to spend your otherwise productive time in court or out earning money to support a staff of lawyers or accountants to "protect" your rights, consider placing your patent in the public domain to prevent others from filing on your claim. Offer your services for pay as a consultant or author to help others make use of your knowledge. Encourage others to improve on your ideas. You will be busy going to the bank depositing all that money you earn rather than going to the bank to withdraw all that money to pay your spies and mouthpieces.

Sharing knowledge in the past created the industry which is earning your living today. Don't louse it up. Loosen it up.

J.A.W.

REFERENCE 34

The National Shipbuilding Research Program
1991 Ship Production Symposium
Pan Pacific Hotel, San Diego, California
September 3–9, 1991

PERMANENT COMPOSITE CLADDING OF DETERIORATING STEEL HULLS

by

Albert W. Horsmon, Jr.

ABSTRACT

The 42.7 m (140 ft) steel steam yacht (S/Y) **Medea** was nearly condemned in 1988 because of deteriorating steel hull plate. However, it was recently restored with a structural foam and composite skin bonded to the outside of the remaining steel structure. The composite repair was completed at a cost of $220,000 compared to the $1.7 million estimated to crop and replace the wasted steel plate.

The repair, the events leading up to the repair, including U.S. Coast Guard approval, the structural and production decision making processes involved, and the projected use of an integrated production system for similar future applications are described in this paper. The use of similar processing technology to apply the glass epoxy composite coating on the wooden coastal minehunters (MHCs) is also discussed.

INTRODUCTION

Steel became the marine construction material of choice in the late 1800s due to its stiffness, strength and damage tolerance. Coating systems of that time were crude but, with early ships being overbuilt, excess wastage was acceptable, as were occasional leaks. Current steel construction is to a much tighter standard with very little excess plating for wastage and sophisticated coatings to preserve the relatively thin shell plating.

Composites, mostly fiberglass reinforced plastics (FRP), became common marine construction materials in the 1960s. FRP has the advantages of light weight, corrosion resistance, ease of construction, and lower cost in comparison to steel, wood and aluminum vessels in lengths of 21 m (69 ft)

and less. Sandwich composites take some of the FRP advantages one step further by using relatively thin FRP skins (inner and outer layers) "sandwiching" a low density foam or balsa core to achieve adequate panel stiffness at even further reduced weights. FRP vessels have steadily grown in size to where 40m (130 ft) yachts are common, one 49m (160 ft) yacht is under construction, and the U.S. Navy is building 55m (180 ft) MHCs.

The **Medea,** built of steel in 1904, falls between these two extremes of building philosophies. The vessel had been well cared for but many years of salt water use had deteriorated much of its structure. Permanent repairs of the steel structure were beyond the financial means of its owners, but a repair that combined advantages of both steel and FRP materials was feasible and attractive from the standpoint of both engineering and cost.

MEDEA HISTORY

Tracing the vessel's history leading up to the actual repair to the **Medea** helps put the repair into perspective. Much of this historical tracking describes working with Coast Guard authorities to achieve acceptable levels of safety for operation in U.S. waters, a procedure that is often misunderstood. More details about the vessel's full history are available from the San Diego Maritime Museum (1), the current owners of the vessel.

The **Medea** was built in England in 1904 of 6.4 mm (0.25 in.) mild steel shell plate with fairly close 500 mm (20 in.) spaced transverse frames. The vessel spent much of its life as a well cared for private yacht, with other periods in the hands of members of British Parliament and the builder's family (2). The **Medea** did service during both world wars and passed through a number of other owners. It was finally purchased and transported from Scandinavia to Whidby Island in Los Angeles for restoration in the early 1970s. It was then sailed under its own power to San Diego and donated to the Museum there in

*The steam yacht **Medea** sailing in San Diego Bay.*

1971. It was first certified by the U.S. Coast Guard as a "miscellaneous" vessel under Title 46, U.S. Code of Federal Regulations (46 CFR), Part 90.05-1 (3) in 1977 because it had a steam plant operating in U.S. waters.

Coast Guard Certification

When the *Medea* was first certificated, the Coast Guard accepted a number of existing repairs to the hull plate and framing that had been performed to a standard less than normally required by the Coast Guard. The repairs were permitted because of the vessel's limited service and because of the ample availability of rapid rescue or grounding to avert the consequences of minor flooding. These "temporary" repairs consisted of around 30 doublers, clad welding and epoxy patches to maintain the watertight integrity of the hull.

Doublers are additional plates welded over areas where the original hull plate is severely deteriorated, usually beyond 25 per cent wastage, which is the allowance built into the American Bureau of Shipping Rules for Building and Classing Steel Vessels Under 200 Feet (61m) (4), (ABS Rules). This is normally allowed by the Coast Guard before renewals are required. It is a simpler repair than cutting out the bad plate and welding or, in the case of the *Medea,* much riveting, to make permanent repairs to the plating. Simple fillet welds and roughly fit plates are used for doublers as opposed to the careful fitting and two side welding normally required for insert plates.

Clad welding is a method of building up the steel plate thickness by overlaying numerous layers of weld metal in way of localized pitting and pinholes. This method is not widely accepted for permanent repairs because of the large welding heat input to thin plate areas causing locked in stresses, and because of the susceptibility of the overlapped welds to increased corrosion attack.

When the *Medea* was hauled out for a drydock inspection in 1986, numerous additional holes, wasted areas and loose rivets were discovered. The Coast Guard allowed 12 additional doublers and more clad welding, rivet ring welding, and epoxy patches. But a definitive plan for permanent repairs was also required or the *Medea* would have had its certificate removed.

Repair Proposals

In early 1987 the owners of the *Medea* first proposed the FRP cladding of the vessel. The Coast Guard's San Diego Marine Safety Office initial response to this proposal was that Navigation and Vessel Inspection Circular (NVIC) 7-68, Notes on Repairs to Steel Hulls (5), required repairs that were to "renew as original" the steel hull plate. The Coast Guard was slightly mistaken in stating that the NVIC "required" renewal of the steel plating as original. Because NVIC is a Coast Guard produced document, publishing recommended practice without the official public comment and legal procedure

followed for regulations that are promulgated from U.S. Law, a NVIC can not be made a requirement. Nonetheless, most marine industry people accept NVICs the same as regulation, as was the case initially for the *Medea* owners.

The Coast Guard was also going to consider the FRP cladding repair a complete alteration, but invoked the requirements of regulations in 46 CFR 92.07-10 (3), supposedly requiring the vessel to be constructed of steel or "other suitable material, having in mind the risk of fire." Even though imposing that particular regulation on a vessel the size and type of the *Medea* was beyond the applicability of that regulation, the owners of the vessel, especially considering its poor condition, had little basis for appeal.

The Coast Guard finally withdrew certification for the *Medea* in September of 1988, citing the lack of progress towards or a plan for permanent repairs. Bids were sought for making the required repairs in steel, but the estimates ranged from $1.2 to $1.7 million, far beyond the means of the San Diego Maritime Museum.

However, another attempt was made to obtain approval for the composite cladding repair, this time appealing the decision of the local Coast Guard office to Coast Guard Headquarters, commercial vessel safety technical Office of Merchant Marine Safety, Security and Environmental Protection (Commandant [G-M]), Marine Technical and Hazardous Materials Division (G-MTH). The headquarters office reviewed the proposal based on its overall technical merits and the provisions for "equivalent safety," 46 CFR 90.15-1 (4). Approval was given as long as some additional conditions were met, those being to show:

1. An acceptable method for strengthening the internal structure;

2. An adequate midship section modulus with the FRP sheathing; and

3. Sufficient strength of the FRP to steel interface.

THE PERMANENT REPAIR

The basics of the FRP cladding are shown in Figure 1 (6). The *Medea's* steel hull was blasted to white metal and given a thin coat of vinylester resin to quickly seal the bare steel. A linear polyvinyl chloride (PVC) foam was vacuum bonded to the hull with a putty resin and faired, and three layers of woven glass fibers alternating with chopped strand mat (CSM) were bonded to the foam. Finally the FRP was faired, then painted with epoxy primer and anti-fouling paint. The repair will be described from the structural aspect and from the aspect of producibility.

Steel and Fiberglass Composite

The main structural concerns that had to be addressed for the *Medea* were local panel strength and longitudinal hull bending strength. A full description of the structural interactions between FRP and steel skins sandwiching a low density core material for panel stiffness is fairly complex and beyond the